Problems and Solutions
in
Partnership Tax

Problems and Solutions
in
Partnership Tax

Joni Larson

CAROLINA ACADEMIC PRESS

Durham, North Carolina

Library of Congress Cataloging-in-Publication Data

Larson, Joni.
  Problems and solutions in partnership tax / Joni Larson.
    pages cm
  Includes bibliographical references and index.
  ISBN 978-1-61163-491-4 (alk. paper)
  1. Partnership--Taxation--United States. I. Title.

KF6452.L375 2013
343.7306'62--dc23   2013025646

Carolina Academic Press
700 Kent Street
Durham, NC 27701
Telephone (919) 489-7486
Fax (919) 493-5668
www.cap-press.com

Printed in the United States of America

Contents

Introduction

Partnership taxation is often considered one of the most difficult areas of tax. However, given the growing number of limited liabilities companies (which generally are taxed as partnerships for tax purposes), it is extremely beneficial to have a working knowledge of this area. In addition, partnership tax provides a flexibility found nowhere else in the Code, affording the attorney or accountant an unparalleled opportunity to engage in tax planning on behalf of his client.

In approaching partnership tax, it is helpful to understand a few basic concepts. First, a partnership is a "flow-through" entity. It does not pay any tax. Rather, the taxable items flow through the partnership and are reported by the partners. Second, in designing the flow-through system, Congress was not always consistent in its treatment of the status of the partnership. Sometimes it is respected as an entity, separate and distinct from its partners. At other times, the entity is ignored and instead the arrangement is treated as an aggregation of the partners. And, finally, at other times, a hybrid approach is used.

The chapters that follow organize the partnership tax concepts and provisions into cohesive groups. However, one of the things that makes partnership tax so difficult is that the provisions are often interrelated and intertwined. In some respects, it is only after the entire area has been studied that the overall system will make sense. As a result, trying to fit the pieces together along the way can feel a bit like putting together a puzzle without having seen the picture. But, once the pieces are in place, the overall picture does make sense. And then, planning can begin.

Problems and Solutions
in
Partnership Tax

Chapter I

Formation of a Partnership

A. Requirements for Tax-Free Transaction

A partnership is a legal entity, separate from the taxpayer-partner. Thus, a transfer of property by a partner to a partnership is a disposition of property. Gain must be recognized, unless authority provides otherwise, and loss can be recognized if provided for under Section 165.

When a taxpayer disposes of property by transferring it to a partnership in exchange for a partnership interest, he continues to have an indirect ownership interest in the property. Stated differently, he has a continuity of his investment. Accordingly, Congress chose not to require taxpayers to recognize gain or loss from the transfer of property to a partnership in which the taxpayer is a partner. Rather, any gain or loss is deferred. Similarly, from the perspective of the partnership, no gain or loss is recognized.

To come within the non-recognition provision (Section 721), property must be transferred to the partnership in exchange for an interest in the partnership. (Services are not considered property for purposes of the non-recognition provision.) This rule applies regardless of whether the partnership is being created or a contribution is being made to a partnership already in existence. In addition, unlike with corporations, there is no requirement that the partner have a certain amount of control over the partnership in order to come within the non-recognition provision.

1. Special Rules

Contribution of an installment note. If a taxpayer sells property to an unrelated party and at least one payment for the property is to be received in a year after the year of disposition, the gain[1] from the disposition can be reported using the installment method. Rather than the gain being reported all in the year of sale, a portion of the gain is reported each time an installment payment is received.[2]

---

1. The gain must qualify to be reported using the installment method. In general, gain from inventory and Section 1245 recapture is not eligible to be reported using the installment method. Section 453(b)(2), (i).
2. See Section 453.

If an installment note is disposed of, the disposition is treated as a disposition of property.[3] Gain or loss is recognized based on the difference between the amount realized and the remaining adjusted basis. However, if an installment note is transferred to a partnership in exchange for a partnership interest, the non-recognition provision controls and no gain or loss is recognized.

Recapture. In general, if a taxpayer disposes of tangible or intangible personal depreciable property and realizes a gain, he must characterize the gain as ordinary to the extent of depreciation previously claimed. This gain commonly is referred to as "recapture" gain.[4]

If a taxpayer disposes of depreciable real property, he generally must characterize the gain as ordinary to the extent of depreciation taken in excess of that allowed under the straightline method.[5] Because the straightline method is the only method available for property placed in service after 1986, the recapture provision applicable to real property generally does not re-characterize any of the gain.

If the transfer qualifies as a tax-free contribution to a partnership under Section 721, for both depreciable personal property and depreciable real property, no gain is recognized and no depreciation recapture is required.

Noncompensatory options. A taxpayer may contribute property to the partnership in exchange for an option to acquire a partnership interest. The transfer of property in exchange for the option does not come within Section 721. The taxpayer recognizes gain or loss on the transfer and the partnership takes a cost basis in the property.[6] When the taxpayer transfers property to the partnership to exercise the option, the transfer is covered by Section 721. While the taxpayer holds a noncompensatory option, he is not treated as a partner for purposes of allocating partnership income. However, if the option gives the taxpayer rights substantially similar to those of a partner, then he is treated as a partner for purposes of allocating partnership income.[7]

2. Failing Tax-Free Status

Sale or rental to partnership. Rather than make a contribution, a partner may sell the property to the partnership or lease or rent the property to the partnership. If the transaction is structured as a sale or lease, the property has not been contributed to the partnership. The partner must include any rental or lease payment in his gross income and the partnership, to the extent allowed, may claim a deduction for the payments. The substance of the transaction, rather than the form, will be determinative of whether the transaction is a contribution, sale, or rental of property.[8]

Section 721(b)—diversification of appreciated securities. If partners owning various securities were allowed to transfer them to a partnership without recognizing gain, they could use the non-recognition provisions to diversify their appreciated securities on a

---

3. See Section 453B.

4. See Section 1245.

5. See Section 1250.

6. Prop. Reg. § 1.721-2(a), (b).

7. Prop. Reg. § 1.761-3(a).

8. For a complete discussion of the tax treatment of a partner not acting in the capacity of a partner, see Chapter XIII.

tax-free basis. The Code does not permit such tax-free diversification.[9] Rather, if the partnership would be treated as an investment company if incorporated, the partner must recognize any gain in the securities contributed to the partnership.

The transfer of property will be considered a transfer to a partnership treated as an investment company if the transfer results, directly or indirectly, in diversification of the partner's interests and the transfer is made to a partnership, more than 80 percent of the value of whose assets are held for investment and are:

- readily marketable stocks or securities;
- interests in regulated investment companies; or
- real estate investment trusts.

In making this determination, the following items are treated as stocks and securities:

- money;
- stocks and other equity interests in a corporation, evidence of indebtedness, options, forward or futures contracts, notional principal contracts, and derivatives;
- Foreign currency;
- Any interest in a real estate investment trust, a common trust fund, a regulated investment company, a publicly traded partnership, or other equity interest; and
- Any interest in precious metals, unless such metal is used or held in the active conduct of a business after contribution.

A transfer ordinarily results in the diversification of the partner's interest if two or more partners transfer non-identical assets to a partnership. A transfer of stock and securities is not treated as resulting in a diversification of the partners' interests if each partner transfers a diversified portfolio of stocks and securities. For purposes of determining whether there has been diversification, if any transaction involves one or more transfers of non-identical assets that, taken in the aggregate, constitute an insignificant portion of the total value of assets transferred, such transfers are disregarded in determining whether diversification has occurred.

If the transfer is part of a plan to achieve diversification without recognition of gain, the original transfer will be treated as resulting in diversification. For example, a plan that contemplates a subsequent transfer, however delayed, of the partnership assets to a partnership treated as an investment company in a transaction purporting to qualify for non-recognition treatment will be treated as resulting in diversification.

If the partnership is treated as an investment company, gain is recognized on all transfers, not just on transfers of securities. In addition, if a loss is realized upon contribution of property, it cannot be recognized.

B. Basis

The partner. For purposes of determining the partner's basis in his continuing interest (the partnership), the Code follows the entity approach. Thus, rather than owning an

---

9. Section 721(b).

interest in the underlying assets of the partnership, the partner owns an interest in the partnership (which, in turn, owns all the assets contributed).

The contribution of property to a partnership generally is not a taxable event. However, the ability of a partner to transfer property to a partnership free of any tax consequences does not completely relieve the partner from the tax liability associated with appreciation in the asset. Nor generally does it eliminate any loss. Rather, it postpones the recognition event, generally until the time the partnership disposes of the asset or the partner disposes of his partnership interest.

The gain or loss inherent in the property is preserved in the partner's basis in the partnership interest. This concept is similar to the treatment of the basis of property received in a like-kind exchange, replacement property acquired after an involuntary conversion, and property transferred from a spouse or former spouse. Any gain or loss that has been deferred is reflected in the basis of the new property.

The partner's basis in his partnership interest is the amount of money and the adjusted basis of contributed property at the time of the contribution, increased by the amount (if any) of gain recognized under Section 721(b).[10] The partner's basis in his partnership interest is referred to as his "outside basis."

If a partner contributes his promissory note to the partnership, it is not treated as cash. Rather, it is considered a contractual obligation to the partnership, and the partner has basis from the note only to the extent he makes payments on the note.

If a cash basis taxpayer contributes accounts receivable to the partnership, the basis in the accounts receivable is zero. The zero basis reflects the fact that the accounts receivable have not been reported in income.

The partnership. The partnership is continuing the ownership interest in the assets contributed by its partners. Because the gain or loss inherent in that property has not yet been recognized, it must be preserved in the basis of the asset. In essence, the partnership steps into the shoes of the contributing partner.

The basis of assets contributed to a partnership is the basis in the hands of the contributing partner, increased by the amount (if any) of gain recognized under Section 721(b) by the contributing partner at the time of the contribution.[11] The partnership's transferred basis in the assets is referred to as the "inside basis."

The partner's basis as assumed by the partnership is used for all purposes. Such purposes include determining gain or loss upon disposition of the asset, calculating depreciation, and determining availability of credits. For depreciable property, in addition to the partner's basis being transferred to the partnership, the partnership succeeds to the cost recovery method used by the partner.[12]

Note that, by treating the partnership as an entity separate from the partners, one asset can be viewed from two different perspectives. First, the basis of all the assets contributed will be reflected cumulatively in the partner's basis in his partnership interest.

---

10. Section 722.

11. Section 723. If the property being contributed to the partnership was not being used in a business or investment activity, the basis in the hands of the partnership is the lesser of its adjusted basis or fair market value.

12. Section 168(i)(7).

Second, the partnership will have a basis in each individual asset that has been contributed to the partnership.

C. Holding Period

The partner. In general, a partnership interest is a capital asset. Because the partnership interest represents a continuation of the partner's interest in the contributed assets, the length of time the individual held contributed capital assets should tack onto the length of time the partner has held the partnership interest. Thus, by including the time the underlying capital assets were held, if the partner held the partnership interest for more than one year, the gain would be eligible for long-term capital gain preferential treatment. Similarly, if the property contributed by the partner to the partnership is a hotchpot (Section 1231) asset, the partner's holding period in the asset is tacked onto the holding period of his partnership interest. If the partner contributes cash or ordinary income assets, the holding period of the partnership interest begins on the day following the date of contribution.[13] If a partner contributes assets whose holding period tacks and those that do not, the holding period will be allocated between the two.[14] For purposes of this determination, Section 1245 recapture gain is not treated as a capital or Section 1231 asset.

The partnership. Consistent with the concept of continuing the partner's interest in the property and preserving the tax ramifications inherent in the property until disposition of the asset by the partnership, the partnership can tack the partner's holding period in the asset onto the partnership's holding period.[15] However, there is no distinction between the various types of assets; the holding period for all assets tacks. Because each asset continues to be a separate and distinct asset, the character of the gain or loss and holding period can be determined at the partnership level.

D. Partnership Interest Received in Exchange for Services

A partner can receive a capital interest or profits interest in the partnership. A capital interest is an interest that would give the partner a share of the proceeds if the partnership's assets were sold at fair market value and then the proceeds were distributed in a complete liquidation of the partnership. A profits interest is only the right to participate in the earnings and profits of the partnership.

Capital interest. When a partner receives a capital interest in a partnership in exchange for services provided (or to be provided) to the partnership, the non-recognition provision does not apply to the entire transaction. Rather, the tax consequences are based on the two component parts of the transaction. First, the partner receives compensation in exchange for his services. The amount of the compensation received will

---

13. Rev. Rul. 99-5, 99-1 C.B. 434; Rev. Rul. 66-7, 1966-1 C.B. 188.
14. Treas. Reg. § 1.1223-3(a)(2).
15. Section 1223(2).

be the value of the capital account; this amount must be included in his gross income. Second, the partner contributes the amount received as compensation for services to the partnership in exchange for the partnership interest. The contribution is tax-free.

In *McDougal v. Commissioner*,[16] the McDougals' horse trainer, Gilbert McClanahan, encouraged them to buy Iron Card, a two-year-old race horse that suffered from a protein allergy. The McDougals purchased Iron Card for $10,000 and entered into an agreement with McClanahan. If McClanahan trained and attended to Iron Card, he would receive a one-half interest in the horse after the McDougals recovered their costs and acquisition expenses. McClanahan successfully treated Iron Card's protein allergy and the horse had great success as a race horse. When the McDougals had recovered their costs and expenses from the race winnings, they transferred a one-half interest in the horse to McClanahan.

The Tax Court found that when the one-half ownership interest in Iron Card was transferred by the McDougals to McClanahan, a partnership was formed; the McDougals contributed the horse and McClanahan contributed past services. However, the court analyzed the transaction in three steps.

First, the McDougals transferred a one-half interest in Iron Card to McClanahan. Because the McDougals had disposed of property, they had to recognize gain to the extent the amount realized (value of the services performed by McClanahan) exceeded their adjusted basis. Second, McClanahan received a one-half interest in Iron Card as compensation for his prior services. This amount of compensation paid to him had to be included in his gross income. He had a basis in his one-half of Iron Card equal to the amount of compensation income he reported. Finally, the McDougals and McClanahan each contributed their respective one-half interests in Iron Card to the partnership. This transfer was tax-free.[17]

Profits interest. When a partner receives a profits interest in a partnership in exchange for services provided to the partnership, generally the partner does not have any income to report. This result is due to the fact that the profits interest does not have any current value or is too difficult to value because it is speculative. However, there are situations where the taxpayer was in fact able to sell his partnership interest, belying any argument that the profits interest was valueless or was too difficult to value.

In *Hale v. Commissioner*,[18] in exchange for future services, the taxpayer received a right to the partnership's future profits. Before receiving any income from the partnership, the taxpayer sold 90 percent of its interest. The issue before the court was the character of the income received. The taxpayer argued that it disposed of a capital asset, a partnership interest, and, therefore, that the gain should be capital.

The Tax Court found that what the taxpayer disposed of was not a partnership interest, but the right to receive future income. Because the taxpayer received the present value of what would otherwise have been ordinary income (compensation for services paid at some point in the future), it had received ordinary income in exchange for its profits interest.

---

16. 62 T.C. 720 (1974).

17. See Section 721(a).

18. T.C. Memo. 1965-274.

In *Diamond v. Commissioner*,[19] the taxpayer received a profits interest in exchange for services. After the taxpayer had rendered his services but before the partnership showed any profit, the taxpayer sold his partnership interest for $40,000. As in *Hale*, the taxpayer argued that the character of the gain should be capital due to the disposition of a partnership interest. The Seventh Circuit followed the holding of the Tax Court and concluded that the value of the partnership interest was $40,000 and that the interest was received as compensation for services.

Both *Hale* and *Diamond* support the proposition that if you dispose of a right to receive compensation for services, the amount received in the exchange must be included in income as ordinary income. However, neither the value of the profits interest nor the year the accession to wealth occurred was at issue in either case.

In *Campbell v. Commissioner*,[20] the court addressed the issue of whether receipt of a profits interest could result in ordinary income upon receipt and before sale. In this case, the taxpayer did not sell the profits interest. The Tax Court used a present value methodology to value the profits interest and find that the taxpayer had gross income. On appeal, the Eighth Circuit reversed the Tax Court on the valuation issue, finding the interest too speculative for the value to be determined.

To provide some certainty in this area, the Service issued Revenue Procedure 93-27. The Service stated that receipt of a profits interest in a partnership is not required to be included in income unless:

- The profits interest relates to a "substantially certain and predictable stream of income from partnership assets";
- Within two years of receipt, the partner disposes of the profits interest; or
- The profits interest is a limited partnership interest in a publicly traded partnership.

Further guidance from the Service provides that the determination of whether an interest given to a service provider is a tax-free receipt of a profits interest is made at the time of the grant, irrespective of whether the interest has vested. However, the service provider and partnership must treat the service provider as owning a partnership interest from the date of the grant.[21]

Vesting issues. If the interest is not substantially vested when acquired, arguably, the timing of when it should be included in income is governed by Section 83. Section 83 provides that if a taxpayer is paid for services with property, the taxpayer must include the value of the property in gross income unless the property is subject to a substantial risk of forfeiture. In such situations, the taxpayer can either elect to include the fair market value of the property valued, without the restriction, in gross income in the year the property is received. Or the taxpayer can include the fair market value of the property in income in the year the property is no longer subject to the substantial risk of forfeiture. If the taxpayer elects to include the property in the year of receipt, but

---

19. 492 F.2d 286 (7th Cir. 1974), *aff'g* 56 T.C. 530 (1971).

20. 943 F.2d 815 (8th Cir. 1991), *aff'g in part and rev'g in part* T.C. Memo. 1990-162.

21. *See* Rev. Proc. 2001-43, 2001-2 C.B. 191. The ruling also provides some guidance with respect to the applicability of Section 83.

the right never vests, the taxpayer cannot subsequently take a deduction for the previously included amount.

The Service has issued proposed regulations[22] and a proposed Revenue Procedure[23] addressing the receipt of a partnership interest in exchange for services. They treat both a capital and a profits interest as property for purposes of Section 83. They provide a safe harbor provision for valuing the transferred interest. In addition, they permit the partnership to make the transfer tax-free.

E. Partnership Balance Sheet

A partnership balance sheet is a document that can be used to keep track of the relationship of the partnership to the partners and the partners to each other, both from a tax perspective and an economic perspective.

The left half of the balance sheet reflects the assets from the partnership's perspective. Generally, assets are listed starting with the most liquid and moving towards the most illiquid.

For each asset, both the adjusted basis (inside basis) and the fair market value are reflected. The adjusted basis is the partnership's basis (inside basis) in each asset. Generally, the fair market value will be the value of the asset upon contribution (book value), reduced to reflect any depreciation taken by the partnership. In general, for purposes of the balance sheet, except to reflect depreciation, the fair market value, or book value, does not change, even if it does change in the marketplace.[24]

The right half of the balance sheet reflects partnership liabilities and ownership from the perspective of the partners. Liabilities include not only obligations to third parties, but also obligations to partners who have loaned funds to the partnership, acting other than in their capacity as a partner.

For each partner, both the adjusted basis of the partner in his partnership interest (outside basis) and his economic investment are reflected. A partner's economic investment is his "capital account" or the "book value" of his partnership interest.

The method of computing a partner's capital account is set forth in the regulations. The partner's initial capital account is computed by adding the amount of money and the net fair market value of property contributed to the partnership. "Net fair market value" is the fair market value of the property, less any liabilities the property is taken subject to. The regulations provide detailed rules for how the capital accounts are adjusted during the life of the partnership.

In general, except to reflect depreciation claimed by the partnership and allocated among the partners, the partner's capital account is not adjusted to reflect changes in the value of the contributed assets.[25]

Finally, a partner's capital account reflects the amount each partner would receive if the partnership were liquidated, all assets were sold for their fair market value, all

---

22. Treas. Reg. § 1.83-3(e); REG-105346-03, 70 Fed. Reg. 29675 (May 24, 2005).
23. Notice 2005-43, 2005-1 C.B. 1221.
24. There are some events that trigger a revaluation of the partnership assets.
25. There are some events that trigger a restatement of capital accounts.

debts were paid, and the net proceeds distributed among the partners. It also reflects the ownership interest of each partner as compared to the other partners. Noteworthy, the method of computing a partner's capital account does not follow Generally Accepted Accounting Principles (GAAP).

Example:

Asset	Adj. Basis	FMV		Adj. Basis	Cap. Acct.
Cash	$ 500	$ 500	Ann:	$ 300	$1,000
Equipment	700	500	Bob:	1,200	1,000
Land	300	1,000			
Total	$1,500	$2,000		$1,500	$2,000

Summary

Contribution to a partnership: No gain or loss is recognized when property is transferred to a partnership in exchange for a partnership interest. Services are not considered property.

Partner's basis (no liabilities):

$$\begin{array}{r}
\text{Adjusted basis of the asset(s) contributed to the partnership} \\
+ \qquad \qquad \text{Cash contributed to the partnership} \\
\hline
\text{Partner's (outside basis) in the partnership interest}
\end{array}$$

Partner's holding period in partnership interest:

- The percentage of the partnership interest that has a holding period that tacks is:

$$\frac{\text{Fair market value of capital and Section 1231 assets}}{\text{Fair market value of entire partnership interest}}$$

- The percentage of the partnership interest that has a holding period that does not tack is:

$$\frac{\text{Fair market value of ordinary income assets and cash}}{\text{Fair market value of entire partnership interest}}$$

Partnership's basis: The partnership takes the partner's basis in the asset.

Partnership's holding period: The partnership takes the partner's holding period in the asset.

Profits interest: Receipt of a profits interest in a partnership is not required to be included in income unless:

- The profits interest relates to a "substantially certain and predictable stream of income from partnership assets";
- Within two years of receipt, the partner disposes of the profits interest; or
- The profits interest is a limited partnership interest in a publicly traded partnership.

Balance sheet: Snapshot of the situation of the partnership and the partners at a particular time.

In general, the partnership's basis in the assets (inside basis) will equal the basis of the partners in their partnership interest (outside basis) and the fair market value of the partnership assets will equal the debts plus the capital accounts.

	Basis	FMV		Debt:	Basis	$0 Cap. Acct.
Cash:	$ 5,000	$ 5,000	Ann:		$ 5,000	$ 5,000
Land:	10,000	5,000	Bob:		10,000	5,000
Total:	$15,000	$10,000			$15,000	$10,000

Questions

1.   Ann and Bob formed a general partnership. Ann contributed land with a basis of $300 and fair market value of $1,000. Ann had held the land as investment property and had purchased it five years earlier. Bob contributed $500 and equipment with a basis of $700 and fair market value of $500. Bob had used the equipment for two years in his sole proprietorship business and had claimed $200 of deprecation.

   a. What are the tax consequences to each of Ann and Bob?

   b. What are the tax consequences to the partnership?

   c. Construct a balance sheet to reflect the situation of the partners and the partnership at the time of formation.

2.   Carl, Deb, and Ellen formed an equal general partnership. They contributed the following assets:

Carl:	Asset	Adjusted Basis	Fair Market Value
	Equipment (all § 1245 gain)	$1,000	$3,000
	Goodwill	0	5,000
	Accounts receivable	0	1,000

Deb:	Asset	Adjusted Basis	Fair Market Value
	Cash	$ 3,000	$3,000
	Whiteacre	10,000	4,000
	Installment note	500	2,000

Ellen:	Asset	Adjusted Basis	Fair Market Value
	Cash	$7,000	$7,000
	Greenacre	1,000	2,000

   Carl had held the equipment for two years and generated the goodwill in his sole proprietorship business, which he had been operating for ten years.

   Deb had held Whiteacre for five years prior to contribution and had held it for investment purposes. Her installment note was from the sale of land she had held for investment for five years prior to sale.

   Ellen had held Greenacre for two years prior to contribution and had held it for investment purposes.

   a. What are the tax consequences to each of Carl, Deb, and Ellen?

   b. What are the tax consequences to the partnership?

   c. Construct a balance sheet to reflect the situation of the partners and the partnership at the time of formation.

3.   Frank, Greg, Hal, and Ira formed a limited partnership in which they each had an equal interest. They contributed the following assets:

Frank:	Asset	Adjusted Basis	Fair Market Value
	Cash	$10,000	$10,000

Greg:	Asset	Adjusted Basis	Fair Market Value
	Cash	$5,000	$5,000
	Accounts receivable	0	5,000

Hal:	**Asset**	**Adjusted Basis**	**Fair Market Value**
	Cash	$5,000	$5,000
	Land	9,000	5,000
Ira:	**Asset**	**Adjusted Basis**	**Fair Market Value**
	Cash	$3,000	$3,000
	Equipment	3,000	7,000

Hal had held the land for three years prior to contribution.

Ira had used the equipment in his sole proprietorship business for three years and had claimed $4,000 in depreciation.

a. What are the tax consequences to each of Frank, Greg, Hal, and Ira?

b. What are the tax consequences to the partnership?

c. Construct a balance sheet to reflect the situation of the partners and the partnership at the time of formation.

4. A general partnership operates a small resort area in Florida. Jeb is given the opportunity to receive a capital interest in the partnership in exchange for managing the resort from February through July. If Jeb accepts, what are the tax consequences to him?

5. A general partnership is beginning an online publishing business. Kent is given the opportunity to receive a one-quarter non-forfeitable profits interest in the partnership in exchange for providing editing services. He is not required to contribute any property to the partnership. If Kent accepts, is the profits interest taxable?

6. A general partnership is beginning a marketing consulting business. Len is given the opportunity to receive a one-third non-forfeitable profits interest in the partnership. Len accepts, but one year later sells his partnership interest. What are the tax consequences to Len?

7. A partnership owns a building. The building is leased to a nationally recognized chain food restaurant on a net basis. The lessee pays all interest, taxes, insurance, and mortgage related to the building. Mike is given the opportunity to receive a one-fifth non-forfeitable profits interest in the partnership. He would not be required to contribute any property to the partnership, but would be expected to render accounting services to the partnership. If Mike accepts, is the profits interest taxable?

Solutions

1. Ann and Bob formed a general partnership. Ann contributed land with a basis of $300 and fair market value of $1,000. Ann had held the land as investment property and had purchased it five years earlier. Bob contributed $500 and equipment with a basis of $700 and fair market value of $500. Bob had used the equipment for two years in his sole proprietorship business and had claimed $200 of deprecation.

 a. What are the tax consequences to each of Ann and Bob?

Ann: She recognizes no gain or loss on contribution of the land to the partnership. (Section 721(a); Treas. Reg. § 1.721-1(a))

 Ann's outside basis in the partnership interest is (Section 722; Treas. Reg. § 1.722-1):

Basis in land:	$300
Cash contributed:	—
Total → outside basis:	$300

 The five year holding period in the land will tack, giving her a five year holding period in her partnership interest. (Section 1223(1); Treas. Reg. § 1.1223-3(a))

Bob: He recognizes no gain or loss on contribution of the cash and equipment to the partnership. (Section 721(a); Treas. Reg. § 1.721-1(a))

 Bob's outside basis in the partnership interest is (Section 722; Treas. Reg. § 1.722-1):

Basis in equipment:	$ 700
Cash contributed:	500
Total → outside basis:	$1,200

 The holding period attributable to the equipment will tack (hotchpot property with no recapture) and the holding period attributable to the cash will begin the day following contribution. Thus, the portion of Bob's partnership interest for which the two year holding period will tack is:

$$\frac{\text{fmv equipment)}}{\text{(fmv of all entire partnership interest)}} \quad \frac{500}{1,000} = \frac{1}{2}$$

 The portion of Bob's holding period that does not tack, and which begins the day following contribution, is:

$$\frac{\text{cash}}{\text{fmv of all entire partnership interest}} \quad \frac{500}{1,000} = \frac{1}{2}$$

(Section 1223(1); Treas. Reg. § 1.1223-3(b)(1))

 b. What are the tax consequences to the partnership?

 The partnership's basis for each item is (Section 723; Treas. Reg. § 1.723-1):

Asset	Adjusted Basis
Cash	$500
Equipment	700
Land	300

The partners' holding period for each asset tacks onto the partnership's holding period. Accordingly, upon formation the partnership holds the assets for the same length of time each partner held each asset. Thus, it has held the land for five years and the equipment for two years. (Section 1223(2))

c. **Construct a balance sheet to reflect the situation of the partners and the partnership at the time of formation.**

Asset	Adj. Basis	FMV		Adj. Basis	Cap. Acct.
Cash	$ 500	$ 500	Ann:	$ 300	$1,000
Equipment	700	500	Bob:	1,200	1,000
Land	300	1,000			
Total:	$1,500	$2,000		$1,500	$2,000

The fact the partners are equal partners is reflected in the capital accounts—they each own an equal economic interest in the partnership. Or, seen from another perspective, if the partnership sold all its assets (ignoring selling costs), the $2,000 received would be distributed according to Ann and Bob's capital accounts, or $1,000 each.

Note that the total of the partnership's inside bases is equal to the total of all partners' outside bases and that the total fair market value of the partnership assets is equal to the total of all liabilities plus the partners' capital accounts.

2. Carl, Deb, and Ellen formed an equal general partnership. They contributed the following assets:

Carl:	Asset	Adjusted Basis	Fair Market Value
	Equipment (all § 1245 gain)	$1,000	$3,000
	Goodwill	0	5,000
	Accounts receivable	0	1,000
Deb:	Asset	Adjusted Basis	Fair Market Value
	Cash	$ 3,000	$3,000
	Whiteacre	10,000	4,000
	Installment note	500	2,000
Ellen:	Asset	Adjusted Basis	Fair Market Value
	Cash	$7,000	$7,000
	Greenacre	1,000	2,000

Carl had held the equipment for two years and generated the goodwill in his sole proprietorship business, which he had been operating for ten years.

Deb had held Whiteacre for five years prior to contribution and had held it for investment purposes. Her installment note was from the sale of land she had held for investment for five years prior to sale.

Ellen had held Greenacre for two years prior to contribution and had held it for investment purposes.

a. **What are the tax consequences to each of Carl, Deb, and Ellen?**

Carl: He recognizes no gain or loss on contribution of the equipment, goodwill, and accounts receivable to the partnership. (Section 721(a); Treas. Reg. § 1.721-1(a))

Carl's outside basis in the partnership interest is (Section 722; Treas. Reg. § 1.722-1):

Basis in equipment:	$1,000
Basis in goodwill:	0
Basis in accounts rec.:	0
Cash contributed:	—
Total → outside basis:	$1,000

The holding period for the basis in the equipment (the portion that is not Section 1245 gain) and the holding period in the goodwill will tack. Thus, the portion of Carl's partnership interest for which the holding period will tack is:

$$\frac{\text{(basis in equipment + fmv of goodwill)}}{\text{(fmv of all entire partnership interest)}} \quad \frac{1{,}000 + 5{,}000}{9{,}000} = \frac{6{,}000}{9{,}000} = \frac{6}{9}$$

The portion of Carl's holding period that does not tack, and which begins the day following contribution, is:

$$\frac{\text{(Section 1245 gain + fmv of acct rec.)}}{\text{(fmv of all entire partnership interest)}} \quad \frac{2{,}000 + 1{,}000}{9{,}000} = \frac{3{,}000}{9{,}000} = \frac{3}{9}$$

(Section 1223(1); Treas. Reg. § 1.1223-3(b)(1))

Deb: She recognizes no gain or loss on contribution of the cash, land, and installment note to the partnership. (Section 721(a); Treas. Reg. § 1.721-1(a))

Deb's outside basis in the partnership interest is (Section 722; Treas. Reg. § 1.722-1):

Basis in Whiteacre:	$10,000
Basis in installment note:	500
Cash contributed:	3,000
Total → outside basis:	$13,500

The holding period for Whiteacre and the installment note will tack. Thus, the portion of Deb's partnership interest for which the holding period will tack is:

$$\frac{\text{(fmv of Whiteacre + fmv of note)}}{\text{(fmv of all entire partnership interest)}} \quad \frac{2{,}000 + 4{,}000}{9{,}000} = \frac{6{,}000}{9{,}000} = \frac{6}{9}$$

The portion of Deb's holding period that does not tack, and which begins the day following contribution, is:

$$\frac{\text{cash}}{\text{fmv of all entire partnership interest}} \quad \frac{3{,}000}{9{,}000} = \frac{3}{9}$$

(Section 1223(1); Treas. Reg. § 1.1223-3(b)(1))

Ellen: She recognizes no gain or loss on contribution of the cash and land to the partnership. (Section 721(a); Treas. Reg. § 1.721-1(a))

Ellen's outside basis in the partnership interest is (Section 722; Treas. Reg. § 1.722-1):

Basis in Greenacre:	$1,000
Cash contributed:	7,000
Total → outside basis:	$8,000

The holding period for Greenacre will tack. Thus, the portion of Ellen's partnership interest for which the holding period will tack is:

$$\frac{\text{fmv of Greenacre}}{\text{fmv of all entire partnership interest}} \quad \frac{2{,}000}{9{,}000} = \frac{2}{9}$$

The portion of Ellen's holding period that does not tack, and which begins the day following contribution, is:

$$\frac{cash}{fmv\ of\ all\ entire\ partnership\ interest} \quad \frac{7,000}{9,000} = \frac{7}{9}$$

(Section 1223(1); Treas. Reg. §1.1223-3(b)(1))

b. What are the tax consequences to the partnership?

The partnership's basis for each item is (Section 723; Treas. Reg. §1.723-1):

Asset	Adjusted Basis
Cash	$10,000
Accounts receivable	0
Installment note	500
Equipment	1,000
Whiteacre	10,000
Greenacre	1,000
Goodwill	0

The partners' holding period for each asset tacks onto the partnership's holding period. Accordingly, upon formation the partnership holds the assets for the same length of time each partner held each asset. Thus, it has held the equipment for two years, the goodwill for ten years, Whiteacre for five years, the installment note for five years, and Greenacre for two years (and the accounts receivable for the length of time Carl held them). (Section 1223(2))

c. Construct a balance sheet to reflect the situation of the partners and the partnership at the time of formation.

Asset	Adj. Basis	FMV		Adj. Basis	Cap. Acct.
Cash	$10,000	$10,000	Carl:	$ 1,000	$ 9,000
Acct rec	0	1,000	Deb:	13,500	9,000
Note	500	2,000	Ellen:	8,000	9,000
Equipment	1,000	3,000			
Whiteacre	10,000	4,000			
Greenacre	1,000	2,000			
Goodwill	0	5,000			
Total:	$22,500	$27,000		$22,500	$27,000

The fact the partners are equal partners is reflected in the capital accounts—they each own an equal economic interest in the partnership. Or, seen from another perspective, if the partnership sold all its assets (ignoring selling costs), the $27,000 received would be distributed according to Carl, Deb, and Ellen's capital accounts, or $9,000 each.

Note that the total of the partnership's inside bases is equal to the total of all partners' outside bases and that the total fair market value of the partnership assets is equal to the total of all liabilities plus the partners' capital accounts.

3. Frank, Greg, Hal, and Ira formed a limited partnership in which they each had an equal interest. They contributed the following assets:

Frank:	Asset	Adjusted Basis	Fair Market Value
	Cash	$10,000	$10,000

Greg:	Asset	Adjusted Basis	Fair Market Value
	Cash	$5,000	$5,000
	Accounts receivable	0	5,000

Hal:	Asset	Adjusted Basis	Fair Market Value
	Cash	$5,000	$5,000
	Land	9,000	5,000

Ira:	Asset	Adjusted Basis	Fair Market Value
	Cash	$3,000	$3,000
	Equipment	3,000	7,000

Hal had held the land for three years prior to contribution.

Ira had used the equipment in his sole proprietorship business for three years and had claimed $4,000 in depreciation.

a. What are the tax consequences to each of Frank, Greg, Hal, and Ira?

Frank: He recognizes no gain or loss on contribution of the cash to the partnership. (Section 721(a); Treas. Reg. § 1.721-1(a))

Frank's outside basis in the partnership interest is (Section 722; Treas. Reg. § 1.722-1):

Basis in property:	$ —
Cash contributed:	10,000
Total → outside basis:	$10,000

His holding period begins the day following contribution of the cash. (Section 1223(1); Treas. Reg. § 1.1223-3(a))

Greg: He recognizes no gain or loss on contribution of the cash and accounts receivable to the partnership. (Section 721(a); Treas. Reg. § 1.721-1(a))

Greg's outside basis in the partnership interest is (Section 722; Treas. Reg. § 1.722-1):

Step 1: Basis in accounts rec.:	$ 0
Step 2: Cash contributed:	5,000
Step 3: Total → outside basis:	$5,000

The holding period begins the day following contribution of the cash and accounts receivable (no tacking). (Section 1223(1); Treas. Reg. § 1.1223-3(a))

Hal: He recognizes no gain or loss on contribution of the cash and land to the partnership. (Section 721(a); Treas. Reg. § 1.721-1(a))

Hal's outside basis in the partnership interest is (Section 722; Treas. Reg. § 1.722-1):

Basis in land:	$ 9,000
Cash contributed:	5,000
Total → outside basis:	$14,000

The three year holding period for the land will tack. Thus, the portion of Hal's partnership interest for which the holding period will tack is:

$$\frac{\text{fmv of land}}{\text{fmv of all entire partnership interest}} \quad \frac{5,000}{10,000} = \frac{1}{2}$$

The portion of Hal's holding period that does not tack, and which begins the day following contribution, is:

$$\frac{\text{cash}}{\text{fmv of all entire partnership interest}} \quad \frac{5,000}{10,000} = \frac{1}{2}$$

(Section 1223(1); Treas. Reg. § 1.1223-3(b)(1))

Ira: He recognizes no gain or loss on contribution of the cash and equipment to the partnership. (Section 721(a); Treas. Reg. § 1.721-1(a))

Ira's outside basis in the partnership interest is (Section 722; Treas. Reg. § 1.722-1):

Basis in equipment	$3,000
Cash contributed	3,000
Total → outside basis	$6,000

The holding period for the basis in the equipment (the portion that is not Section 1245 gain) will tack. Thus, the portion of Ira's partnership interest for which the holding period will tack is:

$$\frac{\text{basis in equipment}}{\text{fmv of all entire partnership interest}} \quad \frac{3,000}{10,000} = \frac{3}{10}$$

The portion of Ira's holding period that does not tack, and which begins the day following contribution, is:

$$\frac{\text{(Section 1245 gain + cash)}}{\text{(fmv of all entire partnership interest)}} \quad \frac{4,000 + 3,000}{10,000} = \frac{7,000}{10,000} = \frac{7}{10}$$

(Section 1223(1); Treas. Reg. § 1.1223-3(b)(1))

b. What are the tax consequences to the partnership?

The partnership's basis for each item is (Section 723; Treas. Reg. § 1.723-1):

Asset	Adjusted Basis
Cash	$23,000
Accounts receivable	0
Equipment	3,000
Land	9,000

The partners' holding period for each asset tacks onto the partnership's holding period. Accordingly, upon formation the partnership holds the assets for the same length of time each partner held each asset. Thus, it has held the land for three years and the equipment for three years (and the accounts receivable for the length of time Greg held them). (Section 1223(2))

c. Construct a balance sheet to reflect the situation of the partners and the partnership at the time of formation.

Asset	Adj. Basis	FMV		Adj. Basis	Cap. Acct.
Cash	$23,000	$23,000	Frank:	$10,000	$10,000
Acct rec	0	5,000	Greg:	5,000	10,000
Equipment	3,000	7,000	Hal:	14,000	10,000
Land	9,000	5,000	Ira:	6,000	10,000
Total:	$35,000	$40,000		$35,000	$40,000

The fact the partners are equal partners is reflected in the capital accounts—they each own an equal economic interest in the partnership. Or, seen from another perspective, if the partnership sold all its assets (ignoring selling costs), the $40,000 received would be distributed according to Frank, Greg, Hal, and Ira's capital accounts, or $10,000 each.

Note that the total of the partnership's inside bases is equal to the total of all partners' outside bases and that the total fair market value of the partnership assets is equal to the total of all liabilities plus the partners' capital accounts.

4. A general partnership operates a small resort area in Florida. Jeb is given the opportunity to receive a capital interest in the partnership in exchange for managing the resort from February through July. If Jeb accepts, what are the tax consequences to him?

Jeb has received a capital interest in exchange for his services. Section 721 does not apply to a contribution of services. (Treas. Reg. § 1.721-1(b); Prop. Reg. § 1.721-1(b)(1)) Accordingly, Jeb has received a payment that represents compensation for services and he must include the amount in his gross income. He then contributes the amount reported (*i.e.*, the salary paid to him) to the partnership. His outside basis is equal to the amount of the contribution, the amount of the salary.

5. A general partnership is beginning an online publishing business. Kent is given the opportunity to receive a one-quarter non-forfeitable profits interest in the partnership in exchange for providing editing services. He is not required to contribute any property to the partnership. If Kent accepts, is the profits interest taxable?

Kent has received a profits interest in exchange for his services. Note that the services are to be performed in the future and it will be difficult to value his profits interest. More importantly, the receipt of the profits interest is not within any of the exceptions set forth in Rev Proc. 93-27. Thus, the profits interest currently is not taxable.

6. A general partnership is beginning a marketing consulting business. Len is given the opportunity to receive a one-third non-forfeitable profits interest in the partnership. Len accepts, but one year later sells his partnership interest. What are the tax consequences to Len?

Len has received a profits interest in exchange for his services. Note that the services are to be performed in the future and it will be difficult to value his profits interest. The profits interest will not be taxable unless it comes within any of the exceptions set forth in Rev Proc. 93-27. Because Len disposed of his profits interest within two years of receipt he comes within one of the exceptions. The interest is taxable when it was received.

7.   A partnership owns a building. The building is leased to a nationally recognized chain food restaurant on a net basis. The lessee pays all interest, taxes, insurance, and mortgage related to the building. Mike is given the opportunity to receive a one-fifth non-forfeitable profits interest in the partnership. He would not be required to contribute any property to the partnership, but would be expected to render accounting services to the partnership. If Mike accepts, is the profits interest taxable?

Mike has received a profits interest in exchange for his services. Note that the services are to be performed in the future and it will be difficult to value his profits interest. The profits interest will not be taxable unless it comes within any of the exceptions set forth in Rev Proc. 93-27.

The profits interest does come within one of the exceptions if it relates to a "substantially certain and predictable" stream of income, such as income from a "high-quality" net lease. To the extent it does, and the facts make it appear that it does, Mike must determine the value of the interest and include that amount in his income upon receipt of the profits interest.

Chapter II

Partnership Debt — The Basics

In this chapter, the most basic rules with respect to partnership debt are addressed. Later chapters address the more complicated aspects of partnership debt.

A. Definition of Liability

The regulations provide a specific definition of what constitutes a liability. An obligation is a liability to the extent that incurring the obligation:[1]

- Creates or increases the basis of the obligor's assets;
- Gives rise to an immediate deduction to the obligor; or
- Gives rise to an expense that is not deductible and not properly chargeable to capital.

If a cash basis taxpayer contributes accounts payable to a partnership, the accounts payable are not treated as a liability for purposes of Section 752.[2]

B. Capital Accounts and Obligation of Partners to Partnership to Make Capital Contributions

Recall that capital accounts reflect a partner's economic interest in the partnership. The account is increased by cash and the net value of property contributed to the partnership. The account is increased by gain or income allocated to the partner. Similarly, the account is decreased by partnership expenses and losses allocated to the partner and the amount cash and the net value of property distributed to the partner from the partnership.[3]

---

1. Treas. Reg. § 1.752-1(a)(4)(i).
2. Rev. Rul. 88-77, 1988-2 C.B. 129.
3. Treas. Reg. § 1.704-1(b)(2)(iv)(b).

Because capital accounts reflect a partner's economic interest in the partnership, they reflect the amount a partner generally expects to receive from the partnership upon liquidation. Accordingly, the partnership agreement and, in some situations, state law will impose on the partner an obligation to restore a negative capital account balance.

C. Effect of Liabilities

Decrease in individual liabilities. When property subject to a liability is contributed by a partner to the partnership, the partnership is treated as having assumed the liability to the extent the liability does not exceed the fair market value of the property at the time of contribution.[4] Thus, the partner's individual liability has decreased. Any decrease in a partner's liabilities by reason of the partnership's assumption of the liabilities is treated as a distribution of money by the partnership to that partner. While distributions from a partnership to a partner have not yet been considered, in general, a distribution of cash from a partnership to a partner will result in a decrease in the partner's basis by the amount distributed.[5]

Increase in partnership liabilities. When the partnership acquires debt, the debt generally becomes the responsibility of the general partners. To the extent a partner has increased his share of responsibility for a partnership liability, he is treated as having advanced to the partnership his portion of the funds needed to repay the debt. Because a partner's outside basis reflects all contributions, the partner's outside basis is increased by the amount of the liability for which the partner would be responsible.[6]

Net change in liabilities. If, in a single transaction, there is an increase in the partner's share of the partnership's liabilities and a decrease in the partner's individual liabilities, only the net amount will affect the partner's basis. If there is a net increase, the net amount is considered as a contribution of money by the partner to the partnership. If there is a net decrease, the net amount is considered a distribution of money from the partnership to the partner.[7]

D. Determination of Partner's Share of Recourse Liability

A partner's basis depends, in part, on the partner's share of partnership liabilities. In turn, the extent to which a partner is liable with respect to a partnership liability depends on whether the liability is a recourse or non-recourse liability and on related facts, such as whether a partner has guaranteed the debt or is entitled to be reimbursed for amounts paid with respect to the debt.

---

4. Section 752(c); Treas. Reg. § 1.752-1(e). A liability is treated as having been assumed if the assuming person is personally obligated to pay the liability. A partner assumes a partnership liability if the creditor knows of the assumption and can directly enforce the partner's obligation and no other partner would bear the economic risk of loss for the liability immediately after the assumption. Treas. Reg. § 1.752-1(d).

5. Section 752(b).

6. Section 752(a).

7. Treas. Reg. § 1.752-1(f).

A partnership liability is a recourse liability to the extent that any partner bears the economic risk of loss for that liability or would be obligated to contribute to the partnership to satisfy the liability.[8] To ascertain whether a partner bears the economic risk of loss, the regulations create a doomsday scenario and then consider which partners would have to contribute to the partnership to satisfy the liability. Note that whether a partner is required to contribute to the partnership to satisfy a liability is based on economic, or book, value, not on tax values. Specifically, a partner bears the economic risk of loss if:[9]

- The partnership constructively liquidated;
- As a result of the liquidation, the partner would be obligated to make a payment because the liability became due and payable; and
- The partner would not be entitled to reimbursement from another partner.

When the partnership constructively liquidates, several events are deemed to occur:

- All of the partnership's liabilities become payable in full.
- All of the partnership's assets (including cash) become worthless. The only exception is separately-held property that secures a partnership liability. Such property is transferred to the creditor to fully or partially satisfy the debt.
- Considering fair market, or book, values, the partnership sells all of its assets in a taxable transaction. Any property that secures a non-recourse debt is sold for the amount of the debt. Because all other property has become worthless, it is sold for nothing.
- All resulting items of book gain or loss are allocated among the partners and their capital accounts are adjusted accordingly.[10]
- The partnership liquidates.

Whether a partner has an obligation to make a contribution to the partnership is based on all the facts and circumstances.[11] All obligations are taken into consideration, such as guarantees. In addition, obligations imposed by the partnership agreement or state law are taken into consideration, including the obligation to restore negative capital account balances.[12] Similarly, if the partner is entitled to be reimbursed or indemnified by another partner, in determining the amount of that partner's required contribution,

---

8. Treas. Reg. § 1.752-2(a).

9. Treas. Reg. § 1.752-2(b)(1).

10. In general, all allocations will be based on each partner's respective ownership interest in the partnership. See Section 704(a). This issue is discussed in Chapter III.

11. Treas. Reg. § 1.752-2(b)(3). In determining the extent to which a partner bears the risk of loss, obligations of related parties are also taken into consideration. A related person includes a person related to a partner as defined in Section 267(b) or 707(b)(1), except that 80 percent is substituted for 50 percent; brother and sisters are excluded; and Section 267(e)(1) and 267(f)(1)(A) are disregarded. Treas. Reg. § 1.752-4(b)(1).

If the obligation to make a payment is not required to be satisfied within a reasonable time after the liability becomes due, or the obligation to make a contribution to the partnership is not required to be satisfied before the later of the end of the year in which the partnership interest is liquidated or 90 days after the liquidation, then the liability is only taken into account to the extent of its value. Treas. Reg. § 1.752-2(g)(1).

12. Treas. Reg. § 1.752-2(b)(3).

the amount of reimbursement or indemnification is taken into consideration.[13] There is a presumption that any partner required to reimburse another partner does so, even if the partner does not have the funds to make the payment (unless there is a plan to circumvent or avoid the payment).[14] However, if an obligation is subject to a contingency that makes it unlikely it would ever be paid, the obligation is disregarded.[15]

E. Determination of Partner's Share of Non-Recourse Liability

In general, a recourse liability is one for which the borrower is personally liable. A non-recourse liability is one for which the borrower is not personally liable. Most often, a non-recourse loan is secured by the property purchased with the borrowed funds.

Pursuant to the regulations, a partnership liability is a non-recourse liability to the extent that no partner bears the economic risk of loss for that liability.[16] Accordingly, the constructive liquidation of the doomsday scenario can be used to determine which liabilities are recourse liabilities. Any remaining liabilities will be non-recourse liabilities.

Noteworthy, because no partner will bear the economic risk of loss for a non-recourse liability, such risk cannot be used to allocate the liability among the partners. However, because a partnership generally finances the repayment of a non-recourse debt out of profits, it makes sense to allocate non-recourse debt based on how the partners share profits. As will be addressed in later chapters, other principles come into play to require that some or all of the non-recourse liability be allocated based on something other than how the partners share profits.[17]

F. Effect on Balance Sheet

Each partner's outside basis will reflect the amount of recourse or non-recourse liability for which he is responsible.

Capital accounts reflect only a partner's economic investment in the partnership. Stated another way, it reflects the amount a partner would expect to receive if the partnership where liquidated. Because all recourse creditors would be paid before any net proceeds were distributed to a partner and an asset that secured a non-recourse debt would be used to satisfy the debt, a partner's capital account does not include any liabilities. Thus, the total of all capital accounts must equal the value of all the partnership assets less all partnership liabilities.

---

13. Treas. Reg. § 1.752-2(b)(5).

14. Treas. Reg. § 1.752-2(b)(6). Special rules apply if the partner is a disregarded entity. See Treas. Reg. § 1.752-2(k).

15. Treas. Reg. § 1.752-2(b)(4).

16. Treas. Reg. § 1.752-1(a)(2).

17. Treas. Reg. § 1.752-3(a)(1), (2).

Summary

Recourse Debt:

- A partnership liability is a recourse liability to the extent that any partner bears the economic risk of loss for that liability or would be obligated to contribute to the partnership to satisfy the liability.

- To ascertain whether a partner bears the economic risk of loss, utilize the doomsday scenario and then consider which partners would have to contribute to the partnership to satisfy the liability. A partner bears the economic risk of loss if:
  - The partnership constructively liquidated;
  - As a result of the liquidation, the partner would be obligated to make a payment because the liability became due and payable; and
  - The partner would not be entitled to reimbursement from another partner.

Non-Recourse Debt:

- A partnership liability is a non-recourse liability to the extent that no partner bears the economic risk of loss for that liability.

- Non-recourse debt is allocated based on how the partners share profits.

Constructive Liquidation:

Step 1: All of the partnership liabilities become due and payable.

Step 2: Any separate property pledged by a partner to secure a partnership liability is transferred to the creditor in full or partial satisfaction of the liability.

Step 3: Any asset subject to a non-recourse debt is sold for the amount of the debt.

Step 4: All remaining partnership assets (including cash) become worthless.

Step 5: Considering fair market value, the partnership sells the remaining assets in a taxable transaction for nothing.

Step 6: Any resulting gain or loss is allocated among the partners based on how they have agreed to share profits and losses. Their capital accounts are adjusted accordingly.

Step 7: The partnership liquidates.

Taking into account all relevant agreements or laws, as a result of the liquidation, is a partner obligated to make a payment to the partnership so that the partnership can discharge a liability that has become due and payable?

Rules:

- A partner's outside basis is decreased by any decrease in his share of partnership liabilities or decrease in his individual liabilities due to the partnership's assumption of the liability.

- A partner's outside basis is increased by any increase in his share of partnership liabilities.

- If, in a single transaction, there is an increase in the partner's share of the partnership's liabilities and a decrease in the partner's individual liabilities (or vice versa), only the net amount will affect the partner's basis.

Formula: A partner's basis in a partnership interest where the partnership has liabilities is:

Adjusted basis of the asset(s) contributed to the partnership
+   Cash contributed to the partnership
+ _____ Net change in liabilities*
Partner's outside basis

* Amount of partnership debt assumed – amount of individual debt relief

Questions

1.   Ann and Bob formed an equal general partnership and each contributed $5,000. The partnership agreement provided that, upon liquidation, each partner must restore a negative capital account. The partnership purchased land for $15,000. It paid $10,000 in cash and obtained a $5,000 recourse loan for the remaining purchase price.

   a. Use a constructive liquidation to determine how the $5,000 debt should be allocated between Ann and Bob.

   b. Determine Ann and Bob's outside basis in the partnership.

   c. Prepare a balance sheet to reflect the situation of the partnership after purchase of the land.

2.   Carl and Deb formed a general partnership. Carl contributed $10,000 for a one-third interest, and Deb contributed $20,000 for a two-thirds interest. All partnership items were to be allocated one-third to Carl and two-thirds to Deb. The partnership agreement provided that, upon liquidation, each partner must restore a negative capital account. The partnership purchased land for $39,000. It paid $30,000 in cash and obtained a $9,000 recourse loan for the remaining purchase price.

   a. Use a constructive liquidation to determine how the $9,000 debt should be allocated between Carl and Deb.

   b. Determine Carl and Deb's outside basis in the partnership.

   c. Prepare a balance sheet to reflect the situation of the partnership after purchase of the land.

3.   Ellen and Frank formed a general partnership. Ellen contributed $10,000 for a one-third interest, and Frank contributed $20,000 for a two-thirds interest. All partnership items were to be allocated one-third to Ellen and two-thirds to Frank. The partnership agreement provided that, upon liquidation, each partner must restore a negative capital account. The partnership purchased land for $39,000. It paid $30,000 in cash and obtained a $9,000 recourse loan for the remaining purchase price. Frank signed a personal guaranty, guarantying payment of the debt.

   a. Use a constructive liquidation to determine how the $9,000 debt should be allocated between Ellen and Frank.

   b. Determine Ellen and Frank's outside basis in the partnership.

   c. Prepare a balance sheet to reflect the situation of the partnership after purchase of the land.

4.   Greg and Hal formed an equal general partnership. Greg contributed $5,000 and Hal contributed land with a basis of $7,000, with a fair market value of $7,000, and subject to a $2,000 recourse liability. The partnership agreement provided that, upon liquidation, all partners must restore a negative capital account.

   a. Use a constructive liquidation to determine how the $2,000 debt should be allocated between Greg and Hal.

   b. Determine Greg and Hal's outside basis in the partnership.

   c. Prepare a balance sheet to reflect the situation of the partnership at formation.

5.   Ira and Jeb formed an equal general partnership. Ira contributed $50,000 and Jeb contributed land with a basis of $30,000 and fair market value of $50,000. The partnership agreement provided that, upon liquidation, all partners must restore a negative capital account. The partnership purchased a building for $20,000 with $10,000 of cash and financed the remainder of the purchase with a $10,000 recourse liability.

   a. Use a constructive liquidation to determine how the $10,000 debt should be allocated between Ira and Jeb.

   b. Determine Ira and Jeb's outside basis in the partnership.

   c. Prepare a balance sheet to reflect the situation of the partnership after purchase of the building.

6.   Kent and Len formed a general partnership. Kent contributed $10,000 and Len contributed land with a basis of $7,000, with a fair market value of $10,000. The partnership agreement provided that all income, gain, deductions, and losses would be allocated 20 percent to Kent and 80 percent to Len, and that, upon liquidation, all partners must restore a negative capital account. The partnership purchased a building for $50,000 and financed the entire purchase price with a $50,000 recourse liability.

   a. Use a constructive liquidation to determine how the $50,000 debt should be allocated between Kent and Len.

   b. Determine Kent and Len's outside basis in the partnership.

   c. Prepare a balance sheet to reflect the situation of the partnership after purchase of the building.

7.   Mike and Ned formed a general partnership. Mike contributed $10,000 and Ned contributed $20,000. All partnership items were to be allocated one-third to Mike and two-thirds to Ned. The partnership agreement provided that, upon liquidation, all partners must restore a negative capital account. The partnership purchased land for $30,000, financing the purchase price with a non-recourse debt.

   a. Can you use a constructive liquidation to determine how the $30,000 debt should be allocated between Mike and Ned?

   b. Determine Mike and Ned's outside basis in the partnership.

   c. Prepare a balance sheet to reflect the situation of the partnership after purchase of the land.

8.   Opie and Paul formed a limited partnership. Opie contributed $10,000 in exchange for a limited partnership interest, and Paul contributed $20,000 for a general partnership interest. All partnership items were to be allocated one-third to Opie and two-thirds to Paul. The partnership agreement provided that, upon liquidation, Paul must restore a negative capital account. The partnership purchased land for $30,000, financing the purchase price with a non-recourse debt.

   a. Can you use a constructive liquidation to determine how the $30,000 debt should be allocated between Opie and Paul?

   b. Determine Opie and Paul's outside basis in the partnership.

   c. Prepare a balance sheet to reflect the situation of the partnership after purchase of the land.

Solutions

1.   Ann and Bob formed an equal general partnership and each contributed $5,000. The partnership agreement provided that, upon liquidation, each partner must restore a negative capital account. The partnership purchased land for $15,000. It paid $10,000 in cash and obtained a $5,000 recourse loan for the remaining purchase price.

   a. Use a constructive liquidation to determine how the $5,000 debt should be allocated between Ann and Bob.

   Ann and Bob's basis depends, in part, on their share of partnership liabilities. The partnership's $5,000 liability is a recourse liability to the extent that any partner bears the economic risk of loss for that liability or would be obligated to contribute to the partnership to satisfy the liability. (Treas. Reg. § 1.752-1(a)(1)) To ascertain whether Ann or Bob bears the economic risk of loss, the partnership must go though the constructive liquidation of the doomsday scenario. (Treas. Reg. § 1.752-2(b))

   First, the partnership is constructively liquidated. As part of the liquidation, the $5,000 obligation becomes due. All assets become worthless. Considering fair market, or book, value, the partnership sells the land for nothing. The tax consequences from the sale are as follows:

Amount realized:	$ 0
Book basis:	15,000
Loss:	<$15,000>

   The $15,000 loss is allocated equally between Ann and Bob, or <$7,500> each. The impact to Ann and Bob's capital accounts would be as follows:

	Ann	Bob
Capital account on formation:	$5,000	$5,000
Loss from sale of land:	<7,500>	<7,500>
Balance:	<$2,500>	<$2,500>

   The partnership liquidates. The partnership agreement requires the partners to restore a negative capital account upon liquidation. Thus, both Ann and Bob have an obligation to contribute $2,500 to the partnership. The total of the contributions, $5,000, would be used to satisfy the $5,000 debt.

   The liability is a recourse liability because one or more partners bear the economic risk of loss. Specifically, Ann and Bob each bears an economic risk of loss of $2,500. The liability should be allocated equally, or $2,500 each. (Treas. Reg. §§ 1.752-1(a)(1); 1.752-2(a))

   b. Determine Ann and Bob's outside basis in the partnership.

   Ann and Bob's basis would be determined as follows (Sections 722; 752(a)):

	Ann	Bob
Cash:	$5,000	$5,000
Increase in liabilities:	2,500	2,500
Basis:	$7,500	$7,500

   c. Prepare a balance sheet to reflect the situation of the partnership after purchase of the land.

After the partnership purchases the land, the balance sheet would appear as follows:

Asset	Adj. Basis	FMV	Liabilities:		$5,000
Land	$15,000	$15,000		Basis	Cap. Acct.
			Ann:	$ 7,500	$ 5,000
			Bob:	7,500	5,000
Total:	$15,000	$15,000		$15,000	$15,000

2.   Carl and Deb formed a general partnership. Carl contributed $10,000 for a one-third interest, and Deb contributed $20,000 for a two-thirds interest. All partnership items were to be allocated one-third to Carl and two-thirds to Deb. The partnership agreement provided that, upon liquidation, each partner must restore a negative capital account. The partnership purchased land for $39,000. It paid $30,000 in cash and obtained a $9,000 recourse loan for the remaining purchase price.

   a. Use a constructive liquidation to determine how the $9,000 debt should be allocated between Carl and Deb.

Carl and Deb's basis depends, in part, on their share of partnership liabilities. The partnership's $9,000 liability is a recourse liability to the extent that any partner bears the economic risk of loss for that liability or would be obligated to contribute to the partnership to satisfy the liability. (Treas. Reg. § 1.752-1(a)(1)) To ascertain whether Carl or Deb bears the economic risk of loss, the partnership must go though the constructive liquidation of the doomsday scenario. (Treas. Reg. § 1.752-2(b))

First, the partnership is constructively liquidated. As part of the liquidation, the $9,000 obligation becomes due. All assets become worthless. Considering fair market, or book, value, the partnership sells the land for nothing. The tax consequences from the sale are as follows:

Amount realized: $ 0
Book basis: 39,000
Loss: <$39,000>

The $39,000 loss is allocated one-third to Carl and two-thirds to Deb, or <$13,000> to Carl and <$26,000> to Deb. The impact to Carl and Deb's capital accounts would be as follows:

	Carl	Deb
Capital account on formation:	$10,000	$20,000
Loss from sale of land:	<13,000>	<26,000>
Balance:	<$3,000>	<$6,000>

The partnership liquidates. The partnership agreement requires the partners to restore a negative capital account upon liquidation. Thus, both Carl and Deb have an obligation to contribute, Carl to contribute $3,000 and Deb to contribute $6,000. The total of the contributions, $9,000, would be used to satisfy the $9,000 debt.

The liability is a recourse liability because one or more partners bear the economic risk of loss. Specifically, Carl bears an economic risk of loss of $3,000 and Deb bears an economic risk of loss of $6,000 and the liability should be allocated accordingly. (Treas. Reg. §§ 1.752-1(a)(1); 1.752-2(a))

b. **Determine Carl and Deb's outside basis in the partnership.**

Carl and Deb's basis would be determined as follows (Section 722; 752(a)):

	Carl	Deb
Cash:	$10,000	$20,000
Increase in liabilities:	3,000	6,000
Basis:	$13,000	$26,000

c. **Prepare a balance sheet to reflect the situation of the partnership after purchase of the land.**

After the partnership purchases the land, the balance sheet would appear as follows:

Asset	Adj. Basis	FMV	Liabilities:		$9,000
Land	$39,000	$39,000		**Basis**	**Cap. Acct.**
			Carl:	$13,000	$10,000
			Deb:	26,000	20,000
Total:	$39,000	$39,000		$39,000	$39,000

3. Ellen and Frank formed a general partnership. Ellen contributed $10,000 for a one-third interest, and Frank contributed $20,000 for a two-thirds interest. All partnership items were to be allocated one-third to Ellen and two-thirds to Frank. The partnership agreement provided that, upon liquidation, each partner must restore a negative capital account. The partnership purchased land for $39,000. It paid $30,000 in cash and obtained a $9,000 recourse loan for the remaining purchase price. Frank signed a personal guaranty, guarantying payment of the debt.

a. **Use a constructive liquidation to determine how the $9,000 debt should be allocated between Ellen and Frank.**

Ellen and Frank's basis depends, in part, on their share of partnership liabilities. The partnership's $9,000 liability is a recourse liability to the extent that any partner bears the economic risk of loss for that liability or would be obligated to contribute to the partnership to satisfy the liability. (Treas. Reg. § 1.752-1(a)(1)) To ascertain whether Ellen or Frank bears the economic risk of loss, the partnership must go though the constructive liquidation of the doomsday scenario. (Treas. Reg. § 1.752-2(b))

First, the partnership is constructively liquidated. As part of the liquidation, the $9,000 obligation becomes due. All assets become worthless. Considering fair market, or book, value, the partnership sells the land for nothing. The tax consequences from the sale are as follows:

Amount realized:	$ 0
Book basis:	39,000
Loss:	<$39,000>

The $39,000 loss is allocated one-third to Ellen and two-thirds to Frank, or <$13,000> to Ellen and <$26,000> to Frank. The impact to Ellen and Frank's capital accounts would be as follows:

	Ellen	Frank
Capital account on formation:	$10,000	$20,000
Loss from sale of land:	<13,000>	<26,000>
Balance:	<$3,000>	<$6,000>

The partnership liquidates. The partnership agreement requires the partners to restore a negative capital account upon liquidation. Thus, both Ellen and Frank have an obligation to contribute, Ellen to contribute $3,000 and Frank to contribute $6,000. The total of the contributions, $9,000, would be used to satisfy the $9,000 debt. Frank would not be called upon to pay the debt pursuant to his guaranty.

The liability is a recourse liability because one or more partners bear the economic risk of loss. Specifically, Ellen bears an economic risk of loss of $3,000 and Frank bears an economic risk of loss of $6,000 and the liability should be allocated accordingly. (Treas. Reg. §§ 1.752-1(a)(1); 1.752-2(a), -2(b)(6))

b. Determine Ellen and Frank's outside basis in the partnership.

Ellen and Frank's basis would be determined as follows (Sections 722; 752(a)):

	Ellen	Frank
Cash:	$10,000	$20,000
Increase in liabilities:	3,000	6,000
Basis:	$13,000	$26,000

c. Prepare a balance sheet to reflect the situation of the partnership after purchase of the land.

After the partnership purchases the land, the balance sheet would appear as follows:

Asset	Adj. Basis	FMV	Liabilities:		$9,000
Land	$39,000	$39,000		Basis	Cap. Acct.
			Ellen:	$13,000	$10,000
			Frank:	26,000	20,000
Total:	$39,000	$39,000		$39,000	$39,000

4.   Greg and Hal formed an equal general partnership. Greg contributed $5,000 and Hal contributed land with a basis of $7,000, with a fair market value of $7,000, and subject to a $2,000 recourse liability. The partnership agreement provided that, upon liquidation, all partners must restore a negative capital account.

a. Use a constructive liquidation to determine how the $2,000 debt should be allocated between Greg and Hal.

Greg and Hal's basis depends, in part, on their share of partnership liabilities. The partnership's $2,000 liability is a recourse liability to the extent that any partner bears the economic risk of loss for that liability or would be obligated to contribute to the partnership to satisfy the liability. (Treas. Reg. § 1.752-1(a)(1)) To ascertain whether Greg or Hal bears the economic risk of loss, the partnership must go though the constructive liquidation of the doomsday scenario. (Treas. Reg. § 1.752-2(b))

First, the partnership is constructively liquidated. As part of the liquidation, the $2,000 obligation becomes due. All assets become worthless. Considering fair market, or book, value, the partnership sells the land for nothing. The tax consequences from the sale are as follows:

Amount realized:	$ 0
Book basis:	7,000
Loss:	<$7,000>

The $7,000 loss is allocated equally between them, or $3,500 each. The $5,000 cash also becomes worthless. The loss is allocated equally between them, or $2,500 each. The impact to Greg and Hal's capital accounts would be as follows:

	Greg	Hal
Capital account on formation:	$5,000	$5,000
Loss from cash:	<2,500>	<2,500>
Loss from sale of land:	<3,500>	<3,500>
Balance:	<$1,000>	<$1,000>

The partnership liquidates. The partnership agreement requires the partners to restore a negative capital account upon liquidation. Thus, both Greg and Hal have an obligation to contribute $1,000 to the partnership. The total of the contributions, $2,000, would be used to satisfy the $2,000 debt.

The liability is a recourse liability because one or more partners bear the economic risk of loss. Specifically, Greg and Hal each bears an economic risk of loss of $1,000. The liability should be allocated equally, or $1,000 each. (Treas. Reg. §§ 1.752-1(a)(1); 1.752-2(a))

b. Determine Greg and Hal's outside basis in the partnership.

Greg and Hal's basis would be determined as follows (Sections 722; 752(a)):

	Greg	Hal
Cash:	$5,000	—
Property:	—	$7,000
Net change in liabilities:	1,000	<1,000>*
Basis:	$6,000	$6,000

* $1,000 of partnership debt assumed, less $2,000 of individual debt relief. (Treas. Reg. § 1.752-1(f))

c. Prepare a balance sheet to reflect the situation of the partnership at formation.

After the partnership purchases the land, the balance sheet would appear as follows:

Asset	Adj. Basis	FMV	Liabilities:		$2,000
Cash	$ 5,000	$ 5,000		Basis	Cap. Acct.
Land	7,000	7,000	Greg:	$ 6,000	$ 5,000
			Hal:	6,000	5,000
Total:	$12,000	$12,000		$12,000	$12,000

5. Ira and Jeb formed an equal general partnership. Ira contributed $50,000 and Jeb contributed land with a basis of $30,000 and fair market value of $50,000. The partnership agreement provided that, upon liquidation, all partners must restore a negative capital account. The partnership purchased a building for $20,000 with $10,000 of cash and financed the remainder of the purchase with a $10,000 recourse liability.

a. Use a constructive liquidation to determine how the $10,000 debt should be allocated between Ira and Jeb.

Ira and Jeb's basis depends, in part, on their share of partnership liabilities. The partnership's $10,000 liability is a recourse liability to the extent that any partner bears the economic risk of loss for that liability or would be obligated to contribute to the partnership to satisfy the liability. (Treas. Reg. § 1.752-1(a)(1)) To ascertain whether Ira or Jeb bears the economic risk of loss, the partnership must go though the constructive liquidation of the doomsday scenario. (Treas. Reg. § 1.752-2(b))

First, the partnership is constructively liquidated. As part of the liquidation, the $10,000 obligation becomes due. All assets become worthless. Considering fair market, or book, value, the partnership sells the land for nothing. The tax consequences from the sale of the land are as follows:

Amount realized:	$ 0
Book basis:	50,000
Loss:	<$50,000>

The $50,000 loss is allocated equally between them, or $25,000 each.

The partnership sells the building for nothing. The tax consequences from the sale of the building are as follows:

Amount realized:	$ 0
Book basis:	20,000
Loss:	<$20,000>

The $20,000 loss is allocated equally between them, or $10,000 each.

After purchase of the building, there is $40,000 of cash remaining, and it also becomes worthless. The loss is allocated equally between them, or $20,000 each. The impact to Ira and Jeb's capital accounts would be as follows:

	Ira	Jeb
Capital account on formation:	$50,000	$50,000
Loss from cash:	<20,000>	<20,000>
Loss from sale of land:	<25,000>	<25,000>
Loss from sale of building:	<10,000>	<10,000>
Balance:	<$ 5,000>	<$ 5,000>

The partnership liquidates. The partnership agreement requires the partners to restore a negative capital account upon liquidation. Thus, both Ira and Jeb have an obligation to contribute $5,000 to the partnership. The total of the contributions, $10,000, would be used to satisfy the $10,000 debt.

The liability is a recourse liability because one or more partners bear the economic risk of loss. Specifically, Ira and Jeb each bears an economic risk of loss of $5,000. The liability should be allocated equally, or $5,000 each. (Treas. Reg. §§ 1.752-1(a)(1); 1.752-2(a))

b. Determine Ira and Jeb's outside basis in the partnership.

Ira and Jeb's basis would be determined as follows (Sections 722; 752(a)):

	Ira	Jeb
Cash:	$50,000	$ —
Property:	—	30,000
Increase in liabilities:	5,000	5,000
Basis:	$55,000	$35,000

c. Prepare a balance sheet to reflect the situation of the partnership after purchase of the building.

After the partnership purchases the building, the balance sheet would appear as follows:

Asset	Adj. Basis	FMV	Liabilities:		$ 10,000	
Cash	$40,000	$ 40,000		**Basis**	**Cap. Acct.**	
Building	20,000	20,000	Ira:	$55,000	$ 50,000	
Land	30,000	50,000	Jeb:	35,000	50,000	
Total:	$90,000	$110,000		$90,000	$110,000	

6. Kent and Len formed a general partnership. Kent contributed $10,000 and Len contributed land with a basis of $7,000, with a fair market value of $10,000. The partnership agreement provided that all income, gain, deductions, and losses would be allocated 20 percent to Kent and 80 percent to Len, and that, upon liquidation, all partners must restore a negative capital account. The partnership purchased a building for $50,000 and financed the entire purchase price with a $50,000 recourse liability.

a. Use a constructive liquidation to determine how the $50,000 debt should be allocated between Kent and Len.

Kent and Len's basis depends, in part, on their share of partnership liabilities. The partnership's $50,000 liability is a recourse liability to the extent that any partner bears the economic risk of loss for that liability or would be obligated to contribute to the partnership to satisfy the liability. (Treas. Reg. § 1.752-1(a)(1)) To ascertain whether Kent or Len bears the economic risk of loss, the partnership must go though the constructive liquidation of the doomsday scenario. (Treas. Reg. § 1.752-2(b))

First, the partnership is constructively liquidated. As part of the liquidation, the $50,000 obligation becomes due. All assets become worthless. Considering fair market, or book, value, the partnership sells the land for nothing. The tax consequences from the sale of the land are as follows:

Amount realized:	$	0
Book basis:		10,000
Loss:		<$10,000>

The $10,000 loss is allocated 20 percent to Kent and 80 percent to Len, or $2,000 to Kent and $8,000 to Len.

The partnership sells the building for nothing. The tax consequences from the sale of the building are as follows:

Amount realized:	$	0
Book basis:		50,000
Loss:		<$50,000>

The $50,000 loss is allocated 20 percent to Kent and 80 percent to Len, or $10,000 to Kent and $40,000 to Len.

The $10,000 cash also becomes worthless. The loss is allocated 20 percent to Kent and 80 percent to Len, or $2,000 to Kent and $8,000 to Len. The impact to Kent and Len's capital accounts would be as follows:

	Kent	Len
Capital account on formation:	$10,000	$10,000
Loss from cash:	<2,000>	<8,000>
Loss from sale of land:	<2,000>	<8,000>
Loss from sale of building:	<10,000>	<40,000>
Balance:	<$ 4,000>	<$46,000>

The partnership liquidates. The partnership agreement requires the partners to restore a negative capital account upon liquidation. Thus, Kent has an obligation to contribute $4,000 and Len has an obligation to contribute $46,000. The total of the contributions, $50,000, would be used to satisfy the $50,000 debt.

The liability is a recourse liability because one or more partners bear the economic risk of loss. Specifically, Kent bears an economic risk of loss of $4,000 and Len bears an economic risk of loss of $46,000. The liability should be allocated $4,000 to Kent and $46,000 to Len. (Treas. Reg. §§ 1.752-1(a)(1); 1.752-2(a))

b. **Determine Kent and Len's outside basis in the partnership.**

Kent and Len's basis would be determined as follows (Section 722; 752(a)):

	Kent	Len
Cash:	$10,000	$ —
Property:	—	7,000
Increase in liabilities:	4,000	46,000
Basis:	$14,000	$53,000

c. **Prepare a balance sheet to reflect the situation of the partnership after purchase of the building.**

After the partnership purchases the building, the balance sheet would appear as follows:

Asset	Adj. Basis	FMV	Liabilities:			$50,000
Cash	$10,000	$10,000			**Basis**	**Cap. Acct.**
Building	50,000	50,000	Kent:	$14,000	$10,000
Land	7,000	10,000	Len:	53,000	10,000
Total:	$67,000	$70,000		$67,000	$70,000

7. Mike and Ned formed a general partnership. Mike contributed $10,000 and Ned contributed $20,000. All partnership items were to be allocated one-third to Mike and two-thirds to Ned. The partnership agreement provided that, upon liquidation, all partners must restore a negative capital account. The partnership purchased land for $30,000, financing the purchase price with a non-recourse debt.

a. Can you use a constructive liquidation to determine how the $30,000 debt should be allocated between Mike and Ned?

No, because no partner will be at risk for the liability. (Treas. Reg. § 1.752-1(a)(2)) The constructive liquidation establishes this to be true. (Treas. Reg. § 1.752-2(b))

First, the partnership is constructively liquidated. As part of the liquidation, the $30,000 obligation becomes due. Any asset subject to a non-recourse debt is sold for the amount of the debt. The land is sold for the amount of the debt.

Amount realized:	$30,000
Book basis:	30,000
Loss:	0

All other assets become worthless. The $30,000 cash becomes worthless. The loss is allocated one-third to Mike and two-thirds to Ned, or $10,000 to Mike and $20,000 to Ned. The impact to Mike and Ned's capital accounts would be as follows:

	Mike	Ned
Capital account on formation:	$10,000	$20,000
Loss from cash:	<10,000>	<20,000>
Balance:	$ 0	$ 0

The partnership liquidates. Because neither partner has a negative capital account, neither partner bears the economic risk of loss. The liability is a non-recourse liability.

Non-recourse liabilities generally are allocated according to the ratio in which the partners share profits. (Treas. Reg. § 1.752-3(a)(3)) An increase in a partner's share of partnership liabilities is treated as a cash contribution by the partner to the partnership. (Section 752(a)) The liability is allocated one-third to Mike and two-thirds to Ned, or $10,000 to Mike and $20,000 to Ned.

b. **Determine Mike and Ned's outside basis in the partnership.**

Mike and Ned's basis would be determined as follows (Sections 722; 752(a)):

	Mike	Ned
Cash:	$10,000	$20,000
Increase in liabilities:	10,000	20,000
Basis:	$20,000	$40,000

c. **Prepare a balance sheet to reflect the situation of the partnership after purchase of the land.**

After the partnership purchases the land, the balance sheet would appear as follows:

Asset	Adj. Basis	FMV	Liabilities:			$30,000
Cash	$30,000	$30,000			**Basis**	**Cap. Acct.**
Land	30,000	30,000	Mike:	$20,000		$10,000
			Ned:	40,000		20,000
Total:	$60,000	$60,000		$60,000		$60,000

8.   Opie and Paul formed a limited partnership. Opie contributed $10,000 in exchange for a limited partnership interest, and Paul contributed $20,000 for a general partnership interest. All partnership items were to be allocated one-third to Opie and two-thirds to Paul. The partnership agreement provided that, upon liquidation, Paul must restore a negative capital account. The partnership purchased land for $30,000, financing the purchase price with a non-recourse debt.

a. Can you use a constructive liquidation to determine how the $30,000 debt should be allocated between Opie and Paul?

No, because no partner will be at risk for the liability. (Treas. Reg. § 1.752-1(a)(2)) The constructive liquidation establishes this to be true. (Treas. Reg. § 1.752-2(b))

First, the partnership is constructively liquidated. As part of the liquidation, the $30,000 obligation becomes due. Any asset subject to a non-recourse debt is sold for the amount of the debt. The land is sold for the amount of the debt.

Amount realized:	$30,000
Book basis:	30,000
Loss:	$ 0

All other assets become worthless. The $30,000 cash becomes worthless. The loss is allocated one-third to Opie and two-thirds to Paul, or $10,000 to Opie and $20,000 to Paul. The impact to Opie and Paul's capital accounts would be as follows:

	Opie	Paul
Capital account on formation:	$10,000	$20,000
Loss from cash:	<10,000>	<20,000>
Balance:	$ 0	$ 0

The partnership liquidates. Because neither partner has a negative capital account, neither partner bears the economic risk of loss. The liability is a non-recourse liability.

Non-recourse liabilities generally are allocated according to the ratio in which the partners share profits. (Treas. Reg. § 1.752-3(a)(3)) An increase in a partner's share of partnership liabilities is treated as a cash contribution by the partner to the partnership. (Section 752(a)) The liability is allocated one-third to Opie and two-thirds to Paul, or $10,000 to Opie and $20,000 to Paul.

b. Determine Opie and Paul's outside basis in the partnership.

Opie and Paul's basis would be determined as follows (Sections 722; 752(a)):

	Opie	Paul
Cash:	$10,000	$20,000
Increase in liabilities:	10,000	20,000
Basis:	$20,000	$40,000

c. Prepare a balance sheet to reflect the situation of the partnership after purchase of the land.

After the partnership purchases the land, the balance sheet would appear as follows:

Asset	Adj. Basis	FMV	Liabilities:			$30,000
Cash	$30,000	$30,000			**Basis**	**Cap. Acct.**
Land	30,000	30,000	Opie:	$20,000		$10,000
			Paul:	40,000		20,000
Total:	$60,000	$60,000		$60,000		$60,000

Chapter III

Operating Provisions

A. Partnership Return

A partnership is treated as a separate entity (*i.e.*, separate from the partners) for some purposes and as an aggregation of partners for other purposes.

Partnership return. For purposes of computing the partnership's taxable income, the partnership is treated as a separate entity.[1] The partnership is required to prepare and file an information income tax return, reflecting income, gains, deductions, losses and credits.[2] The information return is a Form 1065, U.S. Return of Partnership Income. If the partnership is a calendar year taxpayer, it must file its return on or before April 15 (without consideration of any available extensions). If a fiscal year taxpayer, the partnership must file its return on or before the 15th day of the fourth month after the close of its taxable year.

Partnership accounting method. The partnership's accounting method will dictate when items must be reported on the partnership tax return. In general, it may select any method of accounting, as long as it clearly reflects the partnership's income, even if that method differs from its partners' method of accounting.[3] However, there are some limitations.

If the partnership is a "tax shelter," it may not use the cash method of accounting.[4] A partnership is a "tax shelter" if:

- Interests in the partnership have been offered for sale in an offering required to be registered with any federal or state securities agency;
- More than 35 percent of the partnership's losses during the tax year are allocable to limited partners or limited entrepreneurs who do not actively participate in management of the partnership; or

---

1. Section 703(a).
2. Sections 6031; 6072(a).
3. Sections 446(c); 703(b).
4. Sections 448(a), (d)(3); 461(i)(3).

- A significant purpose of the partnership is the avoidance or evasion of federal income tax.

If a C corporation is a partner in the partnership, the partnership may not use the cash method of accounting.[5] The prohibition on use of the cash method does not apply if:[6]

- The C corporation is a qualified personal service corporation;[7]
- The business is farming; or
- Average annual gross receipts do not exceed $5,000,000 for the three-year period preceding the taxable year.

Flow-through of partnership items. The partnership does not pay any tax.[8] Rather, for such purposes, the partnership is treated as an aggregate of its partners and the partners are responsible for reporting partnership income, gain, deduction, and loss on their individual income tax returns.[9] A partner includes his share of partnership items on his tax return for the taxable year in which the partnership's taxable year ends.[10]

Given that both the partnership and the partners file on a yearly basis, a partner may attempt to utilize the disparity between the time a partnership files an information return and the time partnership items are included on the partner's individual return to defer income. To prohibit this deferral, the Code limits the taxable year that may be used by the partnership.

B. Taxable Year

To prohibit taxpayer-partners from deferring the reporting of partnership items, the Code sets forth three mechanical rules that identify the partnership's taxable year. There are three exceptions to the mechanical rules.

Mechanical rules. The mechanical rules are applied in order. The first rule that is satisfied will determine the taxable year of the partnership.

First, if the owners of more than 50 percent of the partnership profits and/or capital interests have the same taxable year, that taxable year is the partnership's taxable year.[11] If a partnership is required to change its taxable year under this rule, it is not required to change to another tax year for either of the two tax years following the year of change.[12]

---

5. Section 448(a), (b)(2).

6. Sections 447; 448(a), (b)(1), (b)(2), (c).

7. A corporation is a "qualified personal service corporation" if substantially all its activities involve the performance of services in the fields of health, law, engineering, architecture, accounting, actuarial service, performing arts, or consulting and substantially all its stock is owned by employees, retired employees, or their estates. Section 448(d)(2).

8. Section 701.

9. Id.

10. Treas. Reg. § 1.706-1(a)(1).

11. Section 706(b)(1)(B)(i), (b)(4).

12. Section 706(b)(4)(B).

Second, if all the principal partners have the same taxable year, that taxable year is the partnership's taxable year.[13] A partner is considered a principal partner if he owns a five percent or more interest in the partnership profits or capital.[14]

Third, the partnership taxable year is the year that would result in the least aggregate amount of deferral of income to the partners.[15] For this test, the aggregate deferral with respect to each partner's taxable year must be determined. For each such year, first determine the number of months of deferral for each partner. The months of deferral is the number of months from the end of the partnership's taxable year forward to the end of the partner's taxable year. Then, multiply the number of months of deferral for each partner by the partner's interest in partnership profits for that year. Finally, add together all the products to determine the aggregate deferral with respect to that taxable year. The partner's taxable year that produces the lowest sum when compared to the other partners' taxable years is the taxable year that results in the least aggregate deferral of income.

If the calculation results in more than one taxable year qualifying as the taxable year with the least aggregate deferral, the partnership may select any one of those taxable years as its taxable year. But, if one of the qualifying taxable years is the partnership's existing taxable year, the partnership must maintain its existing taxable year.[16]

Exceptions to mechanical rules. There are three exceptions to the statute's mechanical rules.

First, a partnership can use a taxable year not provided for in the mechanical rules if it can establish a business purpose.[17] While both tax and non-tax factors must be considered, generally those that relate to taxpayer convenience are not sufficient to establish a business purpose. Non-tax factors include:[18]

- The use of a particular year for regulatory or financial accounting purposes;
- The seasonal hiring patterns of a business;
- The use of a particular year for administrative purposes, such as retirements, promotions, or salary increases; and
- The fact that a business involves the use of price lists, a model year, or other items that change annually.

Second, a partnership can use a taxable year not provided for in the mechanical rules if it can establish a business purpose and obtain approval from the Service under Section 442.[19] A business purpose can be established by showing there is a "natural business year" under the gross receipts test.[20] A natural business year exists if 25 percent or more of the partnership's gross receipts for the selected year are earned in the last two months. This test must be satisfied in each of the preceding three 12-month periods that correspond to the requested fiscal year.

---

13. Section 706(b)(1)(B)(ii).
14. Section 706(b)(3).
15. Section 706(b)(1)(B)(iii); Treas. Reg. § 1.706-1(b)(2)(i)(C).
16. Treas. Reg. § 1.706-1(b)(3)(i).
17. Code Sec. 706(b)(1)(C).
18. Rev. Rul. 87-57, 1987-2 C.B. 117.
19. Treas. Reg. § 1.706-1(b)(2)(ii).
20. Rev. Proc. 2002-38, 2002-1 C.B. 1037.

Under the third exception, a partnership may elect a taxable year that results in up to three months of deferral. However, because the rules for determining a partnership's taxable year are designed to prevent partners from deferring the reporting of income (and payment of tax) to later years, the deferral is allowed only if the partnership is willing to pay the tax on the deferred income.[21] Because of the required tax payment, there is no tax benefit to deferring the income. Accordingly, the partnership must have some other reason for selecting a taxable year other than the one provided for in the statute or regulations.

C. Computation of Taxable Income

In general, the partnership's taxable income is computed in the same manner as an individual's taxable income.[22] First, the partnership must report all gross income for the taxable year. Next, it reduces its gross income by all allowable deductions. It is allowed the same deductions as an individual, except it is not allowed a deduction for the following items:

- Personal exemptions;
- Taxes paid to foreign countries or U.S. possessions;
- Charitable contributions;
- Net operating losses;
- Certain itemized deductions including:
  - Expenses incurred in the production of income;
  - Medical and dental expenses;
  - Alimony paid;
  - Moving expenses;
  - Qualified retirement contributions;
  - Interest paid on education loans;
  - Qualified tuition and related expenses; and
  - Amounts paid to a health savings account.

To the extent a partnership has the above expenses (except the personal exemption and certain of the itemized deductions), they are separately stated and may be deductible by the partners.

Elections. To ensure consistency among the partners, the partnership is responsible for making elections that will impact the computation of its taxable income.[23] The election applies only with respect to partnership items. It does not impact the partner's tax items from sources other than the partnership.

The following decisions are made by the partnership:

- Accounting method;
- Inventory method;

---

21. Sections 444; 7519; Treas. Reg. § 1.706-1(b)(2)(ii).
22. Section 703(a).
23. Section 703(b).

- Depreciation method and whether to claim bonus depreciation;
- Election to amortize start-up expenses;
- Whether to report gain using the installment method;
- Election to deduct research and development expenses;
- Election to adjust the basis of partnership property under Section 754; and
- Election to defer gain from an involuntary conversion of partnership property.

A small number of elections are made by the individual partners. They include items such as elections related to income from discharge of indebtedness and the recapture of certain mining exploration expenditures.[24]

Separately stated items. While the items are reported on the partnership's tax return, the partnership does not pay tax. Rather, the items pass through the partnership and are reported on the partner's individual income tax return.

Because the character of items may impact how they must be included on the partner's individual income tax return, some partnership items must be reported separately to the partners. The character of such items is determined as if each such item were realized directly from the source from which the partnership realized the item or as if the item had been incurred in the same manner as incurred by the partnership.[25]

Those items that must be separately stated when reported to the partners include:[26]

- Short-term capital gain and loss;
- Long-term capital gain and loss;
- Gain and loss from hotchpot (Section 1231) property;
- Charitable contributions;
- Dividends;
- Taxes paid to foreign countries and U.S. possessions; and
- Other items identified in the regulations that may affect the partner's individual income tax liability.

Those items that are not specially treated on an individual partner's income tax return can be netted together before being reported to the partners.

D. Start-Up Costs

Qualified expenses. A partnership may elect to amortize the cost of organizational expenses.[27] To be an organizational expense, the expense must meet a three-part test.

First, the expense must be incident to the creation of the partnership.[28] To be incident to the creation of the partnership, the expense must have been incurred a reasonable time before the partnership began business and ending before the date its partnership tax return was due to be filed for the year the partnership began business, without

---

24. Id.
25. Section 702(b).
26. Section 702(a).
27. Section 709(a), (b)(1).
28. Section 709(b)(3)(A).

taking into consideration any extensions. In contrast, an expense incurred for operating or starting operation of a partnership is not incident to the creation of partnership.[29]

Second, the expense must be one that is chargeable to capital account.[30] Third, the expense must be of a character that, if expended incident to the creation of a partnership having an ascertainable life, would be amortizable over such life.[31] To satisfy this requirement, the expense should be for an item that would normally benefit the partnership throughout its entire life.[32]

Examples of organizational expenses include:[33]

- Legal fees for services incident to the organization of the partnership such as negotiation and preparation of a partnership agreement or operating agreement;
- Accounting fees for services incident to the organization of the partnership; and
- Filing fees.

Examples of expenses that are not organizational expenses include:[34]

- Expenses connected with acquiring assets for the partnership or transferring assets to the partnership;
- Expenses connected with the admission or removal of partners or members other than at the time the partnership is first organized;
- Expenses connected with a contract relating to the operation of the partnership business; and
- Syndication expenses.

Syndication expenses are expenses connected with the issuing and marketing of interests in the partnership.[35] They include:

- brokerage fees;
- registration fees;
- legal fees of the underwriter or placement agent and the issuer for securities advice and for advice pertaining to the adequacy of tax disclosures in the prospectus or placement memorandum for securities law purposes;
- accounting fees for preparation of representations to be included in the offering materials;
- printing costs of the prospectus;
- printing cost of the placement memorandum; and
- printing cost of other selling and promotional material.

Because syndication expenses do not constitute organizational expenses, they must be capitalized.[36]

---

29. Treas. Reg. § 1.709-2(a).
30. Section 709(b)(3)(B).
31. Section 709(b)(3)(C).
32. Treas. Reg. § 1.709-2(a).
33. Id.
34. Id.
35. Treas. Reg. § 1.709-2(b).
36. Section 709(a); Treas. Reg. § 1.709-2(b).

To be entitled to make the election to amortize organizational expenses, the partnership must have begun a business.[37] Whether or not a partnership has begun a business is a question of fact, based on all the facts and circumstances.

The mere signing of a partnership agreement is generally insufficient to establish that the partnership has engaged in a business. Similarly, mere organizational activities, such as obtaining the certificate or articles of formation, is not sufficient to show the beginning of business. In contrast, if the partnership has the operating assets necessary for the type of business contemplated or otherwise starts the business operations for which it was organized, the partnership has begun business.[38]

The election. A partnership is deemed to have made the election for the taxable year in which it begins business. If the partnership wants to forgo the election, it can do so by clearly electing to capitalize the organizational expenses on the return for the year in which it begins business.[39]

Once the election is made, whether the deemed election to amortize organizational expenses or the election to forgo amortization, it applies to all organizational expenses of the partnership. In addition, the election is irrevocable.[40]

Calculating the amount of the deduction. The amount the partnership can deduct is determined by a two-step process. First, the partnership can take an amount in the year it begins its business. The amount is the lesser of two amounts: the total amount of organizational expenses or $5,000 reduced by the amount by which the organizational expenses exceed $50,000 (but not below zero). Thus, if the partnership incurs more than $55,000 in organizational expenses, it is not entitled to any deduction under the first step. The expenses must be recovered entirely through the second step.[41] Conversely, if the total amount of organizational expenditures can be claimed under the first step no calculation need be done under the second step.

Under the second step, any remaining organizational expenses are amortized ratably over 180 months beginning in the month the partnership begins business.[42]

If a partnership goes out of business and is liquidated prior to the end of the amortization period, any remaining unamortized organizational expenses can be deducted as provided in Section 165 in the partnership's final taxable year. However, no deduction is allowed with respect to capitalized syndication expenses.[43]

E. Allocation of Partnership Items

Partnership items must be allocated among and reported by the partners. Under the Code the partnership is treated as an aggregate of the partners for purposes of reporting and paying tax on the partnership's income, gains, deductions, and losses. In general,

---

37. Section 709(b)(1).
38. Treas. Reg. § 1.709-2(c).
39. Treas. Reg. § 1.709-1(b)(2).
40. Treas. Reg. § 1.709-1(b)(3).
41. Section 709(b)(1)(A).
42. Section 709(b)(1)(B).
43. Section 709; Treas. Reg. § 1.709-1(b)(3).

partnership items are allocated among the partners based on the partnership agreement.[44] If the partnership agreement does not provide an allocation or there is no partnership agreement, the items will be allocated based on the partner's interest in the partnership.[45] The partners report their allocable share on their individual tax return.

Partner's interest in the partnership. A partner's interest in the partnership is determined by considering all the facts and circumstances related to the economic arrangement of the partners.[46] Relevant factors to consider include:[47]

- The partners' relative contributions to the partnership;
- The partners' interests in economic profits and losses (if different from their interests in taxable income or loss);
- The partners' interests in cash flow and other non-liquidating distributions; and
- The partners' rights to distributions of capital upon liquidation.

Effect of allocation on basis. A partner's basis is increased for any income or gain that is allocated from the partnership to the partner.[48] It is also increased for any tax-exempt income allocated to the partner.[49]

A partner's basis is decreased for any expenses or losses that are allocated to the partner. It also is decreased for any expenses that are not deductible and not properly chargeable to capital account.[50] Examples of nondeductible, non-capital expenditures include illegal bribes and kickbacks, expenses relating to tax-exempt income, and disallowed losses between related parties. However, a partner's outside basis cannot be reduced below zero.[51]

Effect of allocation on capital account. A partner's capital account is increased for any income or gain that is allocated from the partnership to the partner. It also is increased for any tax exempt income allocated to the partner. The partner's capital account is decreased for any deductible expenses, depreciation, losses, and nondeductible expenses that are allocated to the partner.

F. Varying Interests in the Partnership

A partner's interest in the partnership can change during the year for a number of reasons, including the entry of a new partner or a partner making a capital contribution. However, the partnership's taxable year does not close when there is a change. Rather, each partner's distributive share of partnership income or loss is determined by taking into account such varying interests in the partnership during the year.

To determine the amount allocated to each partner when their interests have varied over the year, either of two methods may be used. First, under the interim closing of

---

44. Section 704(a); Treas. Reg. § 1.704-1(a).
45. Treas. Reg. § 1.704-1(b)(1)(i).
46. Treas. Reg. § 1.704-1(b)(3)(i).
47. Treas. Reg. § 1.704-1(b)(3)(ii).
48. Section 705(a)(1)(A).
49. Section 705(a)(1)(B).
50. Section 705(a)(2).
51. Section 705(a)(2).

the books method, income and deductions are traced back to the time they are paid or incurred. A partner is entitled to a share of items paid or incurred while he is a partner in the partnership.

In determining when items are paid by the partnership, a cash basis method taxpayer must allocate certain items to when they were economically attributable, irrespective of when they are paid. In essence, it places a cash basis method taxpayer on the accrual method with respect to certain items. The items that must be so allocated are called "allocable cash basis items" and include interest, taxes, payments for services or for the use of property, and items specified by the Internal Revenue Service.[52]

If a cash basis item is allocable to a period before the year of payment, it is assigned entirely to the first day of the year. Then, the item is allocated among those partners who were partners at the time the deduction accrued based on their ownership interest at that time. If the payment is allocable to a period after the year of the payment, it is assigned entirely to the last day of the year.[53] If a partner would be entitled to an allocable share of the deduction but is no longer a partner in the partnership, that portion of the deduction must be capitalized and added to the basis of the partnership's assets.

Alternatively, under the proration method, all partnership items are prorated over the taxable year. Then, each partner's share of the items is determined by the number of days he is a partner in the partnership.

G. Limitation of Losses

Losses in excess of basis. A partner's basis in his partnership interest, to an extent, reflects his tax investment in the partnership. Just as when no additional depreciation is permitted when the basis of an asset reaches zero, no deductions (whether expenses, depreciation, losses, etc.) are permitted once the partner's basis in his partnership interest reaches zero.[54]

Carry forward of deferred loss. Any loss that is not allowed because of an insufficiency of basis is deferred and carried forward until it can be used.[55] If necessary, the character of the loss allowed and the character of the loss deferred must be determined based on the composition of the loss.[56] The partner can deduct the proportion that each loss item bears to the total of all the partner's allocated partnership losses for the year. Losses that have been carried forward can be claimed by the partner when his basis rises above zero and continues to be above zero after current year losses are taken into consideration.

---

52. Section 706(d)(2)(A), (d)(2)(B).
53. Section 706(d)(2).
54. Sections 705(a)(2); 704(d).
55. Section 704(d).
56. Treas. Reg. § 1.704-1(d)(4) Ex. 3.

Summary

Mechanical rules for partnership's taxable year: Use the first rule the partnership satisfies:

1. If the owners of more than 50 percent of the partnership profits and/or capital interests have the same taxable year, that taxable year is the partnership's taxable year.

2. If all the principal partners have the same taxable year, that taxable year is the partnership's taxable year.

3. The partnership taxable year is the year that would result in the least aggregate amount of deferral of income to the partners.

Items reported by the partners: Those items that must be separately stated when reported to the partners include:

-   Short-term capital gain and loss;

-   Long-term capital gain and loss;

-   Gain and loss from hotchpot (Section 1231) property;

-   Charitable contributions;

-   Dividends;

-   Taxes paid to foreign countries and U.S. possessions; and

-   Other items identified in the regulations that may affect the partner's individual income tax liability.

Those items that are not specially treated on an individual partner's income tax return can be netted together before being reported to the partners.

Varying interest of partners during the year: Each partner's distributive share is determined by taking into account the varying interest.

Steps to determine a partner's outside basis:

Step 1: Determine the partner's initial outside basis in the partnership.

Step 2: Increase the basis by the partner's allocable share of partnership taxable income and gain (both separately stated and non-separately stated).

Step 3: Increase the basis by the partner's allocable share of tax-exempt income.

Step 4: Decrease the basis by the partner's allocable share of expenses, depreciation, and losses (both separately stated and non-separately stated).

Step 5: Decrease the basis by the partner's allocable share of partnership expenditures that are neither deductible in computing partnership taxable income nor properly chargeable to capital account.

The partner's basis can never go below zero.

Steps to determine the partner's capital account balance:

Step 1: Determine the partner's initial capital account.

Step 2: Increase the capital account by the partner's allocable share of partnership taxable income and gain (both separately stated and non-separately stated).

Step 3: Increase the capital account by the partner's allocable share of tax-exempt income.

Step 4: Decrease the capital account by the partner's allocable share of expenses, depreciation, and losses (both separately stated and non-separately stated).

Step 5: Decrease the capital account by the partner's allocable share of partnership expenditures that are neither deductible in computing partnership taxable income nor properly chargeable to capital account.

Questions

1.   Ann, Bob, and Carl are general partners. Their ownership interest and individual taxable years are as follows:

Partner	Ownership	Taxable Year
Ann	30%	December 31
Bob	30%	March 31
Carl	40%	March 31

   The partnership makes no elections. What is the taxable year of the partnership?

2.   Deb, Ellen, and Frank are general partners. Their ownership interest and individual taxable years are as follows:

Partner	Ownership	Taxable Year
Deb	55%	December 31
Ellen	25%	March 31
Frank	20%	May 31

   The partnership makes no elections. What is the taxable year of the partnership?

3.   Greg owns 16 percent of the partnership. His taxable year ends September 30. The remaining 84 percent is held by 21 different partners, each of whom owns 4 percent. Of the 21 partners, 10 have a taxable year that ends December 31 and 11 have a taxable year that ends July 31. The partnership makes no elections. What is the taxable year of the partnership?

4.   The partnership has 20 partners. The ownership interest of each partner and the taxable year ending is as follows:

No. of Partners	Percentage Ownership	Tax Year Ending
2	15% each	September 30
12	4% each	December 31
5	4% each	June 30
1	2%	July 31

   The partnership has made no elections. What taxable year must the partnership use?

5.   Hal and Ira are equal partners in the general partnership. Hal's taxable year ends March 31 and Ira's taxable year ends April 30. The partnership makes no elections. What is the taxable year of the partnership?

6.   The partnership sold land and recognized a gain. The buyer made payments over the next three years. Who is permitted to elect out of the installment method? A partner? The partnership?

7.   Jeb owns oil paintings as investments. He is also a member of a partnership that owns and operates an art gallery. The partnership sold three paintings during the year, recognizing $100,000 of gain. What is the character of the allocable share of gain Jeb must report?

8.   During the year Kent earned a $60,000 salary. He also sold Blackacre, recognizing a $30,000 long term capital gain, and Whiteacre, recognizing a $10,000 long term capital gain. He also had a 30 percent interest in a partnership.

The partnership earned $150,000 from consulting services. It incurred the following costs:

Rent: $15,000
Electricity: 4,000
Salaries: 11,000

The partnership also sold stock and recognized a $90,000 short term capital loss. What are the tax consequences to Kent?

9.   Len and Mike are equal partners. The partnership agreement provides that allocations are to be made equally between the partners and that, when the partnership liquidates, distributions are to be made in accordance with capital account balances. At the beginning of the year, Len's basis was $10,000 and his capital account was $75,000. Mike's basis was $30,000 and his capital account was $75,000. During the year the partnership had the following income and expenses:

Income from services:	$200,000
Salaries:	50,000
Rent:	20,000
Depreciation:	6,000
Advertising expenses:	2,000
Gain from the sale of equipment held for three years	
Section 1245 gain:	4,000
Section 1231 gain:	2,000
Dividends:	5,000
Charitable contributions:	1,000
Tax-exempt interest:	2,000
Long-term capital gain on sale of Whiteacre:	10,000
Long-term capital gain on sale of Blackacre:	6,000
Short-term capital loss on sale of stock:	2,000
Short-term capital gain on sale of Redacre:	10,000

What is Len and Mike's basis and capital account at the end of the year?

10.   The partnership was formed to own and operate a large series of chain hotels. Which of the following expenses are organizational expenses?

- Legal fees incurred to organize the partnership.
- State filing fee for partnership documents.
- Amount paid to accountant to set up the books and records.
- Amounts paid to prepare a prospectus to be given to prospective investors.

11.   The partnership incurred $3,000 in organizational expenses and properly elected to amortize them. How much may the partnership deduct in the first year?

12.   The partnership incurred $72,000 in organizational expenses and properly elected to amortize them. The partnership began business in March. How much may the partnership deduct in the first year? In the second year?

13.   The partnership incurred $51,000 in organizational expenses and properly elected to amortize them. The partnership began business in November. How much may the partnership deduct in the first year? In the second year?

14. Ned, Opie, and Paul are equal partners. The partnership is a cash basis taxpayer and uses the interim closing of the books method. On October 1 Quinn joins the partnership, and the four become equal partners. On March 1 the partnership paid $30,000 in salaries. On November 1 the partnership paid $10,000 to an independent contractor for consulting services. How is the deduction for the salary and payment for consulting services allocated among the partners?

15. Roy, Sam, and Tess are equal partners. The partnership is an accrual basis taxpayer and uses the interim closing of the books method. On September 1 Vince joins the partnership and the four become equal partners. On December 1 the partnership pays $90,000 in rent for the year. How is the deduction for the rent payment allocated among the partners?

16. Wes, Xander, and Yolanda are equal partners. The partnership is a cash basis taxpayer and uses the proration method. On October 1 Zelda joins the partnership, and the four become equal partners. For the year, the partnership has a net $80,000 loss. How is the loss allocated among the partners?

17. Ann, Bob, and Carl are equal partners. The partnership is a cash basis taxpayer and uses the interim closing of the books method. On October 1 Deb joins the partnership, and the four become equal partners. The partnership incurred a $40,000 expense on March 1, but did not pay the amount until November 1. How will the expense be allocated among the partners?

18. Ellen, Frank, and Greg are equal partners. The partnership is a cash basis taxpayer and uses the interim closing of the books method. On October 1 Hal joins the partnership, and the four become equal partners. In the prior year the partnership incurred a $30,000 expense but did not pay the amount until March 1. How will the expense be allocated among the partners?

19. Ira's basis in the partnership was $50,000. At the end of the year, he was allocated a $30,000 loss from the partnership. What is Ira's basis after taking into consideration the allocation?

20. Jeb's basis in the partnership was $50,000. At the end of the year, he was allocated a $60,000 loss from the partnership. What are the tax consequences to Jeb?

21. Kent's basis in the partnership was $50,000. At the end of the year, he was allocated a $30,000 ordinary loss and $50,000 long term capital loss from the partnership. What are the tax consequences to Kent?

22. Len's basis in the partnership was $50,000. At the end of the first year, he was allocated a $70,000 loss from the partnership. At the end of the second year he was allocated $100,000 of net income. What are the tax consequences to Len at the end of the first and second year?

Solutions

1. Ann, Bob, and Carl are general partners. Their ownership interest and individual taxable years are as follows:

Partner	Ownership	Taxable Year
Ann	30%	December 31
Bob	30%	March 31
Carl	40%	March 31

The partnership makes no elections. What is the taxable year of the partnership?

Together, Bob and Carl own more than 50 percent of the partnership and they have the same taxable year. Thus, the partnership's taxable year is the year ending March 31. (Section 706(b)(1)(B)(i), (b)(4))

2. Deb, Ellen, and Frank are general partners. Their ownership interest and individual taxable years are as follows:

Partner	Ownership	Taxable Year
Deb	55%	December 31
Ellen	25%	March 31
Frank	20%	May 31

The partnership makes no elections. What is the taxable year of the partnership?

Deb owns more than 50 percent of the partnership. The partnership's taxable year is the same as Deb's taxable year, or taxable year ending December 31. (Section 706(b)(1)(B)(i), (b)(4))

3. Greg owns 16 percent of the partnership. His taxable year ends September 30. The remaining 84 percent is held by 21 different partners, each of whom owns 4 percent. Of the 21 partners, 10 have a taxable year that ends December 31 and 11 have a taxable year that ends July 31. The partnership makes no elections. What is the taxable year of the partnership?

No combination of partners who own more than 50 percent of the partnership have the same taxable year. Thus, there is no majority-interest taxable year. (Section 706(b)(1)(B)(i), (b)(4))

Greg is a 16-pecent owner of the partnership. The remaining 84 percent interest is held by 21 partners, none of whom owns five percent. As the only owner of a 5-percent interest, Greg is the only principal partner. (Section 706(b)(3)) Thus, the partnership taxable year is the same as his taxable year, or September 30. (Section 706(b)(1)(B)(ii))

4. The partnership has 20 partners. The ownership interest of each partner and the taxable year ending is as follows:

No. of Partners	Percentage Ownership	Tax Year Ending
2	15% each	September 30
12	4% each	December 31
5	4% each	June 30
1	2%	July 31

The partnership has made no elections. What taxable year must the partnership use?

No combination of partners who own more than 50 percent of the partnership have the same taxable year. Thus, there is no majority-interest taxable year. (Section 706(b)(1)(B)(i), (b)(4))

Two partners own more than 5 percent of the partnership. Of the remaining 18 partners, none owns 5 percent. As the owners of a 5-percent interest, the two 15-percent partners are the only principal partners. (Section 706(b)(3)) Thus, the partnership taxable year is the same as their taxable year, or September 30. (Section 706(b)(1)(B)(ii))

5.   Hal and Ira are equal partners in the general partnership. Hal's taxable year ends March 31 and Ira's taxable year ends April 30. The partnership makes no elections. What is the taxable year of the partnership?

No combination of partners who own more than 50 percent of the partnership have the same taxable year. There is no majority interest taxable year. (Section 706(b)(1)(B)(i), (b)(4))

Hal and Ira are both principal partners. (Section 706(b)(3)) However, because they do not have the same taxable year, there is no principal partner taxable year. (Section 706(b)(1)(B)(i), (b)(4))

Thus, the partnership must use whichever of Hal's or Ira's taxable year would result in the least aggregate deferral. That determination is made as follows:

Amount of deferral if the partnership used Hal's taxable year:

Partner	Ownership	Taxable year	Deferral from 3/31	Interest × deferral
Hal	50%	March 31	0	0.0
Ira	50%	April 30	1	0.5
Aggregate deferral:				0.5

Amount of deferral if the partnership used Ira's taxable year:

Partner	Ownership	Taxable year	Deferral from 4/30	Interest × deferral
Hal	50%	March 31	11	5.5
Ira	50%	April 30	0	0.0
Aggregate deferral:				5.5

The partnership is required to have a taxable year ending March 31 because it results in the least aggregate deferral of income.

6.   The partnership sold land and recognized a gain. The buyer made payments over the next three years. Who is permitted to elect out of the installment method? A partner? The partnership?

Only the partnership is entitled to elect out of reporting using the installment method. (Section 703(b))

7.   Jeb owns oil paintings as investments. He is also a member of a partnership that owns and operates an art gallery. The partnership sold three paintings during the year, recognizing $100,000 of gain. What is the character of allocable share of gain Jeb must report?

The character of the gain from the sale of the paintings (inventory) is determined at the partnership level as ordinary income. (Section 702(b)) The fact that the character would have been different if the paintings had been sold by Jeb (capital gain) is irrelevant.

8.   During the year Kent earned a $60,000 salary. He also sold Blackacre, recognizing a $30,000 long term capital gain, and Whiteacre, recognizing a $10,000 long term capital gain. He also had a 30 percent interest in a partnership.

The partnership earned $150,000 from consulting services. It incurred the following costs:

Rent:	$15,000
Electricity:	4,000
Salaries:	11,000

The partnership also sold stock and recognized a $90,000 short term capital loss. What are the tax consequences to Kent?

The partnership does not need to separately state the income or the related expenses. (Section 703(a)) Thus, its net income is

Income:	$150,000
Expenses:	
Rent	$ 15,000
Electricity	4,000
Salaries	11,000
	$120,000

The partnership must separately state the $90,000 short term capital loss from the sale of the stock. (Sections 703(a)(1); 702(a)(2))

The partnership items are allocated to Kent as follows:

Item	Partnership Level	Kent's 30% share
Net income	$120,000	$36,000
Short-term capital loss	90,000	27,000

Combined with his individual items, Kent must report:

- $96,000 of ordinary income ($60,000 of salary and $36,000 of net income from the partnership)
- $40,000 of long-term capital gain ($30,000 long term capital gain from sale of the Blackacre and $10,000 long term capital gain from the sale of Whiteacre)
- $27,000 of short-term capital loss from the partnership

The $40,000 net long term capital gain can be netted with the $27,000 short term capital loss, for a net $13,000 long term capital gain.

9.   Len and Mike are equal partners. The partnership agreement provides that allocations are to be made equally between the partners and that, when the partnership liquidates, distributions are to be made in accordance with capital account balances. At the beginning of the year, Len's basis was $10,000 and his capital account was $75,000. Mike's basis was $30,000 and his capital account was $75,000. During the year the partnership had the following income and expenses:

Income from services:	$200,000
Salaries:	50,000
Rent:	20,000
Depreciation:	6,000
Advertising expenses:	2,000
Gain from the sale of equipment held for three years	
Section 1245 gain:	4,000
Section 1231 gain:	2,000
Dividends:	5,000
Charitable contributions:	1,000
Tax-exempt interest:	2,000
Long-term capital gain on sale of Whiteacre:	10,000
Long-term capital gain on sale of Blackacre:	6,000
Short-term capital loss on sale of stock:	2,000
Short-term capital gain on sale of Redacre:	10,000

What is Len and Mike's basis and capital account at the end of the year?

The partnership does not need to separately state the following amounts:

Income:		
Income from services:	$200,000	
Section 1245 gain:	4,000	
Total:	$204,000	$204,000
Deductions:		
Salaries:	$50,000	
Rent:	20,000	
Depreciation:	6,000	
Adv. exp.:	2,000	
Total:	$78,000	<78,000>
Net income:		$126,000

One half, or $63,000, is allocated to each of Len and Mike.

The partnership must separately state the following:

Gain from the sale of equipment held for three years	
Section 1231 gain:	2,000
Dividends:	5,000
Charitable contributions:	<1,000>
Tax-exempt interest:	2,000
Long-term capital gain on sale of Whiteacre:	10,000
Long-term capital gain on sale of Blackacre:	6,000
Short-term capital loss on sale of stock:	2,000
Short-term capital gain on sale of Redacre:	10,000

For each item, one-half is allocated to each of Len and Mike.

Their basis are adjusted as follows:

	Len	Mike	
Beginning of year:	$10,000	$ 30,000	
Net income:	63,000	63,000	(Sec 705(a)(1)(A); 703(a))
Section 1231 gain:	1,000	1,000	(Section 702(a)(3))
Dividends:	2,500	2,500	(Section 702(a)(5))
Net long-term capital gain:	8,000	8,000	(Section 702(a)(2))
Net short-term capital gain:	4,000	4,000	(Section 702(a)(1))
Tax-exempt interest:	1,000	1,000	(Section 705(a)(1)(B))
Charitable contributions:	<500>	<500>	(Section 705(a)(2)(B))
End of year:	$89,000	$109,000	

Their capital accounts are adjusted as follows:

	Len	Mike
Beginning of year:	$ 75,000	$ 75,000
Net income:	63,000	63,000
Section 1231 gain:	1,000	1,000
Dividends:	2,500	2,500
Net long-term capital gain:	8,000	8,000
Net short-term capital gain:	4,000	4,000
Tax-exempt interest:	1,000	1,000
Charitable contributions:	<500>	<500>
End of year:	$154,000	$154,000

10. **The partnership was formed to own and operate a large series of chain hotels. Which of the following expenses are organizational expenses?**

- **Legal fees incurred to organize the partnership.**
- **State filing fee for partnership documents.**
- **Amount paid to accountant to set up the books and records.**
- **Amounts paid to prepare a prospectus to be given to prospective investors.**

Amounts paid to an attorney to draft a partnership agreement would be an organizational expense. (Section 709(b)(3); Treas. Reg. § 1.709-2(a)) The state filing fee would be an organizational expense. (Section 709(b)(3); Treas. Reg. § 1.709-2(a)) Amounts paid to the accountant related to formation of the partnership would be an organizational expense. (Section 709(b)(3); Treas. Reg. § 1.709-2(a))

An amount paid in connection with preparing the offering documents is a syndication expense. A syndication expense does not qualify as an organizational expense, is not subject to the election under Section 709(b), and must be capitalized. (Treas. Reg. § 1.709-2(a), (b))

11. **The partnership incurred $3,000 in organizational expenses and properly elected to amortize them. How much may the partnership deduct in the first year?**

The partnership can deduct the entire $3,000 in the year it begins its business. (Section 709(b)(1)(A))

12. **The partnership incurred $72,000 in organizational expenses and properly elected to amortize them. The partnership began business in March. How much may the partnership deduct in the first year? In the second year?**

Under the first step, the partnership can deduct the lesser of two amounts: the total amount of organizational expenses or $5,000 reduced by the amount by which the organizational expenses exceed $50,000 (but not below zero). (Section 709(b)(1)(A)) Because the organizational expenses exceed $50,000 by $22,000, the $5,000 is reduced to zero and the partnership is not entitled to any deduction under the first step.

Under the second step, the partnership may amortize the entire $72,000 of organizational expenses ratably over 180 months, or $400 each month, beginning in the month the partnership begins business. (Section 709(b)(1)(B)) In the first year, the partnership can deduct $4,000.

$$\$400 \text{ per month} \times 10 \text{ months} = \$4,000$$

In the second year the partnership can deduct $4,800

$$\$400 \text{ per month} \times 12 \text{ months} = \$4,800$$

13. The partnership incurred $51,000 in organizational expenses and properly elected to amortize them. The partnership began business in November. How much may the partnership deduct in the first year? In the second year?

Under the first step, the partnership can deduct the lesser of two amounts: the total amount of organizational expenses or $5,000 reduced by the amount by which the organizational expenses exceed $50,000 (but not below zero). (Section 709(b)(1)(A)) Because the organizational expenses exceed $50,000 by $1,000, the $5,000 is reduced to $4,000 and the amount under the first step is $4,000.

Under the second step, the partnership may amortize the remaining $47,000 ($51,000, less $4,000) over 180 months, or $261 each month beginning in the month the partnership begins business. (Section 709(b)(1)(B)) In the first year, the amount under the second step is $522.

$$\$261 \text{ per month} \times 2 \text{ months} = \$522$$

The total amount the partnership can deduct in the first years is $4,522.

First step:	$4,000
Second step:	522
Total:	$4,522

In the second year the partnership can deduct $3,132.

$$\$261 \text{ per month} \times 12 \text{ months} = \$3,132$$

14. Ned, Opie, and Paul are equal partners. The partnership is a cash basis taxpayer and uses the interim closing of the books method. On October 1 Quinn joins the partnership, and the four become equal partners. On March 1 the partnership paid $30,000 in salaries. On November 1 the partnership paid $10,000 to an independent contractor for consulting services. How is the deduction for the salary and payment for consulting services allocated among the partners?

Under the interim closing of the books method, income and deductions are traced back to the time they are paid or incurred. A partner is entitled to a share of items paid while he is a partner in the partnership. (Section 706(d)(1)) On March 1, Ned, Opie, and Paul were equal partners in the partnership.

However, in determining when items are paid by the partnership, a cash basis method taxpayer must allocate "allocable cash basis items" to when they were economically attributable, irrespective of when they are paid. Salary is an "allocable cash basis item" and must be allocated ratably over the year. (Section 706(d)(2)(A), (d)(2)(B)(iii)) For January through September, the salary is allocated between Ned, Opie, and Paul. For October through December, the salary is allocated between Ned, Opie, Paul, and Quinn.

Partner	Ownership	Months	Computation	Partner Allocation
Ned	one-third	9	$9/12 \times 1/3 \times \$30,000$	$ 7,500
	one-fourth	3	$3/12 \times 1/4 \times \$30,000$	1,875
Opie	one-third	9	$9/12 \times 1/3 \times \$30,000$	7,500
	one-fourth	3	$3/12 \times 1/4 \times \$30,000$	1,875
Paul	one-third	9	$9/12 \times 1/3 \times \$30,000$	7,500
	one-fourth	3	$3/12 \times 1/4 \times \$30,000$	1,875
Quinn	one-fourth	3	$3/12 \times 1/4 \times \$30,000$	1,875
Total:				$30,000

Under the interim closing of the books method, income and deductions are traced back to the time they are paid or incurred. A partner is entitled to a share of items paid while he is a partner in the partnership. (Section 706(d)(1)) On November 1 Ned, Opie, Paul, and Quinn were equal partners in the partnership. The $10,000 deduction is allocated equally between the four, or $2,500 each.

To summarize, each partner is allocated the following deductions:

	Ned	Opie	Paul	Quinn
Salary:	$ 9,375	$ 9,375	$ 9,375	$1,875
Ind. Cont.:	2,500	2,500	2,500	2,500
Total:	$11,875	$11,875	$11,875	$4,375

15. Roy, Sam, and Tess are equal partners. The partnership is an accrual basis taxpayer and uses the interim closing of the books method. On September 1 Vince joins the partnership and the four become equal partners. On December 1 the partnership pays $90,000 in rent for the year. How is the deduction for the rent payment allocated among the partners?

Under the interim closing of the books method, income and deductions are traced back to the time they are paid or incurred. A partner is entitled to a share of items paid while he is a partner in the partnership. (Section 706(d)(1)) As an accrual basis taxpayer, the rent accrues ratably over the year. Roy, Sam, and Tess were equal partners for the first 8 months; Roy, Sam, Tess, and Vince were equal partners for the last 4 months. The rent would be allocated as follows:

Partner	Ownership	Months	Computation	Partner Allocation
Roy	one-third	8	$8/12 \times 1/3 \times \$90,000$	$20,000
	one-fourth	4	$4/12 \times 1/4 \times \$90,000$	7,500
Sam	one-third	8	$8/12 \times 1/3 \times \$90,000$	20,000
	one-fourth	4	$4/12 \times 1/4 \times \$90,000$	7,500
Tess	one-third	8	$8/12 \times 1/3 \times \$90,000$	20,000
	one-fourth	4	$4/12 \times 1/4 \times \$90,000$	7,500
Vince	one-fourth	4	$4/12 \times 1/4 \times \$90,000$	7,500
Total:				$90,000

In sum, for the year, Roy, Sam, and Tess would be allocated a $27,500 deduction for the rent. Vince would be allocated a $7,500 deduction.

16. **Wes, Xander, and Yolanda are equal partners. The partnership is a cash basis taxpayer and uses the proration method. On October 1 Zelda joins the partnership, and the four become equal partners. For the year, the partnership has a net $80,000 loss. How is the loss allocated among the partners?**

The loss must be prorated among the partners based on their interest in the partnership. (Section 706(d)(1)) Allocation of the loss would be as follows:

Partner	Ownership	Months	Computation	Partner Allocation
Wes	one-third	9	9/12 × 1/3 × $80,000	$20,000
	one-fourth	3	3/12 × 1/4 × $80,000	5,000
Xander	one-third	9	9/12 × 1/3 × $80,000	20,000
	one-fourth	3	3/12 × 1/4 × $80,000	5,000
Yolanda	one-third	9	9/12 × 1/3 × $80,000	20,000
	one-fourth	3	3/12 × 1/4 × $80,000	5,000
Zelda	one-fourth	3	3/12 × 1/4 × $80,000	5,000
Total:				$80,000

For the year, Wes, Xander, and Yolanda would be allocated a loss of $25,000 and Zelda would be allocated a loss of $5,000.

17. **Ann, Bob, and Carl are equal partners. The partnership is a cash basis taxpayer and uses the interim closing of the books method. On October 1 Deb joins the partnership, and the four become equal partners. The partnership incurred a $40,000 expense on March 1, but did not pay the amount until November 1. How will the expense be allocated among the partners?**

Under the interim closing of the books method, income and deductions are traced back to the time they are paid or incurred. A partner is entitled to a share of items paid while he is a partner in the partnership. (Section 706(d)(1)) The expense was paid on November 1. At that time, Ann, Bob, Carl, and Deb were equal partners. The expense is allocated equally between them, or $10,000 each.

18. **Ellen, Frank, and Greg are equal partners. The partnership is a cash basis taxpayer and uses the interim closing of the books method. On October 1 Hal joins the partnership, and the four become equal partners. In the prior year the partnership incurred a $30,000 expense but did not pay the amount until March 1. How will the expense be allocated among the partners?**

Under the interim closing of the books method, income and deductions are traced back to the time they are paid or incurred. A partner is entitled to a share of items paid while he is a partner in the partnership. (Section 706(d)(1))

However, in determining when items are paid by the partnership, a cash basis method taxpayer must allocate "allocable cash basis items" to when they were economically attributable, irrespective of when they are paid. Rent is an "allocable cash basis item" and must be allocated ratably over the year. (Section 706(d)(2)(A), (d)(2)(B))

If a cash basis item is allocable to a period before the year of payment, it is assigned entirely to the first day of the year. Then, the item is allocated among those partners who were partners at the time the deduction accrued based on their ownership interest at that time. (Section 706(d)(2)(C)(i))

Because Ellen, Frank, and Greg were equal partners on the first day of the year, the expense is allocated equally between them, or $10,000 each.

19. Ira's basis in the partnership was $50,000. At the end of the year, he was allocated a $30,000 loss from the partnership. What is Ira's basis after taking into consideration the allocation?

Ira's basis in the partnership is reduced to $20,000 ($50,000 less $30,000).

Basis:	$50,000	
Loss:	<30,000>	(Section 705(a)(2)(A))
Basis:	$20,000	

20. Jeb's basis in the partnership was $50,000. At the end of the year, he was allocated a $60,000 loss from the partnership. What are the tax consequences to Jeb?

Jeb may claim only $50,000 of the loss. His basis in the partnership is reduced to zero and he carries forward a $10,000 loss.

Basis:	$50,000	
Loss:	<60,000>	(Section 705(a)(2)(A))
Basis:	$0	$10,000 loss deferred (Section 704(d))

21. Kent's basis in the partnership was $50,000. At the end of the year, he was allocated a $30,000 ordinary loss and $50,000 long term capital loss from the partnership. What are the tax consequences to Kent?

Kent may claim only $50,000 of loss, while $30,000 must be deferred.

Basis:	$50,000	
Loss:	<80,000>	(Section 705(a)(2)(A))
Basis:	$ 0	$30,000 loss deferred (Section 704(d))

To determine the character of the loss allowed, a proportionate share of each character of loss must be allowed.

$$\frac{\$30,000}{\$80,000} \times \$30,000 = \$11,250 \text{ ordinary loss is deferred (\$18,750 allowed)}$$

$$\frac{\$50,000}{\$80,000} \times \$30,000 = \$18,750 \text{ capital loss is deferred (\$31,250 allowed)}$$

Basis:	$50,000	
Ord. loss:	<18,750>	
Cap. loss:	<31,250>	(Section 705(a)(2)(A))
Basis:	$ 0	

22. Len's basis in the partnership was $50,000. At the end of the first year, he was allocated a $70,000 loss from the partnership. At the end of the second year he was allocated $100,000 of net income. What are the tax consequences to Len at the end of the first and second year?

Len may claim only $50,000 of the loss. His basis in the partnership is reduced to zero and he carries forward a $20,000 loss.

Basis:	$50,000	
Loss:	<70,000>	(Section 705(a)(2)(A))
Basis:	$ 0	$20,000 loss deferred (Section 704(d))

In the second year, his basis is adjusted for the allocation of net income. Len also may claim the loss carried forward.

Basis:	$ 0	
Income:	100,000	(Section 705(a)(1)(A))
Loss carried forward:	<u><20,000></u>	(Section 705(a)(2)(A), 704(d))
Basis:	$ 80,000	

Chapter IV

Special Rules Relating to Allocations

A. Allocation of Recourse Deductions

In some situations, the partnership rules provide a means for a shifting of the income, gain, deductions, or losses that was prohibited in *Lucas v. Earl*[1] and *Horst v. Helvering*.[2] Specifically, through an allocation of partnership items, an allocation not based on the partners' respective interests in the partnership, such a shifting can occur. It is this flexibility that makes partnerships popular for tax planning.

Example: Ann and Bob form an equal general partnership. They each contribute $50 to the partnership. If the partnership made allocations based on their interest in the partnership, each partner would receive an allocation of one-half of all partnership items. However, Ann and Bob agree upon a special allocation. All net income will be allocated to Ann and all net losses will be allocated to Bob.

In the first year of partnership operations, the partnership has net income of $25. Based on the partners' agreement, the net income is allocated entirely to Ann. In general, Ann must report $25 of income on her individual income tax return, increase her outside basis by $25, and increase her capital account by $25.

In the second year of partnership operations, the partnership has a net loss of $25. Based on the partners' agreement, the net loss is allocated entirely to Bob. In general, Bob must report $25 of loss on his individual income tax return, decrease his outside basis by $25, and decrease his capital account by $25.

For an allocation to be respected, it must have substantial economic effect. This requirement is broken down into two parts. First, the allocation must have economic effect. Second, the economic effect must be substantial. The test is applied to all

---

1. 281 U.S. 111 (1930).
2. 311 U.S. 112 (1940).

allocations from the partnership, whether a separately-stated or a net amount.[3] In addition, it is applied on an annual basis.[4]

1. Economic Effect

For the allocation to have economic effect, it must be consistent with what the partners have agreed to from an economic perspective. In other words, the partner receiving the allocation must bear the tax burden and receive the economic benefit of the allocation.[5] To understand how this requirement is applied, some basic partnership concepts must be understood.

Maintenance of capital accounts. The regulations provide rules for maintaining capital accounts.[6] If these rules are followed, the capital accounts will reflect the partner's economic situation in the partnership and his economic situation as compared to the other partners. Pursuant to the rules set forth in the regulations, a partner's capital account is increased by:

- The amount of cash contributed by the partner;
- The value of property contributed by the partner, reduced by any liabilities the property is subject to; and
- Any allocations of income or gain to the partner.

The partner's capital account is decreased by:

- The amount of cash withdrawn by the partner from the partnership;
- The value of property distributed by the partnership to the partner, reduced by any liabilities the property is subject to; and
- Any allocations of deductions or loss to the partner.

Liquidating distributions based on capital account balances. If capital accounts are maintained according to the rules set forth in the regulations, they reflect the partner's economic situation in the partnership and his economic situation as compared to the other partners. Thus, if the partnership were to liquidate, each partner would expect to receive from the partnership the amount reflected in his capital account.

Restoration of negative capital account balance. A partner's capital account reflects his investment in the partnership relative to the other partners. It also reflects what he is entitled to receive upon distribution. Thus, a negative capital account reflects the fact that the partner has received more from the partnership than what he had a right to receive on liquidation. In essence, he has received a loan from the partnership. If he is not obligated to restore the negative capital account, a portion of partnership assets have been shifted away from other partners and to this partner.

---

3. Treas. Reg. § 1.704-1(b)(1)(i).
4. Treas. Reg. § 1.704-1(b)(2)(i).
5. Treas. Reg. § 1.704-1(b)(2)(ii)(*a*).
6. Treas. Reg. § 1.704-1(b)(2)(iv)(*b*).

Example: Carl and Deb formed an equal general partnership, each contributing $50 to the partnership. They agreed that all net income would be allocated to Carl and all net losses allocated to Deb. At the time of formation, the partnership balance sheet would appear as follows:

Asset	Basis	FMV	Partner	Basis	Cap. Acct.
Cash	$100	$100	Carl	$ 50	$ 50
	$100	$100	Deb	$ 50	$ 50
				$100	$100

In year 1, the partnership has a net loss of $75, which is allocated to Deb. Deb's basis can be reduced only to zero ($50 reduced by the $75 loss, limited by her outside basis) and her capital account is reduced to <$25> ($50 less net loss of $75). After the first year, the balance sheet would appear as follows:

Asset	Basis	FMV	Partner	Basis	Cap. Acct.
Cash	$25	$25	Carl	$50	$50
	$25	$25	Deb	$ 0	<25>
				$50	$25

If the partnership were to liquidate, Carl would expect to receive $50 from the partnership. However, the partnership has only $25. Deb's negative capital account reflects the fact that she has received more from the partnership than she contributed.

If Deb is not obligated to restore her negative capital account balance, $25 that properly belongs to Carl has been shifted to Deb.

If Deb is obligated to restore her negative capital account balance, she must contribute $25 to the partnership. The partnership then would have $50 available to distribute to Carl in liquidation of his partnership interest. As Deb's capital account would be zero (<$25> increased by the $25 contribution), she would not be entitled to any liquidating distribution.

---

a. General Test for Economic Effect

For an allocation to be respected, the partner receiving the allocation must bear the tax burden and receive the economic benefit of the allocation. For this result to occur, a three-part test must be satisfied:[7]

- The partnership must maintain capital accounts in accordance with Treas. Reg. § 1.704-1(b)(2)(iv)(*b*);
- All partners must have an obligation to restore negative capital account balances upon liquidation before the later of the end of the taxable year of liquidation of the partner's interest or 90 days after the date of the liquidation; and
- Liquidating distributions must be made in accordance with capital account balances.

b. Alternate Test for Economic Effect

If the partner is a limited partner, the partner likely will be unwilling to enter into a partnership agreement that requires him to make additional contributions to the part-

---

7. Treas. Reg. § 1.704-1(b)(2)(ii)(*b*), -1(b)(2)(ii)(*c*).

nership (*i.e.*, restore a negative capital account balance). Thus, the partnership will not be able to meet the general test for economic effect.

Through the alternate test for economic effect, the regulations address this issue simply by not allowing the limited partner's capital account to become negative beyond any amount the partner has agreed to contribute to the partnership.

For this approach to work, and result in the least chance possible that the partner's capital account will go below zero, adjustments to the partner's capital account must be anticipated prior to considering any allocations to the partner. Thus, certain temporary adjustments must be made for any allocations that are reasonably expected to occur. Some of the adjustments that must be anticipated include:

- Allocations due to reasonably expected changes in interests in the partnership in future years; and
- Any distributions that are expected to be made to the partner, less any increases due to reasonably expected allocations of income.

If, by chance, the partner's capital account does go negative, the partnership must allocate items of income to the partner until his capital account is no longer negative. The obligation to allocate income items to the partner is called a qualified income offset.

For an allocation to be respected under the alternate economic effect test, a four-part test must be satisfied:[8]

- The partnership must maintain capital accounts in accordance with Treas. Reg. § 1.704-1(b)(2)(iv)(*b*);
- Liquidating distributions must be made in accordance with capital account balances;
- The allocation of recourse deductions cannot cause or increase a deficit in the partner's capital account in excess of any limited amount the partner is obligated to restore; and
- The partnership agreement must contain a qualified income offset.

c. Failure to Meet General or Alternate Test

Economic effect equivalence. If the allocation fails to meet either the general test or the alternate test, the allocation can still be respected if the allocation would have been the same if the above criteria had been met. In other words, even though the partnership failed to include such provisions in its agreement, the partner who was allocated gain or income increased his investment in the partnership and a partner who was allocated a deduction or loss decreased his investment in the partnership.[9]

Allocation in accordance with the partners' interest in the partnership. If the allocation fails to have substantial economic effect and the economic effect equivalence test is not applicable, the allocations will be reallocated in accordance with the partners' respective interests in the partnership.[10] In other words, allocations will be made based on the

---

8. Treas. Reg. § 1.704-1(b)(2)(ii)(*d*).
9. Treas. Reg. § 1.704-1(b)(2)(ii)(*i*).
10. Treas. Reg. § 1.704-1(b)(3).

manner in which the partners have agreed to share the economic benefit or burden that corresponds with the allocation.

A partner's interest in the partnership is determined by considering all the facts and circumstances related to the economic arrangement of the partners.[11] Relevant factors to consider include:[12]

- The partner's relative contributions to the partnership;
- The interests of the partners in the economic profits and loss (if different from their interests in taxable income or loss);
- The interest of the partners in cash flow and other nonliquidating distributions; and
- The rights of the partners to distributions of capital upon liquidation.

There is an exception to using the factors to determine the partner's interest in the partnership. Specifically, if the reason the partnership allocation fails the substantial economic effect test is because it lacked a deficit makeup obligation, the partner's interest in the partnership is determined using a comparative liquidation test. The manner in which distributions would be made if all partnership property were sold at book value and the partnership were liquidated immediately following the end of the taxable year to which the allocation relates is compared with the manner in which distributions would be made if all partnership property were sold at book value and the partnership were liquidated immediately following the end of the prior table year (and certain other adjustments are made).[13]

2. Substantiality

In addition to having economic effect, the effect must be substantial.[14] The economic effect will be considered substantial if the allocation substantially alters the way the partners share items economically and not just the way the allocation affects them for tax purposes. In other words, it must affect substantially the dollar amounts that the partners will receive from the partnership, independent of tax consequences.

In general, the allocation is not substantial if at the time the allocation is agreed upon, its inclusion causes the after-tax economic position of at least one partner to be enhanced while there is a strong likelihood that the after-tax economic position of no partner will be diminished. Accordingly, the allocation contained in the partnership agreement is compared to an allocation made in accordance with the partners' interest in the partnership, and, in determining the after-tax consequences to the partner, both the partner's partnership items and individual items are considered.[15]

---

11. Treas. Reg. § 1.704-1(b)(3)(i).
12. Treas. Reg. § 1.704-1(b)(3)(ii).
13. Treas. Reg. § 1.704-1(b)(3)(iii).
14. Id.
15. The tax attributes of a de minimis partner does not have to be taken into consideration. A de minimis partner is any partner that owns directly or indirectly less than 10 percent of the capital and profits of a partnership and is allocated less than 10 percent of each partnership item of income, gain, loss, deduction and credit. Treas. Reg. § 1.704-1(b)(2)(iii)(e).

Shifting tax consequences test. Under the shifting allocation test, allocations during just one year are considered. First, at the time the allocation is agreed upon, there must be a strong likelihood that the net change in the respective partners' capital accounts for the year with the allocation would not differ substantially from the net change that would occur without the allocation. Second, the total tax liability of the partners (determined by including their individual tax attributes) will be less with the allocation than without the allocation. If this result in fact occurs, it is presumed that there was a strong likelihood that that would be the result.[16]

Transitory allocation test. Under the transitory allocation test, allocations over two or more years are considered. First, at the time the allocation is agreed upon, there must be a strong likelihood that the net change in the respective partners' capital accounts over a span of years with the allocation would not differ substantially from the net change that would occur without the allocation. Second, the total tax liability of the partners (determined by including their individual tax attributes) over the same span of years will be less with the allocation than without the allocation.[17] An allocation and a subsequent offsetting allocation will not be considered transitory if there is a strong likelihood that the offsetting allocation will not, in large part, be made within five years of the original allocation.[18]

Failure to pass substantiality tests. If the special allocation is considered not substantial, the allocation will be disregarded and the partnership items will be reallocated based on the partners' interests in the partnership.[19]

Note that the regulations provide that the adjusted basis of property is presumed to be its fair market value. Thus, to the extent the basis is reduced for deprecation, the value of the property is reduced. Upon sale of the property, using this presumption, there will not be a presumption of gain. As there will not be any gain, there can never be a strong likelihood that the economic effect of an allocation of deprecation will be offset by a subsequent gain on disposition.[20]

3. Areas of Special Concern

Depreciation recapture. When property subject to depreciation has been sold, the gain on disposition will be the difference between the selling price and the basis, as adjusted for depreciation taken. To the extent of the gain that is due solely to the depreciation that was taken, the character of the gain will be ordinary. This portion of the gain is often referred to as depreciation recapture. The character of the remainder of the gain will depend on the use of the property. Because depreciation recapture only affects the character of the gain, and not the amount of the gain, an allocation based on such character will only alter the tax results of the partners. Accordingly, an allocation of gain based on its characterization as recapture gain will not have substantial economic effect.

---

16. Treas. Reg. § 1.704-1(b)(2)(iii)(*b*).
17. Treas. Reg. § 1.704-1(b)(2)(iii)(*c*).
18. Id.
19. Treas. Reg. § 1.704-1(b)(3).
20. Treas. Reg. § 1.704-1(b)(2)(iii)(*c*).

The regulations provide some guidance as to how the gain from the sale of depreciable property should be allocated. The objective is to match an allocation of recapture gain to a previous allocation of depreciation. A partner's share of recapture gain generally is equal to the lesser of:

- The partner's share of the total gain from the disposition of the property; or
- The total amount of depreciation previously allocated to the partner with respect to the property.

The partner's allocation of recapture gain may be limited by that partner's share of total gain.

Allocation of credits. Partnership credits are not reflected in a partner's capital account. Thus, a special allocation of partnership credits cannot have substantial economic effect. Accordingly, generally, all allocations of credits must be made in accordance with the partners' interests in the partnership.[21]

B. Allocation of Non-Recourse Deductions

Non-recourse liability. A non-recourse deduction is a deduction that is financed by a non-recourse liability of the partnership. Recall that a partnership liability is a recourse liability to the extent that any partner bears the economic risk of loss for that liability or would be obligated to contribute to the partnership to satisfy the liability.[22] The amount of partnership liability that has not been characterized as a recourse liability, the amount for which no partner bears the economic risk of loss, is a non-recourse liability.[23]

1. Relevance of *Tufts*, or Phantom, Gain

Relevance of Tufts, *or phantom, gain.* The allocation of deductions that arise out of property encumbered by a non-recourse liability cannot be addressed in the same manner as the allocation of deductions that arise out of property encumbered by a recourse liability. Allocation of the latter is based on the premise that the allocation reflects the economic risk of loss of the partners; one or more of the partners will be liable to pay the outstanding balance of the loan.

In contrast, because the non-recourse lender, and not any of the partners, bears the economic risk of loss for the loan proceeds, an allocation of deductions that arises out of property encumbered by a non-recourse liability does not reflect an economic risk of loss of the partners. Accordingly, the allocation will not pass the test of substantial economic effect.

However, the fact that a partner is not liable for repayment of the loan proceeds is only part of the consequences associated with a non-recourse liability. From a tax perspective, upon disposition, the least amount of gain the partnership must recognize is

---

21. Treas. Reg. § 1.704-1(b)(4)(ii).
22. Treas. Reg. § 1.752-2(a).
23. Treas. Reg. §§ 1.752-1(a)(2), 1.704-2(b)(2).

the amount of the non-recourse debt, less the adjusted basis of the property that secures the debt (*Tufts* or phantom gain). If the *Tufts* gain is allocated to a partner to the extent the partner was allocated deductions from the property, the partner who received the tax benefit of the deduction will bear the tax burden on disposition of the property.

Example: In Year 1, the partnership purchased an apartment building for $50,000. It was financed entirely with a $50,000 non-recourse loan, secured by the apartment building. The partnership was not required to make any principal payments on the non-recourse loan until Year 5. It was allowed to claim $10,000 of depreciation each year. The partnership allocated all depreciation deductions to Ellen, a partner in partnership. At the end of Year 3, Ellen had claimed a total of $30,000 in depreciation.

Year	Depreciation	Adjusted Basis of Building
1	$10,000	$40,000
2	10,000	30,000
3	10,000	20,000
Total:	$30,000	

Notice that the total depreciation deductions Ellen has been able to claim exceeds the partnership's investment in the property by $30,000.

From the perspective of the lender, if the partnership abandons the property and the fair market value of the property was equal to its adjusted basis, the lender would bear the $30,000 loss (the difference between the $50,000 outstanding loan balance and the $20,000 value of the building).

From the perspective of the partnership, if the property is abandoned or sold for the amount of the outstanding liability, the partnership will recognize $30,000 of gain (amount realized of $50,000 non-recourse debt, less adjusted basis of $20,000). Note that the gain is due entirely to the depreciation claimed with respect to the property. Ellen will bear the burden of the $30,000 depreciation deductions she received if she is required to report the correlative $30,000 gain on disposition of the property.

---

2. Safe Harbor Requirements

The partners can agree to an allocation of non-recourse deductions. However, for the allocation to be respected, the partnership agreement must include four safe harbor requirements. In general, the safe harbor requirements are centered around the concept that the partner who received the deductions generated by the non-recourse debt should be allocated the *Tufts* (or phantom) gain upon disposition of the property.

The safe harbor requirements include several technical terms that must be understood before the requirements can be understood.

a. Underlying Concepts

Partnership minimum gain. In general, partnership minimum gain (PMG) is the excess of the non-recourse liability over the adjusted basis of the encumbered property.[24]

---

24. Treas. Reg. § 1.704-2(d)(1).

In other words, partnership minimum gain includes the amount of potential *Tufts* gain or phantom gain. Similarly, a net increase in partnership minimum gain for the year reflects a net increase in potential *Tufts* (or phantom) gain for the year.

Partnership minimum gain can arise through three methods, two of them are based solely on *Tufts*, or phantom, gain. First, partnership minimum gain may be created through deductions associated with the property that secures the non-recourse liability, most often depreciation deductions.

Example: In Year 1, the partnership purchased an apartment building for $50,000. It was financed entirely with a $50,000 non-recourse loan, secured by the apartment building. The partnership was not required to make any principal payments on the non-recourse loan until Year 5. It was allowed to claim $10,000 of depreciation each year. The partnership allocated all depreciation deductions to Ellen, a partner in the partnership.

At the end of Year 1, Ellen had claimed $10,000 in depreciation and the adjusted basis of the building was $40,000. The amount of partnership minimum gain (or *Tufts* or phantom gain) was $10,000.

At the end of Year 2, Ellen had claimed an additional $10,000 in depreciation and the adjusted basis of the building was $30,000. The total amount of partnership minimum gain (or *Tufts* or phantom gain) was $20,000. The increase in partnership minimum gain for the year was $10,000.

At the end of Year 3, Ellen had claimed an additional $10,000 in depreciation and the adjusted basis of the building was $20,000. The total amount of partnership minimum gain (or *Tufts* or phantom gain) was $30,000. The increase in partnership minimum gain for the year was $10,000.

In summary:

Year	Depreciation	Adjusted Basis	Increase in PMG	Total PMG
1	$10,000	$40,000	$10,000	$10,000
2	10,000	30,000	10,000	20,000
3	10,000	20,000	10,000	30,000

In determining the excess of the non-recourse liability over the property's adjusted basis, there potentially may be two different adjusted bases that may be used. The "adjusted tax basis" refers to the partner's basis in the property at the time it was contributed to the partnership, adjusted by depreciation deductions. "Adjusted book basis" refers to the fair market value of the property at the time it was contributed to the partnership (or purchased by the partnership), adjusted by book depreciation deductions. If the adjusted tax basis differs from the adjusted book basis, the adjusted book basis is used for purposes of computing minimum gain.[25]

Second, partnership minimum gain may be created when the amount of non-recourse liability is increased.

---

25. Treas. Reg. § 1.704-2(d)(3). There also may be a difference between the two bases when there has been a revaluation of the partnership property. Treas. Reg. § 1.704-2(d)(4).

> **Example:** In Year 1, the partnership purchased an apartment building for $50,000. It was allowed to claim $10,000 of depreciation each year. In Year 3, when the adjusted basis of the building was $20,000, the partnership obtained a $50,000 non-recourse loan, secured by the building.
>
> Upon obtaining the non-recourse liability, the non-recourse liability, $50,000, exceeded the building's adjusted basis, $20,000, by $30,000. Thus, the partnership now has $30,000 of partnership minimum gain.

Finally, partner's share of partnership minimum gain is increased when a partner receives a distribution of proceeds from a non-recourse loan allocable to an increase in partnership minimum gain. The reason why there is partnership minimum gain in such a situation can be best understood by considering the ramifications of such a distribution.

A distribution of loan proceeds may cause a deficit balance in the partner's capital account. If the partnership has a qualified income offset, the partnership then would be required to allocate items of income or gain to the partner until his account was brought back to zero. However, by creating partnership minimum gain to the extent of the distribution, the partner can be allocated a correlative portion of the gain upon disposition of the property securing the non-recourse liability. It follows that, in anticipation of the future allocation of gain, under the alternate economic effect test the partner can be treated as having an obligation to restore a negative capital account balance to the extent of his share of partnership minimum gain.[26]

> **Example:** In Year 1, the partnership purchased an apartment building for $50,000. It was allowed to claim $10,000 of depreciation each year. In Year 3, when the adjusted basis of the building was $20,000, the partnership obtained a $50,000 non-recourse loan, secured by the building.
>
> Upon obtaining the non-recourse liability, the non-recourse liability, $50,000, exceeded the building's adjusted basis, $20,000, by $30,000. Thus, the partnership now has $30,000 of partnership minimum gain.
>
> The partnership distributed the $30,000 of non-recourse loan proceeds to Frank, a partner in the partnership. If his capital account was zero before the distribution, it will be <$30,000> after the distribution.
>
> Note that the non-recourse loan proceeds are no longer part of the partnership property, no partner has an obligation to repay the loan, and, because the proceeds did not generate any deductions, there is no correlation between an allowable depreciation deduction and potential future gain. In addition, Frank is not obligated to restore a negative capital account balance. Under the qualified income offset, the partnership would be obligated to begin allocating income and gain to Frank.
>
> However, Frank's share of partnership minimum gain is increased through the distribution of loan proceeds allocable to an increase in partnership minimum gain. Because of the allocation of partnership minimum gain, Frank will be treated as having an obligation to contribute $30,000 to the partnership.

---

26. Treas. Reg. § 1.704-2(g)(1), flush language.

Note that this result makes sense. If the partnership immediately sold the property for the amount of the debt, the partnership would have $30,000 of gain ($50,000 non-recourse debt, less $20,000 adjusted basis). Based on the minimum gain chargeback all $30,000 will be allocated to Frank, bringing his capital account from <$30,000> to zero.

Thus, by increasing the partner's share of partnership minimum gain when there has been a distribution of non-recourse loan proceeds allocable to an increase in partnership minimum gain, the qualified income offset is not triggered and Frank will be responsible for the tax liability associated with the distribution upon disposition of the property securing the debt.

Non-recourse deduction. A non-recourse deduction is equal to the net increase in partnership minimum gain, less distributions of proceeds of a non-recourse liability that are allocable to an increase in partnership minimum gain.[27]

Example: In Year 1, the partnership purchased an apartment building for $50,000. It was financed entirely with a $50,000 non-recourse loan, secured by the apartment building. The partnership was not required to make any principal payments on the non-recourse loan until Year 5. It was allowed to claim $10,000 of depreciation each year. Each year the depreciation deductions will create a $10,000 increase in partnership minimum gain. Accordingly, each year the partnership has $10,000 in non-recourse deductions.

Minimum gain chargeback. When there is a decrease in a partner's share of partnership minimum gain, a corresponding amount of gain must be allocated, or chargedback, to that partner.[28] Two different events may cause a decrease in a partner's share of partnership minimum gain.

First, the property subject to the non-recourse debt may be sold, triggering gain at least in the amount of the *Tufts* gain. Second, a decrease can occur when the amount of non-recourse debt is reduced, either by repayment of any portion of the liability or by conversion of any portion of a non-recourse debt into a recourse debt.

Example: In Year 1, the partnership purchased an apartment building for $50,000. It was financed entirely with a $50,000 non-recourse loan, secured by the apartment building. The partnership was not required to make any principal payments on the non-recourse loan until Year 5. It was allowed to claim $10,000 of depreciation each year. The partnership allocated all depreciation deductions to Ellen, a partner in the partnership. Ellens initial capital account was $100,000.

At the end of Year 1, Ellen had claimed $10,000 in depreciation and the adjusted basis of the building was $40,000. The amount of non-recourse deduction (*i.e.*, the increase in the amount of partnership minimum gain or *Tufts* or phantom gain) was $10,000. Her capital account was reduced by $10,000 to $90,000.

At the end of Year 2, Ellen claimed an additional $10,000 in depreciation and the adjusted basis of the building was $30,000. The total amount of partnership minimum gain (or

27. Treas. Reg. §1.704-2(c).
28. Treas. Reg. §1.704-2(f)(1).

Tufts or phantom gain) was $20,000. The amount of non-recourse deduction (*i.e.*, the increase in the amount of partnership minimum gain or *Tufts* or phantom gain) was $10,000. Her capital account was reduced by $10,000 to $80,000.

At the end of Year 3, Ellen claimed an additional $10,000 in depreciation and the adjusted basis of the building was $20,000. The total amount of partnership minimum gain (or *Tufts* or phantom gain) was $30,000. The amount of non-recourse deduction (*i.e.*, the increase in the amount of partnership minimum gain or *Tufts* or phantom gain) was $10,000. Her capital account was reduced by $10,000 to $70,000.

In summary:

Year	Depreciation	Building Adj. Bas.	NR ded.	Total PMG
1	$10,000	$40,000	$10,000	$10,000
2	10,000	30,000	10,000	20,000
3	10,000	20,000	10,000	30,000

At the beginning of Year 4 (ignoring any applicable depreciation for the year) the partnership sold the building for the amount of the non-recourse debt, $50,000. It recognized $30,000 or gain (amount realized of $50,000, less adjusted basis of $20,000). After the sale, because the partnership no longer has any partnership minimum gain, there has been a $30,000 decrease in partnership minimum gain ($30,000 partnership minimum gain to zero partnership minimum gain). This decrease triggers a minimum gain chargeback to Ellen, the partner who was allocated the correlative non-recourse deductions. Her capital account is increased by the $30,000 of gain from $70,000 to $100,000.

There are some exceptions to the requirement of a minimum gain chargeback. First, the outstanding balance of the non-recourse liability may be reduced by funds contributed by the partner to the partnership to pay down a non-recourse liability. Because the partner's capital account will be increased by the amount of the contribution, to this extent the reduction in the partner's share of partnership minimum gain will not trigger any qualified income offset. Similarly, to this extent, there is no need to allocate income to the partner through a minimum gain chargeback.[29]

Second, if any portion of the non-recourse debt is converted to recourse debt, the partner may bear the economic risk of loss for the debt. To such an extent, there is no need for a minimum gain chargeback.[30]

Finally, there is no minimum gain chargeback if it would cause a distortion in the economic arrangement of the partners and there is sufficient other income to correct the distortion.[31] Because the partner will be allocated gain equal to the amount of non-recourse deductions that have been allocated to him (in general, his share of partnership minimum gain), under the alternate economic effect test he is treated as having an obligation to restore a negative capital account balance to the extent of his share of partnership minimum gain.[32]

---

29. Treas. Reg. § 1.704-2(f)(3).
30. Treas. Reg. § 1.704-2(f)(2).
31. Treas. Reg. § 1.704-2(f)(4).
32. Treas. Reg. § 1.704-2(g)(1), flush language.

Partner's share of partnership minimum gain. The partnership's total partnership minimum gain is allocated among the partners. Each partner's share of partnership minimum gain is important:

- For determining the extent to which a partner is treated as having an obligation to restore a negative capital account balance (so as to not trigger a qualified income offset);
- To determine the amount of *Tufts*, or phantom, gain that must be allocated to the partner; and
- As will be seen in a later chapter, to determine the partner's share of a non-recourse liability.

A partner's share of partnership minimum gain is the sum of the non-recourse deductions allocated to the partner throughout the life of the partnership and the partner's share of distributions of non-recourse liability proceeds allocable to an increase in minimum gain, less the partner's share of any prior net decreases in partnership minimum gain.[33]

A partner's minimum gain chargeback is equal to his share of the net decrease in partnership minimum gain. In general, a partner's share of the net decrease is the amount of the total net decrease, multiplied by the partner's percentage share of the partnership minimum gain at the end of the immediately preceding taxable year.[34] The allocation consists first of gains recognized from disposition of the property subject to a non-recourse liability. Second, it consists of a ratable share of other items of partnership income and gain for the year.[35] A minimum gain chargeback must be made before any other allocations of partnership items for the year.[36] If the partnership does not have sufficient items of income or gain to satisfy the chargeback, such items must be allocated in the subsequent years to cure the deficiency as soon as possible.[37]

b. Safe Harbor Requirements

The allocation of deductions and losses attributable to non-recourse liabilities will be deemed to have been made in accordance with the partner's interest in the partnership and, therefore will be respected, if the safe harbor requirements set forth in the regulations are met.[38]

The first requirement is that the partnership agreement must meet either the general economic effect test or the alternate economic effect test.[39]

The second requirement is that, beginning in the first taxable year in which the partnership has non-recourse deductions, allocation of non-recourse deductions must be reasonably consistent with allocations of some other significant partnership item attributable to the property securing the non-recourse liabilities of the partnership

---

33. Treas. Reg. § 1.704-2(g)(1)
34. Treas. Reg. § 1.704-2(g)(2).
35. Treas. Reg. § 1.704-2(f)(6).
36. Treas. Reg. § 1.704-2(j).
37. Treas. Reg. § 1.704-2(f)(6), (j)(1).
38. Treas. Reg. § 1.704-2(e).
39. Treas. Reg. § 1.704-2(e)(1).

(other than allocation of minimum gain). Such other allocations must have substantial economic effect.[40]

The third requirement is that, in the first year in which the partnership has non-recourse deductions or makes a distribution of proceeds of a non-recourse liability allocable to an increase in partnership minimum gain, the partnership agreement must contain a minimum gain chargeback.[41]

The fourth requirement is that all other material allocations and capital account adjustments under the partnership agreement must comply with the basic Section 704(b) regulations.[42]

If the allocation of non-recourse deductions does not meet the safe harbor requirements, it will be reallocated in accordance with the partner's interest in the partnership.[43]

---

40. Treas. Reg. § 1.704-2(e)(2).
41. Treas. Reg. § 1.704-2(e)(3).
42. Treas. Reg. § 1.704-2(e)(4).
43. Treas. Reg. §§ 1.704-1(b)(3), -2(b)(1)

Summary

Recourse Deductions and Tests for Economic Effect: For an allocation to have economic effect, one of the following tests must be met.

General Test:
- Partners' capital accounts must be maintained according to the regulations;
- Liquidating distributions must be made in accordance with positive capital account balances; and
- If, following a liquidation, a partner has a deficit balance in his capital account, he must be unconditionally obligated to restore the amount of such deficit balance.

Alternate Test:
- Partners' capital accounts must be maintained according to the regulations;
- Liquidating distributions must be made in accordance with positive capital account balances;
- The allocation of recourse deductions cannot cause or increase a deficit in the partner's capital account in excess of any limited amount the partner is obligated to restore; and
- The partnership agreement contains a qualified income offset.

General Rule for Substantiality: The economic effect of an allocation is *not* substantial if:
- The after-tax economic consequences of at least one partner may, in present value terms, be enhanced compared to such consequences if the allocation were not contained in the partnership agreement; and
- There is a strong likelihood that the after-tax economic consequences of no partner will, in present value terms, be substantially diminished compared to such consequences if the allocation were not contained in the partnership agreement.

Shifting: Allocations that impact one year are considered.

Transitory: Allocations that impact two or more years are considered.

Definitions Related to Non-Recourse Deductions:

$$\frac{\text{Non-recourse debt}}{\text{Partnership minimum gain } (\textit{Tufts} \text{ gain or phantom income})} - \text{Book adjusted basis}$$

$$\frac{\text{Net increase in PMG} - \text{Distributions made during the year of proceeds of non-recourse liability that are allocable to an increase in PMG}}{\text{Non-recourse deductions}}$$

$$\frac{\text{Non-recourse deduction allocations} + \text{distributions of non-recourse liability proceeds allocable to increase in PMG}}{\text{Partner's share of PMG}}$$

Minimum gain chargeback: if there is a net decrease in PMG, each partner must be allocated items of income/gain equal to that partner's share of the net decrease in PMG unless the decrease is due to:
- The liability becoming recourse to that partner; or
- A contribution to capital that is used to repay the non-recourse liability.

A partner's share of the net decrease in PMG = (total net decrease) × (partner's percentage share of PMG at the end of prior year).

Safe Harbor Requirements for Allocations of Non-recourse Deductions:
- The economic effect test must be met (either the general or the alternate);
- Beginning in the year the partnership has non-recourse deductions, the allocation must be reasonably consistent with other allocations (which have substantial economic effect) attributable to the property securing the non-recourse debt;
- There must be a minimum gain chargeback provision; and
- Allocations of other material items must have substantial economic effect.

Questions

1. Ann and Bob each contributed $50,000 in exchange for a general partnership interest. The partnership agreement provided that Ann and Bob would share profits and losses equally, but that all depreciation would be allocated to Bob. The agreement also provided that capital accounts would be maintained in accordance with the regulations, but that, upon liquidation, distributions would be made equally between the partners (and not in accordance with capital account balances). The agreement does not require that a partner restore a negative capital account balance.

The partnership used the cash to purchase a building for $100,000. The partnership was entitled to $10,000 of depreciation each year.

In the first year, before taking into consideration the depreciation, income equaled expenses. Will the allocation of all depreciation to Bob be respected?

2. Carl and Deb each contributed $50,000 in exchange for a general partnership interest. The partnership agreement provided that Carl and Deb would share profits and losses equally, but that all depreciation would be allocated to Carl. The agreement also provided that capital accounts would be maintained in accordance with the regulations, that a partner must restore a negative capital account balance, and that liquidating distributions would be made in accordance with capital account balances.

The partnership used the cash to purchase a building for $100,000. The partnership was entitled to $20,000 of depreciation each year.

a. In the first year, before taking into consideration the depreciation, income equaled expenses. Will the allocation of all depreciation to Carl be respected? Prepare a balance sheet to reflect the situation of the partners at the end of the first year.

b. If at the beginning of the second year the partnership sold the building for $80,000 and liquidated, how would the proceeds from the sale be distributed? (For purposes of simplicity, assume no depreciation is allocated in the second year and that there are no selling costs.)

c. Alternatively, if at the beginning of the second year, the partnership sold the building for $140,000 and liquidated, how would the proceeds from the sale be distributed? (For purposes of simplicity, assume no depreciation is allocated in the second year and that there are no selling costs.)

d. Alternatively, if at the beginning of the second year, the partnership sold the building for $60,000 and liquidated, how would the proceeds from the sale be distributed? (For purposes of simplicity, assume no depreciation is allocated in the second year and that there are no selling costs.)

3. Ellen and Frank each contributed $50,000 in exchange for a general partnership interest. The partnership agreement provided that Ellen and Frank would share profits and losses equally, but that all depreciation would be allocated to Frank. The agreement also provided that capital accounts would be maintained in accordance with the regulations, that a partner must restore a negative capital account balance, and that liquidating distributions would be made in accordance with capital account balances.

The partnership used the cash to purchase a building for $100,000. The partnership was entitled to $25,000 of depreciation each year. In each year, before taking into consideration the depreciation, income equaled expenses.

   a. Will the allocation of all depreciation to Frank in the first year be respected? Prepare a balance sheet to reflect the situation of the partners at the end of year one.

   b. Will the allocation of all depreciation to Frank in year two be respected? Prepare a balance sheet to reflect the situation of the partners at the end of year two.

   c. Will the allocation of all depreciation to Frank in year three be respected? Prepare a balance sheet to reflect the situation of the partners at the end of year three.

   d. At the beginning of the fourth year, the partnership sold the building for $25,000 and liquidated. What are the tax consequences to the partners? (For purposes of simplicity, assume no depreciation is allocated in the fourth year and that there are no selling costs.)

4.   Greg contributed $50,000 in exchange for a general partnership interest and Hal contributed $50,000 in exchange for a limited partnership interest. The partnership agreement provided that Greg and Hal would share profits and losses equally, but that all depreciation would be allocated to Hal. The agreement also provided that capital accounts would be maintained in accordance with the regulations and that liquidating distributions would be made in accordance with capital account balances. Greg has an unconditional obligation to restore a negative capital account balance. Hal was not required to restore any deficit balance in his account, but the agreement contained a qualified income offset with respect to him.

The partnership used the cash to purchase a building for $100,000. The partnership was entitled to $25,000 of depreciation each year. In each year, before taking into consideration the depreciation, income equaled expenses.

   a. In the first year will the allocation of depreciation to Hal be respected? Prepare a balance sheet to reflect the situation of the partners at the end of year one.

   b. In the second year will the allocation of depreciation to Hal be respected? Prepare a balance sheet to reflect the situation of the partners at the end of the second year.

   c. In the third year will the allocation of depreciation to Hal be respected? Prepare a balance sheet to reflect the situation of the partners at the end of the third year.

5.   Ira contributed $150,000 in exchange for a general partnership interest and Jeb contributed $50,000 in exchange for a limited partnership interest. The partnership agreement provided that 75 percent of profits and losses would be allocated to Ira and 25 percent to Jeb, but that all depreciation would be allocated to Jeb. The agreement also provided that capital accounts would be maintained in accordance with the regulations and that liquidating distributions would be made in accordance with capital account balances. Ira has an unconditional obligation to restore a negative capital account balance. Jeb was not required to restore any deficit balance in his account, but the agreement contained a qualified income offset with respect to him.

The partnership used the cash to purchase a building for $200,000. The partnership was entitled to $25,000 of depreciation each year. In each year, before taking into consideration the depreciation, income equaled expenses.

a. In the first year will the allocation of depreciation to Jeb be respected? Prepare a balance sheet to reflect the situation of the partners at the end of year one.

b. The partners agree that the partnership will distribute $25,000 to each of Ira and Jeb at the beginning of the third year. In the second year will the allocation of depreciation to Jeb be respected? Prepare a balance sheet to reflect the situation of the partners at the end of the second year.

6. Kent contributed $150,000 in exchange for a general partnership interest and Len contributed $50,000 in exchange for a limited partnership interest. The partnership agreement provided that 75 percent of profits and losses would be allocated to Kent and 25 percent to Len, but that all depreciation would be allocated to Len. The agreement also provided that capital accounts would be maintained in accordance with the regulations and that liquidating distributions would be made in accordance with capital account balances. Kent has an unconditional obligation to restore a negative capital account balance. Len was not required to restore any deficit balance in his account, but the agreement contained a qualified income offset with respect to him.

The partnership used the cash to purchase a building for $200,000. The partnership was entitled to $50,000 of depreciation each year. In each year, before taking into consideration the depreciation, income equaled expenses.

a. In the first year will the allocation of depreciation to Len be respected? Prepare a balance sheet to reflect the situations of the partners at the end of year one.

b. At the beginning of the second year, the partnership distributed $50,000 to each of Kent and Len. At the end of the second year, the partnership had the $50,000 of depreciation and had also earned $25,000 of income. What is each partner's capital account at the end of the year?

7. Mike contributed $50,000 in exchange for a general partnership interest and Ned contributed $50,000 in exchange for a limited partnership interest. The partnership agreement provided that Mike and Ned would share profits and losses equally, but that all depreciation would be allocated to Ned. The agreement also provided that capital accounts would be maintained in accordance with the regulations and that liquidating distributions would be made in accordance with capital account balances. Mike has an unconditional obligation to restore a negative capital account balance. Ned was not required to restore any deficit balance in his account, but the agreement contained a qualified income offset with respect to him.

The partnership used the cash to purchase a building for $100,000. The partnership was entitled to $50,000 of depreciation each year. In each year, before taking into consideration the depreciation, income equaled expenses.

a. In the first year will the allocation of depreciation to Ned be respected? Prepare a balance sheet to reflect the situation of the partners at the end of year one.

b. In the second year, Ned contributed his promissory note in the amount of $100,000 to the partnership. Will the allocation of depreciation to Ned be respected?

8. Opie contributed $50,000 in exchange for a general partnership interest and Paul contributed $50,000 in exchange for a limited partnership interest. The partnership

agreement provided only that Opie and Paul would share profits and losses equally, but that all depreciation would be allocated to Paul.

The partnership used the cash to purchase a building for $100,000. The partnership was entitled to $25,000 of depreciation each year. In each year, before taking into consideration the depreciation, income equaled expenses.

   a. In the first year will the allocation of depreciation to Paul be respected? Prepare a balance sheet to reflect the situation of the partners at the end of year one.

   b. In the second year will the allocation of depreciation to Paul be respected? Prepare a balance sheet to reflect the situation of the partners at the end of the second year.

   c. In the third year will the allocation of depreciation to Paul be respected? Prepare a balance sheet to reflect the situation of the partners at the end of the third year.

9.   Quinn and Roy are equal partners. Quinn does not pay any United States tax. The partnership expects to earn $50,000 in profits and $50,000 of interest from tax-exempt bonds. The partners agree that all profits will be allocated to Quinn and all income from the tax-exempt bonds will be allocated to Roy.

The partnership agreement provided that capital accounts would be maintained in accordance with the regulations, that liquidating distributions would be made in accordance with capital account balances, and that all partners have an obligation to restore a negative capital account balance.

Will the allocation be respected?

10. Sam and Tess are equal partners. Sam is an unemployed student, but expects to graduate and obtain a job in three years and expects the money he earns from that job to be taxed at the 25 percent rate. Tess is employed as a doctor and has a substantial amount of income taxed at the 35 percent rate. She expects to retire in three years. The partners agree to allocate all profits to Sam and all deductions to Tess for three years. During the following three years, the partners will allocate all profits to Tess and all deductions to Sam. Beginning in year seven, they will allocate all items equally. The partnership expects to earn $100,000 of income and incur $100,000 of deductions over the next six years.

The partnership agreement provided that capital accounts would be maintained in accordance with the regulations, that liquidating distributions would be made in accordance with capital account balances, and that all partners have an obligation to restore a negative capital account balance.

Will the allocation be respected?

11. Vince and Wes each contributed $50,000 in exchange for a general partnership interest. The partnership agreement provided that Vince and Wes would share profits and losses equally. The agreement also provided that capital accounts would be maintained in accordance with the regulations, that a partner must restore a negative capital account balance, and that liquidating distributions would be made in accordance with capital account balances.

The partnership purchased equipment for $50,000 and was entitled to claim $10,000 of depreciation each year. The partners agreed to allocate 60 percent of the depreciation to Vince and 40 percent to Wes. When the equipment was sold, the gain would be allocated in such a way so as to equalize the partners' capital accounts. Any remaining gain would be allocated equally between Vince and Wes.

   a. In the first year, before taking into consideration the depreciation, income equaled expenses. How is the depreciation allocated? Prepare a balance to reflect the situation of the partners at the end of the first year.

   b. The partnership sold the equipment at the beginning of the second year for $60,000. (For purposes of simplicity, ignore any allowable depreciation for the second year.) What is the character of gain Vince and Wes must report?

12. Xander contributed $10,000 in exchange for a general partnership interest and Yolanda contributed $90,000 in exchange for a limited partnership interest. The partnership obtained a $200,000 non-recourse loan and purchased a building for $300,000. The loan was secured by the building and no payments were due on the loan for five years.

The partnership agreement provided that capital accounts would be maintained according to the regulations, liquidating distributions would be make according to capital account balances and that Xander would be required to restore any deficit balance in his capital account. Yolanda was not required to restore any deficit balance in her account, but the agreement contained a qualified income offset with respect to her. The partnership agreement also contained a minimum gain chargeback. Finally, the partnership agreement provided that, except as otherwise required by its qualified income offset and minimum gain chargeback provisions, all partnership items would be allocated 90 percent to Yolanda and 10 percent to Xander, except non-recourse deductions which would be allocated 80 percent to Yolanda and 20 percent to Xander, until the first time when the partnership had recognized items of income and gain that exceeded the items of loss and deduction it had recognized over its life. Then, all partnership items would be allocated equally between Xander and Yolanda.

At the end of each partnership taxable year, no items are reasonably expected to cause or increase a deficit balance in Yolanda's capital account.

   a. In the first year, the partnership generates income equal to its expenses and is entitled to $50,000 of depreciation. What are the partners' capital accounts at the end of the year?

   b. In the second year, the partnership generates income equal to its expenses and is entitled to $50,000 of depreciation. What are the partners' capital accounts at the end of the second year?

   c. In the third year, the partnership generates income equal to its expenses and is entitled to $50,000 of depreciation. What are the partners' capital accounts at the end of the third year?

   d. In the fourth year, the partnership generates income equal to its expenses. It also forfeited the building to the lender. (For the sake of simplicity, ignore any allowable depreciation for the fourth year.) What are the partners' capital accounts at the end of the fourth year?

13. Zelda contributed $40,000 in exchange for a general partnership interest and Ann contributed $60,000 in exchange for a limited partnership interest. The partnership

obtained a $200,000 non-recourse loan and purchased a building for $300,000. The loan was secured by the building and no payments were due on the loan for five years.

The partnership agreement provided that capital accounts would be maintained according to the regulations, liquidating distributions would be made according to capital account balances and that Zelda would be required to restore any deficit balance in her capital account. Ann was not required to restore any deficit balance in her account, but the agreement contained a qualified income offset with respect to her. The partnership agreement also contained a minimum gain chargeback. Finally, the partnership agreement provided that, except as otherwise required by its qualified income offset and minimum gain chargeback provisions, all partnership items would be allocated 60 percent to Ann and 40 percent to Zelda, except non-recourse deductions which would be allocated 50 percent to Ann and 50 percent to Zelda, until the first time when the partnership had recognized items of income and gain that exceeded the items of loss and deduction it had recognized over its life. Then, all partnership items would be allocated equally between Zelda and Ann.

At the end of each partnership taxable year, no items are reasonably expected to cause or increase a deficit balance in Ann's capital account.

   a. In the first year, the partnership generates income equal to its expenses and is entitled to $50,000 of depreciation. What are the partners' capital accounts at the end of the year?

   b. In the second year, the partnership generates income equal to its expenses and is entitled to $50,000 of depreciation. What are the partners' capital accounts at the end of the second year?

   c. In the third year, the partnership generates income equal to its expenses and is entitled to $50,000 of depreciation. What are the partners' capital accounts at the end of the third year?

   d. In the fourth year, the partnership converts the non-recourse debt to a recourse debt. Is a minimum gain chargeback triggered?

Solutions

1. Ann and Bob each contributed $50,000 in exchange for a general partnership interest. The partnership agreement provided that Ann and Bob would share profits and losses equally, but that all depreciation would be allocated to Bob. The agreement also provided that capital accounts would be maintained in accordance with the regulations, but that, upon liquidation, distributions would be made equally between the partners (and not in accordance with capital account balances). The agreement does not require that a partner restore a negative capital account balance.

The partnership used the cash to purchase a building for $100,000. The partnership was entitled to $10,000 of depreciation each year.

In the first year, before taking into consideration the depreciation, income equaled expenses. Will the allocation of all depreciation to Bob be respected?

The partnership is entitled to claim $10,000 of depreciation in the first year.

Building (tax and book)

Basis:	$100,000
Depreciation:	− 10,000
Adjusted basis:	$ 90,000

The depreciation is allocated all to Bob. Adjustments would be made as follows (Section 705(a)(2)):

	Ann			Bob	
	Basis	**Capital Account**		**Basis**	**Capital Account**
	$50,000	$50,000		$50,000	$50,000
depr.:	—	—		− 10,000	− 10,000
	$50,000	$50,000		$40,000	$40,000

At the end of the first year, the balance sheet would be as follows:

Asset	Basis	FMV	Partner	Basis	Cap. Acct.
Building	$90,000	$90,000	Ann	$50,000	$50,000
	$90,000	$90,000	Bob	$40,000	$40,000
				$90,000	$90,000

If the partnership liquidated at the end of the year, pursuant to the partnership agreement Ann and Bob would each receive $45,000 (recall that liquidating distributions were to be made equally). Under this method of distribution, Bob did not bear the full risk of the economic loss corresponding to the deduction he received. Thus, the allocation of depreciation to Bob lacks economic effect and will be disregarded. (Treas. Reg. § 1.704-1(b)(2)(ii)(b)(2)) The depreciation deduction must be reallocated based on the partners' interests in the partnership. (Treas. Reg. §§ 1.704-1(b)(1)(i), -1(b)(3))

Because the Ann and Bob made equal contributions to the partnership, shared equally in operating income and losses, and shared equally in liquidating distributions, they both had a 50-percent interest in the partnership. (See Treas. Reg. § 1.704-1(b)(3)) Accordingly, the depreciation will be re-allocated equally between Ann and Bob.

	Ann			Bob	
	Basis	**Capital Account**	**Basis**	**Capital Account**	
	$50,000	$50,000	$50,000	$50,000	
depr.:	−5,000	−5,000	−5,000	−5,000	
	$45,000	$45,000	$45,000	$45,000	

At the end of the first year, the balance sheet would be as follows:

Asset	Basis	FMV	Partner	Basis	Cap. Acct.
Building	$90,000	$90,000	Ann	$45,000	$45,000
	$90,000	$90,000	Bob	$45,000	$45,000
				$90,000	$90,000

2. Carl and Deb each contributed $50,000 in exchange for a general partnership interest. The partnership agreement provided that Carl and Deb would share profits and losses equally, but that all depreciation would be allocated to Carl. The agreement also provided that capital accounts would be maintained in accordance with the regulations, that a partner must restore a negative capital account balance, and that liquidating distributions would be made in accordance with capital account balances.

The partnership used the cash to purchase a building for $100,000. The partnership was entitled to $20,000 of depreciation each year.

a. In the first year, before taking into consideration the depreciation, income equaled expenses. Will the allocation of all depreciation to Carl be respected? Prepare a balance sheet to reflect the situation of the partners at the end of the first year.

All depreciation is allocated to Carl. All allocations are respected because the general test has been met and the allocations have substantial economic effect. (Treas. Reg. § 1.704-1(b)(2)(ii)(b)) Adjustments would be made as follows (Section 705(a)(2)):

Building (tax and book)

Basis:	$100,000		Carl:	Basis	Capital Account
Depreciation:	−20,000			$50,000	$50,000
Adjusted basis:	$80,000		depreciation	−20,000	−20,000
				$30,000	$30,000

Incorporating the above information, the partnership balance sheet would appear as follows:

Asset	Basis	FMV	Partner	Basis	Cap. Acct.
Building	$80,000	$80,000	Carl	$30,000	$30,000
	$80,000	$80,000	Deb	50,000	50,000
				$80,000	$80,000

b. If at the beginning of the second year the partnership sold the building for $80,000 and liquidated, how would the proceeds from the sale be distributed? (For purposes of simplicity, assume no depreciation is allocated in the second year and that there are no selling costs.)

Upon sale of the building, tax and book gain must be determined.

Building

	Tax	Book
AR:	$80,000	$80,000
AB:	80,000	80,000
	$ 0	$ 0

Just after the sale and prior to liquidation, the balance sheet would appear as follows:

Asset	Basis	FMV	Partner	Basis	Cap. Acct.
Cash	$80,000	$80,000	Carl	$30,000	$30,000
	$80,000	$80,000	Deb	50,000	50,000
				$80,000	$80,000

On liquidation, there would be $80,000 to distribute to the partners. Because liquidating distributions are made based on capital account balances, $30,000 is distributed to Carl and $50,000 is distributed to Deb.

    c. **Alternatively, if at the beginning of the second year, the partnership sold the building for $140,000 and liquidated, how would the proceeds from the sale be distributed? (For purposes of simplicity, assume no depreciation is allocated in the second year and that there are no selling costs.)**

Upon sale of the building, tax and book gain must be determined.

Building

	Tax	Book
AR:	$140,000	$140,000
AB:	80,000	80,000
	$ 60,000	$ 60,000

The $60,000 of gain must be allocated equally between the partners, or $30,000 each. Adjustments would be made as follows:

	Carl		Deb
Basis	**Capital Account**	**Basis**	**Capital Account**
$30,000	$30,000	$50,000	$50,000
gain: + 30,000	+ 30,000	+ 30,000	+ 30,000
$60,000	$60,000	$80,000	$80,000

Just after the sale and prior to liquidation, the balance sheet would appear as follows:

Asset	Basis	FMV	Partner	Basis	Cap. Acct.
Cash	$140,000	$140,000	Carl	$ 60,000	$ 60,000
	$140,000	$140,000	Deb	80,000	80,000
				$140,000	$140,000

On liquidation, there would be $140,000 to distribute to the partners. Because liquidating distributions are made based on capital account balances, $60,000 is distributed to Carl and $80,000 is distributed to Deb.

d. Alternatively, if at the beginning of the second year, the partnership sold the building for $60,000 and liquidated, how would the proceeds from the sale be distributed? (For purposes of simplicity, assume no depreciation is allocated in the second year and that there are no selling costs.)

Upon sale of the building, tax and book loss must be determined.

Building

	Tax	Book
AR:	$60,000	$60,000
AB:	80,000	80,000
	<$20,000>	<$20,000>

The $20,000 of loss must be allocated equally between the partners, or $10,000 each. Adjustments would be made as follows:

	Carl		Deb	
	Basis	Capital Account	Basis	Capital Account
	$30,000	$30,000	$50,000	$50,000
Loss	− 10,000	− 10,000	− 10,000	− 10,000
	$20,000	$20,000	$40,000	$40,000

Just after the sale and prior to liquidation, the balance sheet would appear as follows:

Asset	Basis	FMV	Partner	Basis	Cap. Acct.
Cash	$60,000	$60,000	Carl	$20,000	$20,000
	$60,000	$60,000	Deb	40,000	40,000
				$60,000	$60,000

On liquidation, there would be $60,000 to distribute to the partners. Because liquidating distributions are made based on capital account balances, $20,000 is distributed to Carl and $40,000 is distributed to Deb.

3. Ellen and Frank each contributed $50,000 in exchange for a general partnership interest. The partnership agreement provided that Ellen and Frank would share profits and losses equally, but that all depreciation would be allocated to Frank. The agreement also provided that capital accounts would be maintained in accordance with the regulations, that a partner must restore a negative capital account balance, and that liquidating distributions would be made in accordance with capital account balances.

The partnership used the cash to purchase a building for $100,000. The partnership was entitled to $25,000 of depreciation each year. In each year, before taking into consideration the depreciation, income equaled expenses.

a. Will the allocation of all depreciation to Frank in the first year be respected? Prepare a balance sheet to reflect the situation of the partners at the end of year one.

All depreciation is allocated to Frank. All allocations are respected because the general test has been met and the allocations have substantial economic effect. (Treas. Reg. § 1.704-1(b)(2)(ii)(b)) Adjustments would be made as follows:

Building (tax and book)			**Frank**	
			Basis	**Capital Account**
Basis:	$100,000		$50,000	$50,000
Depreciation:	− 25,000		− 25,000	− 25,000
Adjusted basis:	$ 75,000	depreciation:	$25,000	$25,000

Incorporating the above information, the partnership balance sheet would appear as follows:

Asset	Basis	FMV	Partner	Basis	Cap. Acct.
Building	$75,000	$75,000	Ellen	$50,000	$50,000
	$75,000	$75,000	Frank	25,000	25,000
				$75,000	$75,000

b. Will the allocation of all depreciation to Frank in year two be respected? Prepare a balance sheet to reflect the situation of the partners at the end of year two.

All depreciation is allocated to Frank. All allocations are respected because the general test has been met and the allocations have substantial economic effect. (Treas. Reg. § 1.704-1(b)(2)(ii)(*b*)) Adjustments would be made as follows:

Building (tax and book)			**Frank**	
			Basis	**Capital Account**
Basis:	$75,000		$25,000	$25,000
Depreciation:	− 25,000		− 25,000	− 25,000
Adjusted basis:	$50,000	depreciation:	$ 0	$ 0

Incorporating the above information, the partnership balance sheet would appear as follows:

Asset	Basis	FMV	Partner	Basis	Cap. Acct.
Building	$50,000	$50,000	Ellen	$50,000	$50,000
	$50,000	$50,000	Frank	0	0
				$50,000	$50,000

c. Will the allocation of all depreciation to Frank in year three be respected? Prepare a balance sheet to reflect the situation of the partners at the end of year three.

All depreciation is allocated to Frank. All allocations are respected because the general test has been met and the allocations have substantial economic effect. (Treas. Reg. § 1.704-1(b)(2)(ii)(*b*)) Adjustments would be made as follows:

Building (tax and book)			**Frank**	
			Basis	Capital Account
Basis:	$50,000		$ 0	$ 0
Depreciation:	− 25,000		− 25,000	− 25,000
Adjusted basis:	$25,000	depreciation:	$ 0	<$25,000>

Frank's basis cannot go below zero. Rather, the $25,000 loss is disallowed and carried forward. (Section 704(d))

Incorporating the above information, the partnership balance sheet would appear as follows:

Asset	Basis	FMV	Partner	Basis	Cap. Acct.
Building	$25,000	$25,000	Ellen	$50,000	$50,000
	$25,000	$25,000	Frank	0	<25,000>
				$50,000	$25,000

Upon liquidation, Frank has an obligation to contributed $25,000 to the partnership.

> d. At the beginning of the fourth year, the partnership sold the building for $25,000 and liquidated. What are the tax consequences to the partners? (For purposes of simplicity, assume no depreciation is allocated in the fourth year and that there are no selling costs.)

Upon sale of the building, there is no tax or book gain or loss.

Building

	Tax	Book
AR:	$25,000	$25,000
AB:	25,000	25,000
	$ 0	$ 0

Just after the sale and prior to liquidation, the balance sheet would appear as follows:

Asset	Basis	FMV	Partner	Basis	Cap. Acct.
Cash	$25,000	$25,000	Ellen	$50,000	$50,000
	$25,000	$25,000	Frank	0	<25,000>
				$50,000	$25,000

Frank has an obligation to contribute $25,000 to the partnership (bringing his capital account balance to zero). The $25,000 contributed by Frank and the $25,000 already in the partnership would be distributed to Ellen.

(Also, upon Frank's contribution of $25,000, his basis will be increased to $25,000 and he would be allowed to claim the disallowed loss carried forward from the preceding year, reducing his basis again to zero.)

4. Greg contributed $50,000 in exchange for a general partnership interest and Hal contributed $50,000 in exchange for a limited partnership interest. The partnership agreement provided that Greg and Hal would share profits and losses equally, but that all depreciation would be allocated to Hal. The agreement also provided that capital accounts would be maintained in accordance with the regulations and that liquidating distributions would be made in accordance with capital account balances. Greg has an unconditional obligation to restore a negative capital account balance. Hal was not required to restore any deficit balance in his account, but the agreement contained a qualified income offset with respect to him.

The partnership used the cash to purchase a building for $100,000. The partnership was entitled to $25,000 of depreciation each year. In each year, before taking into consideration the depreciation, income equaled expenses.

a. In the first year will the allocation of depreciation to Hal be respected? Prepare a balance sheet to reflect the situation of the partners at the end of year one.

All depreciation is allocated to Hal. All allocations are respected because the general and alternate tests have been met; the allocations have substantial economic effect. (Treas. Reg. § 1.704-1(b)(2)(ii)(b), (d)) Adjustments would be made as follows:

Building (tax and book)				Hal	
				Basis	Capital Account
Basis:	$100,000			$50,000	$50,000
Depreciation:	− 25,000		depreciation:	− 25,000	− 25,000
Adjusted basis:	$ 75,000			$25,000	$25,000

Incorporating the above information, the partnership balance sheet would appear as follows:

Asset	Basis	FMV	Partner	Basis	Cap. Acct.
Building	$75,000	$75,000	Greg	$50,000	$50,000
	$75,000	$75,000	Hal	25,000	25,000
				$75,000	$75,000

b. In the second year will the allocation of depreciation to Hal be respected? Prepare a balance sheet to reflect the situation of the partners at the end of the second year.

All depreciation is allocated to Hal. All allocations are respected because the general and alternate tests have been met; the allocations have substantial economic effect. (Treas. Reg. § 1.704-1(b)(2)(ii)(b), (d)) Adjustments would be made as follows:

Building (tax and book)				Hal	
				Basis	Capital Account
Basis:	$75,000			$25,000	$25,000
Depreciation:	− 25,000		depreciation:	− 25,000	− 25,000
Adjusted basis:	$50,000			$ 0	$ 0

Incorporating the above information, the partnership balance sheet would appear as follows:

Asset	Basis	FMV	Partner	Basis	Cap. Acct.
Building	$50,000	$50,000	Greg	$50,000	$50,000
	$50,000	$50,000	Hal	0	0
				$50,000	$50,000

c. In the third year will the allocation of depreciation to Hal be respected? Prepare a balance sheet to reflect the situation of the partners at the end of the third year.

All depreciation is allocated to Hal. Adjustments would be made as follows:

	Building (tax and book)		Hal
Basis:	$50,000		**Capital Account**
Depreciation:	– 25,000		$ 0
Adjusted basis:	$25,000	depreciation:	– 25,000
			<$25,000>

Because an allocation of depreciation would result in Hal's capital account going negative, the allocation would not have economic effect. (Treas. Reg. § 1.704-1(b)(2)(ii)(*d*)(3)) Accordingly, the depreciation must be reallocated in accordance with the partners' interests in the partnership. (Treas. Reg. § 1.704-1(b)(3))

Because the first two elements of the alternate economic effect test were met, the partner's interest in the partnership is determined using a comparative liquidation test. (Treas. Reg. § 1.704-1(b)(3)(iii))

If the building had been sold at book value at the end of year two, it would have been sold for $50,000 and the $50,000 of proceeds allocated entirely to Greg.

Year Two: Building sale proceeds = $50,000

Greg = $50,000   Hal = $0

If the building had been sold at book value at the end of year three, it would have been sold for $25,000 and the $25,000 of proceeds allocated entirely to Greg.

Year Three: Building sale proceeds = $25,000

Greg = $25,000   Hal = $0

However, because Greg's capital account was $50,000 and he would receive only $25,000, he bears the burden of the $25,000 depreciation. Accordingly, the $25,000 of depreciation should be reallocated to him.

Greg:	Basis	Capital Account
	$50,000	$50,000
depreciation:	– 25,000	– 25,000
	$25,000	$25,000

Incorporating the above information, the partnership balance sheet would appear as follows:

Asset	Basis	FMV	Partner	Basis	Cap. Acct.
Building	$25,000	$25,000	Greg	$25,000	$25,000
	$25,000	$25,000	Hal	0	0
				$25,000	$25,000

5. Ira contributed $150,000 in exchange for a general partnership interest and Jeb contributed $50,000 in exchange for a limited partnership interest. The partnership agreement provided that 75 percent of profits and losses would be allocated to Ira and

25 percent to Jeb, but that all depreciation would be allocated to Jeb. The agreement also provided that capital accounts would be maintained in accordance with the regulations and that liquidating distributions would be made in accordance with capital account balances. Ira has an unconditional obligation to restore a negative capital account balance. Jeb was not required to restore any deficit balance in his account, but the agreement contained a qualified income offset with respect to him.

The partnership used the cash to purchase a building for $200,000. The partnership was entitled to $25,000 of depreciation each year. In each year, before taking into consideration the depreciation, income equaled expenses.

a. In the first year will the allocation of depreciation to Jeb be respected? Prepare a balance sheet to reflect the situation of the partners at the end of year one.

All depreciation is allocated to Jeb. All allocations are respected because the general and alternate tests have been met; the allocations have substantial economic effect. (Treas. Reg. § 1.704-1(b)(2)(ii)(b), (d)) Adjustments would be made as follows:

Building (tax and book)				Jeb	
				Basis	Capital Account
Basis:	$200,000			$50,000	$50,000
Depreciation:	– 25,000				
Adjusted basis:	$175,000	depreciation:		– 25,000	– 25,000
				$25,000	$25,000

Incorporating the above information, the partnership balance sheet would appear as follows:

Asset	Basis	FMV	Partner	Basis	Cap. Acct.
Building	$175,000	$175,000	Ira	$150,000	$150,000
	$175,000	$175,000	Jeb	25,000	25,000
				$175,000	$175,000

b. The partners agree that the partnership will distribute $25,000 to each of Ira and Jeb at the beginning of the third year. In the second year will the allocation of depreciation to Jeb be respected? Prepare a balance sheet to reflect the situation of the partners at the end of the second year.

All depreciation is allocated to Jeb.

Building (tax and book)
Basis:	$175,000
Depreciation:	– 25,000
Adjusted basis:	$150,000

Under the alternate economic effect test, to result in the least chance possible that the partner's capital account will go below zero, adjustments to the partner's capital account must be anticipated prior to considering any allocations to the partner. Thus, certain temporary adjustments must be made for any allocations that are reasonably expected to occur. Some of the adjustments that must be anticipated include:

- Allocations due to reasonably expected changes in interests in the partnership in future years; and

- Any distributions that are expected to be made to the partner, less any increases due to reasonably expected allocations of income.

(Treas. Reg. § 1.704-1(b)(2)(ii)(d)(6); 1.704-2(b)(2)(iv)(e)(1))

Because the partnership will be making a distribution in the following year, Jeb's capital account must be temporarily adjusted for the distribution.

Capital Account

	$25,000
Distribution	– 25,000
	$ 0

When the depreciation is also considered, it would result in his capital account going negative.

Capital Account

	$ 0
Depreciation:	<25,000>
	<$25,000>

Thus, the allocation of depreciation would not have economic effect. (Treas. Reg. § 1.704-1(b)(2)(ii)(d)(3), (6)) Accordingly, the depreciation must be reallocated in accordance with the partners' interests in the partnership. (Treas. Reg. § 1.704-1(b)(3))

Because the first two elements of the alternate economic effect test were met, the partner's interest in the partnership is determined using a comparative liquidation test. (Treas. Reg. § 1.704-1(b)(3)(iii)) Accordingly, the depreciation is reallocated all to Ira.

	Ira		Jeb	
	Basis	Capital Account	Basis	Capital Account
$150,000:	$150,000	$150,000	$25,000	$25,000
depreciation:	– 25,000	– 25,000	—	—
	$125,000	$125,000	$25,000	$25,000

Incorporating the above information, the partnership balance sheet would appear as follows:

Asset	Basis	FMV	Partner	Basis	Cap. Acct.
Building	$150,000	$150,000	Ira	$125,000	$125,000
	$150,000	$150,000	Jeb	25,000	25,000
				$150,000	$150,000

Note that this result makes sense. When the distribution is made to Jeb in year three, his basis and capital account would be adjusted as follows:

Jeb:	Basis	Capital Account
	$25,000	$25,000
Distribution:	– 25,000	– 25,000
	$ 0	$ 0

6.   Kent contributed $150,000 in exchange for a general partnership interest and Len contributed $50,000 in exchange for a limited partnership interest. The partnership agreement provided that 75 percent of profits and losses would be allocated to Kent

and 25 percent to Len, but that all depreciation would be allocated to Len. The agreement also provided that capital accounts would be maintained in accordance with the regulations and that liquidating distributions would be made in accordance with capital account balances. Kent has an unconditional obligation to restore a negative capital account balance. Len was not required to restore any deficit balance in his account, but the agreement contained a qualified income offset with respect to him.

The partnership used the cash to purchase a building for $200,000. The partnership was entitled to $50,000 of depreciation each year. In each year, before taking into consideration the depreciation, income equaled expenses.

  a. In the first year will the allocation of depreciation to Len be respected? Prepare a balance sheet to reflect the situation of the partners at the end of year one.

All depreciation is allocated to Len. All allocations are respected because the general and alternate tests have been met; the allocations have substantial economic effect. (Treas. Reg. § 1.704-1(b)(2)(ii)(b), (d)) Adjustments would be made as follows:

Building (tax and book)				Len	
Basis:	$200,000			Basis	Capital Account
Depreciation:	− 50,000			$50,000	$50,000
Adjusted basis:	$150,000	depreciation:		− 50,000	− 50,000
				$ 0	$ 0

Incorporating the above information, the partnership balance sheet would appear as follows:

Asset	Basis	FMV	Partner	Basis	Cap. Acct.
Building	$150,000	$150,000	Kent	$150,000	$150,000
	$150,000	$150,000	Len	0	0
				$150,000	$150,000

  b. At the beginning of the second year, the partnership distributed $50,000 to each of Kent and Len. At the end of the second year, the partnership had the $50,000 of depreciation and had also earned $25,000 of income. What is each partner's capital account at the end of the year?

After the distribution, the partners' capital accounts would be adjusted as follows:

	Kent	Len
	$150,000	$ 0
distribution:	− 50,000	− 50,000
	$100,000	<$50,000>

Because Len improperly has a negative capital account, he must be allocated income and gain to bring his capital account back to zero. Any allocation of depreciation to him would not have economic effect. (Treas. Reg. § 1.704-1(b)(2)(ii)(d) flush language) Thus, the depreciation is allocated to Kent and all income is allocated to Len. The capital accounts would be adjusted as follows:

	Kent	Len
	$100,000	<$50,000>
Income		+ 25,000
depreciation:	– 50,000	– 0
	$50,000	<$25,000>

Because Len's capital account is still negative, in the following year(s), income must be allocated to him until his capital account is brought back to zero.

7.   Mike contributed $50,000 in exchange for a general partnership interest and Ned contributed $50,000 in exchange for a limited partnership interest. The partnership agreement provided that Mike and Ned would share profits and losses equally, but that all depreciation would be allocated to Ned. The agreement also provided that capital accounts would be maintained in accordance with the regulations and that liquidating distributions would be made in accordance with capital account balances. Mike has an unconditional obligation to restore a negative capital account balance. Ned was not required to restore any deficit balance in his account, but the agreement contained a qualified income offset with respect to him.

The partnership used the cash to purchase a building for $100,000. The partnership was entitled to $50,000 of depreciation each year. In each year, before taking into consideration the depreciation, income equaled expenses.

   a. In the first year will the allocation of depreciation to Ned be respected? Prepare a balance sheet to reflect the situation of the partners at the end of year one.

All depreciation is allocated to Ned. All allocations are respected because the general and alternate tests have been met; the allocations have substantial economic effect. (Treas. Reg. § 1.704-1(b)(2)(ii)(b), (d)) Adjustments would be made as follows:

Building (tax and book)			Ned	
			Basis	Capital Account
Basis:	$100,000		$ 50,000	$ 50,000
Depreciation:	– 50,000	depreciation	– 50,000	– 50,000
Adjusted basis:	$ 50,000		$ 0	$ 0

Incorporating the above information, the partnership balance sheet would appear as follows:

Asset	Basis	FMV	Partner	Basis	Cap. Acct.
Building	$50,000	$50,000	Mike	$50,000	$50,000
	$50,000	$50,000	Ned	0	0
				$50,000	$50,000

   b. In the second year, Ned contributed his promissory note in the amount of $100,000 to the partnership. Will the allocation of depreciation to Ned be respected?

All depreciation is allocated to Ned. Adjustments would be made as follows:

	Building (tax and book)		Ned
Basis:	$50,000		Capital Account
Depreciation:	− 50,000		$ 0
Adjusted basis:	$ 0	depreciation:	− 50,000
			<$50,000>

Because Ned has contributed a promissory note to the partnership, he is treated as having an obligation to contribute an additional $100,000 and his capital account can go negative to this extent. (Treas. Reg. § 1.704-1(b)(2)(ii)(c)(1), -1(b)(2)(iv)(d)(2)) Thus, the allocation of $50,000 of depreciation to Ned satisfies the alternate economic effect test and will be respected.

8.   Opie contributed $50,000 in exchange for a general partnership interest and Paul contributed $50,000 in exchange for a limited partnership interest. The partnership agreement provided only that Opie and Paul would share profits and losses equally, but that all depreciation would be allocated to Paul.

The partnership used the cash to purchase a building for $100,000. The partnership was entitled to $25,000 of depreciation each year. In each year, before taking into consideration the depreciation, income equaled expenses.

a. In the first year will the allocation of depreciation to Paul be respected? Prepare a balance sheet to reflect the situation of the partners at the end of year one.

All depreciation is allocated to Paul. However, neither the general nor the alternate tests have been met. (Treas. Reg. § 1.704-1(b)(2)(ii)(b), (d)) If the allocation fails to meet either the general test or the alternate test, the allocation can still be respected if the allocation would have been the same if the criteria had been met. In other words, even though the partnership failed to include such provisions in its agreement, the partner who was allocated gain or income increased his investment in the partnership and a partner who was allocated a deduction or loss decreased his investment in the partnership. (Treas. Reg. § 1.704-1(b)(2)(ii)(i))

The allocation will be respected in the first year, as the allocation would have been respected if the partnership agreement contained the general and alternate tests. Adjustments would be made as follows:

	Building (tax and book)		Paul	
			Basis	Capital Account
Basis:	$100,000			
Depreciation:	− 25,000		$50,000	$50,000
Adjusted basis:	$ 75,000	depreciation:	− 25,000	− 25,000
			$25,000	$25,000

Incorporating the above information, the partnership balance sheet would appear as follows:

Asset	Basis	FMV	Partner	Basis	Cap. Acct.
Building	$75,000	$75,000	Opie	$50,000	$50,000
	$75,000	$75,000	Paul	25,000	25,000
				$75,000	$75,000

b. In the second year will the allocation of depreciation to Paul be respected? Prepare a balance sheet to reflect the situation of the partners at the end of the second year.

All depreciation is allocated to Paul. However, neither the general nor the alternate tests have been met. (Treas. Reg. §1.704-1(b)(2)(ii)(b), (d)) If the allocation fails to meet either the general test or the alternate test, the allocation can still be respected if the allocation would have been the same if the criteria had been met. In other words, even though the partnership failed to include such provisions in its agreement, the partner who was allocated gain or income increased his investment in the partnership and a partner who was allocated a deduction or loss decreased his investment in the partnership. (Treas. Reg. §1.704-1(b)(2)(ii)(i))

The allocation will be respected in the second year, as the allocation would have been respected if the partnership agreement contained the general and alternate tests. Adjustments would be made as follows:

Building (tax and book)			Paul	
			Basis	Capital Account
Basis:	$75,000			
Depreciation:	− 25,000		$25,000	$25,000
Adjusted basis:	$50,000	depreciation:	− 25,000	− 25,000
			$ 0	$ 0

Incorporating the above information, the partnership balance sheet would appear as follows:

Asset	Basis	FMV	Partner	Basis	Cap. Acct.
Building	$50,000	$50,000	Opie	$50,000	$50,000
	$50,000	$50,000	Paul	0	0
				$50,000	$50,000

c. In the third year will the allocation of depreciation to Paul be respected? Prepare a balance sheet to reflect the situation of the partners at the end of the third year.

All depreciation is allocated to Paul. However, neither the general nor the alternate tests have been met. (Treas. Reg. §1.704-1(b)(2)(ii)(b), (d)) If the allocation fails to meet either the general test or the alternate test, the allocation can still be respected if the allocation would have been the same if the criteria had been met. In other words, even though the partnership failed to include such provisions in its agreement, the partner who was allocated gain or income increased his investment in the partnership and a partner who was allocated a deduction or loss decreased his investment in the partnership. (Treas. Reg. §1.704-1(b)(2)(ii)(i))

The allocation would cause Paul's capital account to go negative and he has no obligation to restore the negative balance. Accordingly, the allocation will not be respected and depreciation will be allocated based on the partner's interest in the partnership. (Treas. Reg. §1.704-1(b)(3)(i), (ii)) The depreciation will be re-allocated to Opie. Adjustments would be made as follows:

Building (tax and book)				Opie	
				Basis	Capital Account
Basis:	$50,000			$50,000	$50,000
Depreciation:	– 25,000		depreciation:	– 25,000	– 25,000
Adjusted basis:	$25,000			$ 25,000	$ 25,000

Incorporating the above information, the partnership balance sheet would appear as follows:

Asset	Basis	FMV	Partner	Basis	Cap. Acct.
Building	$25,000	$25,000	Opie	$25,000	$25,000
	$25,000	$25,000	Paul	0	0
				$25,000	$25,000

9. Quinn and Roy are equal partners. Quinn does not pay any United States tax. The partnership expects to earn $50,000 in profits and $50,000 of interest from tax-exempt bonds. The partners agree that all profits will be allocated to Quinn and all income from the tax-exempt bonds will be allocated to Roy.

The partnership agreement provided that capital accounts would be maintained in accordance with the regulations, that liquidating distributions would be made in accordance with capital account balances, and that all partners have an obligation to restore a negative capital account balance.

Will the allocation be respected?

Because the economic portion of the test has been met, the focus is on the substantiality portion of the test. (Treas. Reg. § 1.704-1(b)(2)(ii)(b)) Under the general rule for substantiality:

- The after-tax economic effect of at least one partner may, in present value terms, be enhanced compared to such consequences if the allocation were not contained in the partnership agreement; and
- There is a strong likelihood that the after-tax economic consequences of no partner will, in present value terms, be substantially diminished compared to such consequences if the allocation were not contained in the partnership agreement.

(Treas. Reg. § 1.704-1(b)(2)(iii)(a)) Under the shifting tax consequences test, allocations during just one year are considered. (Treas. Reg. § 1.704-1(b)(2)(iii)(b))

It may be helpful to note that, if the partners receive the same dollar amounts from the partnership during the year, but with the special allocation one of the partners pays less in individual tax while no other partner pays more individual tax, the allocation will not pass the substantiality test. It also may be helpful to begin the analysis by considering the allocation based on the partners' interest in the partnership and compare the tax consequences to the allocation as agreed to by the partners.

The allocation based on the partners' interest in the partnership *without* the special allocation would be as follows:

	Quinn	Roy
Profits:	$25,000	$25,000
Interest:	25,000	25,000
Total:	$50,000	$50,000
Total taxable:	$ 0	$25,000

The allocation based on the partners' interest in the partnership *with* the special allocation would be as follows:

	Quinn	Roy
Profits:	$50,000	$ 0
Interest:	0	50,000
Total:	$50,000	$50,000
Total taxable:	$0	$0

Roy's after-tax economic effect is enhanced because the dollar amount he receives has stayed the same ($50,000), but his taxable income has decreased from $25,000 to zero. Moreover, the dollar amount Quinn receives has stayed the same ($50,000) and his after-tax economic consequences have stayed the same. Thus, the allocation fails the substantiality test and the items must be reallocated in accordance with the partners' interest in the partnership. (Treas. Reg. § 1.704-1(b)(2)(iii)(*a*))

10. Sam and Tess are equal partners. Sam is an unemployed student, but expects to graduate and obtain a job in three years and expects the money he earns from that job to be taxed at the 25 percent rate. Tess is employed as a doctor and has a substantial amount of income taxed at the 35 percent rate. She expects to retire in three years. The partners agree to allocate all profits to Sam and all deductions to Tess for three years. During the following three years, the partners will allocate all profits to Tess and all deductions to Sam. Beginning in year seven, they will allocate all items equally. The partnership expects to earn $100,000 of income and incur $100,000 of deductions over the next six years.

The partnership agreement provided that capital accounts would be maintained in accordance with the regulations, that liquidating distributions would be made in accordance with capital account balances, and that all partners have an obligation to restore a negative capital account balance.

Will the allocation be respected?

Because the economic portion of the test has been met, the focus is on the substantiality portion of the test. (Treas. Reg. § 1.704-1(b)(2)(ii)(*b*)) Under the general rule for substantiality:

- The after-tax economic effect of at least one partner may, in present value terms, be enhanced compared to such consequences if the allocation were not contained in the partnership agreement; and

- There is a strong likelihood that the after-tax economic consequences of no partner will, in present value terms, be substantially diminished compared to such consequences if the allocation were not contained in the partnership agreement.

(Treas. Reg. § 1.704-1(b)(2)(iii)(*a*)) Under the transitory allocation test, allocations over more than one year are considered. At the time the allocation is agreed upon:

- there must be a strong likelihood that the net change in the respective partners' capital accounts over a span of years with the special allocation will not differ substantially from the net change that would occur with the special allocation; and

- the total tax liability of the partners (determined by including their individual tax attributes) over the same span of years will be less with the special allocation than without the special allocation.

(Treas. Reg. § 1.704-1(b)(2)(iii)(*c*))

It may be helpful to note that, if the partners receive the same dollar amounts from the partnership over a period of time, but with the special allocation one of the partners pays less in individual tax during that same period while no other partner pays more individual tax, the allocation will not pass the substantiality test.

Over the next six years, the allocation of profits and depreciation will be as follows:

Year	Sam	Tess
1	$100,000	<$100,000>
2	100,000	<100,000>
3	100,000	<100,000>
4	<100,000>	100,000
5	<100,000>	100,000
6	<100,000>	100,000
Net change	$ 0	$ 0

Due to the benefit of the deductions in the first three years, Tess can offset her income from other sources and, arguably, be taxed at a lower rate. In the later years, when she will not have income from other sources, she will receive income from the partnership and most likely be taxed at a lower rate. When considering her individual tax attributes, her tax liability over the six years should be lower with the special allocation than without it. However, there is no economic change to her capital account when the 6 years are viewed together.

In the first three years, when he does not have income from other sources, he will receive income from the partnership and likely pay tax at a low rate. Due to the benefit of the deductions in the last three years, Sam can offset his income from other sources and, arguably, be taxed at a lower rate. When considering his individual income tax attributes, his tax liability over the six years should be lower with the special allocation than without it. However there is no economic change to his capital account when the 6 years are viewed together.

The fact that neither partner's capital account will be different and both their individual tax liabilities likely will be lower with the allocation suggests that the allocation is a transitory allocation. Thus, the allocation fails the substantiality test and the items must be reallocated in accordance with the partners' interest in the partnership. (Treas. Reg. § 1.704-1(b)(2)(iii)(*a*))

11. Vince and Wes each contributed $50,000 in exchange for a general partnership interest. The partnership agreement provided that Vince and Wes would share profits and losses equally. The agreement also provided that capital accounts would be maintained in accordance with the regulations, that a partner must restore a negative

capital account balance, and that liquidating distributions would be made in accordance with capital account balances.

The partnership purchased equipment for $50,000 and was entitled to claim $10,000 of depreciation each year. The partners agreed to allocate 60 percent of the depreciation to Vince and 40 percent to Wes. When the equipment was sold, the gain would be allocated in such a way so as to equalize the partners' capital accounts. Any remaining gain would be allocated equally between Vince and Wes.

a. In the first year, before taking into consideration the depreciation, income equaled expenses. How is the depreciation allocated? Prepare a balance to reflect the situation of the partners at the end of the first year.

All allocations are respected because the general test has been met; the allocations have substantial economic effect. (Treas. Reg. § 1.704-1(b)(2)(ii)(b)) The basis of the equipment is reduced for depreciation.

Building

Basis:	$50,000
Depreciation:	− 10,000
Adjusted basis:	$40,000

In the first year, the depreciation was allocated $6,000 to Vince and $4,000 to Wes. Their basis and capital accounts are adjusted as follows:

	Vince		Wes	
	Basis	**Capital Account**	**Basis**	**Capital Account**
Cash:	$50,000	$50,000	$50,000	$50,000
Depreciation:	− 6,000	− 6,000	− 4,000	− 4,000
Total:	$44,000	$44,000	$46,000	$46,000

Incorporating the above information, the partnership balance sheet would appear as follows:

Asset	Basis	FMV	Partner	Basis	Cap. Acct.
Cash	$50,000	$50,000	Vince	$44,000	$44,000
Equipment	40,000	40,000	Wes	46,000	46,000
	$90,000	$90,000		$90,000	$90,000

b. The partnership sold the equipment at the beginning of the second year for $60,000. (For the sake of simplicity, ignore any allowable depreciation for the second year.) What is the character of gain Vince and Wes must report?

Upon sale of the equipment, tax and book gain must be determined.

Building

	Tax	Book
AR:	$60,000	$60,000
AB:	40,000	40,000
	$20,000	$20,000

Of the tax gain, $10,000 is characterized as ordinary recapture gain and $10,000 is characterized as hotchpot (Section 1231) gain.

Based on the partnership agreement, the first $2,000 of gain is allocated to Vince to equalize their capital accounts. The remaining $18,000 of gain ($20,000, less $2,000) is allocated equally between them, or $9,000 each. Thus, a total of $11,000 of gain will be allocated to Vince ($2,000, plus $9,000) and $9,000 will be allocated to Wes. Each partner's share of the gain that is characterized as depreciation recapture gain is the lesser of:

- The partner's share of the total gain from the disposition of the property; or

- The total amount of depreciation previously allocated to the partner with respect to the property.

For Vince, his total share of gain from disposition of the equipment is $11,000. The total amount of depreciation previously allocated to him was $6,000. The lesser of the two amounts is $6,000. For Wes, his total share of gain from the disposition of the equipment is $9,000. The total amount of depreciation previously allocated to him was $4,000. The lesser of the two amounts is $4,000. Accordingly, the character of the gain allocated to Vince and Wes would be as follows:

Partner	Recapture	Hotchpot	Total Gain
Vince	$6,000	$5,000	$11,000
Wes	4,000	5,000	9,000
Total:	$10,000	$10,000	$20,000

12. Xander contributed $10,000 in exchange for a general partnership interest and Yolanda contributed $90,000 in exchange for a limited partnership interest. The partnership obtained a $200,000 non-recourse loan and purchased a building for $300,000. The loan was secured by the building and no payments were due on the loan for five years.

The partnership agreement provided that capital accounts would be maintained according to the regulations, liquidating distributions would be make according to capital account balances and that Xander would be required to restore any deficit balance in his capital account. Yolanda was not required to restore any deficit balance in her account, but the agreement contained a qualified income offset with respect to her. The partnership agreement also contained a minimum gain chargeback. Finally, the partnership agreement provided that, except as otherwise required by its qualified income offset and minimum gain chargeback provisions, all partnership items would be allocated 90 percent to Yolanda and 10 percent to Xander, except non-recourse deductions which would be allocated 80 percent to Yolanda and 20 percent to Xander, until the first time when the partnership had recognized items of income and gain that exceeded the items of loss and deduction it had recognized over its life. Then, all partnership items would be allocated equally between Xander and Yolanda.

At the end of each partnership taxable year, no items are reasonably expected to cause or increase a deficit balance in Yolanda's capital account.

a. In the first year, the partnership generates income equal to its expenses and is entitled to $50,000 of depreciation. What are the partners' capital accounts at the end of the year?

All allocations are respected because the general and alternate tests have been met; the allocations have substantial economic effect. (Treas. Reg. § 1.704-1(b)(2)(ii)(*b*), (*d*)) The basis for the building is reduced for depreciation.

Building

Basis:	$300,000
Depreciation:	− 50,000
Adjusted basis:	$250,000

There is no partnership minimum gain.

Debt:	$200,000
Basis:	− 250,000
	No PMG

(Treas. Reg. § 1.704-2(d)(1))

Thus, the depreciation is allocated $5,000 to Xander and $45,000 to Yolanda and their capital accounts at the end of the year are:

	Xander	Yolanda
	$10,000	$90,000
Depreciation:	− 5,000	− 45,000
	$ 5,000	$45,000

b. **In the second year, the partnership generates income equal to its expenses and is entitled to $50,000 of depreciation. What are the partners' capital accounts at the end of the second year?**

All allocations are respected because the general and alternate tests have been met; the allocations have substantial economic effect. (Treas. Reg. § 1.704-1(b)(2)(ii)(*b*), (*d*)) The basis for the building is reduced for depreciation.

Building

Basis:	$250,000
Depreciation:	− 50,000
Adjusted basis:	$200,000

There is no partnership minimum gain.

Debt:	$200,000
Basis:	− 200,000
	No PMG

(Treas. Reg. § 1.704-2(d)(1))

Thus, the depreciation is allocated $5,000 to Xander and $45,000 to Yolanda and their capital accounts at the end of the second year are:

	Xander	Yolanda
	$5,000	$45,000
Depreciation:	− 5,000	− 45,000
	$ 0	$ 0

c. **In the third year, the partnership generates income equal to its expenses and is entitled to $50,000 of depreciation. What are the partners' capital accounts at the end of the third year?**

All allocations are respected because the general and alternate tests have been met; the allocations have substantial economic effect. (Treas. Reg. § 1.704-1(b)(2)(ii)(*b*), (*d*)) In addition, the safe harbor for allocations of non-recourse deductions has been met. (Treas. Reg. § 1.704-2(e)) The basis for the building is reduced for depreciation.

Building

Basis:	$200,000
Depreciation:	– 50,000
Adjusted basis:	$150,000

There is a $50,000 increase in partnership minimum gain in the third year. (Treas. Reg. § 1.704-2(d)(1)) Thus, there is a $50,000 of non-recourse deduction. (Treas. Reg. § 1.704-2(c))

Debt:	$200,000
Basis:	– 150,000
	$ 50,000

Allocation of non-recourse deductions, 80 percent to Yolanda and 20 percent to Xander, is consistent with the allocation of other significant items related to the building. The other items are allocated in a manner that has substantial economic effect. The partnership agreement contains a minimum gain chargeback. Other material allocations and capital account adjustments under the partnership agreement comply with the basic Section 704(b) regulations. (Treas. Reg. § 1.704-2(e)) The partners' capital accounts would appear as follows:

	Xander	Yolanda
	$ 0	$ 0
Depreciation:	– 10,000	– 40,000
	<$10,000>	<$40,000>

Note that Yolanda is treated as having an obligation to restore a deficit capital account balance of $40,000 (the amount of her partnership minimum gain). Thus, even though she is a limited partner and does not have an obligation to restore a negative capital account, to the extent of her share of partnership minimum gain, her negative capital account balance does not trigger the qualified income offset. (Treas. Reg. § 1.704-2(g)(1) flush language) In sum, Xander's share of partnership minimum gain is $10,000 and Yolanda's is $40,000. (Treas. Reg. § 1.704-2(g)(1))

d. **In the fourth year, the partnership generates income equal to its expenses. It also forfeited the building to the lender. (For the sake of simplicity, ignore any allowable depreciation for the fourth year.) What are the partners' capital accounts at the end of the fourth year?**

Upon the forfeit of the building, tax and book gain must be determined. The least amount the partnership can dispose of the building for is the amount of the debt.

Building

	Tax	Book
AR:	$200,000	$200,000
AB:	150,000	150,000
	$50,000	$50,000

There has been a $50,000 decrease in partnership minimum gain ($50,000 at the end of year three, zero in year four). (Treas. Reg. § 1.704-2(d)(1)) The decrease in partnership minimum gain triggers a partnership minimum gain chargeback and each partner must be allocated items of partnership income and gain equal to the partner's share of the net decrease in partnership minimum gain. (Treas. Reg. § 1.704-2(f)(1)) Xander's share of partnership minimum gain decrease is $10,000 and Yolanda's is $40,000. (Treas. Reg. § 1.704-2(g)(2)) Thus, the gain is allocated $10,000 to Xander and $40,000 to Yolanda. Their capital accounts would be adjusted as follows:

	Xander	Yolanda
	<$10,000>	<$40,000>
Gain:	+ 10,000	+ 40,000
	$ 0	$ 0

13. Zelda contributed $40,000 in exchange for a general partnership interest and Ann contributed $60,000 in exchange for a limited partnership interest. The partnership obtained a $200,000 non-recourse loan and purchased a building for $300,000. The loan was secured by the building and no payments were due on the loan for five years.

The partnership agreement provided that capital accounts would be maintained according to the regulations, liquidating distributions would be made according to capital account balances and that Zelda would be required to restore any deficit balance in her capital account. Ann was not required to restore any deficit balance in her account, but the agreement contained a qualified income offset with respect to her. The partnership agreement also contained a minimum gain chargeback. Finally, the partnership agreement provided that, except as otherwise required by its qualified income offset and minimum gain chargeback provisions, all partnership items would be allocated 60 percent to Ann and 40 percent to Zelda, except non-recourse deductions which would be allocated 50 percent to Ann and 50 percent to Zelda, until the first time when the partnership had recognized items of income and gain that exceeded the items of loss and deduction it had recognized over its life. Then, all partnership items would be allocated equally between Zelda and Ann.

At the end of each partnership taxable year, no items are reasonably expected to cause or increase a deficit balance in Ann's capital account.

a. In the first year, the partnership generates income equal to its expenses and is entitled to $50,000 of depreciation. What are the partners' capital accounts at the end of the year?

All allocations are respected because the general and alternate tests have been met; the allocations have substantial economic effect. (Treas. Reg. § 1.704-1(b)(2)(ii)(b), (d)) The basis for the building is reduced for depreciation.

Building

Basis:	$300,000
Depreciation:	– 50,000
Adjusted basis:	$250,000

There is no partnership minimum gain.

Debt:	$200,000
Basis:	– 250,000
	No PMG

(Treas. Reg. § 1.704-2(d)(1))

Thus, the depreciation is allocated $20,000 to Zelda and $30,000 to Ann and their capital accounts at the end of the year are:

	Zelda	**Ann**
	$40,000	$60,000
Depreciation:	– 20,000	– 30,000
	$20,000	$30,000

b. In the second year, the partnership generates income equal to its expenses and is entitled to $50,000 of depreciation. What are the partners' capital accounts at the end of the second year?

All allocations are respected because the general and alternate tests have been met; the allocations have substantial economic effect. (Treas. Reg. § 1.704-1(b)(2)(ii)(*b*), (*d*)) The basis for the building is reduced for depreciation.

Building

Basis:	$250,000
Depreciation:	– 50,000
Adjusted basis:	$200,000

There is no partnership minimum gain.

Debt:	$200,000
Basis:	– 200,000
	No PMG

(Treas. Reg. § 1.704-2(d)(1))

Thus, the depreciation is allocated $20,000 to Zelda and $30,000 to Ann and their capital accounts at the end of the year are:

	Zelda	**Ann**
	$20,000	$30,000
Depreciation:	– 20,000	– 30,000
	$ 0	$ 0

c. In the third year, the partnership generates income equal to its expenses and is entitled to $50,000 of depreciation. What are the partners' capital accounts at the end of the third year?

All allocations are respected because the general and alternate tests have been met; the allocations have substantial economic effect. (Treas. Reg. § 1.704-1(b)(2)(ii)(*b*), (*d*)) In addition, the safe harbor for allocations of non-recourse deductions has been met. (Treas. Reg. § 1.704-2(e)) The basis for the building is reduced for depreciation.

Building

Basis:	$200,000
Depreciation:	– 50,000
Adjusted basis:	$150,000

There is a $50,000 increase in partnership minimum gain in the third year. (Treas. Reg. § 1.704-2(d)(1)) Thus, there is a $50,000 non-recourse deduction. (Treas. Reg. § 1.704-2(c))

Debt:	$200,000
Basis:	– 150,000
	$50,000

Allocation of non-recourse deductions, 50 percent to Ann and 50 percent to Zelda, is consistent with the allocation of other significant items related to the building. The other items are allocated in a manner that has substantial economic effect. The partnership agreement contains a minimum gain chargeback. And, other material allocations and capital account adjustments under the partnership agreement comply with the basic Section 704(b) regulations. (Treas. Reg. § 1.704-2(e)) Thus, the depreciation is allocated $12,500 to Zelda and $12,500 to Ann and their capital accounts at the end of the year are:

	Zelda	Ann
	$ 0	$ 0
Depreciation:	– 12,500	– 12,500
	<$12,500>	<$12,500>

Note that Ann is treated as having an obligation to restore a deficit capital account balance of $12,500 (the amount of her partnership minimum gain). Thus, even though she is a limited partner and does not have an obligation to restore a negative capital account, to the extent of her share of partnership minimum gain, her negative capital account balance does not trigger the qualified income offset. (Treas. Reg. § 1.704-2(g)(1) flush language) In sum, Zelda's share of partnership minimum gain is $12,500 and Ann's is $12,500. (Treas. Reg. § 1.704-2(g)(1))

d. In the fourth year, the partnership converts the non-recourse debt to a recourse debt. Is a minimum gain chargeback triggered?

There is a $50,000 decrease in partnership minimum gain in the fourth year ($50,000 in year three, zero in year four). (Treas. Reg. § 1.704-2(d)(1)) Usually, a decrease in partnership minimum gain would trigger a partnership minimum gain chargeback and each partner must be allocated items of partnership income and gain equal to the partner's share of the net decrease in partnership minimum gain. (Treas. Reg. § 1.704-2(f)(1)) However, there is no gain chargeback required when the reduction is due to a conversion to recourse debt and the partners bear the economic risk of loss. (Treas. Reg. § 1.704-2(f)(2))

Chapter V

Allocations Deemed to Have Economic Effect

A. Allocation of Depreciation

When partners are forming a partnership, they evaluate their respective economic positions based on the fair market value (less any liabilities the property is taken subject to) of the property contributed to the partnership.

The tax treatment of the item may differ from the treatment for economic purposes. More specifically, for tax purposes, depreciation is determined based on the adjusted basis of the property. If the property had been purchased by the partnership, the cost of the property is recovered through depreciation or amortization and there will be no disparity between the depreciation determined for tax purposes and the depreciation determined for economic, or book, purposes. However, if the property had been contributed to the partnership by a partner, the partnership assumes the basis of the property and the partner's recovery method. Accordingly, there likely will be a disparity between the depreciation determined for tax purposes and the depreciation determined for economic, or book, purposes.

Example: Ann and Bob formed an equal general partnership. Ann contributed $200,000 and Bob contributed equipment with a fair market value of $200,000 and adjusted basis of $100,000. There are four years remaining on the life of the equipment. Assume for purposes of simplicity that the remaining basis is recovered using the straightline method (with no conventions).

From an economic perspective, the value of the property, $200,000, is recovered over the next four years, or $50,000 each year. As a 50-percent partner, Ann will expect to receive an allocation of one-half of the depreciation, or $25,000 each year.

At the time of contribution, Bob's adjusted basis in the equipment was $100,000. For tax purposes, the adjusted basis is recovered over the next four years, or $25,000 each year. As a 50-percent partner, Ann would be entitled to $12,500.

There is a disparity between how much depreciation Ann expects from an economic perspective, $25,000, and how much she would be allocated for tax purposes, $12,500.

---

1. General Rule

To address the disparity that will exist when tax and economic, or book, depreciation are not the same, the regulations provide that the noncontributing partner is allocated the same amount of depreciation for tax purposes as he is allocated for economic, or book, purposes. Any remaining amount of depreciation is allocated to the contributing partner.[1] When computing the amount of depreciation, the same method and recovery period must be used for computing tax and economic, or book, depreciation.

Example: Ann and Bob formed an equal general partnership. Ann contributed $200,000 and Bob contributed equipment with a fair market value of $200,000 and adjusted basis of $100,000. There are four years remaining on the life of the equipment. Assume for purposes of simplicity that the remaining basis is recovered using the straightline method (with no conventions).

From an economic perspective, the value of the property, $200,000, is recovered over the next four years, or $50,000 each year. As a 50-percent partner, Ann will expect to receive an allocation of one-half of the depreciation, or $25,000 each year.

At the time of contribution, Bob's adjusted basis in the equipment was $100,000. For tax purposes, the adjusted basis is recovered over the next four years, or $25,000 each year.

As the non-contributing partner, Ann is allocated the same amount of depreciation for tax purposes as she is allocated for economic, or book, purposes, or $25,000. There is no remaining amount of depreciation to be allocated to the contributing partner, Bob.

Note that this result makes sense. As a partner with an indirect one-half ownership interest in the equipment, Ann was entitled to depreciation with respect to one-half of the equipment. Bob, as the contributing partner, was able to claim depreciation prior to contribution. To the extent he previously claimed depreciation with respect to the equipment, he has claimed depreciation with respect to his indirect one-half ownership interest.

Assume that Bob had previously purchased the equipment for $200,000 and that he was entitled to claim $25,000 of depreciation each year (ignoring any conventions). If he contributed the property in the fifth year, the total amount of depreciation claimed by Ann and Bob would be as follows:

Year	Bob	Ann	Basis in property
1	$ 25,000	—	$175,000
2	25,000	—	150,000
3	25,000	—	125,000
4	25,000	—	100,000
	- equipment contributed to partnership -		
5	—	$ 25,000	75,000
6	—	$ 25,000	50,000
7	—	$ 25,000	25,000
8	—	$ 25,000	0
Total:	$100,000	$100,000	

When the equipment is fully depreciated, both Ann and Bob will have claimed one-half of the total cost of the property, $200,000, as depreciation, or $100,000 each.

---

1. Section 704(c)(1)(A); Treas. Reg. § 1.704-3(b)(1).

Exception for small disparity. If the amount of built-in gain or loss is small, the allocation required by Section 704(c) can be disregarded. The disparity is small if the total fair market value of all property contributed by a partner during the taxable year does not differ from the total adjusted basis of the property by more than 15 percent of the adjusted basis and the total gross disparity does not exceed $20,000.[2]

Example: Carl purchased land for $90,000. When the land had increased in value to $100,000, he contributed it to a partnership in exchange for a 50-percent general partnership interest. Deb contributed $100,000.

Fifteen percent of the adjusted basis of the land is $13,500 (15% x 90,000). The fair market value of the land, $100,000, does not differ from the basis of the property, $90,000, by more than $13,500. And, the total disparity does not exceed $20,000. Accordingly, the disparity between basis and fair market value is a small disparity and may be disregarded.

---

2. Ceiling Rule

In certain circumstances, the amount of tax depreciation will be less than the amount of economic, or book, depreciation. When this result occurs, the regulations provide that the maximum amount of depreciation that can be allocated to the noncontributing partner is the amount of tax depreciation. The rule is referred to as the ceiling rule. Under the traditional method, no adjustments are made to address the disparity between the amount of tax depreciation that is available to be allocated to the noncontributing partners and the amount of economic, or book, depreciation.

Example: Ann and Bob formed an equal general partnership. Ann contributed $200,000 and Bob contributed equipment with a fair market value of $200,000 and adjusted basis of $75,000. There are three years remaining on the life of the equipment. Assume for purposes of simplicity that the remaining basis is recovered using the straightline method (with no conventions).

From an economic perspective, the value of the property, $200,000, is recovered over the next three years, or $66,667 each year. As a 50-percent partner, Ann will expect to receive an allocation of one-half of the depreciation, or $33,333 each year.

At the time of contribution, Bob's adjusted basis in the equipment was $75,000. For tax purposes, the adjusted basis is recovered over the next three years, or $25,000 each year.

As the non-contributing partner, Ann should be allocated the same amount of depreciation for tax purposes as she is allocated for economic, or book, purposes, or $33,333. However, there is only $25,000 of tax depreciation available to be allocated to Ann.

Note that this result creates a disparity. As a partner with an indirect one-half ownership interest in the equipment, Ann should be entitled to depreciation with respect to one-half of the equipment. Bob, as the contributing partner, was able to claim depreciation prior to contribution. To the extent he previously claimed depreciation with respect to the equipment, he has claimed more than his one-half of the depreciation.

---

2. Treas. Reg. § 1.704-3(e)(1).

Assume that Bob had previously purchased the equipment for $200,000 and that he was entitled to claim $25,000 of depreciation each year (ignoring any conventions). If he contributed the property in the sixth year, the total amount of depreciation claimed by Ann and Bob would be as follows:

Year	Bob	Ann	Basis in property
1	$ 25,000	—	$175,000
2	25,000	—	150,000
3	25,000	—	125,000
4	25,000	—	100,000
5	25,000	—	75,000
- equipment contributed to partnership -			
6	—	$25,000	50,000
7	—	25,000	25,000
8	—	25,000	0
Total:	$125,000	$75,000	

When the ceiling rule applies there is an insufficient amount of tax depreciation available to be allocated to the non-contributing partner. Under the traditional method, this disparity is not corrected.[3] However, the shortfall can be corrected through one of two methods, the traditional method with curative allocations or the remedial method.

a. Traditional Method with Curative Allocations

Under the traditional method with curative allocations, the partnership can allocate depreciation in the amount of the shortfall to the noncontributing partner from a different asset. Alternatively, the partnership can reduce the amount of ordinary income allocated to the noncontributing partner in an amount equal to the amount of the shortfall.[4] The curative allocation only impacts the partner's outside basis. It does not impact the partner's capital account.

b. Remedial Allocations

Under the remedial method, the partnership creates the necessary amount of depreciation to make up the shortfall caused by the ceiling rule. In addition, it creates an offsetting amount of ordinary income that is allocated to the contributing partner. The remedial allocation only impacts the partner's outside basis.[5]

If the remedial method is used, the economic, or book, depreciation is calculated in a different manner. The economic, or book, basis is divided into two portions, the first portion is equal to the tax basis and the second portion is equal to the remainder. With respect to the first portion, the amount equal to tax basis, depreciation is computed in the same manner as it is computed for tax purposes. With respect to the second portion, the remainder amount, depreciation is computed using the applicable recovery

3. Treas. Reg. § 1.704-3(b)(1).
4. Treas. Reg. § 1.704-3(c).
5. Treas. Reg. § 1.704-3(d).

period and method that would be used if the partnership had just acquired the property.[6] Remedial allocations impact the partner's outside basis. They do not impact the partner's capital account.

B. Allocations Related to Sale of Contributed Property

1. General Rule

Pre-contribution gain or loss. Prior to contribution of property to a partnership, the partner is the owner of the property. Thus, any gain or loss that arises in the property prior to contribution belongs to the partner individually and must be allocated to, and reported by, the contributing partner. It cannot be shifted to the other partners.[7]

Example: Ellen purchased land for $10,000. When the land had increased in value to $50,000, she contributed it to a partnership in exchange for a 50-percent general partnership interest. Frank contributed $50,000 in exchange for a 50-percent general partnership interest. The partnership agreement provided that allocations would be made based on ownership interests.

Eight years later, the partnership sold the land for $50,000, realizing a tax gain of $40,000 (amount realized of $50,000, less adjusted basis of $10,000). It did not recognize any book gain (amount realized of $50,000, less book basis of $50,000).

All of the $40,000 of tax gain represents Ellen's pre-contribution gain. Thus, even though the partnership agreement provides that allocations are made based on ownership interests, the $40,000 of gain must be allocated solely to Ellen.

The tax allocation associated with the built-in gain or loss does not have a correlative economic allocation or adjustment to the partner's capital account. There has been no change at the partnership level.

The amount of built-in gain or loss is the difference between the fair market value, or book value, and the adjusted tax basis of the property.[8]

Example: Greg purchased equipment for $10,000. When the equipment had an adjusted basis of $7,000 and fair market value of $8,000, he contributed it to a partnership in exchange for a 50-percent general partnership interest. Hal contributed $8,000 in exchange for a 50-percent general partnership interest. The partnership agreement provided that allocations would be made based on ownership interests.

Eight years later, when the equipment had an adjusted basis of $5,000 and book value of $6,000, the partnership sold the equipment for $6,000. The partnership realized a tax gain of $1,000 (amount realized of $6,000, less adjusted basis of $5,000). It did not recognize any book gain (amount realized of $6,000, less book basis of $6,000).

---

6. Treas. Reg. § 1.704-3(d)(2).
7. Section 704(c)(1)(A); Treas. Reg. § 1.704-3(a)(1).
8. Treas. Reg. § 1.704-3(a)(3)(ii).

> The amount of built-in gain is the different between the fair market value, $6,000, and the adjusted basis, $5,000. Accordingly, all of the $1,000 of tax gain represents Greg's pre-contribution gain. Thus, even though the partnership agreement provides that allocations are made based on ownership interests, the $1,000 of gain must be allocated solely to Greg.

The allocation of pre-contribution gain or loss cannot be addressed through a special allocation. Because the tax gain or loss associated with the built-in gain or loss does not have a correlative capital account adjustment, a special allocation of the tax gain or loss would not have substantial economic effect.

The property has a built-in gain when, at the time the property is contributed to the partnership, the fair market value (book value) is greater than the adjusted basis. The property has a built-in loss when, at the time the property is contributed to the partnership, the adjusted basis is greater than the fair market value (book value).[9]

Post-contribution gain or loss. After contribution of the property, the partnership is the owner of the property. Any gain or loss that arises after contribution must be allocated among and reported by the partners. The amount of post-contribution gain or loss is measured by the difference between the selling price and the property's fair market, or book, value. Unlike pre-contribution gain or loss, post-contribution gain or loss is reflected in the partners' capital accounts.

> **Example:** Ira purchased land for $10,000. When the land had increased in value to $50,000, he contributed it to a partnership in exchange for a 50-percent general partnership interest. Jeb contributed $50,000 in exchange for a 50-percent general partnership interest. The partnership agreement provided that allocations would be made based on ownership interests.
>
> Eight years later, the partnership sold the land for $60,000, realizing a tax gain of $50,000 (amount realized of $60,000, less adjusted basis of $10,000). It recognized $10,000 of book gain (amount realized of $60,000, less book basis of $50,000).
>
> The $40,000 of tax gain represents Ira's pre-contribution gain. Thus, even though the partnership agreement provides that allocations are made based on ownership interests, $40,000 of gain must be allocated solely to Ira. The remaining $10,000 of gain is post-contribution gain that is allocated equally between Ira and Jeb. Similarly, the $10,000 of book gain is allocated equally between Ira and Jeb.
>
> | Ira | | Jeb | |
> |---|---|---|---|
> | Tax | Book | Tax | Book |
> | $45,000 | $5,000 | $5,000 | $5,000 |

Exception for small disparity. If the amount of built-in gain or loss is small, the allocation required by Section 704(c) can be disregarded. The disparity is small if the total fair market value of all property contributed by a partner during the taxable year

---

9. Treas. Reg. § 1.704-3(a)(3)(ii).

does not differ from the total adjusted basis of the property by more than 15 percent of the adjusted basis and the total gross disparity does not exceed $20,000.[10]

Example: Kent purchased land for $90,000. When the land had increased in value to $100,000, he contributed it to a partnership in exchange for a 50-percent general partnership interest. Len contributed $100,000.

Fifteen percent of the adjusted basis of the land is $13,500 (15% × 90,000). The fair market value of the land, $100,000, does not differ from the basis of the property, $90,000, by more than $13,500. And, the total disparity does not exceed $20,000. Accordingly, the disparity between basis and fair market value is a small disparity and may be disregarded.

Anti-abuse rule for property with built-in loss. If a partner contributes property with a built-in loss, special rules apply.[11] First, the built-in loss is taken into consideration only when considering allocations to the contributing partner. Second, except when provided for in the regulations, when considering allocations to the noncontributing partners, the property is treated as if its basis was its fair market value at the time of contribution.

Reverse Section 704(c). While a Section 704(c) issue may arise when a partner contributes property to a partnership, it is not the only time a partnership may have to address built-in gain or loss in partnership assets. When a new partner joins an existing partnership, there may be gain or loss in the assets at the time he joins. This pre-existing gain or loss should be allocated to the old (existing) partners, and not the new partner. Then, any gain or loss that occurs after the new partner joins should be allocated among all the partners.

To address this issue, the partners can use one of two methods. First, it can provide for a special allocation of the gain or loss at the time the new partner joins the old (existing) partners.[12]

Example: Mike and Ned were equal partners in the partnership. The partnership had previously purchased land for $100,000. Its current fair market value was $200,000. Opie joined the partnership by contributing $100,000 in exchange for a one-third interest.

At the time Opie joined the partnership, the land had $100,000 of built-in gain that occurred while only Mike and Ned were partners. When then land is sold, tax gain will equal book, or economic, gain. Of this gain the built-in gain at the time Opie joined the partnership should be specially allocated to Mike and Ned. Any gain attributable to the time after Opie joined the partnership should be allocated among the three partners.

For example, if the land was later sold for $290,000, the tax (and book) gain would be $190,000. Of this gain, $100,000 should be specially allocated equally between Mike and Ned. The remaining $90,000 should be allocated equally among Mike, Ned, and Opie. Thus, Mike and Ned each will recognize $80,000 and Opie will recognize $30,000 of gain (both tax and book).

---

10. Treas. Reg. § 1.704-3(e)(1).
11. Section 704(c)(1)(C).
12. Treas. Reg. § 1.704-1(b)(5) Ex. (14)(iv).

Alternatively, the partnership can restate its assets at their fair market value at the time the new partner joins the partnership. The built-in gain or loss reflected in the revalued assets will be allocated to the old (existing) partners.[13]

> **Example:** Mike and Ned were equal partners in the partnership. The partnership had previously purchased land for $100,000. Its current fair market value was $200,000. Opie joined the partnership by contributing $100,000 in exchange for a one-third interest.
>
> At the time Opie joined the partnership, the land had $100,000 of built-in gain that occurred while only Mike and Ned were partners. The partnership elected to restate its assets at their fair market value. The balance sheet then would reflect the land with a basis of $100,000 and fair market value of $200,000. The $100,000 of gain is treated as built-in gain, allocable to Mike and Ned. When the land is sold, the book, or economic, gain will reflect the gain that occurred after Opie joined the partnership. It should be allocated between the three partners. The difference between the book and tax gain represents the built-in gain and is allocated to Mike and Ned.
>
> For example, if the land was later sold for $290,000, the tax gain would be $190,000 and the book, or economic, gain would be $90,000. The difference between the book and tax gain, $100,000, represents the built-in gain and is allocated to Mike and Ned. The book gain should be allocated between the three partners. Thus, Mike and Ned each will recognize $80,000 and Opie will recognize $30,000 of tax gain. They will each have $30,000 of book, or economic, gain.

2. Ceiling Rule

In certain circumstances, the sale of a contributed partnership asset may not generate sufficient gain or loss to allocate the pre-contribution gain or loss to the contributing partner. When this result occurs, the regulations provide that the maximum amount of built-in gain or loss that can be allocated to the partner is the amount of tax gain or loss generated by the sale of the asset. The rule is referred to as the ceiling rule.

When the ceiling rule applies to property with a built-in gain, the property has depreciated in value from the time of contribution to the partnership. Thus, the partners have experienced an economic loss. When the ceiling rule applies to property with a built-in loss, the property has increased in value from the time of contribution to the partnership. Thus, the partners have experienced an economic increase.

> **Example:** Quinn purchased land for $10,000. When the land had increased in value to $50,000, she contributed it to a partnership in exchange for a 50-percent general partnership interest. Roy contributed $50,000 in exchange for a 50-percent general partnership interest. The partnership agreement provided that allocations would be made based on ownership interests.
>
> Eight years later, the partnership sold the land for $40,000, realizing a tax gain of $30,000 (amount realized of $40,000, less adjusted basis of $10,000). It recognized $10,000 of book loss (amount realized of $40,000, less book basis of $50,000).

---

13. Treas. Reg. § 1.704-1(b)(4)(i), -1(b)(5) Ex. (14)(i).

Even though Quinn should be allocated $40,000 of tax gain, there is only $30,000 available to allocate to her. All $30,000 of gain must be allocated solely to Quinn. There has been an economic loss at the partnership level. This $10,000 loss is allocated equally between Quinn and Roy.

	Quinn		Roy	
Tax	Book	Tax	Book
$30,000	<$5,000>	—	<$5,000>

When there is a shortfall due to the ceiling rule, there will be a disparity between the partner's built-in gain or loss and the tax gain or loss. Under the traditional method, the disparity is not corrected.[14] However, the shortfall can be corrected through either of two methods, the traditional method with curative allocations or the remedial method.[15]

Anti-abuse rule. Each method is subject to an anti-abuse rule. The allocation method will not be respected if the contribution of property and allocation of associated gain or loss is made with a view to shifting the tax consequences of the built-in gain or loss among the partners so as to substantially reduce the present value of their aggregate tax liability.[16]

Choice of method. Only one method may be used for any one piece of property contributed with a built-in gain or loss. However, the partnership may use different methods for different properties, as long as the combination of methods is reasonable based on the facts and circumstances.[17]

a. Traditional Method with Curative Allocations

When the ceiling rule applies because the sale of a contributed partnership asset did not generate sufficient gain or loss to allocate the pre-contribution gain or loss to the contributing partner, there will be a disparity between the partner's outside basis and capital account in the amount of the shortfall. Under the traditional method with curative allocations, this disparity can be corrected at the time of sale by allocating gain or loss (as appropriate) from items other than the sale of the property.[18] Because the shortfall is a tax shortfall, the curative allocation only impacts the partner's outside basis; it does not impact the partner's capital account.

For the curative allocation to be respected, it must:[19]

- Not exceed the amount necessary to correct the disparity caused by the ceiling rule; and
- Be of the same character and have the same tax consequences as the contributed property.

---

14. Treas. Reg. § 1.704-3(b)(1).

15. Treas. Reg. § 1.704-3(a)(1), -3(b), -3(c), -3(d). The regulations also provide that any reasonable method may be used, as long as it is consistent with the purposes of Section 704(c). Treas. Reg. § 1.704-3(a)(1).

16. Treas. Reg. § 1.704-3(a)(10).

17. Treas. Reg. § 1.704-3(a)(2).

18. Treas. Reg. § 1.704-3(c).

19. Treas. Reg. § 1.704-3(c)(3).

A curative allocation may be made only if the partnership has income or loss in a sufficient amount and in the right character. Accordingly, in some situations, it will not be possible for the partnership to make the necessary curative allocations. Thus, the partnership may make an allocation in a year subsequent to the year the property was sold, as long as the allocation is made within a reasonable amount of time and the partnership agreement provided for curative allocations in the year the property was contributed to the partnership.[20] Curative allocations impact the partner's outside basis. They do not impact the partner's capital account.

b. Remedial Method

When the ceiling rule applies because the sale of a contributed partnership asset did not generate sufficient gain or loss to allocate the pre-contribution gain or loss to the contributing partner, there will be a disparity between the partner's outside basis and capital account in the amount of the shortfall. Under the remedial method, the partnership creates the necessary amount of gain or loss (of the correct character) to make up the shortfall caused by the ceiling rule. In addition, it creates an offsetting gain or loss to allocate to the non-contributing partners.[21] Because the shortfall is a tax shortfall, the remedial allocation only impacts the partner's outside basis; it does not impact the partner's capital account.[22]

3. Characterization Issues

Congress was concerned that partner-taxpayers would attempt to change the character of gain or loss from the sale of property by contributing the property to a partnership and having the partnership sell the property (generally converting ordinary income into capital gain and capital losses into ordinary losses). For example, a taxpayer may be in the business of developing lots for sale. Any gain from the sale of such lots would be ordinary income, taxed at regular rates. The taxpayer may attempt to convert the ordinary gain into long-term capital gain by contributing the property to a partnership and having the partnership hold the property for investment purposes, then sell it to recognize long-term capital gain.

To curb this abuse, Congress identified three types of property and set forth specific characterization rules that apply to each specific category. The three categories are: unrealized receivables, inventory items, and capital loss property.

Unrealized receivables. Unrealized receivables include, to the extent not previously included in income, any right to payment for services rendered. It also includes the right to payment for goods delivered to the extent the proceeds would be treated as amounts received from the sale or exchange of property other than a capital asset. It also includes any gain that would be characterized as ordinary income under the depreciation recapture provisions.[23]

---

20. Treas. Reg. § 1.704-3(c)(3)(ii).
21. Treas. Reg. § 1.704-3(d)(1).
22. Treas. Reg. § 1.704-3(d)(4)(ii).
23. Code Secs. 724(a), (d)(1); 751(c).

> **Example:** The partnership holds only accounts receivable. If the partnership is a cash method taxpayer, the accounts receivable are unrealized receivables. In contrast, if the partnership is an accrual method taxpayer, the accounts receivable are not unrealized receivables.

Any gain or loss recognized by the partnership from the sale or disposition of unrealized receivables contributed by a partner to the partnership will be characterized as ordinary.[24]

Inventory items. Inventory includes those assets held for sale to customers and any items that are not characterized as a capital or hotchpot (Section 1231) item.[25] For five years from the time of contribution of inventory by a partner to the partnership, any gain or loss recognized by the partnership from the sale will be characterized as ordinary.[26] At the end of the five year period, the character of the gain or loss is determined under the regular rules, *i.e.*, at the partnership level.

Capital loss property. Capital loss property includes any capital asset held by the contributing partner that had a built-in loss immediately before the partner contributed the property to the partnership. For five years from the time of contribution to the partnership, the loss, up to the amount of the built-in loss, will retain its character as a capital loss. Any additional loss is characterized at the partnership level.[27] At the end of the five year period, the character of the loss (or gain) is determined under the regular rules, *i.e.*, at the partnership level.

If the partnership exchanges the unrealized receivable, inventory, or capital loss property for other property in a like-kind exchange, the characterization rules apply to the property received in the exchange to the same extent they applied to the property transferred.[28] When determining the five-year time period, the five years begins as of the date the original property was contributed to the partnership. The only exception is if the property received is stock in a corporation acquired in an exchange governed by Section 351.[29]

---

24. Section 724(a).
25. Sections 724(b), (d)(2); 751(d).
26. Section 724(b).
27. Section 724(c).
28. Section 724(d)(3)(A).
29. Section 724(d)(3)(B).

Summary

Allocating Tax Depreciation Among the Partners—Traditional Method:

Step 1: Determine the total amount of tax depreciation.

Step 2: Determine the total amount of book depreciation.

Step 3: Determine how the book depreciation would be allocated among the partners.

Step 4: Allocate to the noncontributing partners tax depreciation in an amount equal to the amount of book depreciation.

Step 5: Allocate any remaining tax depreciation to the contributing partner.

Allocating Pre-Contribution Tax Gain or Loss—Traditional Method:

Step 1: Determine the total amount of tax gain or loss.

Step 2: Determine the total amount of pre-contribution gain or loss (book value, less adjusted basis).

Step 3: Allocate the pre-contribution tax gain or loss to the contributing partner.

Step 4: Allocate to the remaining tax gain or loss (total gain or loss, less pre-contribution gain or loss) among the partners.

Step 5: Allocate the book gain or loss among the partners.

Questions

1. Ann contributed equipment with a basis of $16,000 and fair market value of $20,000. The equipment had a remaining useful life of four years. Bob contributed $20,000. With respect to Section 704(c) the partnership used the traditional method of allocation. In the first year, how would the depreciation be allocated? Prepare a balance sheet to reflect the situation of the partners and the partnership at the end of the first year.

2. Carl contributed equipment with a basis of $30,000 and fair market value of $50,000. The equipment had a remaining useful life of five years. Deb contributed $50,000. With respect to Section 704(c) the partnership used the traditional method of allocation. In the first year, how would the depreciation be allocated? Prepare a balance sheet to reflect the situation of the partners and the partnership at the end of the first year.

3. Ellen contributed equipment with a basis of $8,000 and fair market value of $20,000. The equipment had a remaining useful life of four years. Frank contributed $20,000. With respect to Section 704(c) the partnership used the traditional method of allocation. In the first year, how would the depreciation be allocated? Prepare a balance sheet to reflect the situation of the partners and the partnership at the end of the first year.

4. Greg contributed equipment with a basis of $60,000 and fair market value of $50,000. The equipment had a remaining useful life of five years. Hal contributed $50,000. With respect to Section 704(c) the partnership used the traditional method of allocation. In the first year, how would the depreciation be allocated? Prepare a balance sheet to reflect the situation of the partners and the partnership at the end of the first year.

5. Ira contributed equipment with a basis of $8,000 and fair market value of $20,000. The equipment had a remaining useful life of four years. Jeb contributed $20,000. With respect to Section 704(c) the partnership used the traditional method with curative allocations.

    The partnership used the $20,000 to purchase a small shed. The shed had a useful life of five years. In the first year, how would the depreciation be allocated? Prepare a balance sheet to reflect the situation of the partners and the partnership at the end of the first year.

6. Kent contributed equipment with a basis of $8,000 and fair market value of $20,000. The equipment had a remaining useful life of five years. Len contributed $20,000. With respect to Section 704(c) the partnership used the traditional method with curative allocations. During the year, the partnership earned $5,000 in income. In the first year, how would the depreciation and income be allocated? Prepare a balance sheet to reflect the situation of the partners and the partnership at the end of the first year.

7. Mike contributed equipment with a basis of $8,000 and fair market value of $20,000. The equipment had a remaining useful life of four years. Ned contributed $20,000. If the partnership had just acquired the property, it could recover the cost over ten years, using the straightline method (assuming no conventions). With respect to Section 704(c) the partnership used the remedial allocation method. How would the depreciation be allocated over the next five years?

8.   Opie contributed land with a basis of $20,000 and fair market value of $50,000. Paul contributed $50,000. Five years later, the partnership sold the land for $60,000. How is the gain allocated between the partners? Assuming no other changes to the partnership, prepare a balance sheet to reflect the situation of the partners after the sale.

9.   Quinn contributed land with a basis of $50,000 and fair market value of $60,000. Roy contributed $60,000. Four years later, the partnership sold the land for $80,000. How is the gain allocated between the partners? Assuming no other changes to the partnership, prepare a balance sheet to reflect the situation of the partners after the sale.

10. Sam contributed land with a basis of $20,000 and fair market value of $50,000. Tess contributed $50,000. With respect to Section 704(c), the partnership uses the traditional method of allocation. Five years later, the partnership sold the land for $40,000. How is the gain allocated between the partners? Assuming no other changes to the partnership, prepare a balance sheet to reflect the situation of the partners after the sale.

11. Vince contributed land with a basis of $20,000 and fair market value of $50,000. Wes contributed $50,000. The partnership used the $50,000 to purchase stock. With respect to Section 704(c), the partnership uses the traditional method with curative allocations. Five years later, the partnership sold the land for $40,000 and the stock for $70,000. How is the gain from each sale allocated between the partners? Assuming no other changes to the partnership, prepare a balance sheet to reflect the situation of the partners after the sales.

12. Xander contributed land with a basis of $20,000 and fair market value of $50,000. Yolanda contributed $50,000. With respect to Section 704(c), the partnership uses the remedial allocation method. Five years later, the partnership sold the land for $40,000. How is the gain allocated between the partners? Assuming no other changes to the partnership, prepare a balance sheet to reflect the situation of the partners after the sale.

13. Zelda contributed land with a basis of $50,000 and fair market value of $20,000. Ann contributed $20,000. Five years later, the partnership sold the land for $10,000. How is the loss allocated between the partners? Assuming no other changes to the partnership, prepare a balance sheet to reflect the situation of the partners after the sale.

14. Bob contributed land with a basis of $50,000 and fair market value of $40,000. Carl contributed $40,000. Four years later, the partnership sold the land for $30,000. How is the loss allocated between the partners? Assuming no other changes to the partnership, prepare a balance sheet to reflect the situation of the partners after the sale.

15. Deb contributed land with a basis of $50,000 and fair market value of $40,000. Ellen contributed $40,000. With respect to Section 704(c), the partnership uses the traditional method of allocation. Five years later, the partnership sold the land for $45,000. How is the loss allocated between the partners? Assuming no other changes to the partnership, prepare a balance sheet to reflect the situation of the partners after the sale.

16. Frank contributed land with a basis of $50,000 and fair market value of $40,000. Greg contributed $40,000. The partnership used the $40,000 to purchase stock. With respect to Section 704(c), the partnership uses the traditional method with curative allocations. Five years later, the partnership sold the land for $45,000 and the stock for $20,000. How is the loss from each sale allocated between the partners? Assuming no

other changes to the partnership, prepare a balance sheet to reflect the situation of the partners after the sales.

17. Hal contributed land with a basis of $50,000 and fair market value of $40,000. Ira contributed $40,000. With respect to Section 704(c), the partnership uses the remedial allocation method. Five years later, the partnership sold the land for $45,000. How is the loss allocated between the partners? Assuming no other changes to the partnership, prepare a balance sheet to reflect the situation of the partners after the sale.

18. Jeb contributed equipment with a $10,000 basis and $50,000 fair market value. Kent contributed $50,000. Three years later when the equipment's adjusted basis was $5,000 and book basis was $25,000, the partnership sold the equipment for $30,000. How is the gain allocated between the partners?

19. Len contributed equipment with a $10,000 basis and $50,000 fair market value. Mike contributed $50,000. Three years later when the equipment's adjusted basis was $5,000 and book basis was $25,000, the partnership sold the equipment for $20,000. With respect to Section 704(c), the partnership uses the traditional method of allocation. How is the gain allocated between the partners?

20. Ned contributed land with a basis of $50,000 and a fair market value of $40,000 to a partnership. At the time of contribution, Ned held the land for investment purposes. The partnership held the property as part of its inventory. Three years later, the partnership sold the land for $35,000. What is the character of the loss?

21. Opie contributed accounts receivable to a partnership. The accounts receivable had a basis of zero and fair market value of $10,000. Three years later, the partnership sold the accounts receivable for $10,000. What is the character of the gain?

22. Paul contributed accounts receivable to a partnership. The accounts receivable had a basis of zero and fair market value of $10,000. Six years later, the partnership sold the accounts receivable for $10,000. What is the character of the gain?

23. Quinn contributed inventory to a partnership. The inventory had a basis of zero and fair market value of $10,000. Three years later, the partnership sold the inventory for $15,000. What is the character of the gain?

24. Roy contributed inventory to a partnership. The inventory had a basis of zero and fair market value of $10,000. Six years later, the partnership sold the inventory for $10,000. What is the character of the gain?

Solutions

1.   Ann contributed equipment with a basis of $16,000 and fair market value of $20,000. The equipment had a remaining useful life of four years. Bob contributed $20,000. With respect to Section 704(c) the partnership used the traditional method of allocation. In the first year, how would the depreciation be allocated? Prepare a balance sheet to reflect the situation of the partners and the partnership at the end of the first year.

At the time of formation, the balance sheet would appear as follows:

Asset	Basis	FMV	Partner	Basis	Cap. Acct.
Cash	$20,000	$20,000	Ann	$16,000	$20,000
Equipment	16,000	20,000	Bob	20,000	20,000
	$36,000	$40,000		$36,000	$40,000

The equipment is Section 704(c) property. (Treas. Reg. § 1.704-3(a)(3)(i)) The amount of tax depreciation is $4,000, and the amount of book deprecation is $5,000:

Tax: $16,000/4 = $4,000
Book: $20,000/4 = $5,000

Bob is allocated $2,500 of depreciation for book purposes (one-half of the book depreciation, or ½ × $5,000). Moreover, as the non-contributing partner, he is allocated $2,500 of tax depreciation and Ann is allocated the remainder, or $1,500 ($4,000, less $2,500). (Section 704(c)(1)(A); Treas. Reg. § 1.704-3(a)(1), -3(b)(1)) Thus, the depreciation is allocated as follows:

Ann		Bob	
Tax	Book	Tax	Book
<$1,500>	<$2,500>	<$2,500>	<$2,500>

After the allocation of depreciation, the balance sheet would appear as follows:

Asset	Basis	FMV	Partner	Basis	Cap. Acct.
Cash	$20,000	$20,000	Ann	$14,500	$17,500
Equipment	12,000	15,000	Bob	17,500	17,500
	$32,000	$35,000		$32,000	$35,000

2.   Carl contributed equipment with a basis of $30,000 and fair market value of $50,000. The equipment had a remaining useful life of five years. Deb contributed $50,000. With respect to Section 704(c) the partnership used the traditional method of allocation. In the first year, how would the depreciation be allocated? Prepare a balance sheet to reflect the situation of the partners and the partnership at the end of the first year.

At the time of formation, the balance sheet would appear as follows:

Asset	Basis	FMV	Partner	Basis	Cap. Acct.
Cash	$50,000	$ 50,000	Carl	$30,000	$ 50,000
Equipment	30,000	50,000	Deb	50,000	50,000
	$80,000	$100,000		$80,000	$100,000

The equipment is Section 704(c) property. (Treas. Reg. § 1.704-3(a)(3)(i)) The amount of tax depreciation is $6,000, and the amount of book deprecation is $10,000:

Tax: $30,000/5 = $6,000
Book: $50,000/5 = $10,000

Deb is allocated $5,000 of depreciation for book purposes (one-half of the book depreciation, or ½ × $10,000). Moreover, as the non-contributing partner, she is allocated $5,000 of tax depreciation and Carl is allocated the remainder, or $1,000 ($6,000, less $1,000). (Section 704(c)(1)(A); Treas. Reg. § 1.704-3(a)(1), -3(b)(1)) Thus, the depreciation is allocated as follows:

Carl		Deb	
Tax	Book	Tax	Book
<$1,000>	<$5,000>	<$5,000>	<$5,000>

After the allocation of depreciation, the balance sheet would appear as follows:

Asset	Basis	FMV	Partner	Basis	Cap. Acct.
Cash	$50,000	$50,000	Carl	$29,000	$45,000
Equipment	24,000	40,000	Deb	45,000	45,000
	$74,000	$90,000		$74,000	$90,000

3. Ellen contributed equipment with a basis of $8,000 and fair market value of $20,000. The equipment had a remaining useful life of four years. Frank contributed $20,000. With respect to Section 704(c) the partnership used the traditional method of allocation. In the first year, how would the depreciation be allocated? Prepare a balance sheet to reflect the situation of the partners and the partnership at the end of the first year.

At the time of formation, the balance sheet would appear as follows:

Asset	Basis	FMV	Partner	Basis	Cap. Acct.
Cash	$20,000	$20,000	Ellen	$ 8,000	$20,000
Equipment	8,000	20,000	Frank	20,000	20,000
	$28,000	$40,000		$28,000	$40,000

The equipment is Section 704(c) property. (Treas. Reg. § 1.704-3(a)(3)(i)) The amount of tax depreciation is $2,000, and the amount of book deprecation is $5,000:

Tax: $8,000/4 = $2,000
Book: $20,000/4 = $5,000

Frank is allocated $2,500 of depreciation for book purposes (one-half of the book depreciation, or ½ × $5,000). Moreover, as the non-contributing partner, he should be allocated $2,500 of depreciation for tax purposes. However, there is only $2,000 of tax depreciation to allocate to Frank. Because the partnership uses the traditional method of allocation, the partnership will not correct the disparity. (Section 704(c)(1)(A); Treas. Reg. § 1.704-3(a)(1), -3(b)(1)) Thus, the depreciation is allocated as follows:

	Ellen		Frank	
Tax	Book	Tax	Book
$ 0	<$2,500>	<$2,000>	<$2,500>

After the allocation of depreciation, the balance sheet would appear as follows:

Asset	Basis	FMV	Partner	Basis	Cap. Acct.
Cash	$20,000	$20,000	Ellen	$ 8,000	$17,500
Equipment	6,000	15,000	Frank	18,000	17,500
	$26,000	$35,000		$26,000	$35,000

4. Greg contributed equipment with a basis of $60,000 and fair market value of $50,000. The equipment had a remaining useful life of five years. Hal contributed $50,000. With respect to Section 704(c) the partnership used the traditional method of allocation. In the first year, how would the depreciation be allocated? Prepare a balance sheet to reflect the situation of the partners and the partnership at the end of the first year.

At the time of formation, the balance sheet would appear as follows:

Asset	Basis	FMV	Partner	Basis	Cap. Acct.
Cash	$ 50,000	$ 50,000	Greg	$ 60,000	$ 50,000
Equipment	60,000	50,000	Hal	50,000	50,000
	$110,000	$100,000		$110,000	$100,000

The equipment is Section 704(c) property. (Treas. Reg. § 1.704-3(a)(3)(i)) The amount of tax depreciation is $12,000, and the amount of book deprecation is $10,000:

Tax: $60,000/5 = $12,000
Book: $50,000/5 = $10,000

Hal is allocated $5,000 of depreciation for book purposes (one-half of the book depreciation, or ½ × $10,000). Moreover, as the non-contributing partner, he is allocated $5,000 of tax depreciation and Greg is allocated the remainder, or $7,000 ($12,000, less $5,000). (Section 704(c)(1)(A); Treas. Reg. § 1.704-3(a)(1), -3(b)(1)) Thus, the depreciation is allocated as follows:

	Greg		Hal	
Tax	Book	Tax	Book
<$7,000>	<$5,000>	<$5,000>	<$5,000>

After the allocation of depreciation, the balance sheet would appear as follows:

Asset	Basis	FMV	Partner	Basis	Cap. Acct.
Cash	$50,000	$50,000	Greg	$53,000	$45,000
Equipment	48,000	40,000	Hal	45,000	45,000
	$98,000	$90,000		$98,000	$90,000

5. Ira contributed equipment with a basis of $8,000 and fair market value of $20,000. The equipment had a remaining useful life of four years. Jeb contributed $20,000. With respect to Section 704(c) the partnership used the traditional method with curative allocations.

The partnership used the $20,000 to purchase a small shed. The shed had a useful life of five years. In the first year, how would the depreciation be allocated? Prepare a balance sheet to reflect the situation of the partners and the partnership at the end of the first year.

At the time of formation, and after purchase of the shed, the balance sheet would appear as follows:

Asset	Basis	FMV	Partner	Basis	Cap. Acct.
Equipment	$ 8,000	$20,000	Ira	$ 8,000	$20,000
Shed	20,000	20,000	Jeb	20,000	20,000
	$28,000	$40,000		$28,000	$40,000

The equipment is Section 704(c) property. (Treas. Reg. § 1.704-3(a)(3)(i)) The amount of tax depreciation is $2,000, and the amount of book deprecation is $5,000:

Tax: $8,000/4 = $2,000
Book: $20,000/4 = $5,000

Jeb is allocated $2,500 of depreciation for book purposes (one-half of the book depreciation, or ½ × $5,000). Moreover, as the non-contributing partner, he should be allocated $2,500 of depreciation for tax purposes. However, there is only $2,000 of tax depreciation to allocate to Jeb. Because the partnership uses the traditional method with curative allocations, the partnership will correct the disparity. (Section 704(c)(1)(A); Treas. Reg. § 1.704-3(a)(1), -3(c)(1))

The amount of tax and book depreciation on the shed is $4,000 ($20,000 recovered over five years).

Tax: $20,000/5 = $4,000
Book: $20,000/5 = $4,000

Each partner would be allocated $2,000 ($4,000 × ½). The partnership can use this depreciation to correct the disparity caused by the ceiling rule with respect to the equipment. It can allocate an additional $500 depreciation to Jeb (to account for the fact that he received $500 too little of depreciation from the equipment). Thus, for tax purposes, the depreciation from the shed would be allocated $1,500 to Ira and $2,500 to Jeb. The curative allocation does not impact their capital accounts; for book purposes, they are each allocated $2,000 of depreciation. The allocations would appear as follows:

	Ira		Jeb	
	Tax	Book	Tax	Book
Equipment:	$ 0	<$2,500>	<$2,000>	<$2,500>
Shed:	<1,500>	<2,000>	<2,500>	<2,000>

After the allocation of depreciation from the equipment and the shed, the balance sheet would appear as follows:

Asset	Basis	FMV	Partner	Basis	Cap. Acct.
Equipment	$ 6,000	$15,000	Ira	$ 6,500	$15,500
Shed	16,000	16,000	Jeb	15,500	15,500
	$22,000	$31,000		$22,000	$31,000

6. Kent contributed equipment with a basis of $8,000 and fair market value of $20,000. The equipment had a remaining useful life of five years. Len contributed $20,000. With respect to Section 704(c) the partnership used the traditional method with curative allocations. During the year, the partnership earned $5,000 in income. In the first year, how would the depreciation and income be allocated? Prepare a balance sheet to reflect the situation of the partners and the partnership at the end of the first year.

At the time of formation, and before the income is earned, the balance sheet would appear as follows:

Asset	Basis	FMV	Partner	Basis	Cap. Acct.
Cash	$20,000	$20,000	Kent	$ 8,000	$20,000
Equipment	8,000	20,000	Len	20,000	20,000
	$28,000	$40,000		$28,000	$40,000

The equipment is Section 704(c) property. (Treas. Reg. § 1.704-3(a)(3)(i)) The amount of tax depreciation is $1,600, and the amount of book deprecation is $4,000:

Tax: $8,000/5 = $1,600
Book: $20,000/5 = $4,000

Len is allocated $2,000 of depreciation for book purposes (one-half of the book depreciation, or ½ × $4,000). Moreover, as the non-contributing partner, he should be allocated $2,000 of depreciation for tax purposes. However, there is only $1,600 of tax depreciation to allocate to Len. Because the partnership uses the traditional method with curative allocations, the partnership will correct the disparity. (Section 704(c)(1)(A); Treas. Reg. § 1.704-3(a)(1), -3(c)(1))

Generally, the partnership income would be allocated equally between Kent and Len, or $2,500 each. However, the partnership can use the ordinary income to correct the disparity caused by the ceiling rule. It can allocate $400 less of the partnership income to Len (to account for the fact that he received $400 less of a depreciation deduction). Thus, the income, for tax purposes, would be allocated $2,900 to Kent and $2,100 to Len. The curative allocation does not impact their capital accounts; for book purposes, they are each allocated $2,500 of income. The allocations would appear as follows:

	Kent		Len	
	Tax	Book	Tax	Book
Depreciation:	$ 0	<$2,000>	<$1,600>	<$2,000>
Income:	2,900	2,500	2,100	2,500

After the allocation of income and depreciation, the balance sheet would appear as follows:

Asset	Basis	FMV	Partner	Basis	Cap. Acct.
Cash	$25,000	$25,000	Kent	$10,900	$20,500
Equipment	6,400	16,000	Len	20,500	20,500
	$31,400	$41,000		$31,400	$41,000

7. Mike contributed equipment with a basis of $8,000 and fair market value of $20,000. The equipment had a remaining useful life of four years. Ned contributed $20,000. If the partnership had just acquired the property, it could recover the cost over ten years, using the straightline method (assuming no conventions). With respect to Section 704(c) the partnership used the remedial allocation method. How would the depreciation be allocated over the next five years?

At the time of formation, the balance sheet would appear as follows:

Asset	Basis	FMV	Partner	Basis	Cap. Acct.
Cash	$20,000	$20,000	Mike	$ 8,000	$20,000
Equipment	8,000	20,000	Ned	20,000	20,000
	$28,000	$40,000		$28,000	$40,000

The equipment is Section 704(c) property. (Treas. Reg. § 1.704-3(a)(3)(i)) The amount of tax depreciation is $2,000, and the amount of book deprecation is $5,000:

> Tax: $8,000/4 = $2,000
> Book: $20,000/4 = $5,000

Ned is allocated $2,500 of depreciation for book purposes (one-half of the book depreciation, or ½ × $5,000). Moreover, as the non-contributing partner, he should be allocated $2,500 of depreciation for tax purposes. However, there is only $2,000 of tax depreciation to allocate to Ned. Because the partnership uses the remedial allocation method, the partnership will correct the disparity. (Section 704(c)(1)(A); Treas. Reg. § 1.704-3(a)(1), -3(d)(1))

Under the remedial allocation method, book depreciation is calculated by dividing the book basis into two portions. The first portion is equal to the tax basis, $8,000. (Treas. Reg. § 1.704-3(d)(2)) The second portion is equal to the remainder, $12,000 ($20,000, less $8,000). (Treas. Reg. § 1.704-3(d)(2))

With respect to the first portion, depreciation is computed in the same manner as it is computed for tax purposes, or $2,000 each year. With respect to the second portion, depreciation is computed using the applicable recovery period and method which would be used if the partnership had just acquired the property. (Treas. Reg. § 1.704-3(d)(2)) If the partnership had just acquired the property, it could recover the cost over ten years, using the straightline method (assuming no conventions). Accordingly, the second portion is $1,200 ($12,000 recovered over ten years).

For the first year, there is a total book depreciation of $3,200.

> First portion: $2,000
> Second portion: $1,200
> Total: $3,200

This $3,200 is allocated equally between Mike and Ned, or $1,600 each. Ned, as the non-contributing partner, is allocated $1,600 of tax depreciation and Mike is allocated the remainder, or $400 each. No remedial allocations are needed yet as there is sufficient tax depreciation to allocate to Ned. The depreciation is allocated as follows:

Mike		Ned	
Tax	Book	Tax	Book
<$400>	<$1,600>	<$1,600>	<$1,600>

The results are the same for the following three years.

Equipment

	Tax	Book
	$ 8,000	$20,000
Yr. 1 depr.:	<2,000>	< 3,200>
Yr. 2 depr.:	<2,000>	< 3,200>
Yr. 3 depr.:	<2,000>	< 3,200>
Yr. 4 depr.:	<2,000>	< 3,200>
Adj. basis:	$ 0	$ 7,200

In the fifth year, the first portion of the book depreciation has been fully recovered. Accordingly, an amount is recovered only under the second portion. Thus, there is a total of $1,200 of book depreciation for the year, which is allocated equally between Mike and Ned, or $600 each. However, there is no tax depreciation to allocate to Ned. Because the partnership uses the remedial method it can correct the disparity by creating an additional $600 of depreciation to allocate to Ned and creating an offsetting $600 allocation of income to allocate to Mike. The allocations created under the remedial method do not impact the partners' capital accounts. The allocations are as follows:

	Mike		Ned	
	Tax	Book	Tax	Book
Depreciation:	—	<$600>	—	<$600>
Remedial:	$600		<$600>	

Note that at the end of the tenth year the book basis of the equipment would be zero.

Equipment

	Book
Adj basis:	$7,200
Yr. 5 depr.:	<1,200>
Yr. 6 depr.:	<1,200>
Yr. 7 depr.:	<1,200>
Yr. 8 depr.:	<1,200>
Yr. 9 depr.:	<1,200>
Yr. 10 depr.:	<1,200>
Adj. basis:	$ 0

8.   Opie contributed land with a basis of $20,000 and fair market value of $50,000. Paul contributed $50,000. Five years later, the partnership sold the land for $60,000. How is the gain allocated between the partners? Assuming no other changes to the partnership, prepare a balance sheet to reflect the situation of the partners after the sale.

At formation the balance sheet would appear as follows:

Asset	Basis	FMV	Partner	Basis	Cap. Acct.
Cash	$50,000	$ 50,000	Opie	$20,000	$ 50,000
Land	20,000	50,000	Paul	50,000	50,000
	$70,000	$100,000		$70,000	$100,000

Five years later, the partnership sold the land for $60,000.

	Tax	Book
AR:	$60,000	$60,000
AB:	20,000	50,000
	$40,000	$10,000

The land is Section 704(c) property. (Treas. Reg. § 1.704-3(a)(3)(i)) From the tax gain, $30,000 is pre-contribution gain (fair market value of $50,000, less $20,000 basis) and must be allocated to Opie. (Treas. Reg. § 1.704-3(a)(3)(ii)) The remaining tax gain, $10,000 ($40,000 gain, less $30,000 pre-contribution gain), is post-contribution gain and is allocated equally between Opie and Paul, or $5,000 each. Thus, Opie is allocated a total of $35,000 gain ($30,000 pre-contribution, plus $5,000 post-contribution) and Paul is allocated a total of $5,000 (post-contribution) gain. (Section 704(c)(1)(A); Treas. Reg. § 1.704-3(a)(1), -3(b)(1)) Each of their bases is increased by the amount of the allocation.

From an economic perspective, the property has increased in value $10,000 from the time of contribution ($50,000 at the time of contribution to $60,000 at the time of sale). This economic appreciation is allocated equally between the partners. Each partner's capital account is increased by $5,000.

The allocations would be as follows:

	Opie		Paul	
	Tax	Book	Tax	Book
	$20,000	$50,000	$50,000	$50,000
Gain:	35,000	5,000	5,000	5,000
	$55,000	$55,000	$55,000	$55,000

After the sale, the balance sheet would appear as follows:

Asset	Basis	FMV	Partner	Basis	Cap. Acct.
Cash	$110,000	$110,000	Opie	$ 55,000	$ 55,000
	$110,000	$110,000	Paul	55,000	55,000
				$110,000	$110,000

9. Quinn contributed land with a basis of $50,000 and fair market value of $60,000. Roy contributed $60,000. Four years later, the partnership sold the land for $80,000. How is the gain allocated between the partners? Assuming no other changes to the partnership, prepare a balance sheet to reflect the situation of the partners after the sale.

At formation the balance sheet would appear as follows:

Asset	Basis	FMV	Partner	Basis	Cap. Acct.
Cash	$ 60,000	$ 60,000	Quinn	$ 50,000	$ 60,000
Land	50,000	60,000	Roy	60,000	60,000
	$110,000	$120,000		$110,000	$120,000

Four years later, the partnership sold the land for $80,000.

	Tax	Book
AR:	$80,000	$80,000
AB:	50,000	60,000
	$30,000	$20,000

The land is Section 704(c) property. (Treas. Reg. § 1.704-3(a)(3)(i)) From the tax gain, $10,000 is pre-contribution gain (fair market value of $60,000, less $50,000 basis) and must be allocated to Quinn. (Treas. Reg. § 1.704-3(a)(3)(ii)) The remaining tax gain, $20,000 ($30,000 gain, less $10,000 pre-contribution gain), is post-contribution gain and is allocated equally between Quinn and Roy, or $10,000 each. Thus, Quinn is allocated a total of $20,000 gain ($10,000 pre-contribution, plus $10,000 post-contribution) and Roy is allocated a total of $10,000 (post-contribution) gain. (Section 704(c)(1)(A); Treas. Reg. § 1.704-3(a)(1), -3(b)(1)) Each of their bases is increased by the amount of the allocation.

From an economic perspective, the property has increased in value $20,000 from the time of contribution ($60,000 at the time of contribution to $80,000 at the time of sale). This economic appreciation is allocated equally between the partners. Each partner's capital account is increased by $10,000.

The allocations would be as follows:

	Quinn		Roy	
	Tax	Book	Tax	Book
	$50,000	$60,000	$60,000	$60,000
Gain:	20,000	10,000	10,000	10,000
	$70,000	$70,000	$70,000	$70,000

After the sale, the balance sheet would appear as follows:

Asset	Basis	FMV	Partner	Basis	Cap. Acct.
Cash	$140,000	$140,000	Quinn	$ 70,000	$ 70,000
	$140,000	$140,000	Roy	70,000	70,000
				$140,000	$140,000

10. Sam contributed land with a basis of $20,000 and fair market value of $50,000. Tess contributed $50,000. With respect to Section 704(c), the partnership uses the traditional method of allocation. Five years later, the partnership sold the land for $40,000. How is the gain allocated between the partners? Assuming no other changes to the partnership, prepare a balance sheet to reflect the situation of the partners after the sale.

At formation the balance sheet would appear as follows:

Asset	Basis	FMV	Partner	Basis	Cap. Acct.
Cash	$50,000	$ 50,000	Sam	$20,000	$ 50,000
Land	20,000	50,000	Tess	50,000	50,000
	$70,000	$100,000		$70,000	$100,000

Five years later, the partnership sold the land for $40,000.

	Tax	Book
AR:	$40,000	$ 40,000
AB:	20,000	50,000
	$20,000	<$10,000>

The land is Section 704(c) property. (Treas. Reg. § 1.704-3(a)(3)(i)) The pre-contribution gain ($30,000: fair market value of $50,000, less $20,000 basis) must be allocated to Sam. (Treas. Reg. § 1.704-3(a)(3)(ii)) However, there is only $20,000 of tax gain. The ceiling rule provides that the maximum amount of built-in gain that can be allocated to Sam is the amount of tax gain generated by the sale, or $20,000. The disparity is not corrected. (Treas. Reg. § 1.704-3(a)(3)(i), -3(b)(1)) Sam's basis is increased by the $20,000 gain. No gain is allocated to Tess.

When the ceiling rule applies to property with a built-in gain, the property has decreased in value from the time of contribution to the partnership to the time of sale. Thus, the partners have experienced an economic loss. The amount of book loss is $10,000 and is allocated equally between Sam and Tess, or $5,000 each.

The allocations would be as follows:

	Sam		Tess	
	Tax	Book	Tax	Book
	$20,000	$50,000	$50,000	$50,000
Sale:	20,000	<5,000>	0	<5,000>
	$40,000	$45,000	$50,000	$45,000

After sale of the land, the balance sheet would appear as follows:

Asset	Basis	FMV	Partner	Basis	Cap. Acct.
Cash	$90,000	$90,000	Sam	$40,000	$45,000*
	$90,000	$90,000	Tess	50,000	45,000
				$90,000	$90,000

* Because the partnership uses the traditional method of allocation and the ceiling rule applies, the partnership's balance sheet will reflect the fact that not all of the built-in gain was allocated to Sam on sale of the land.

Built-in gain:	$30,000
Gain recognized:	− 20,000
Share of decrease in value:	− 5,000
Remaining amount:	$ 5,000 = the difference between Sam's capital account and basis.

11. Vince contributed land with a basis of $20,000 and fair market value of $50,000. Wes contributed $50,000. The partnership used the $50,000 to purchase stock. With respect to Section 704(c), the partnership uses the traditional method with curative allocations. Five years later, the partnership sold the land for $40,000 and the stock for $70,000. How is the gain from each sale allocated between the partners? Assuming no other changes to the partnership, prepare a balance sheet to reflect the situation of the partners after the sales.

At formation, but after the purchase of the stock, the balance sheet would appear as follows:

Asset	Basis	FMV	Partner	Basis	Cap. Acct.
Stock	$50,000	$ 50,000	Vince	$20,000	$ 50,000
Land	20,000	50,000	Wes	50,000	50,000
	$70,000	$100,000		$70,000	$100,000

Five years later, the partnership sold the land for $40,000.

	Tax	Book
AR:	$40,000	$40,000
AB:	20,000	50,000
	$20,000	<$10,000>

The land is Section 704(c) property. (Treas. Reg. § 1.704-3(a)(3)(i)) The pre-contribution gain ($30,000: fair market value of $50,000, less $20,000 basis) must be allocated to Vince. (Treas. Reg. § 1.704-3(a)(3)(ii)) However, there is only $20,000 of tax gain. The ceiling rule provides that the maximum amount of built-in gain that can be allocated to Vince is the amount of tax gain generated by the sale, or $20,000. Because the partnership uses the traditional method with curative allocations, the disparity is corrected. (Treas. Reg. § 1.704-3(a)(3)(i), -3(c)(1)) Vince's basis is increased by the $20,000 gain. No gain is allocated to Wes.

When the ceiling rule applies to property with a built-in gain, the property has decreased in value from the time of contribution to the partnership to the time of sale. Thus, the partners have experienced an economic loss. The amount of book loss is $10,000 and is allocated equally between Vince and Wes, or $5,000 each.

The partnership sold the stock for $70,000.

	Tax	Book
AR:	$70,000	$70,000
AB:	50,000	50,000
	$20,000	$20,000

Under the traditional method with curative allocations, the disparity caused by the ceiling rule to Vince can be corrected at the time of sale by allocating gain (of the same character) from items other than the sale of the land. (Treas. Reg. § 1.704-3(c)(1), (3)(iii)) A curative allocation may be made because, with the sale of the stock, the partnership had gain in a sufficient amount and in the right character. The amount of the curative allocation is determined as follows:

Built-in gain:	$30,000
Gain recognized:	− 20,000
Share of decrease in value:	− 5,000
Remaining amount:	$ 5,000

Thus, $5,000 of the gain from the sale of the stock is allocated away from Wes and to Vince.

There is a book gain of $20,000 from the sale of the stock. The curative allocation does not impact their capital accounts; for book purposes, they are each allocated $10,000 of income.

The allocations would be as follows:

	Vince		Wes	
	Tax	Book	Tax	Book
Basis:	$20,000	$50,000	$50,000	$50,000
Land:	20,000	< 5,000>	0	< 5,000>
Stock:	15,000	10,000	5,000	10,000
Basis:	$55,000	$55,000	$55,000	$55,000

After sale of the land and stock, the balance sheet would appear as follows:

Asset	Basis	FMV	Partner	Basis	Cap. Acct.
Cash	$110,000	$110,000	Vince	$ 55,000	$ 55,000
	$110,000	$110,000	Wes	55,000	55,000
				$110,000	$110,000

12. Xander contributed land with a basis of $20,000 and fair market value of $50,000. Yolanda contributed $50,000. With respect to Section 704(c), the partnership uses the remedial allocation method. Five years later, the partnership sold the land for $40,000. How is the gain allocated between the partners? Assuming no other changes to the partnership, prepare a balance sheet to reflect the situation of the partners after the sale.

At formation the balance sheet would appear as follows:

Asset	Basis	FMV	Partner	Basis	Cap. Acct.
Cash	$50,000	$ 50,000	Xander	$20,000	$ 50,000
Land	20,000	50,000	Yolanda	50,000	50,000
	$70,000	$100,000		$70,000	$100,000

Five years later, the partnership sold the land for $40,000.

	Tax	Book
AR:	$40,000	$40,000
AB:	20,000	50,000
	$20,000	<$10,000>

The land is Section 704(c) property. (Treas. Reg. § 1.704-3(a)(3)(i)) The pre-contribution gain ($30,000: fair market value of $50,000, less $20,000 basis) must be allocated to Xander. (Treas. Reg. § 1.704-3(a)(3)(ii)) However, there is only $20,000 of tax gain. The ceiling rule provides that the maximum amount of built-in gain that can be allocated to Xander is the amount of tax gain generated by the sale, or $20,000. Because the partnership uses the remedial allocation method, the disparity is corrected. (Treas. Reg. §1.704-3(a)(3)(i), -3(d)(1)) Xander's basis is increased by the $20,000 of tax gain. No gain is allocated to Yolanda.

When the ceiling rule applies to property with a built-in gain, the property has decreased in value from the time of contribution to the partnership to the time of sale. Thus, the partners have experienced an economic loss. The amount of book loss is $10,000 and is allocated equally between Xander and Yolanda, or $5,000 each.

Under the remedial allocation method, the disparity caused by the ceiling rule to Xander can be corrected at the time of sale. The partnership creates the necessary amount of gain (of the correct character) to make up the shortfall caused by the ceiling rule. The amount of the remedial allocation is determined as follows (Treas. Reg. §1.704-3(d)(1), (3)):

Built-in gain:	$30,000
Gain recognized:	– 20,000
Share of decrease in value:	– 5,000
Remaining amount:	$ 5,000

The allocations would be as follows:

	Xander		Yolanda	
	Tax	Book	Tax	Book
Basis:	$20,000	$50,000	$50,000	$50,000
Land:	20,000	<5,000>	0	<5,000>
Remedial Alloc.:	5,000	0	<5,000>	0
Basis:	$45,000	$45,000	$45,000	$45,000

After the sale of the land, the balance sheet would appear as follows:

Asset	Basis	FMV	Partner	Basis	Cap. Acct.
Cash	$90,000	$90,000	Xander	$45,000	$45,000
	$90,000	$90,000	Yolanda	45,000	45,000
				$90,000	$90,000

13. Zelda contributed land with a basis of $50,000 and fair market value of $20,000. Ann contributed $20,000. Five years later, the partnership sold the land for $10,000. How is the loss allocated between the partners? Assuming no other changes to the partnership, prepare a balance sheet to reflect the situation of the partners after the sale.

At formation the balance sheet would appear as follows:

Asset	Basis	FMV	Partner	Basis	Cap. Acct.
Cash	$20,000	$20,000	Zelda	$50,000	$20,000
Land	50,000	20,000	Ann	20,000	20,000
	$70,000	$40,000		$70,000	$40,000

Five years later, the partnership sold the land for $10,000.

	Tax	Book
AR:	$10,000	$10,000
AB:	50,000	20,000
	<$40,000>	<$10,000>

The land is Section 704(c) property. (Treas. Reg. § 1.704-3(a)(3)(i)) From the tax loss, $30,000 is pre-contribution loss (fair market value of $20,000, less $50,000 basis) and must be allocated to Zelda. (Treas. Reg. § 1.704-3(a)(3)(ii)) The remaining tax loss, $10,000 ($40,000 loss, less $30,000 pre-contribution loss), is post-contribution loss and is allocated equally between Zelda and Ann, or $5,000 each. Thus, Zelda is allocated a total of $35,000 loss ($30,000 pre-contribution, plus $5,000 post-contribution) and Ann is allocated a total of $5,000 (post-contribution) loss. (Section 704(c)(1)(A); Treas. Reg. § 1.704-3(a)(1), -3(b)(1)) Each of their bases is decreased by the amount of the allocation.

From an economic perspective, the property has decreased in value $10,000 from the time of contribution ($20,000 at the time of contribution to $10,000 at the time of sale). This economic depreciation is allocated equally between the partners. Each partner's capital account is decreased by $5,000.

The allocations would be as follows:

	Zelda		Ann	
	Tax	Book	Tax	Book
	$50,000	$20,000	$20,000	$20,000
Loss:	<35,000>	<5,000>	<5,000>	<5,000>
	$15,000	$15,000	$15,000	$15,000

After the sale, the balance sheet would appear as follows:

Asset	Basis	FMV	Partner	Basis	Cap. Acct.
Cash	$30,000	$30,000	Zelda	$15,000	$15,000
	$30,000	$30,000	Ann	15,000	15,000
				$30,000	$30,000

14. Bob contributed land with a basis of $50,000 and fair market value of $40,000. Carl contributed $40,000. Four years later, the partnership sold the land for $30,000. How is the loss allocated between the partners? Assuming no other changes to the partnership, prepare a balance sheet to reflect the situation of the partners after the sale.

At formation the balance sheet would appear as follows:

Asset	Basis	FMV	Partner	Basis	Cap. Acct.
Cash	$40,000	$40,000	Bob	$50,000	$40,000
Land	50,000	40,000	Carl	40,000	40,000
	$90,000	$80,000		$90,000	$80,000

Four years later, the partnership sold the land for $30,000.

	Tax	Book
AR:	$30,000	$30,000
AB:	50,000	40,000
	<$20,000>	<$10,000>

The land is Section 704(c) property. (Treas. Reg. § 1.704-3(a)(3)(i)) From the tax loss, $10,000 is pre-contribution loss (fair market value of $40,000, less $50,000 basis) and must be allocated to Bob. (Treas. Reg. § 1.704-3(a)(3)(ii)) The remaining tax loss, $10,000 ($20,000 loss, less $10,000 pre-contribution loss), is post-contribution loss and is allocated equally between Bob and Carl, or $5,000 each. Thus, Bob is allocated a total of $15,000 loss ($10,000 pre-contribution, plus $5,000 post-contribution) and Bob is allocated a total of $5,000 (post-contribution) loss. (Section 704(c)(1)(A); Treas. Reg. § 1.704-3(a)(1), -3(b)(1)) Each of their bases is decreased by the amount of the allocation.

From an economic perspective, the property has decreased in value $10,000 from the time of contribution ($40,000 at the time of contribution to $30,000 at the time of sale). This economic depreciation is allocated equally between the partners. Each partner's capital account is decreased by $5,000.

The allocations would be as follows:

	Bob		Carl	
	Tax	Book	Tax	Book
	$50,000	$40,000	$40,000	$40,000
Loss:	<15,000>	<5,000>	<5,000>	<5,000>
	$35,000	$35,000	$35,000	$35,000

After the sale, the balance sheet would appear as follows:

Asset	Basis	FMV	Partner	Basis	Cap. Acct.
Cash	$70,000	$70,000	Bob	$35,000	$35,000
	$70,000	$70,000	Carl	35,000	35,000
				$70,000	$70,000

15. Deb contributed land with a basis of $50,000 and fair market value of $40,000. Ellen contributed $40,000. With respect to Section 704(c), the partnership uses the traditional method of allocation. Five years later, the partnership sold the land for $45,000. How is the loss allocated between the partners? Assuming no other changes to the partnership, prepare a balance sheet to reflect the situation of the partners after the sale.

At formation the balance sheet would appear as follows:

Asset	Basis	FMV	Partner	Basis	Cap. Acct.
Cash	$40,000	$40,000	Deb	$50,000	$40,000
Land	50,000	40,000	Ellen	40,000	40,000
	$90,000	$80,000		$90,000	$80,000

Five years later, the partnership sold the land for $45,000.

	Tax	Book
AR:	$45,000	$45,000
AB:	50,000	40,000
	<$5,000>	$ 5,000

The land is Section 704(c) property. (Treas. Reg. § 1.704-3(a)(3)(i)) The pre-contribution loss ($10,000: fair market value of $40,000, less $50,000 basis) must be allocated to Deb. (Treas. Reg. § 1.704-3(a)(3)(ii)) However, there is only $5,000 of tax loss. The ceiling rule provides that the maximum amount of built-in loss that can be allocated to Deb is the amount of tax loss generated by the sale, or $5,000. The disparity is not corrected. (Treas. Reg. § 1.704-3(a)(3)(i), -3(b)(1)) Deb's basis is decreased by the $5,000 tax loss. No loss is allocated to Ellen.

When the ceiling rule applies to property with a built-in loss, the property has increased in value from the time of contribution to the partnership to the time of sale. Thus, the partners have experienced an economic gain. The amount of book gain is $5,000 and is allocated equally between Deb and Ellen, or $2,500 each.

The allocations would be as follows:

	Deb		Ellen	
	Tax	Book	Tax	Book
	$50,000	$40,000	$40,000	$40,000
Sale:	<5,000>	2,500	0	2,500
	$45,000	$42,500	$40,000	$42,500

After sale of the land, the balance sheet would appear as follows:

Asset	Basis	FMV	Partner	Basis	Cap. Acct.
Cash	$85,000	$85,000	Deb	$45,000	$42,500*
	$85,000	$85,000	Ellen	40,000	42,500
				$85,000	$85,000

* Because the partnership uses the traditional method of allocation and the ceiling rule applies, the partnership's balance sheet will reflect the fact that not all of the built-in loss was allocated to Deb on sale of the land.

Built-in loss:	<$10,000>
Loss recognized:	– 5,000
Share of increase in value:	+ 2,500
Remaining amount:	<$ 2,500> = the difference between Deb's capital account and basis.

16. Frank contributed land with a basis of $50,000 and fair market value of $40,000. Greg contributed $40,000. The partnership used the $40,000 to purchase stock. With respect to Section 704(c), the partnership uses the traditional method with curative allocations. Five years later, the partnership sold the land for $45,000 and the stock for $20,000. How is the loss from each sale allocated between the partners? Assuming no other changes to the partnership, prepare a balance sheet to reflect the situation of the partners after the sales.

At formation, but after the purchase of the stock, the balance sheet would appear as follows:

Asset	Basis	FMV	Partner	Basis	Cap. Acct.
Stock	$40,000	$40,000	Frank	$50,000	$40,000
Land	50,000	40,000	Greg	40,000	40,000
	$90,000	$80,000		$90,000	$80,000

Five years later, the partnership sold the land for $45,000.

	Tax	Book
AR:	$45,000	$45,000
AB:	50,000	40,000
	<$5,000>	$ 5,000

The land is Section 704(c) property. (Treas. Reg. § 1.704-3(a)(3)(i)) The pre-contribution loss ($10,000: fair market value of $40,000, less $50,000 basis) must be allocated to Frank. (Treas. Reg. § 1.704-3(a)(3)(ii)) However, there is only $5,000 of tax loss. The ceiling rule provides that the maximum amount of built-in loss that can be allocated to Frank is the amount of tax loss generated by the sale, or $5,000. Because the partnership uses the traditional method with curative allocations, the disparity is corrected. (Treas. Reg. § 1.704-3(a)(3)(i), -3(c)(1)) Frank's basis is decreased by the $5,000 of tax loss. No loss is allocated to Greg.

When the ceiling rule applies to property with a built-in loss, the property has increased in value from the time of contribution to the partnership to the time of sale. Thus, the partners have experienced an economic gain. The amount of book gain is $5,000 and is allocated equally between Frank and Greg, or $2,500 each.

The partnership sold the stock for $20.000.

	Tax	Book
AR:	$20,000	$20,000
AB:	40,000	40,000
	<$20,000>	<$20,000>

Under the traditional method with curative allocations, the disparity caused by the ceiling rule to Frank can be corrected at the time of sale by allocating loss (of the same character) from items other than the sale of the land. (Treas. Reg. § 1.704-3(c)(1), (3)(iii)) A curative allocation may be made because, with the sale of the stock, the partnership has a loss in a sufficient amount and in the right character. The amount of the curative allocation is determined as follows:

Built-in loss:	<$10,000>
Loss recognized:	– 5,000
Share of increase in value:	+ 2,500
Remaining amount:	<$ 2,500>

Thus, $2,500 of the loss from the sale of the stock is allocated away from Greg and to Frank.

There is a book loss of $20,000 from the sale of the stock. The curative allocation does not impact their capital accounts; for book purposes, they are each allocated $10,000 of loss.

The allocations would be as follows:

	Frank		Greg	
	Tax	Book	Tax	Book
Basis:	$50,000	$40,000	$40,000	$40,000
Land:	< 5,000>	2,500	0	2,500
Stock	<12,500>	<10,000>	< 7,500>	<10,000>
Basis:	$32,500	$32,500	$32,500	$32,500

After sale of the land and stock, the balance sheet would appear as follows:

Asset	Basis	FMV	Partner	Basis	Cap. Acct.
Cash	$65,000	$65,000	Frank	$32,500	$32,500
	$65,000	$65,000	Greg	32,500	32,500
				$65,000	$65,000

17. Hal contributed land with a basis of $50,000 and fair market value of $40,000. Ira contributed $40,000. With respect to Section 704(c), the partnership uses the remedial allocation method. Five years later, the partnership sold the land for $45,000. How is the loss allocated between the partners? Assuming no other changes to the partnership, prepare a balance sheet to reflect the situation of the partners after the sale.

At formation the balance sheet would appear as follows:

Asset	Basis	FMV	Partner	Basis	Cap. Acct.
Cash	$40,000	$40,000	Hal	$50,000	$40,000
Land	50,000	40,000	Ira	40,000	40,000
	$90,000	$80,000		$90,000	$80,000

Five years later, the partnership sold the land for $45,000.

	Tax	Book
AR:	$45,000	$45,000
AB:	50,000	40,000
	<$5,000>	$ 5,000

The land is Section 704(c) property. (Treas. Reg. §1.704-3(a)(3)(i)) The pre-contribution loss ($10,000: fair market value of $40,000, less $50,000 basis) must be allocated to Hal. (Treas. Reg. §1.704-3(a)(3)(ii)) However, there is only $5,000 of tax loss. The ceiling rule provides that the maximum amount of built-in loss that can be allocated to Hal is the amount of tax loss generated by the sale, or $5,000. Because the partnership uses the remedial allocation method, the disparity is corrected. (Treas. Reg. §1.704-3(a)(3)(i), -3(d)(1)) Hal's basis is decreased by the $5,000 of tax loss. No loss is allocated to Ira.

When the ceiling rule applies to property with a built-in loss, the property has increased in value from the time of contribution to the partnership to the time of sale.

Thus, the partners have experienced an economic gain. The amount of book gain is $5,000 and is allocated equally between Hal and Ira, or $2,500 each.

Under the remedial allocation method, the disparity caused by the ceiling rule to Hal can be corrected at the time of sale. The partnership creates the necessary amount of loss (of the correct character) to make up the shortfall caused by the ceiling rule. The amount of the remedial allocation is determined as follows (Treas. Reg. § 1.704-3(d)(1), (3)):

Built-in loss:	<$10,000>
Loss recognized:	– 5,000
Share of increase in value:	+ 2,500
Remaining amount:	<$ 2,500>

The allocations would be as follows:

	Hal		Ira	
	Tax	Book	Tax	Book
Basis:	$50,000	$40,000	$40,000	$40,000
Land:	< 5,000>	2,500	0	2,500
Remedial Alloc.:	< 2,500>	0	2,500	0
Basis:	$42,500	$42,500	$42,500	$42,500

After the sale of the land, the balance sheet would appear as follows:

Asset	Basis	FMV	Partner	Basis	Cap. Acct.
Cash	$85,000	$85,000	Hal	$42,500	$42,500
	$85,000	$85,000	Ira	42,500	42,500
				$85,000	$85,000

18. Jeb contributed equipment with a $10,000 basis and $50,000 fair market value. Kent contributed $50,000. Three years later when the equipment's adjusted basis was $5,000 and book basis was $25,000, the partnership sold the equipment for $30,000. How is the gain allocated between the partners?

Three years later, the partnership sold the equipment for $30,000. The tax and book results would be as follows:

	Tax	Book
AR:	$30,000	$30,000
AB:	5,000	25,000
	$25,000	$ 5,000

The equipment is Section 704(c) property. (Treas. Reg. § 1.704-3(a)(3)(i)) From the tax gain, $20,000 is pre-contribution gain (book value of $25,000, less $5,000 tax basis (Treas. Reg. § 1.704-3(a)(3)(ii)) and must be allocated to Jeb. (Treas. Reg. § 1.704-3(a)(3)(ii)) The remaining tax gain, $5,000 ($25,000 gain, less $20,000 pre-contribution gain), is post-contribution gain and is allocated equally between Jeb and Kent, or $2,500 each. Thus, Jeb is allocated a total of $22,500 gain ($20,000 pre-contribution, plus $2,500 post-contribution) and Kent is allocated a total of $2,500 (post-contribution) gain. (Section 704(c)(1)(A); Treas. Reg. § 1.704-3(a)(1), -3(b)(1))

From an economic perspective, the property has increased in value $5,000 ($25,000 book value at the time of sale to $30,000 sale price). This economic appreciation is allocated equally between the partners. Each partner's capital account is increased by $2,500.

The allocation is as follows:

	Jeb		Kent	
Tax	Book	Tax	Book
$22,500	$2,500	$2,500	$2,500

19. Len contributed equipment with a $10,000 basis and $50,000 fair market value. Mike contributed $50,000. Three years later when the equipment's adjusted basis was $5,000 and book basis was $25,000, the partnership sold the equipment for $20,000. With respect to Section 704(c), the partnership uses the traditional method of allocation. How is the gain allocated between the partners?

Three years later, the partnership sold the equipment for $20,000. The tax and book results would be as follows:

	Tax	Book
AR:	$20,000	$20,000
AB:	5,000	25,000
	$15,000	<$5,000>

The equipment is Section 704(c) property. (Treas. Reg. § 1.704-3(a)(3)(i)) From the tax gain, $20,000 is pre-contribution gain (book value of $25,000, less $5,000 tax basis (Treas. Reg. § 1.704-3(a)(3)(ii)) and must be allocated to Len. (Treas. Reg. § 1.704-3(a)(3)(ii)) However, there is only $15,000 of tax gain. The ceiling rule provides that the maximum amount of built-in gain that can be allocated to Len is the amount of tax gain generated by the sale, or $15,000. The disparity is not corrected. (Treas. Reg. § 1.704-3(a)(3)(i), -3(b)(1)) No tax gain is allocated to Mike.

From an economic perspective, the property has decreased in value $5,000 ($25,000 book value at the time of sale to $20,000 sale price). This economic depreciation is allocated equally between the partners. Each partner's capital account is decreased by $2,500.

The allocation is as follows:

	Len		Mike	
Tax	Book	Tax	Book
$15,000	<$2,500>	0	<$2,500>

20. Ned contributed land with a basis of $50,000 and a fair market value of $40,000 to a partnership. At the time of contribution, Ned held the land for investment purposes. The partnership held the property as part of its inventory. Three years later, the partnership sold the land for $35,000. What is the character of the loss?

If property would be characterized as a capital asset in the hands of the partner prior to contribution, for five years after contribution to a partnership the loss will be characterized as a capital loss to the extent of the loss in the property at the time of contribution. (Section 724(c))

Ned contributed property that was a capital asset in his hands prior to contribution. For five years after contribution the built-in loss of $10,000 will continue to be characterized as a capital loss. The partnership sold the property within five years from the time of contribution.

Upon sale of the land, there is a tax loss:

	Tax
AR:	$ 35,000
AB:	50,000
	<$15,000>

Pre-contribution tax loss is:

Book value:	$40,000
AB:	50,000
Built-in loss:	<$10,000>

Thus, $10,000 of the loss is a capital loss and the remaining $5,000 of loss is an ordinary loss. (Section 724(c))

21. Opie contributed accounts receivable to a partnership. The accounts receivable had a basis of zero and fair market value of $10,000. Three years later, the partnership sold the accounts receivable for $10,000. What is the character of the gain?

If property would be characterized as an unrealized receivable in the hands of the partner prior to contribution, after the contribution to the partnership the gain or loss will continue to be characterized as ordinary. (Section 724(a), (d)(1))

The accounts receivable were contributed by Opie, a partner, to the partnership and were an unrealized receivable in his hands. Thus, there is $10,000 of ordinary income. (Section 724(a))

22. Paul contributed accounts receivable to a partnership. The accounts receivable had a basis of zero and fair market value of $10,000. Six years later, the partnership sold the accounts receivable for $10,000. What is the character of the gain?

If property would be characterized as an unrealized receivable in the hands of the partner prior to contribution, after the contribution to the partnership the gain or loss will continue to be characterized as ordinary. (Section 724(a), (d)(1))

The accounts receivable were contributed by Paul, a partner, to the partnership and were an unrealized receivable in his hands. Thus, there is $10,000 of ordinary income. (There is no time limit on the characterization provision.) (Section 724(a))

23. Quinn contributed inventory to a partnership. The inventory had a basis of zero and fair market value of $10,000. Three years later, the partnership sold the inventory for $15,000. What is the character of the gain?

If the property would be characterized as inventory in the hands of the partner prior to contribution, for five years after the contribution to the partnership the gain or loss will be characterized as ordinary. (Section 724(b), (d)(2))

Quinn contributed inventory. Three years later, the partnership sold the inventory. Because the inventory was sold within five years of contribution, the $15,000 of gain is characterized as ordinary income. (Section 724(b))

24. Roy contributed inventory to a partnership. The inventory had a basis of zero and fair market value of $10,000. Six years later, the partnership sold the inventory for $10,000. What is the character of the gain?

If property would be characterized as inventory in the hands of the partner prior to contribution, for five years after the contribution to the partnership the gain or loss will be characterized as ordinary. (Section 724(b), (d)(2))

The inventory was contributed by Roy. Because the five-year period has passed, the $10,000 of gain from the sale of the inventory is characterized based on the use of the inventory by the partnership. (Section 724(b))

Chapter VI

Effect of Liabilities — Revisited

This chapter revisits the issue of allocating recourse and non-recourse debt among the partners for purposes of Section 752. A discussion of how to allocate recourse debt began in Chapter II with an understanding of each partner's economic responsibility for recourse debt through use of the doomsday scenario. Chapter II also discussed how to allocate non-recourse debt using the simplest allocation—based on how the partners share profits.

Another concept, the impact of the economic effect test on the allocation of losses, was added in Chapter IV. In addition, Chapter IV discussed how non-recourse deductions must be allocated to be deemed to have economic effect.

Now, in this chapter, with respect to recourse debt, the two concepts are considered together—the impact of the economic effect test on the allocation of recourse debt through the doomsday scenario. And with respect to non-recourse debt, given the broader understanding of the allocation of non-recourse deductions, a more complex method for allocating non-recourse debt is applied.

A. Allocation of Recourse Liabilities

When the partnership acquires debt, either directly or through property contributed by a partner subject to a debt, the debt generally becomes the responsibility of the general partners. To the extent a partner has increased his share of responsibility for a partnership liability, he is treated as having advanced to the partnership his portion of the funds needed to repay the debt. Because a partner's outside basis reflects all contributions, including expected contributions for liabilities, the partner's outside basis is increased by the amount of the liability for which the partner is responsible.[1]

A partner's outside basis depends, in part, on the partner's share of partnership liabilities. In turn, the partner's share of partnership liabilities depends on whether the

---

1. Section 752(a).

liability is a recourse or non-recourse liability and on related facts, such as whether a partner has guaranteed the debt or is entitled to be reimbursed for amounts paid with respect to the debt.

Recall that a partnership liability is a recourse liability to the extent that any partner bears the economic risk of loss for that liability or would be obligated to contribute to the partnership to satisfy the liability.[2] To ascertain whether a partner bears the economic risk of loss, the regulations create a doomsday scenario and then consider which partners would have to contribute to the partnership to satisfy the liability. Note that whether a partner is required to contribute to the partnership to satisfy a liability is based on economic, or book, value, not on tax values. Specifically, a partner bears the economic risk of loss if:[3]

- The partnership constructively liquidated;
- As a result of the liquidation, the partner would be obligated to make a payment because the liability became due and payable; and
- The partner would not be entitled to reimbursement from another partner.

Whether a partner has an obligation to make a contribution to the partnership is based on all the facts and circumstances.[4] All obligations are taken into consideration, including the following:[5]

- Guarantees.
- Any obligations imposed by the partnership agreement, including the obligation to restore a negative capital account balance.
- Any obligations imposed by state law, including the obligation to restore a negative capital account balance.
- Whether a partner is entitled to be reimbursed or indemnified by another partner. There is a presumption that any partner required to reimburse another partner does so, even if the partner does not have the funds to make the payment (unless there is a plan to circumvent or avoid the payment). However, if an obligation is subject to a contingency that makes it unlikely it would ever be paid, the obligation is disregarded.

---

2. Treas. Reg. § 1.752-2(a).

3. Treas. Reg. § 1.752-2(b)(1).

4. Treas. Reg. § 1.752-2(b)(3). In determining the extent to which a partner bears the risk of loss, obligations of related parties are also taken into consideration. A related person includes a person related to a partner as defined in Section 267(b) or 707(b)(1), except that 80 percent is substituted for 50 percent; brothers and sisters are excluded; and section 267(e)(1) and 267(f)(1)(A) are disregarded. Treas. Reg. § 1.752-4(b)(1).

If the obligation to make a payment is not required to be satisfied within a reasonable time after the liability becomes due, or the obligation to make a contribution to the partnership is not required to be satisfied before the later of the end of the year in which the partnership interest is liquidated or 90 days after the liquidation, then the liability is only taken into account to the extent of its value. Treas. Reg. § 1.752-2(g)(1).

5. Treas. Reg. § 1.752-2(b).

B. Allocation of Non-Recourse Liabilities

Partnership non-recourse debt is allocated using a three-tiered system.

First tier. Under the first tier, the partner is allocated a portion of the non-recourse debt equal to his share of partnership minimum gain.

Recall that, because of the basis limitation rules of Section 704(d), a partner only may claim a deduction if the partner has a sufficient amount of basis. Accordingly, to ensure that a partner who has been allocated a non-recourse deduction will have sufficient basis to claim the non-recourse deduction, the partner will be allocated a portion of the debt that corresponds to the amount of non-recourse deduction. This amount is also reflected in the partner's increase in partnership minimum gain for the year.[6]

Example: Ann is a limited partner in the partnership. The partnership purchased a building for $100,000, financed entirely with non-recourse debt. Ignoring all conventions, assume the partnership is entitled to claim $5,000 of depreciation each year. Pursuant to the partnership agreement, Ann is allocated $2,000 of that depreciation each year. Assumer her outside basis is zero.

   Because Ann is a limited partner, no amount of the debt would be allocated to her under the doomsday scenario and her basis would not be increased.

   In the first year, the partnership's partnership minimum gain increased by $5,000 (the amount by which the non-recourse debt, $100,000, exceeded the buildings adjusted basis, $95,000). Thus, the depreciation is a non-recourse deduction.

   Pursuant to the partnership agreement, Ann was allocated $2,000 of the depreciation. If her basis were not adjusted as provided for under the regulations, with a zero basis she would not be able to claim the depreciation. It would be disallowed and carried forward.

   If the partnership later sold the building, Ann would be allocated $2,000 of the gain, based on her share of partnership minimum gain. Her basis would be increased from zero to $2,000 and, at that time, she would be able to claim the suspended depreciation.

   In contrast, by allocating a portion of the liability to Ann equal to the amount of her share of partnership minimum gain, Ann would be able to claim the $2,000 of depreciation in the year it was allocated to her. Her basis would be increased by her share of partnership minimum gain from zero to $2,000. Then, upon allocation of depreciation to her, Ann's basis would be reduced from $2,000 to zero. No amount of the depreciation would be suspended.

Second tier. The second tier is applicable only when property has been contributed by a partner to the partnership (or otherwise has built-in gain or loss). The focus is on the built-in gain in the property. Under the second tier, the partner is allocated a portion of the non-recourse debt equal to the minimum amount of tax built-in gain that would be allocated to the contributing partner upon sale of the property. Because the property can never be disposed of for less than the amount of the non-recourse debt, the minimum amount of tax gain that will be allocated to the contributing partner will always be the excess of the liability over the adjusted basis.

---

6. Treas. Reg. § 1.752-3(a)(1).

Recall that, because of the basis limitation rules of Section 704(d), a partner may only claim a deduction if the partner has a sufficient amount of basis. By allocating to the contributing partner a portion of the debt equal to the amount of built-in tax gain, to that extent, the partner will have basis in his partnership interest that will allow him to claim a non-recourse deduction.[7] These deductions eventually will be offset by the built-in tax gain.

Example: Bob contributed a building with an adjusted basis of $10,000 and subject to a non-recourse debt in the amount of $50,000 to the partnership in exchange for a limited partnership interest. The partnership agreement provided that $2,000 of the depreciation from the building is allocable to Bob each year. Because Bob is a limited partner, no amount of the debt would be allocated to him under the doomsday scenario and his basis would not be increased.

Assume that Bob's basis in the partnership is zero and that the partnership is entitled to $5,000 of depreciation each year.

If his basis were not adjusted as provided for under the regulations, with a zero basis he would not be able to claim the depreciation. It would be disallowed and carried forward.

If the partnership later sold the building, Bob would be allocated gain equal to $45,000, the amount by which the non-recourse debt ($50,000) exceeds the building's adjusted basis ($10,000 adjusted basis upon contribution, reduced by $5,000 of depreciation). His basis would be increased from zero to $45,000 and, at that time, he would be able to claim the suspended depreciation.

In contrast, by allocating a portion of the liability to Bob equal to the amount of the phantom, or *Tufts*, gain allocable to him, he would be able to claim the $2,000 of depreciation in the year it was allocated to him. His basis would be increased by the built-in, or phantom, gain from zero to $45,000. Then, upon allocation of the depreciation to him, Bob's basis would be reduced from $45,000 to $43,000. No amount of the depreciation would be suspended.

Note that the amount of built-in gain, or potential Section 704(c) gain, will never be characterized as partnership minimum gain. Partnership minimum gain is the excess of the non-recourse liability over the fair market value, or book value, of the property. Because the property is incorporated into the partnership's balance sheet upon contribution at its fair market value, there is no partnership minimum gain at that time, only built-in gain. The fair market value, or book value, will always represent the point at which built-in gain ends and partnership minimum gain begins.

An allocation of built-in gain may also apply in a reverse Section 704(c) situation. If a partner joined a pre-existing partnership, there will likely be gain or loss in the partnership assets. The partnership may elect to restate the fair market value of all assets to reflect their current fair market values. The difference between the property's adjusted basis and fair market value at the time the new partner joins the partnership is treated the same as built-in gain or loss at the time of contribution of an asset.[8]

---

7. Treas. Reg. § 1.752-3(a)(2).
8. Treas. Reg. §§ 1.704-1(b)(2)(iv)(f); 1.752-3(a)(2).

Third tier. The third tier allocates the amount of the debt that is remaining after the first and second tier allocations. Sometimes this amount is referred to as the "excess" amount.

In general, the excess amount is allocated based on how the partners share profits, or based on their ownership interests. If the partners have agreed to an allocation of profits associated with partnership assets, an allocation will be respected as long as it is reasonably consistent with an allocation (having substantial economic effect) of any significant item of partnership income or gain.[9] Alternatively, the partners may allocate excess non-recourse liability in a manner in which it is reasonably expected that the deductions attributable to the liability will be allocated.[10] Alternatively, if the non-recourse debt secures property contributed by a partner to the partnership, the partners may allocate excess non-recourse liability to the contributing partner to the extent the built-in gain on the property will be greater than the phantom, or *Tufts,* gain.

Each year, the partners may select a different method for allocating excess non-recourse deductions.[11] If the partners fail to identify how the excess non-recourse liability will be allocated, the allocation will be made consistent with the partners' interest in the partnership.[12]

Part recourse, part non-recourse debt. If the liability is in part a recourse liability and in part a non-recourse liability, the debt must be bifurcated into its two portions. The portion that is recourse is allocated under the recourse rules and the portion that is non-recourse is allocated under the non-recourse rules.

---

9. Treas. Reg. § 1.752-3(a)(3).
10. Treas. Reg. § 1.752-3(b).
11. Id.
12. Treas. Reg. § 1.752-3(a)(3).

Summary

Tests to Determine Whether Allocation Has Economic Effect: For an allocation to have economic effect, one of the following tests must be met.

General Test:
- Partners' capital accounts must be maintained according to the regulations;
- Liquidating distributions must be made in accordance with positive capital account balances; and
- If, following a liquidation, a partner has a deficit balance in his capital account, he must be unconditionally obligated to restore the amount of such deficit balance.

Alternate Test:
- Partners' capital accounts must be maintained according to the regulations;
- Liquidating distributions must be made in accordance with positive capital account balances;
- The allocation of recourse deductions cannot cause or increase a deficit in the partner's capital account in excess of any limited amount the partner is obligated to restore; and
- The partnership agreement contains a qualified income offset.

Safe Harbor Requirements for Allocation of Non-Recourse Deductions:
- The economic effect test must be met (either the general or the alternative);
- Beginning in the year the partnership has non-recourse deductions, the allocation must be reasonably consistent with other allocations (which have substantial economic effect) attributable to the property securing the non-recourse debt;
- There must be a minimum gain chargeback provision; and
- Allocations of other material items must have substantial economic effect.

Formula: A partner's share of a non-recourse debt is the sum of:
- The partner's share of partnership minimum gain;
- If the liability secures property contributed by the partner, the amount of gain that would be generated and allocated to the contributing partner if the partnership sold the property for the amount of the debt; and
- The partner's share of any remaining, or excess, non-recourse liabilities.

Definitions:

Non-recourse debt

– Book adjusted basis

Partnership minimum gain

(*Tufts* gain or phantom income)

Net increase in PMG

– Distributions made during the year of proceeds of non-

recourse liability that are allocable to an increase in PMG

Non-recourse deductions

Non-recourse deduction allocations

+ distributions of non-recourse liability proceeds allocable to increase in PMG

Partner's share of PMG

Minimum gain chargeback: if there is a net decrease in PMG, each partner must be allocated items of income/gain equal to that partner's share of the net decrease in PMG unless the decrease is due to:

- The liability becoming recourse to that partner; or
- A contribution to capital that is used to repay the non-recourse liability.

A partner's share of the net decrease in PMG = (total net decrease) × (partner's percentage share of PMG at the end of prior year)

Rules for Liabilities:

- A partner's outside basis is decreased by any decrease in his share of partnership liabilities or decrease in his individual liabilities due to the partnership's assumption of the liability.
- A partner's outside basis is increased by any increase in his share of partnership liabilities.
- If, in a single transaction, there is an increase in the partner's share of the partnership's liabilities and a decrease in the partner's individual liabilities (or vice versa), only the net amount will affect the partner's basis.

Formula: A partner's basis in a partnership interest where the partnership has liabilities is:

Adjusted basis of the asset(s) contributed to the partnership
+ Cash contributed to the partnership
+ Net change in liabilities*
Partner's outside basis

* Amount of partnership debt assumed – amount of individual debt relief

Questions

1.   Ann and Bob formed a general partnership. Ann contributed $10,000 and Bob contributed $50,000. They agreed to share profits and losses equally. The partnership agreement provided that, upon liquidation, all partners must restore negative capital account balances and that liquidating distributions would be made based on capital account balances.

The partnership purchased a building for $100,000. It paid $60,000 and obtained a $40,000 recourse loan for the remaining purchase price. Prepare a balance sheet to reflect the situation of the partners and the partnership after purchase of the building.

2.   Carl and Deb formed a general partnership. They each contributed $20,000. They agreed to allocate profits and losses 40 percent to Carl and 60 percent to Deb. The partnership agreement provided that, upon liquidation, all partners must restore negative capital account balances and that liquidating distributions would be made based on capital account balances.

The partnership purchased a building for $50,000. It paid $40,000 and obtained a $10,000 recourse loan for the remaining purchase price. Prepare a balance sheet to reflect the situation of the partners and the partnership after purchase of the building.

3.   Ellen and Frank formed a general partnership. Ellen contributed $1,000 and Frank contributed $9,000. They agreed to share profits and losses equally. The partnership agreement provided that, upon liquidation, all partners must restore negative capital account balances and liquidating distributions would be made based on capital account balances.

The partnership purchased a building for $100,000. It paid $10,000 and obtained a $90,000 recourse loan for the remaining purchase price. Prepare a balance sheet to reflect the situation of the partners and the partnership after purchase of the building.

4.   Greg and Hal formed a general partnership. Greg contributed $30,000 and Hal contributed $10,000. They agreed to share profits and losses equally. The partnership agreement provided that, upon liquidation, all partners must restore negative capital account balances and liquidating distributions would be made based on capital account balances.

The partnership purchased a building for $50,000. It paid $40,000 and obtained a $10,000 recourse loan for the remaining purchase price. Prepare a balance sheet to reflect the situation of the partners and the partnership after purchase of the building.

5.   Ira and Jeb formed a limited partnership. Ira contributed $50,000 in exchange for a general partnership interest, and Jeb contributed $50,000 in exchange for a limited partnership interest. The partnership agreement provided that profits and losses would be divided equally between the partners and that, upon liquidation, only Ira had an obligation to restore a negative capital account balance. Jeb was not required to restore any deficit balance in his account, but the partnership agreement contained a qualified income offset with respect to him.

The partnership purchased a building for $150,000. It paid $100,000 and obtained a $50,000 recourse loan for the remaining purchase price. Prepare a balance sheet to reflect the situation of the partners and the partnership after purchase of the building.

6.   Kent and Len formed a general partnership. Kent contributed $1,000 and Len contributed $9,000. They agreed to share profits and losses equally. The partnership agreement provided that, upon liquidation, all partners must restore negative capital account balances and liquidating distributions would be made based on capital account balances.

The partnership purchased a building for $100,000. It paid $10,000 and obtained a $90,000 recourse loan for the remaining purchase price. Kent executed a personal guaranty for the $90,000 liability. Prepare a balance sheet to reflect the situation of the partners and the partnership after purchase of the building.

7.   Mike and Ned formed a limited partnership. Mike contributed $50,000 in exchange for a general partnership interest, and Ned contributed $50,000 in exchange for a limited partnership interest. Ned also contributed a $10,000 promissory note. The partnership agreement provided that profits and losses would be divided equally between the partners and that, upon liquidation, only Mike had an obligation to restore a negative capital account balance. Ned was not required to restore any deficit balance in his account, but the partnership agreement contained a qualified income offset with respect to him.

The partnership purchased a building for $150,000. It paid $100,000 and obtained a $50,000 recourse loan for the remaining purchase price. Prepare a balance sheet to reflect the situation of the partners and the partnership after purchase of the building.

8.   Opie and Paul formed a limited partnership. Opie contributed $20,000 in exchange for a general partnership interest, and Paul contributed $80,000 in exchange for a limited partnership interest. The partnership agreement provided that capital accounts would be maintained in accordance with the regulations, that Opie had an obligation to restore a negative capital account, and that liquidating distributions would be made in accordance with capital account balances. Paul was not required to restore any deficit balance in his account, but the partnership agreement contained a qualified income offset with respect to him. The partnership agreement also contained a minimum gain chargeback provision. It provided that any excess non-recourse debt be allocated 30 percent to Opie and 70 percent to Paul. Finally, the partnership agreement allocated all depreciation 20 percent to Opie and 80 percent to Paul and also allocated all non-recourse deductions 30 percent to Opie and 70 percent to Paul until the first time the partnership recognized items of income and gain that exceeded the items of loss and deduction it had recognized over its life. Then, all further depreciation deductions would be allocated equally between Opie and Paul.

The partnership purchased a building for $300,000, using the $100,000 cash contributed by the partners and financing the remaining $200,000 with a non-recourse debt, secured by the building. No payments were due on the loan for five years. Ignoring all conventions, in each year the partnership was entitled to $50,000 of depreciation. In each year, before taking into consideration the depreciation, partnership income was equal to its expenses.

a. What is each partner's basis at the end of the first year? Create a balance sheet to reflect the situation of the partners and partnership.

b. What is each partner's basis at the end of the second year? Create a balance sheet to reflect the situation of the partners and partnership.

   c. What is each partner's basis at the end of the third year? Create a balance sheet to reflect the situation of the partners and partnership.

9.   Quinn and Roy formed a limited partnership. Quinn contributed $20,000 in exchange for a general partnership interest, and Roy contributed $80,000 in exchange for a limited partnership interest. The partnership agreement provided that capital accounts would be maintained in accordance with the regulations, that Quinn had an obligation to restore a negative capital account, and that liquidating distributions would be made in accordance with capital account balances. Roy was not required to restore any deficit balance in his account, but the partnership agreement contained a qualified income offset with respect to him. The partnership agreement also contained a minimum gain chargeback provision. It provided that any excess non-recourse debt be allocated equally between Quinn and Roy. Finally, the partnership agreement allocated all depreciation 20 percent to Quinn and 80 percent to Roy and allocated all non-recourse deductions 30 percent to Quinn and 70 percent to Roy until the first time the partnership recognized items of income and gain that exceeded the items of loss and deduction it had recognized over its life. Then, all further depreciation deductions would be allocated equally between Quinn and Roy.

The partnership purchased a building for $300,000, using the $100,000 cash contributed by the partners and financing the remaining $200,000 with a non-recourse debt, secured by the building. No payments were due on the loan for five years. Ignoring all conventions, in each year the partnership was entitled to $50,000 of depreciation. In each year, before taking into consideration the depreciation, partnership income was equal to its expenses.

   a. What is each partner's basis at the end of the first year? Create a balance sheet to reflect the situation of the partners and partnership.

   b. What is each partner's basis at the end of the second year? Create a balance sheet to reflect the situation of the partners and partnership.

   c. What is each partner's basis at the end of the third year? Create a balance sheet to reflect the situation of the partners and partnership.

10. Sam and Tess formed a general partnership. Sam contributed $75,000. Tess contributed land with a fair market value of $100,000 and basis of $20,000. The land was subject to a $25,000 non-recourse debt, and the debt was assumed by the partnership.

The partnership agreement provided that capital accounts would be maintained in accordance with the regulations, that the partners have an obligation to restore a negative capital account, and that liquidating distributions would be made in accordance with capital account balances. The partnership agreement also contained a minimum gain chargeback provision. It provided that any excess non-recourse debt would be allocated equally between the partners.

Create a balance sheet to reflect the situation of the partners and partnership.

Solutions

1. Ann and Bob formed a general partnership. Ann contributed $10,000 and Bob contributed $50,000. They agreed to share profits and losses equally. The partnership agreement provided that, upon liquidation, all partners must restore negative capital account balances and that liquidating distributions would be made based on capital account balances.

The partnership purchased a building for $100,000. It paid $60,000 and obtained a $40,000 recourse loan for the remaining purchase price. Prepare a balance sheet to reflect the situation of the partners and the partnership after purchase of the building.

Ann and Bob's basis depends, in part, on their share of partnership liabilities. The partnership's $40,000 liability is a recourse liability to the extent that any partner bears the economic risk of loss for that liability or would be obligated to contribute to the partnership to satisfy the liability. (Treas. Reg. § 1.752-1(a)(1)) To ascertain whether Ann or Bob bears the economic risk of loss, the partnership must go though the constructive liquidation of the doomsday scenario. (Treas. Reg. § 1.752-2(b))

First, the partnership is constructively liquidated. As part of the liquidation, the $40,000 obligation becomes due. Considering fair market, or book, value, the partnership sells the building for nothing. The tax consequences from the sale are as follows:

Amount realized:	$ 0
Book basis:	100,000
Loss:	<$100,000>

The $100,000 book loss is allocated equally between Ann and Bob, or <$50,000> each. The impact to Ann and Bob's capital accounts would be as follows:

	Ann	Bob
Capital account on formation:	$10,000	$50,000
Loss from sale of building:	<50,000>	<50,000>
Balance:	<$40,000>	$ 0

The partnership liquidates. Since a negative capital account represents the amount a partner must contribute to the partnership upon liquidation, Ann would have an obligation to contribute $40,000 and Bob would have no obligation to make a contribution. Ann's contribution of $40,000 would be used to satisfy the $40,000 debt.

The liability is a recourse liability because one or more partners bears the economic risk of loss. (Treas. Reg. §§ 1.752-1(a)(1); 1.752-2(a)) Specifically, Ann bears an economic risk of loss of $40,000. Their basis would be determined as follows (Sections 722; 752(a)):

	Ann	Bob
Cash:	$10,000	$50,000
Increase in liabilities:	40,000	0
Basis:	$50,000	$50,000

After purchase of the building, the balance sheet would appear as follows:

Asset	Adj. Basis	FMV	Liabilities:		$ 40,000
Building	$100,000	$100,000		Adj. Basis	Cap. Acct.
			Ann:	$ 50,000	$ 10,000
			Bob:	50,000	50,000
Total:	$100,000	$100,000		$100,000	$100,000

2.   Carl and Deb formed a general partnership. They each contributed $20,000. They agreed to allocate profits and losses 40 percent to Carl and 60 percent to Deb. The partnership agreement provided that, upon liquidation, all partners must restore negative capital account balances and that liquidating distributions would be made based on capital account balances.

The partnership purchased a building for $50,000. It paid $40,000 and obtained a $10,000 recourse loan for the remaining purchase price. Prepare a balance sheet to reflect the situation of the partners and the partnership after purchase of the building.

Carl and Deb's basis depends, in part, on their share of partnership liabilities. The partnership's $10,000 liability is a recourse liability to the extent that any partner bears the economic risk of loss for that liability or would be obligated to contribute to the partnership to satisfy the liability. (Treas. Reg. § 1.752-1(a)(1)) To ascertain whether Carl or Deb bears the economic risk of loss, the partnership must go though the constructive liquidation of the doomsday scenario. (Treas. Reg. § 1.752-2(b))

First, the partnership is constructively liquidated. As part of the liquidation, the $10,000 obligation becomes due. Considering fair market, or book, value, the partnership sells the building for nothing. The tax consequences from the sale are as follows:

Amount realized: $ 0
Book basis: 50,000
Loss: <$50,000>

The $50,000 book loss is allocated 40 percent to Carl and 60 percent to Deb, or $20,000 to Carl and $30,000 to Deb. The impact to Carl and Deb's capital accounts would be as follows:

	Carl	Deb
Capital account on formation:	$20,000	$20,000
Loss from sale of building:	<20,000>	<30,000>
Balance:	$ 0	<$10,000>

The partnership liquidates. Since a negative capital account represents the amount a partner must contribute to the partnership upon liquidation, Deb would have an obligation to contribute $10,000 and Carl would have no obligation to make a contribution. Deb's contribution of $10,000 would be used to satisfy the $10,000 debt.

The liability is a recourse liability because one or more partners bears the economic risk of loss. (Treas. Reg. §§ 1.752-1(a)(1); 1.752-2(a)) Specifically, Deb bears an economic risk of loss of $10,000. Their basis would be determined as follows (Sections 722; 752(a)):

	Carl	Deb
Cash:	$20,000	$20,000
Increase in liabilities:	0	10,000
Basis:	$20,000	$30,000

After purchase of the building, the balance sheet would appear as follows:

Asset	Adj. Basis	FMV	Liabilities:		$10,000
Building	$50,000	$50,000		Adj. Basis	Cap. Acct.
			Carl:	$20,000	$20,000
			Deb:	30,000	20,000
Total:	$50,000	$50,000		$50,000	$50,000

3. Ellen and Frank formed a general partnership. Ellen contributed $1,000 and Frank contributed $9,000. They agreed to share profits and losses equally. The partnership agreement provided that, upon liquidation, all partners must restore negative capital account balances and liquidating distributions would be made based on capital account balances.

The partnership purchased a building for $100,000. It paid $10,000 and obtained a $90,000 recourse loan for the remaining purchase price. Prepare a balance sheet to reflect the situation of the partners and the partnership after purchase of the building.

Ellen and Frank's basis depends, in part, on their share of partnership liabilities. The partnership's $90,000 liability is a recourse liability to the extent that any partner bears the economic risk of loss for that liability or would be obligated to contribute to the partnership to satisfy the liability. (Treas. Reg. § 1.752-1(a)(1)) To ascertain whether Ellen or Frank bears the economic risk of loss, the partnership must go though the constructive liquidation of the doomsday scenario. (Treas. Reg. § 1.752-2(b))

First, the partnership is constructively liquidated. As part of the liquidation, the $90,000 obligation becomes due. Considering fair market, or book, value, the partnership sells the building for nothing. The tax consequences from the sale are as follows:

Amount realized:	0
Book basis:	100,000
Loss:	<$100,000>

The $100,000 book loss is allocated equally to Ellen and Frank, or $50,00 each. The impact to Ellen and Frank's capital accounts would be as follows:

	Ellen	Frank
Capital account on formation:	$ 1,000	$ 9,000
Loss from sale of building:	<50,000>	<50,000>
Balance:	<$49,000>	<$41,000>

The partnership liquidates. Since a negative capital account represents the amount a partner must contribute to the partnership upon liquidation, Ellen would have an obligation to contribute $49,000 and Frank would have an obligation to contribute $41,000. Their contributions, totaling $90,000, would be used to satisfy the $90,000 debt.

The liability is a recourse liability because one or more partners bears the economic risk of loss. (Treas. Reg. §§ 1.752-1(a)(1); 1.752-2(a)) Specifically, Ellen bears an economic risk of loss of $49,000 and Frank bears an economic risk of loss of $41,000. Their basis would be determined as follows (Sections 722; 752(a)):

	Ellen	Frank
Cash:	$ 1,000	$ 9,000
Increase in liabilities:	49,000	41,000
Basis:	$50,000	$50,000

After purchase of the building, the balance sheet would appear as follows:

Asset	Adj. Basis	FMV	Liabilities:		$ 90,000
Building	$100,000	$100,000		Adj. Basis	Cap. Acct.
			Ellen:	$ 50,000	$ 1,000
			Frank:	50,000	9,000
Total:	$100,000	$100,000		$100,000	$100,000

4.   Greg and Hal formed a general partnership. Greg contributed $30,000 and Hal contributed $10,000. They agreed to share profits and losses equally. The partnership agreement provided that, upon liquidation, all partners must restore negative capital account balances and liquidating distributions would be made based on capital account balances.

The partnership purchased a building for $50,000. It paid $40,000 and obtained a $10,000 recourse loan for the remaining purchase price. Prepare a balance sheet to reflect the situation of the partners and the partnership after purchase of the building.

Greg and Hal's basis depends, in part, on their share of partnership liabilities. The partnership's $10,000 liability is a recourse liability to the extent that any partner bears the economic risk of loss for that liability or would be obligated to contribute to the partnership to satisfy the liability. (Treas. Reg. § 1.752-1(a)(1)) To ascertain whether Greg or Hal bears the economic risk of loss, the partnership must go though the constructive liquidation of the doomsday scenario. (Treas. Reg. § 1.752-2(b))

First, the partnership is constructively liquidated. As part of the liquidation, the $10,000 obligation becomes due. Considering fair market, or book, value, the partnership sells the building for nothing. The tax consequences from the sale are as follows:

Amount realized:	$ 0
Book basis:	50,000
Loss:	<$50,000>

The $50,000 book loss is allocated equally to Greg and Hal, or $25,000 each. The impact to Greg and Hal's capital accounts would be as follows:

	Greg	Hal
Capital account on formation:	$30,000	$10,000
Loss from sale of building:	<25,000>	<25,000>
Balance:	$ 5,000	<$15,000>

The partnership liquidates. Since a negative capital account represents the amount a partner must contribute to the partnership upon liquidation, Hal has an obligation to contribute $15,000 to the partnership. However, only $10,000 of that amount would be used to satisfy the $10,000 debt; the remaining $5,000 would be distributed to Greg in satisfaction of his capital account balance. Thus, the liability is a recourse liability because one or more partners bears the economic risk of loss. (Treas. Reg. §§ 1.752-1(a)(1); 1.752-2(a)) Specifically, Hal bears an economic risk of loss of the $10,000 liability and Greg and Hal's basis would be determined as follows (Sections 722; 752(a)):

	Greg	Hal
Cash:	$30,000	$10,000
Increase in liabilities:	0	10,000
Basis:	$30,000	$20,000

After purchase of the building, the balance sheet would appear as follows:

Asset	Adj. Basis	FMV	Liabilities:		$10,000
Building	$50,000	$50,000		Adj. Basis	Cap. Acct.
			Greg:	$30,000	$30,000
			Hal:	20,000	10,000
Total:	$50,000	$50,000		$50,000	$50,000

5.   Ira and Jeb formed a limited partnership. Ira contributed $50,000 in exchange for a general partnership interest, and Jeb contributed $50,000 in exchange for a limited partnership interest. The partnership agreement provided that profits and losses would be divided equally between the partners and that, upon liquidation, only Ira had an obligation to restore a negative capital account balance. Jeb was not required to restore any deficit balance in his account, but the partnership agreement contained a qualified income offset with respect to him.

The partnership purchased a building for $150,000. It paid $100,000 and obtained a $50,000 recourse loan for the remaining purchase price. Prepare a balance sheet to reflect the situation of the partners and the partnership after purchase of the building.

Ira and Jeb's basis depends, in part, on their share of partnership liabilities. The partnership's $50,000 liability is a recourse liability to the extent that any partner bears the economic risk of loss for that liability or would be obligated to contribute to the partnership to satisfy the liability. (Treas. Reg. § 1.752-1(a)(1)) To ascertain whether Ira or Jeb bears the economic risk of loss, the partnership must go though the constructive liquidation of the doomsday scenario. (Treas. Reg. § 1.752-2(b))

First, the partnership is constructively liquidated. As part of the liquidation, the $50,000 obligation becomes due. Considering fair market, or book, value, the partnership sells the building for nothing. The tax consequences from the sale are as follows:

Amount realized:	$	0
Book basis:		$150,000
Loss:		<$150,000>

The $150,000 book loss is allocated equally between Ira and Jeb, or $75,000 loss each. The impact to the partners' capital accounts would be as follows:

	Ira	Jeb
Capital account on formation:	$50,000	$50,000
Loss from sale of building:	<75,000>	<75,000>
Balance:	<$25,000>	<$25,000>

Because Jeb does not have an obligation to restore a negative capital account balance, the allocation to him would not have economic effect. (Treas. Reg. § 1.704-1(b)(2)(ii)(*d*)(3)) Accordingly, the loss must be reallocated in accordance with the partners' interests in the partnership. (Treas. Reg. § 1.704-1(b)(3))

Because the first two elements of the alternate economic effect test were met, the partner's interest in the partnership is determined using a comparative liquidation test. (Treas. Reg. § 1.704-1(b)(3)(iii)) Only $50,000 of loss can be allocated to Jeb. The remaining $25,000 must be re-allocated to Ira, in accordance with the partners' interests in the partnership. Thus, the impact to the partners' capital accounts would be as follows:

	Ira	Jeb
Capital account on formation:	$ 50,000	$50,000
Loss from sale of building:	<100,000>	<50,000>
Balance:	<$ 50,000>	$ 0

The partnership liquidates. Since a negative capital account represents the amount a partner must contribute to the partnership upon liquidation, Ira would have an obligation to contribute $50,000 to the partnership. This $50,000 would then be used to satisfy the $50,000 debt.

The liability is a recourse liability because one or more partners bears the economic risk of loss. (Treas. Reg. §§ 1.752-1(a)(1); 1.752-2(a)) Specifically, Ira bears the economic risk of loss. The partners' basis would be determined as follows (Sections 722; 752(a)):

	Ira	Jeb
Cash:	$ 50,000	$50,000
Increase in liabilities:	50,000	0
Basis:	$100,000	$50,000

After purchase of the building, the balance sheet would appear as follows:

Asset	Adj. Basis	FMV	Liabilities:		$ 50,000
Building	$150,000	$150,000		Adj. Basis	Cap. Acct.
Total:	$150,000	$150,000	Ira:	$100,000	$ 50,000
			Jeb:	50,000	50,000
				$150,000	$150,000

6.   Kent and Len formed a general partnership. Kent contributed $1,000 and Len contributed $9,000. They agreed to share profits and losses equally. The partnership agreement provided that, upon liquidation, all partners must restore negative capital account balances and liquidating distributions would be made based on capital account balances.

The partnership purchased a building for $100,000. It paid $10,000 and obtained a $90,000 recourse loan for the remaining purchase price. Kent executed a personal guaranty for the $90,000 liability. Prepare a balance sheet to reflect the situation of the partners and the partnership after purchase of the building.

Kent and Len's basis depends, in part, on their share of partnership liabilities. The partnership's $90,000 liability is a recourse liability to the extent that any partner bears the economic risk of loss for that liability or would be obligated to contribute to the partnership to satisfy the liability. (Treas. Reg. § 1.752-1(a)(1)) To ascertain whether Kent or Len bears the economic risk of loss, the partnership must go though the constructive liquidation of the doomsday scenario. (Treas. Reg. § 1.752-2(b))

First, the partnership is constructively liquidated. As part of the liquidation, the $90,000 obligation becomes due. Considering fair market, or book, value, the partnership sells the building for nothing. The tax consequences from the sale are as follows:

Amount realized:	0
Book basis:	100,000
Loss:	<$100,000>

The $100,000 book loss is allocated equally to Kent and Len, or $50,000 each. The impact to Kent and Len's capital accounts would be as follows:

	Kent	Len
Capital account on formation:	$ 1,000	$ 9,000
Loss from sale of building:	<50,000>	<50,000>
Balance:	<$49,000>	<$41,000>

The partnership liquidates. Since a negative capital account represents the amount a partner must contribute to the partnership upon liquidation, Kent would have an obligation to contribute $49,000 and Len would have an obligation to contribute $41,000. Because the partnership now has $90,000 to satisfy the debt, Kent will not be called upon to pay the debt pursuant to his guaranty. (See Treas. Reg. § 1.752-2(b)(6)) Their contributions, totaling $90,000, would be used to satisfy the $90,000 debt.

The liability is a recourse liability because one or more partners bears the economic risk of loss. (Treas. Reg. §§ 1.752-1(a)(1); 1.752-2(a)) Specifically, Kent bears an economic risk of loss of $49,000 and Len bears an economic risk of loss of $41,000. Their basis would be determined as follows (Sections 722; 752(a)):

	Kent	Len
Cash:	$ 1,000	$ 9,000
Increase in liabilities:	49,000	41,000
Basis:	$50,000	$50,000

After purchase of the building, the balance sheet would appear as follows:

Asset	Adj. Basis	FMV	Liabilities:		$ 90,000
Building	$100,000	$100,000		Adj. Basis	Cap. Acct.
			Kent:	$ 50,000	$ 1,000
			Len:	50,000	9,000
Total:	$100,000	$100,000		$100,000	$100,000

7.   Mike and Ned formed a limited partnership. Mike contributed $50,000 in exchange for a general partnership interest, and Ned contributed $50,000 in exchange for a limited partnership interest. Ned also contributed a $10,000 promissory note. The partnership agreement provided that profits and losses would be divided equally between the partners and that, upon liquidation, only Mike had an obligation to restore a negative capital account balance. Ned was not required to restore any deficit balance in his account, but the partnership agreement contained a qualified income offset with respect to him.

The partnership purchased a building for $150,000. It paid $100,000 and obtained a $50,000 recourse loan for the remaining purchase price. Prepare a balance sheet to reflect the situation of the partners and the partnership after purchase of the building.

Mike and Ned's basis depends, in part, on their share of partnership liabilities. The partnership's $50,000 liability is a recourse liability to the extent that any partner bears the economic risk of loss for that liability or would be obligated to contribute to the partnership to satisfy the liability. (Treas. Reg. § 1.752-1(a)(1)) To ascertain whether Mike or Ned bears the economic risk of loss, the partnership must go though the constructive liquidation of the doomsday scenario. (Treas. Reg. § 1.752-2(b))

First, the partnership is constructively liquidated. As part of the liquidation, the $50,000 obligation becomes due. Considering fair market, or book, value, the partnership sells the building for nothing. The tax consequences from the sale are as follows:

Amount realized:	0
Book basis:	$150,000
Loss:	<$150,000>

The $150,000 book loss is allocated equally between Mike and Ned, or $75,000 loss each. The impact to the partners' capital accounts would be as follows:

	Mike	Ned
Capital account on formation:	$50,000	$50,000
Loss from sale of building:	<75,000>	<75,000>
Balance:	<$25,000>	<$25,000>

Because Ned does not have an obligation to restore a negative capital account balance, the allocation to him would not have economic effect. (Treas. Reg. § 1.704-1(b)(2)(ii)(d)(3)) However, because his promissory note is treated as an obligation to contribute to the partnership, Ned's capital account can be negative to the extent of the outstanding amount of the note. (Treas. Reg. § 1.704-1(b)(2)(ii)(c)) Thus, the allocation of $75,000 of loss to Ned satisfies the alternate economic effect test only to the extent of $60,000. The additional loss must be reallocated in accordance with the partners' interests in the partnership. (Treas. Reg. § 1.704-1(b)(3))

Because the first two elements of the alternate economic effect test were met, the partner's interest in the partnership is determined using a comparative liquidation test. (Treas. Reg. § 1.704-1(b)(3)(iii)) The remaining $15,000 of loss must be re-allocated to Mike.

With the loss reallocated, the capital accounts would appear as follows:

	Mike	Ned
Capital account on formation:	$50,000	$50,000
Loss from sale of building:	<90,000>	<60,000>
Balance:	<$40,000>	<$10,000>

The partnership liquidates. Since a negative capital account represents the amount a partner must contribute to the partnership upon liquidation, Mike would have an obligation to contribute $40,000 to the partnership and Ned would have an obligation to contribute $10,000 (the amount of his promissory note). This $50,000 would then be used to satisfy the $50,000 debt.

The liability is a recourse liability because one or more partners bears the economic risk of loss. (Treas. Reg. §§ 1.752-1(a)(1); 1.752-2(a)) Specifically, Mike bears an economic risk of loss of $40,000 and Ned bears an economic risk of loss of $10,000. The partners' basis would be determined as follows (Sections 722; 752(a)):

	Mike	Ned
Cash:	$50,000	$50,000
Increase in liabilities:	40,000	10,000
Basis:	$90,000	$60,000

After purchase of the building, the balance sheet would appear as follows:

Asset	Adj. Basis	FMV	Liabilities:		$ 50,000
Building	$150,000	$150,000		Adj. Basis	Cap. Acct.
Total:	$150,000	$150,000	Mike:	$ 90,000	$ 50,000
			Ned:	60,000	50,000
				$150,000	$150,000

8.   Opie and Paul formed a limited partnership. Opie contributed $20,000 in exchange for a general partnership interest, and Paul contributed $80,000 in exchange for a limited partnership interest. The partnership agreement provided that capital accounts would be maintained in accordance with the regulations, that Opie had an obligation to restore a negative capital account, and that liquidating distributions would be made in accordance with capital account balances. Paul was not required to restore any deficit balance in his account, but the partnership agreement contained a qualified income offset with respect to him. The partnership agreement also contained a minimum gain chargeback provision. It provided that any excess non-recourse debt be allocated 30 percent to Opie and 70 percent to Paul. Finally, the partnership agreement allocated all depreciation 20 percent to Opie and 80 percent to Paul and also allocated all non-recourse deductions 30 percent to Opie and 70 percent to Paul until the first time the partnership recognized items of income and gain that exceeded the items of loss and deduction it had recognized over its life. Then, all further depreciation deductions would be allocated equally between Opie and Paul.

The partnership purchased a building for $300,000, using the $100,000 cash contributed by the partners and financing the remaining $200,000 with a non-recourse debt, secured by the building. No payments were due on the loan for five years. Ignoring all conventions, in each year the partnership was entitled to $50,000 of depreciation.

In each year, before taking into consideration the depreciation, partnership income was equal to its expenses.

    a. What is each partner's basis at the end of the first year? Create a balance sheet to reflect the situation of the partners and partnership.

No partner bears the economic risk of loss with respect to the debt. (Treas. Reg. § 1.752-1(a)(2)) If necessary, the partnership could go through the doomsday scenario which would establish that no one is liable for the debt. Accordingly, the debt is a non-recourse debt.

At the end of the first year, the situation of the partnership is as follows:

Building		PMG	
Basis:	$300,000	Debt:	$200,000
Depr. (Yr. 1):	50,000	AB:	250,000
AB:	$250,000	PMG:	$ 0

The depreciation is not a non-recourse deduction. (Because there is no partnership minimum gain, there cannot be a non-recourse deduction. (Treas. Reg. § 1.704-2(c), -2(d)(1)) The depreciation deduction as allocated as follows:

Opie => 20 percent => $10,000
Paul => 80 percent => $40,000

Their capital accounts would be as follows:

	Opie	Paul
Cash:	$20,000	$ 80,000
Depreciation:	<10,000>	<40,000>
Balance:	$10,000	$40,000

The allocations are respected because the general and alternate tests have been met; the allocations have substantial economic effect. (Treas. Reg. § 1.704-1(b)(2)(ii)(b), (d))

Because there is no partnership minimum gain and no *Tufts*, or phantom, gain, to determine the impact of the debt on the partners' basis, the allocation of the non-recourse debt is made under the third tier. Based on the partnership agreement, third tier allocations are allocated 30 percent to Opie and 70 percent to Paul, or $60,000 to Opie and $140,000 to Paul. The allocation will be respect because it is reasonably consistent with an allocation (having substantial economic effect) of any significant item of partnership income or gain. (Treas. Reg. § 1.752-3(a)(3))

Their basis would be determined as follows (Sections 722; 752(a)):

	Opie	Paul
Cash:	$20,000	$ 80,000
Increase in liabilities:	60,000	140,000
Depreciation:	<10,000>	< 40,000>
Adj. basis:	$70,000	$180,000

At the end of the first year, the balance sheet would appear as follows:

Asset	Adj. Basis	FMV	Liabilities:		$200,000	
Building	$250,000	$250,000		Adj. Basis	Cap. Acct.	
			Opie:	$ 70,000	$ 10,000	
			Paul:	180,000	40,000	
Total:	$250,000	$250,000		$250,000	$250,000	

b. What is each partner's basis at the end of the second year? Create a balance sheet to reflect the situation of the partners and partnership.

At the end of the second year, the situation of the partnership is as follows:

Building			**PMG**	
Basis:	$250,000		debt:	$200,000
Depr. (Yr. 1):	50,000		AB:	200,000
AB:	$200,000		PMG:	$ 0

The depreciation is not a non-recourse deduction. (Because there is no partnership minimum gain, there cannot be a non-recourse deduction. (Treas. Reg. § 1.704-2(c), -2(d)(1)) The depreciation deduction as allocated as follows:

Opie => 20 percent => $10,000
Paul => 80 percent => $40,000

Their capital accounts would be as follows:

	Opie	Paul
Beginning balance:	$10,000	$40,000
Depreciation:	<10,000>	<40,000>
Balance:	$ 0	$ 0

The allocations are respected because the general and alternate tests have been met; the allocations have substantial economic effect. (Treas. Reg. § 1.704-1(b)(2)(ii)(*b*), (*d*))

Because there is no partnership minimum gain and no *Tufts*, or phantom, gain, to determine the impact of the debt on the partners' basis, the allocation of the non-recourse debt is still made under the third tier. Their basis is adjusted as follows (Sections 722; 752(a)):

	Opie	Paul
Beginning basis:	$70,000	$180,000
Depreciation:	<10,000>	<40,000>
Adj. basis:	$60,000	$140,000

At the end of the second year, the balance sheet would appear as follows:

Asset	Adj. Basis	FMV	Liabilities:		$200,000	
Building	$200,000	$200,000		Adj. Basis	Cap. Acct.	
			Opie:	$ 60,000	$ 0	
			Paul:	140,000	0	
Total:	$200,000	$200,000		$200,000	$200,000	

c. What is each partner's basis at the end of the third year? Create a balance sheet to reflect the situation of the partners and partnership.

At the end of the third year, the situation of the partnership is as follows:

Building		PMG	
Basis:	$200,000	debt:	$200,000
Depr. (Yr. 1):	50,000	AB:	150,000
AB:	$150,000	PMG:	$ 50,000

The depreciation is a non-recourse deduction. Because PMG has increased by $50,000, there is a $50,000 non-recourse deduction. (Treas. Reg. § 1.704-2(c), -2(d)(1)) Non-recourse deductions are allocated as follows:

Opie => 30 percent => $15,000
Paul => 70 percent => $35,000

Their capital accounts would be as follows:

	Opie	Paul
Beginning balance:	$ 0	$ 0
Depreciation:	<15,000>	<35,000>
Balance:	<$15,000>	<$35,000>

To the extent Paul, the limited partner, has a negative capital account, he is treated as having an obligation to restore, to the extent of his share of partnership minimum gain. (Treas. Reg. § 1.704-2(g)(1) flush language) His share of partnership minimum gain is $35,000. Thus, the allocation has substantial economic effect and will be respected.

For purposes of determining the impact of the debt on the partners' basis, now that there is partnership minimum gain, there is an amount allocated under the first tier. Of the non-recourse debt, $15,000 is allocated to Opie and $35,000 to Paul. (Treas. Reg. § 1.752-3(a)(1)) There is no *Tufts*, or phantom, gain. Thus, the remaining amount of debt is allocated under the third tier. (Treas. Reg. § 1.752-3(a)(3)) Based on the partnership agreement, third tier allocations are 30 percent to Opie and 70 percent to Paul. Thus, the remaining $150,000 ($200,000, less $50,000 allocated under the first tier) is allocated $45,000 to Opie and $105,000 to Paul.

	Opie	Paul
First tier:	$15,000	$ 35,000
Second tier:	0	0
Third tier:	45,000	105,000
Total debt:	$60,000	$140,000

Note that, because the percentage allocations in the first and third tier are the same, there is no net change in the allocation of the non-recourse debt.

Their basis would be determined as follows (Sections 722; 752(a)):

	Opie	Paul
Beginning basis:	$60,000	$140,000
Depreciation:	<15,000>	<35,000>
Adj. basis:	$45,000	$105,000

At the end of the third year, the balance sheet would appear as follows:

Asset	Adj. Basis	FMV	Liabilities:		$200,000
Building	$150,000	$150,000		Adj. Basis	Cap. Acct.
			Opie:	$ 45,000	<$15,000>
			Paul:	105,000	<35,000>
Total:	$150,000	$150,000		$150,000	$150,000

Note that this result makes sense. If the partnership sold the building for the least amount possible, the amount of the debt, it would have $50,000 of gain.

AR:	$200,000 (debt)
AB:	150,000
Gain:	$ 50,000

Under the minimum gain chargeback provisions, $15,000 of the gain would be allocated to Opie (his share of partnership minimum gain) and $35,000 to Paul (his share of partnership minimum gain). After adjustments are made to their capital accounts for the gain, each would have a zero capital account balance.

	Opie	Paul
Capital account:	<$15,000>	<$35,000>
Gain:	15,000	35,000
Balance:	$ 0	$ 0

9. Quinn and Roy formed a limited partnership. Quinn contributed $20,000 in exchange for a general partnership interest, and Roy contributed $80,000 in exchange for a limited partnership interest. The partnership agreement provided that capital accounts would be maintained in accordance with the regulations, that Quinn had an obligation to restore a negative capital account, and that liquidating distributions would be made in accordance with capital account balances. Roy was not required to restore any deficit balance in his account, but the partnership agreement contained a qualified income offset with respect to him. The partnership agreement also contained a minimum gain chargeback provision. It provided that any excess non-recourse debt be allocated equally between Quinn and Roy. Finally, the partnership agreement allocated all depreciation 20 percent to Quinn and 80 percent to Roy and allocated all non-recourse deductions 30 percent to Quinn and 70 percent to Roy until the first time the partnership recognized items of income and gain that exceeded the items of loss and deduction it had recognized over its life. Then, all further depreciation deductions would be allocated equally between Quinn and Roy.

The partnership purchased a building for $300,000, using the $100,000 cash contributed by the partners and financing the remaining $200,000 with a non-recourse debt, secured by the building. No payments were due on the loan for five years. Ignoring all conventions, in each year the partnership was entitled to $50,000 of depreciation. In each year, before taking into consideration the depreciation, partnership income was equal to its expenses.

a. What is each partner's basis at the end of the first year? Create a balance sheet to reflect the situation of the partners and partnership.

No partner bears the economic risk of loss with respect to the debt. (Treas. Reg. § 1.752-1(a)(2)) If necessary, the partnership could go through the doomsday scenario which would establish that no one is liable for the debt. Accordingly, the debt is a non-recourse debt.

At the end of the first year, the situation of the partnership is as follows:

Building		PMG	
Basis:	$300,000	Debt:	$200,000
Depr. (Yr. 1):	50,000	AB:	250,000
AB:	$250,000	PMG:	$ 0

The depreciation is not a non-recourse deduction. (Because there is no partnership minimum gain, there cannot be a non-recourse deduction. (Treas. Reg. § 1.704-2(c), -2(d)(1)) The depreciation deduction as allocated as follows:

Quinn => 20 percent => $10,000
Roy => 80 percent => $40,000

Their capital accounts would be as follows:

	Quinn	Roy
Cash:	$20,000	$80,000
Depreciation:	<10,000>	<40,000>
Balance:	$10,000	$40,000

The allocations are respected because the general and alternate tests have been met; the allocations have substantial economic effect. (Treas. Reg. § 1.704-1(b)(2)(ii)(*b*), (*d*))

Because there is no partnership minimum gain and no *Tufts*, or phantom, gain, to determine the impact of the debt on the partners' basis, the allocation of the non-recourse debt is made under the third tier. Based on the partnership agreement, third tier allocations are allocated equally, or $100,000 to each of Quinn and Roy. The allocation will be respect because it is reasonably consistent with an allocation (having substantial economic effect) of any significant item of partnership income or gain. (Treas. Reg. § 1.752-3(a)(3))

Their basis would be determined as follows (Sections 722; 752(a)):

	Quinn	Roy
Cash:	$ 20,000	$ 80,000
Increase in liabilities:	100,000	100,000
Depreciation:	<10,000>	<40,000>
Adj. basis:	$110,000	$140,000

At the end of the first year, the balance sheet would appear as follows:

Asset	Adj. Basis	FMV	Liabilities:		$200,000
Building	$250,000	$250,000		Adj. Basis	Cap. Acct.
			Quinn	$110,000	$ 10,000
			Roy	140,000	40,000
Total:	$250,000	$250,000		$250,000	$250,000

b. What is each partner's basis at the end of the second year? Create a balance sheet to reflect the situation of the partners and partnership.

At the end of the second year, the situation of the partnership is as follows:

Building			PMG		
Basis:	$250,000		Debt:	$200,000	
Depr. (Yr. 1):	50,000		AB:	200,000	
AB:	$200,000		PMG:	$ 0	

The depreciation is not a non-recourse deduction. (Because there is no partnership minimum gain, there cannot be a non-recourse deduction. (Treas. Reg. § 1.704-2(c), -2(d)(1)) The depreciation deduction as allocated as follows:

Quinn => 20 percent => $10,000
Roy => 80 percent => $40,000

Their capital accounts would be as follows:

	Quinn	Roy
Beginning balance:	$10,000	$ 40,000
Depreciation:	<10,000>	<40,000>
Balance:	$ 0	$ 0

The allocations are respected because the general and alternate tests have been met; the allocations have substantial economic effect. (Treas. Reg. § 1.704-1(b)(2)(ii)(b), (d))

Because there is no partnership minimum gain and no *Tufts*, or phantom, gain, to determine the impact of the debt on the partners' basis, the allocation of the non-recourse debt is still made under the third tier. Their basis is adjusted as follows (Sections 722; 752(a)):

	Quinn	Roy
Beginning basis:	$110,000	$140,000
Depreciation:	<10,000>	<40,000>
Adj. basis:	$100,000	$100,000

At the end of the second year, the balance sheet would appear as follows:

Asset	Adj. Basis	FMV	Liabilities:		$200,000	
Building	$200,000	$200,000		Adj. Basis	Cap. Acct.	
			Quinn:	$100,000	$ 0	
			Roy:	100,000	0	
Total:	$200,000	$200,000		$200,000	$200,000	

c. What is each partner's basis at the end of the third year? Create a balance sheet to reflect the situation of the partners and partnership.

At the end of the third year, the situation of the partnership is as follows:

Building		**PMG**	
Basis:	$200,000	Debt:	$200,000
Depr. (Yr. 1):	50,000	AB:	150,000
AB:	$150,000	PMG:	$ 50,000

The depreciation is a non-recourse deduction. Because PMG has increased by $50,000, there is a $50,000 non-recourse deduction. (Treas. Reg. §1.704-2(c), -2(d)(1)) Non-recourse deductions are allocated as follows:

Quinn => 30 percent => $15,000
Roy => 70 percent => $35,000

Their capital accounts would be as follows:

	Quinn	**Roy**
Beginning balance:	$ 0	$ 0
Depreciation:	<15,000>	<35,000>
Balance:	<$15,000>	<$35,000>

To the extent Roy, the limited partner, has a negative capital account, he is treated as having an obligation to restore, to the extent of his share of partnership minimum gain. (Treas. Reg. §1.704-2(g)(1) flush language) His share of partnership minimum gain is $35,000. Thus, the allocation has substantial economic effect and will be respected.

For purposes of determining the impact of the debt on the partners' basis, now that there is partnership minimum gain, there is an amount allocated under the first tier. Of the non-recourse debt, $15,000 is allocated to Quinn and $35,000 to Roy. (Treas. Reg. §1.752-3(a)(1)) There is no *Tufts*, or phantom, gain. Thus, the remaining amount of debt is allocated under the third tier. (Treas. Reg. §1.752-3(a)(3)) Based on the partnership agreement, third tier allocations are allocated equally between Quinn and Roy. Thus, the remaining $150,000 ($200,000, less $50,000 allocated under the first tier) is allocated $75,000 to each of Quinn and Roy.

	Quinn	**Roy**
First tier:	$15,000	$ 35,000
Second tier:	0	0
Third tier:	75,000	75,000
Total debt:	$90,000	$110,000

Because the allocation of the debt has changed, the basis needs to be adjusted accordingly. Their basis would be determined as follows (Sections 722; 752(a)):

	Quinn	**Roy**
Cash:	$20,000	$80,000
Debt:	90,000	110,000
First year depr.:	<10,000>	<40,000>
Second year depr.:	<10,000>	<40,000>
Third year depr.:	<15,000>	<35,000>
Adj. Basis:	$75,000	$75,000

At the end of the third year, the balance sheet would appear as follows:

Asset	Adj. Basis	FMV	Liabilities:			$200,000
Building	$150,000	$150,000			Adj. Basis	Cap. Acct.
				Quinn:	$ 75,000	<$15,000>
				Roy:	75,000	<35,000>
Total:	$150,000	$150,000			$150,000	$150,000

Note that this result makes sense. If the partnership sold the building for the least amount possible, the amount of the debt, it would have $50,000 of gain.

AR:	$200,000
AB:	150,000
Gain:	$ 50,000

Under the minimum gain chargeback provisions, $15,000 of the gain would be allocated to Quinn (his share of partnership minimum gain) and $35,000 of the gain would be allocated to Roy (his share of partnership minimum gain). After adjustments are made to their capital accounts for the gain, each would have a zero capital account balance.

	Quinn	Roy
Capital account:	<$15,000>	<$35,000>
Gain:	15,000	35,000
Balance:	$ 0	$ 0

10. **Sam and Tess formed a general partnership. Sam contributed $75,000. Tess contributed land with a fair market value of $100,000 and basis of $20,000. The land was subject to a $25,000 non-recourse debt, and the debt was assumed by the partnership.**

The partnership agreement provided that capital accounts would be maintained in accordance with the regulations, that the partners have an obligation to restore a negative capital account, and that liquidating distributions would be made in accordance with capital account balances. The partnership agreement also contained a minimum gain chargeback provision. It provided that any excess non-recourse debt would be allocated equally between the partners.

Create a balance sheet to reflect the situation of the partners and partnership.

No partner bears the economic risk of loss with respect to the debt. (Treas. Reg. § 1.752-1(a)(2)) If necessary, the partnership could go through the doomsday scenario which would establish that no one is liable for the debt. Accordingly, the debt is a non-recourse debt.

At formation, the situation of the partnership is as follows:

Land		PMG		*Tufts* gain	
Book basis: $100,000	Debt:	$ 25,000	Debt:	$25,000
	Book AB:	100,000	AB:	20,000
	PMG:	$ 0	gain:	$ 5,000

For purposes of determining the impact of the debt on the partners' basis, there is no partnership minimum gain to be allocated under the first tier. (Treas. Reg. § 1.752-3(a)(1))

The second tier takes into consideration the minimum amount of *Tufts*, or phantom, built-in gain that will be allocated to the partner upon sale of the property. (Treas. Reg. § 1.752-3(a)(2)) Because the property can never be disposed of for less than the amount of the non-recourse liability, the minimum amount of gain is the excess of the liability over the adjusted basis, or $5,000 (the excess of $25,000 over $20,000). Accordingly, $5,000 of the liability is allocated to Tess, the contributing partner.

The third tier is the remaining $20,000 ($25,000 debt, less $5,000 allocated under the second tier.) (Treas. Reg. § 1.752-3(a)(3)) It is allocated equally between Sam and Tess, or $10,000 each.

The debt is allocated as follows:

	Sam	Tess
First tier:	$ 0	$ 0
Second tier:	0	5,000
Third tier:	10,000	10,000
Total debt:	$10,000	$15,000

Tess also has debt relief of $25,000 upon contribution of the property to the partnership. Accordingly, the net change in her liabilities is <$10,000> ($15,000 less $25,000). (Treas. Reg. § 1.752-1(f))

Their basis would be determined as follows (Sections 722; 752(a)):

	Sam	Tess
Cash:	$75,000	$ —
Property:		20,000
Debt:	10,000	<10,000>
Adj. Basis:	$85,000	$10,000

On formation, the balance sheet would appear as follows:

Asset	Adj. Basis	FMV	Liabilities:		$ 25,000
Cash	$75,000	$ 75,000		Adj. Basis	Cap. Acct.
Land	20,000	100,000	Sam:	$85,000	$ 75,000
			Tess:	10,000	75,000
Total:	$95,000	$175,000		$95,000	$175,000

Chapter VII

Transfer of a Partnership Interest

A. Tax Consequences to the Transferring Partner

1. General Rule

Character of gain. In general, the disposition of a partnership interest is treated as a disposition of a capital asset. Any gain is a capital gain and any loss is a capital loss.[1]

Holding period of partnership interest. Recall that the holding period of the partnership interest may depend on the assets contributed to the partnership. The partner's holding period in the asset contributed to the partnership tacks onto his holding period of his partnership interest if the asset is a capital asset or hotchpot (Section 1231) asset. The holding period does not tack if the partner contributes cash or ordinary income assets; the holding period begins the day following contribution.[2] If a partner contributes assets whose holding period tacks and those that do not, the holding period will be divided between the two.[3] For purposes of this determination, Section 1245 recapture gain is not treated as a capital or hotchpot (Section 1231) asset. The length of time the partnership interest was held determines whether the gain or loss on disposition is long-term or short-term.

The characterization provisions apply to the partner's total gain or loss on disposition. Note that the amount realized includes any debt relief[4] and the adjusted basis includes any adjustments to the partner's outside basis that reflect his pro rata distribution of partnership items up to the time of sale.[5]

---

1. Section 741.
2. Section 1223(1).
3. Treas. Reg. § 1.1223-3(a)(2).
4. Section 752(d).
5. Section 705.

2. Exceptions to the General Rule

a. Hot Assets

While the general rule is that gain from the disposition of a partnership interest is capital gain, this result allowed taxpayers to convert what would have been ordinary income into capital gain.

Example: Ann became a partner in the partnership five years ago by contributing $100,000 in exchange for a 10-percent general partnership interest. The partnership is a cash basis taxpayer that holds only accounts receivable. Ann's proportionate share of the partnership accounts receivable is $10,000. Her outside basis currently is $100,000.

If Ann waits until the partnership collects the accounts receivable, she would be required to report $10,000 of ordinary income.

In contrast, under the general rule, if Ann sold his partnership interest for $110,000, she would realize and recognize $10,000 of gain (amount realized of $110,000, less adjusted basis of $100,000). Under the general rule, the gain would be long-term capital gain. Effectively, Ann would have been able to convert what would have been ordinary income into long-term capital gain. Section 751(a) prohibits this result.

The statutory provisions return to an aggregate approach, in part, to determine the character of gain or loss when a partner sells all or a portion of his partnership interest. To determine the portion of the gain or loss that must be rechacterized as ordinary, first determine whether the partnership has any unrealized receivables or inventory items. Sometimes, unrealized receivables and inventory are referred to as "hot assets."

Unrealized receivables. Unrealized receivables include, to the extent not previously included in income, any right to payment for services rendered. They also include the right to payment for goods delivered to the extent the proceeds would be treated as amounts received from the sale or exchange of property other than a capital asset. They also include any gain that would be characterized as ordinary income under the depreciation recapture provisions.[6]

Example: The partnership holds only accounts receivable. If the partnership is a cash method taxpayer, the accounts receivable are unrealized receivables. In contrast, if the partnership is an accrual method taxpayer, the accounts receivable are not unrealized receivables.

Inventory items. Inventory includes those assets held for sale to customers and any items held by the partnership that are not characterized as a capital or hotchpot (Section 1231) item.[7]

If an item comes within the definition of both unrealized receivables and inventory items, it is considered only once.

---

6. Section 751(c).

7. Section 751(d). It also includes any property that, if held by the selling partner, would be inventory. Section 751(d)(3).

Example: The partnership is a cash basis partnership that develops lots for sale to customers. Its balance sheet appears as follows:

Asset	Adj. Basis	FMV	Partners	Adj. Basis	Cap. Acct
Cash	$ 3,000	$ 3,000	Bob	$10,000	$20,000
Acct. Rec.	0	14,000	Carl	10,000	20,000
Lots for sale	10,000	20,000		$20,000	$40,000
Land	7,000	3,000			
Total:	$20,000	$40,000			

The accounts receivable come within the definition of unrealized receivables. Both the lots held for sale and the accounts receivable come within the definition of inventory. However, the accounts receivable are considered only once.

In contrast, if the partnership were an accrual basis method taxpayer, its balance sheet would appear as follows:

Asset	Adj. Basis	FMV	Partners	Adj. Basis	Cap. Acct.
Cash	$ 3,000	$ 3,000	Bob	$17,000	$20,000
Acct. Rec.	14,000	14,000	Carl	17,000	20,000
Lots for sale	10,000	20,000		$34,000	$40,000
Land	7,000	3,000			
Total:	$34,000	$40,000			

The accounts receivable do not come within the definition of unrealized receivables. The lots held for sale and the accounts receivable both come within the definition of inventory.

Determination of gain or loss allocable to unrealized receivables and inventory items. To determine how much gain or loss must be recharacterized as ordinary, determine how much gain or loss the partner would have if all unrealized receivables and inventory items were sold for their fair market value and an allocable share allocated to the selling partner.[8] In determining the amount of gain or loss allocable to the partner, take into consideration any special allocations and any allocations required by Section 704(c) (addressing built-in gains and losses), including any remedial allocations. To that extent, the gain or loss is characterized as ordinary income or loss.

Finally, determine the amount necessary so that, when added to the amount of ordinary income, it results in the amount of gain or loss the partner has on disposition of the partnership interest (*i.e.*, the amount of the gain or loss on disposition, less the amount of gain or loss from unrealized receivables or inventory items). This amount continues to be characterized as capital gain or loss. Because Section 751(a) requires a netting of the ordinary income amounts and the gain or loss on disposition, it is possible to have ordinary income and a capital loss or ordinary loss and a capital gain.

b. Lukewarm Assets

Not all capital gains are taxed at the same tax rate. Rather, collectibles and unrecaptured Section 1250 gain are taxed at higher preferential rates. Similarly, the capital gain from the disposition of a partnership interest may be taxed at various rates, depending on

---

8. Treas. Reg. § 1.751-1(a)(2).

the assets held by the partnership.[9] Sometimes, collectibles and unrecaptured Section 1250 gain are referred to as "lukewarm assets."

If the partner held the partnership interest for more than one year, and the partnership holds appreciated collectibles, the regulations use an aggregate approach and look through the partnership. The portion of the gain that would be allocated to the partner if the collectibles were sold for fair market value (taking into consideration Section 704(c)) is taxed as capital gain from a collectible.[10]

The same analysis is used if the partner held the partnership interest for more than one year and the partnership holds unrecaptured Section 1250 gain. The portion of the gain that would be allocated to the partner if the property were sold for fair market value is taxed as gain from an unrecaptured Section 1250 asset.[11]

The remaining amount of capital gain, the total capital gain less the amount allocated to appreciated collectibles and unrecaptured Section 1250 gain, is the adjusted net capital gain.[12]

3. Allocation of Basis and Holding Period

When a partner sells only a portion of his partnership interest, the basis and holding period must be allocated between the portion sold and the portion retained.

> **Example:** Deb is a partner in a partnership. At a time when her basis was $4,000, she sold one-quarter of her interest. The basis in the portion of the interest she sold was $1,000 (one-quarter of $4,000).

A partner may have a divided holding period in his partnership interest.[13] Thus, upon disposition of the partnership interest, a portion of the capital gain may be long-term and a portion may be short-term. The allocation of the holding period is based on the relative portions of the interest that have been held long term and short term.[14]

4. Sale Using the Installment Method

A partner may sell his partnership interest using the installment method. Once again, the partnership provisions return to an aggregate approach in determining the applicability of reporting under the installment method. Specifically, to the extent of gain from unrealized receivables, inventory, or depreciation recapture (generally, to the extent of gain from the hot assets), the partner may not use the installment method. Rather, such gain must be reported in the year of disposition.[15]

---

9. Treas. Reg. § 1.1(h)-1.

10. Treas. Reg. § 1.1(h)-1(b)(2)(ii).

11. Treas. Reg. § 1.1(h)-1(b)(3)(ii).

12. Treas. Reg. § 1.1(h)-1(c).

13. Treas. Reg. § 1.1223-3(a).

14. Treas. Reg. § 1.1223-3(c)(1).

15. Rev. Rul. 89-108, 1989-2 C.B. 100.

5. Death of a Partner

Closing of taxable year. In general, the death of a partner does not close the partnership's taxable year.[16] However, the partnership taxable year closes with respect to the partner.[17]

The death of a partner closes his individual taxable year.[18] His final income tax return must include his allocable share of partnership items for the short taxable year. In addition, if the partnership's prior taxable year's allocations had not yet been included, they must be included in the partner's final tax return.[19]

Built-in loss. If the deceased-partner had contributed property to the partnership with a built-in loss, the loss is eliminated when the partnership interest is transferred.[20]

Transfer of the partnership interest. When a partner passes away, the partnership interest generally becomes property of his estate. The estate may have options as to how to dispose of the interest.

First, the estate may be able to sell the partnership interest. In some circumstances, if required by the partnership agreement or buy-sell agreement, it may be required to sell the interest. The tax consequences of the sale are the same as they would have been if the partner had sold the interest during his lifetime.

Second, the interest may be transferred to a beneficiary of the decedent-partner's estate. The beneficiary takes the partnership interest with a basis equal to its fair market value as of the date of death,[21] increased by the successor's share of partnership liabilities, and decreased by any income in respect of decedent items.

Income in respect of a decedent. The beneficiary-partner will be required to report certain income items that had not been taxed to the decedent-partner. These items also will be required to have the same character they would have had in the hands of the decedent-partner.[22]

Basis elections. If the partnership has made a Section 754 election, the beneficiary's basis in the partnership assets will be adjusted as provided for in Section 743(b). If the partnership's assets have substantially depreciated,[23] it will be required to make the adjustment.[24] If the partnership has not made the election, the beneficiary-partner may elect a basis adjustment for any property distributed to him within two years.[25]

Finally, the partnership may liquidate the deceased partner's interest. If the interest is liquidated, amounts classified under Section 736(a) are treated as income in respect

---

16. Section 706(c)(1).

17. Section 706(c)(2).

18. Section 443(a)(2).

19. Section 706(a).

20. Section 704(c)(1)(C)(ii).

21. If the estate elects an alternative valuation date, the basis is equal to the value as of the alternate date.

22. See Sections 451(a); 691(a)(1), (a)(3); 1014(c). See, *e.g.*, Woodhall v. Commissioner, 454 F.2d 226 (9th Cir. 1972), *aff'g* T.C. Memo. 1969-279.

23. The assets have substantially depreciated if the adjusted basis of its assets exceeds the fair market value of the assets by more than $250,000. Section 743(d)(1).

24. Section 743(a), (d).

25. Section 732(b).

of a decedent.[26] Amounts classified in Section 736(b) are treated as a payment for the partner's interest in partnership property.[27]

B. Tax Consequences to the Buying Partner

1. General Rule

In general, for purposes of determining the partner's basis in a partnership interest that he purchases, the Code follows the entity approach. Thus, rather than purchasing an interest in the underlying assets of the partnership, the partner purchases an interest in the partnership itself. His basis in the partnership interest is the amount he paid for the interest, its cost.[28] In determining the cost of a partnership interest, the amount paid for the interest includes any partnership liabilities assumed by the buyer-partner.[29]

2. Exception to the General Rule

In general, the basis of partnership property is not adjusted as the result of a sale of a partnership interest.[30] Because the buyer-partner has paid the fair market value for his interest, this rule may lead to unexpected results.

Example: Ellen purchased a one-quarter interest in the partnership from Frank for $40,000. The partnership, which uses the cash method, owned $160,000 of accounts receivable with a zero basis.

When the partnership later collected the accounts receivable, one-quarter of the income, or $40,000 of ordinary income, was allocated to Ellen. This result holds true even though Ellen paid $40,000 for the partnership interest and the partnership has not realized any appreciation in its assets from the time Ellen purchased her interest.

In addition, note that, when Frank sold his one-quarter interest, to the extent of the uncollected accounts receivable, he would have been taxed on the $40,000 of gain (characterized as ordinary income under Section 751(a)). It is that same income that is now allocated to Ellen.

In order to avoid this result, the partnership may make an election under Section 754 to adjust the buyer-partner's basis in partnership assets, as provided in Section 743(b). In essence, the buyer-partner is given a cost basis in his share of the partnership's assets.

---

26. Section 753. See also Quick's Trust v. Commissioner, 54 T.C. 1336 (1970), *aff'd*, 444 F.2d 90 (8th Cir. 1971).

27. See discussion of distributions in liquidation of a partner's interest in Chapter XI.

28. Sections 742; 1012.

29. Section 752(d).

30. Section 743(a).

> **Example:** Ellen purchased a one-quarter interest in the partnership from Frank for $40,000. The partnership, which uses the cash method, owned $160,000 of accounts receivable with a zero basis.
>
> If the partnership had elected under Section 754 to adjust Ellen's basis in the partnership's assets, her basis in the accounts receivable would have been $40,000. When the $160,000 of accounts receivable were collected, $40,000 would have been allocated to each of the partners. The other three partners would have recognized $40,000 of ordinary income. However, because Ellen's basis in the accounts receivable was $40,000, she would not have been required to recognize any income.

Substantial built-in loss. If the partnership has a substantial built-in loss immediately after the purchase, the partnership is required to make the election. A substantial built-in loss exists if the partnership's adjusted basis in its assets exceeds the property's fair market value by more than $250,000.[31]

Election. Once the partnership has made the Section 754 election, it is applicable to all subsequent taxable years. It can be revoked only with the consent of the Internal Revenue Service.[32]

Calculating the buyer-partner's basis adjustment. The amount of the overall basis adjustment is the buyer-partner's outside basis, less his share of inside basis:

> outside basis
> − share of inside basis
> overall basis adjustment

The Code and regulations provide a complex formula for determining the buyer-partner's inside basis.[33] The buyer-partner's share of the partnership's inside basis is the buyer-partner's interest in the partnership's previously taxed capital plus the buyer-partner's share of partnership liabilities.

> Inside basis = share of previously taxed capital + share of liabilities

The partner's interest in previously taxed capital is determined by considering a hypothetical disposition by the partnership of all its assets. The assets are sold for cash equal to the asset's fair market value in a taxable transaction. The buyer-partner's interest in previously taxed capital is equal to the amount of cash that the partner would receive, plus (the absolute value of) the amount of tax loss, and minus the amount of tax gain that would have been allocated to the buyer-partner from the hypothetical sale.[34]

> partner's share of cash
> + share of tax loss
> − share of tax gain
> share of previously taxed capital

Next, once the amount of the adjustment has been determined, that amount must be allocated among the partnership's assets.[35] Divide the assets into one group that

---

31. Section 743(a), (d).
32. Treas. Reg. § 1.754-1(c)(1).
33. Sections 743(b); 755; Treas. Reg. §§ 1.743-1; 1.755-1(b).
34. Treas. Reg. § 1.743-1(d).
35. Treas. Reg. §§ 1.743-1(e); 1.755-1(a)(1), -1(b).

consists of all capital and hotchpot (Section 1231) assets and one group that consists of all other property, generally ordinary assets. Allocate the basis adjustment between the two groups. The amount allocated to the ordinary asset group is the total amount of income, gain or loss that would be allocated to the partner from a sale of the ordinary property. The amount allocated to the capital and hotchpot (Section 1231) group is the amount of the total adjustment, less the amount allocated to the ordinary asset group. If necessary, an increase can be made to one group of property while a decrease is made to the other group. However, a decrease in basis allocated to the capital and hotchpot group may not exceed the partnership's basis in the property. If a decrease is greater than the basis, the excess must be applied to reduce the basis of the assets in the ordinary asset group.[36]

Finally, allocate within each group among the properties. For assets in the ordinary asset group, in general, each asset is allocated an amount equal to the amount of income, gain, or loss that would be allocated to the partner from a hypothetical sale.[37]

For assets in the capital and hotchpot group, in general, each asset is allocated an amount equal to the amount of income, gain, or loss that would be allocated to the partner from a hypothetical sale.[38] When making an allocation, the basis of any asset may not be reduced below zero. If the amount allocated to the asset would reduce the basis below zero, the excess amount must be applied to reduce the remaining basis, if any, of other capital gain assets pro rata in proportion to the bases of such assets.[39]

The basis adjustment applies only to the buyer-partner. No actual adjustment is made to the basis of the partnership's assets and no adjustment is taken into consideration when determining the amount of the partnership's income, gains, expenses, deductions, or losses. Rather, the partnership computes its income, computes depreciation, and makes allocations without regard to the adjustment. Then, the partnership adjusts the buyer-partner's share of partnership items, taking into consideration the basis adjustment. In addition, with respect to depreciable property, the amount of the adjustment to depreciable property is treated as a separate asset that can be depreciated.

If partnership property is subsequently distributed to the buyer-partner, the partner's basis in the property is the basis as adjusted under Section 743(b).[40] If the partnership property is distributed to a partner other than the buyer-partner, the amount of the basis adjustment for that property is reallocated to partnership property of the same class.[41]

The basis adjustment allocated to one class of property may be an increase while the allocation to the other class may be a decrease. This result could be true even if the total amount of basis adjustment is zero. Similarly, the portion of the basis adjustment allocated to one item of property within a class may be an increase while the allocation to another is a decrease. This result would be true even though the basis adjustment

---

36. Treas. Reg. § 1.755-1(b)(2).
37. Treas. Reg. § 1.755-1(b)(3)(i).
38. Treas. Reg. § 1.755-1(b)(3)(ii).
39. Treas. Reg. § 1.755-1(b)(3)(iii)(B).
40. Treas. Reg. §§ 1.732-2(b); 1.743-1(g)(1)(i).
41. Treas. Reg. §§ 1.743-1(g)(2), -1(g)(3).

allocated to the class is zero. The basis adjustment under Section 743(b) does not impact the buyer-partner's capital account.[42]

Relationship of Section 743(b) to Section 704(c). If a partner contributes appreciated property to a partnership, then later sells his interest, the built-in gain is transferred to the buyer-partner.[43] However, if the seller-partner contributed property with a built-in loss, this loss cannot be transferred to the buyer-partner as part of the basis adjustment under Section 743(b).[44] Note that, if a partner contributes depreciated property to a partnership, then later sells his interest, the built-in loss is *not* transferred to the buyer-partner.

Allocation of purchase price to intangible assets. When structuring the transaction, the selling partner may sell his partnership interest for more than the amount that is reflected in his capital account. Oftentimes, this additional amount will represent goodwill, going concern value, or some other intangible generated by the partnership. If the partnership has made an election under Section 754, a portion of the purchase price must be allocated to any intangible assets described in Section 179(d).

The amount of the allocation is determined under the residual method of valuation.[45] Under the residual method, the value of all assets other than intangible assets identified under Section 179(d) is subtracted from the total purchase price.[46] This residual amount is allocated to the Section 197(d) intangible assets. If there are intangible assets other than going concern value or goodwill, a portion of the remainder amount is allocated to those intangible assets first, up to the asset's fair market value. Then the remaining amount is allocated to goodwill and going concern value.[47] When the adjustment is made under Section 743(b), the partner will receive an inside basis equal to the amount of the purchase price allocated to the intangible asset.

---

42. Treas. Reg. § 1.743-1(j)(2).
43. Treas. Reg. § 1.704-3(a)(7).
44. Section 704(c)(1)(C).
45. Section 1060(d); Treas. Reg. § 1.755-1(a)(2).
46. Treas. Reg. § 1.755-1(a)(4).
47. Treas. Reg. § 1.755-1(a)(5).

Summary

Seller: Determining Character of Gain on Disposition of a Portion or All of a Partner's Interest in a Partnership:

Step 1: Determine the partner's adjusted basis as of the day of the sale by taking into consideration any allocations to the partner. Determine the amount realized, including any debt relief.

Step 2: Determine the partner's total amount of gain or loss on disposition of the partnership interest.

Step 3: To the extent the partnership has any unrealized receivables or inventory items, determine how much gain or loss the partner would have if these items were sold for their fair market value and an allocable share allocated to the selling partner, taking into consideration any special allocations and any allocations required by Section 704(c). To this extent, the gain or loss is characterized as ordinary income or loss.

Step 4: Determine the amount that, when added to the amount of ordinary income, results in the amount of gain or loss the partner has on disposition of the partnership interest (*i.e.*, the amount of the gain or loss on disposition, less the amount of gain or loss from unrealized receivables or inventory items). This amount is characterized as capital gain or loss.

Step 5: To the extent the partnership has any collectibles or unrecognized Section 1250 gain, determine how much gain or loss the partner would have if the assets were sold for their fair market value and an allocable share allocated to the selling partner; apply the relevant tax rate to each category of gain. Tax any remaining gain, the adjusted net capital gain, at the relevant applicable rate.

Buyer:

General rule: Buyer-partner's outside basis is the amount he paid for the interest.

Exception: The partnership has made a Section 754 election and the buyer-partner's basis is adjusted as provided in Section 743(b).

Formula for Making a Section 743(b) Adjustment:

Step 1: Determine the overall basis adjustment:

outside basis
– share of inside basis
overall basis adjustment

A partner's share of inside basis is his share of previously taxed capital plus his share of liabilities.

Inside basis = share of PTC + share of liabilities

A partner's share of previously taxed capital is the amount of cash the partner would receive on liquidation, plus the amount tax loss, less the amount of tax gain the partner would receive on liquidation.

partner's share of cash
+ share of tax loss
<u>– share of tax gain</u>
share of PTC

Step 2: Divide assets into capital and hotchpot (Section 1231) assets in one group and ordinary assets in another group.

Step 3: Allocate the overall basis adjustment between the two groups.

Step 4: Allocate the group's basis adjustment among the assets in the group.

Step 5: Determine the partner's new inside basis, taking into consideration the adjustment for each asset.

Questions

1.   Ann and Bob are equal partners and had formed the partnership six years earlier. The partnership uses the cash method of accounting. At the end of the year, Ann sold her interest to Carl for $15,000. At the time of the sale, the balance sheet appeared as follows:

Asset	Adj. Basis	FMV	Partners	Adj. Basis	Cap. Acct.
Cash	$10,000	$10,000	Ann	$ 5,000	$15,000
Acct. Rec.	0	20,000	Bob	5,000	15,000
Total:	$10,000	$30,000		$10,000	$30,000

    a. The partnership has made no elections.

        1. What are the tax consequences to Ann and Carl? Prepare a balance sheet to reflect the situation of the partners after the sale.

        2. What are the tax consequences to Carl when the partnership collects the $20,000 of accounts receivable? Prepare a balance sheet to reflect the situation of the partners after collection of the accounts receivable.

    b. Alternatively, the partnership had made an election under Section 754.

        1. What are the tax consequences to Ann and Carl?

        2. What are the tax consequences to Carl when the partnership collects the $20,000 of accounts receivable?

2.   Deb and Ellen are equal partners and had formed the partnership six years earlier. The partnership uses the cash method of accounting and all the asset were purchased by the partnership. At the end of the year, Deb sold her interest to Frank for $15,000. At the time of the sale, the balance sheet appeared as follows:

Asset	Adj. Basis	FMV	Partners	Adj. Basis	Cap. Acct.
Cash	$ 5,000	$ 5,000	Deb	9,000	$15,000
Acct. Rec.	0	10,000	Ellen	9,000	15,000
Inventory	6,000	10,000		$18,000	$30,000
Land	7,000	5,000			
Total:	$18,000	$30,000			

    a. The partnership has made no elections.

        1. What are the tax consequences to Deb?

        2. What are the tax consequences to Frank?

    b. Alternatively, the partnership had made an election under Section 754.

        1. What are the tax consequences to Deb?

        2. What are the tax consequences to Frank?

3.   Greg and Hal are equal partners and had formed the partnership three years earlier. The partnership uses the cash method of accounting, all the assets were purchased by the partnership, and it holds the coins as collectibles. At the end of the year, Greg sold his interest to Ira for $20,000. At the time of the sale, the balance sheet appeared as follows:

Asset	Adj. Basis	FMV	Liabilities:		$ 2,000
Cash	$20,000	$20,000	Partners	Adj. Basis	Cap. Acct.
Acct. Rec.	0	14,000	Greg	$15,000	$20,000
Coins	2,000	4,000	Hal	15,000	20,000
Land	8,000	4,000		$30,000	$42,000
Total:	$30,000	$42,000			

a. The partnership has made no elections.

   1. What are the tax consequences to Greg?

   2. What are the tax consequences to Ira?

b. Alternatively, the partnership had made an election under Section 754.

   1. What are the tax consequences to Greg?

   2. What are the tax consequences to Ira?

4.   Jeb and Kent are equal partners and had formed the partnership three years earlier. The partnership uses the accrual method of accounting and all the assets were purchased by the partnership. At the end of the year, Jeb sold his interest to Len for $15,000. At the time of the sale, the balance sheet appeared as follows:

Asset	Adj. Basis	FMV	Partners	Adj. Basis	Cap. Acct.
Cash	$ 5,000	$ 5,000	Jeb	$16,000	$15,000
Acct. Rec.	10,000	10,000	Kent	16,000	15,000
Inventory	6,000	10,000		$32,000	$30,000
Stock	11,000	5,000			
Total:	$32,000	$30,000			

a. The partnership has made no elections.

   1. What are the tax consequences to Jeb?

   2. What are the tax consequences to Len?

b. Alternatively, the partnership had made an election under Section 754.

   1. What are the tax consequences to Jeb?

   2. What are the tax consequences to Len?

5.   Mike and Ned are equal partners and had formed the partnership three years earlier. The partnership uses the accrual method of accounting, all the assets were purchased by the partnership, and it holds collectibles. At the end of the year, Mike sold his interest to Opie for $20,000. At the time of the sale, the balance sheet appeared as follows:

Asset	Adj. Basis	FMV	Liabilities:		$10,000
Cash	$ 2,000	$ 2,000	Partners	Adj. Basis	Cap. Acct.
Acct. Rec.	14,000	14,000	Mike	$16,000	$20,000
Collectibles	7,000	20,000	Ned	16,000	20,000
Stock	9,000	14,000		$32,000	$50,000
Total:	$32,000	$50,000			

a. The partnership has made no elections.

    1. What are the tax consequences to Mike?

    2. What are the tax consequences to Opie?

b. Alternatively, the partnership had made an election under Section 754.

    1. What are the tax consequences to Mike?

    2. What are the tax consequences to Opie?

Solutions

1. Ann and Bob are equal partners and had formed the partnership six years earlier. The partnership uses the cash method of accounting. At the end of the year, Ann sold her interest to Carl for $15,000. At the time of the sale, the balance sheet appeared as follows:

Asset	Adj. Basis	FMV	Partners	Adj. Basis	Cap. Acct.
Cash	$10,000	$10,000	Ann	$ 5,000	$15,000
Acct. Rec.	0	20,000	Bob	5,000	15,000
Total:	$10,000	$30,000		$10,000	$30,000

    a. The partnership has made no elections.

        1. What are the tax consequences to Ann and Carl? Prepare a balance sheet to reflect the situation of the partners after the sale.

Ann: Upon the sale of her partnership interest, Ann has $10,000 of gain:

    AR: $15,000
    AB: 5,000
    Gain: $10,000

Unrealized receivables: The accounts receivable are an unrealized receivable. (Section 751(c)) If the partnership had sold the accounts receivable for their fair market value, it would have gain recognized of $20,000:

    AR: $20,000
    AB: 0
    Gain: $20,000

One-half, or $10,000, would have been allocated to Ann. To this extent Ann must recognize ordinary income. (Section 751(a); Treas. Reg. § 1.751-1(a)(2))

The amount that, when added to the amount of ordinary income of $10,000, results in the amount of gain Ann has on disposition of the partnership interest, $10,000, is zero.

    Ordinary income: $10,000
    "X"   0
    Gain on disposition: $10,000

Accordingly, Ann must recognize $10,000 of ordinary income (and no capital gain). (Section 751(a); Treas. Reg. § 1.751-1(a)(2))

Carl: Carl purchased the interest for $15,000. Thus, his outside basis in the partnership interest is $15,000. (Section 1012)

Asset	Adj. Basis	FMV	Partners	Adj. Basis	Cap. Acct.
Cash	$10,000	$10,000	Carl	$15,000	$15,000
Acct. Rec.	0	20,000	Bob	5,000	15,000
Total:	$10,000	$30,000		$20,000*	$30,000

* Note the $10,000 disparity between inside and outside basis. This is because, even though Carl paid full value for a proportionate share of all the partnership assets, the inside basis in the accounts receivable does not reflect this cost basis.

2. **What are the tax consequences to Carl when the partnership collects the $20,000 of accounts receivable? Prepare a balance sheet to reflect the situation of the partners after collection of the accounts receivable.**

When the partnership collects the accounts receivable, the $20,000 is allocated equally to Carl and Bob, or $10,000 each. Their basis and capital accounts are adjusted as follows:

	Carl		Bob	
	Basis	**Cap. Acct**	**Basis**	**Cap. Acct.**
	$15,000	$15,000	$ 5,000	$15,000
Gain:	10,000	0	10,000	0
Total:	$25,000	$15,000	$15,000	$15,000

Taking into consideration the adjustments, the balance sheet would appear as follows:

Asset	Adj. Basis	FMV	Partners	Adj. Basis	Cap. Acct
Cash	$30,000	$30,000	Carl	$25,000	$15,000
			Bob	15,000	15,000
Total:	$30,000	$30,000		$40,000*	$30,000

* Note the $10,000 disparity between inside and outside basis. This is because, even though Carl paid full value for a proportionate share of all the partnership assets, including the accounts receivable, when the receivables were collected he was still required to report a share of the income. This $10,000 "over-inclusion" is reflected in the difference between his capital account and adjusted basis. If he sold his interest for $15,000, he would have a $10,000 loss (amount realized of $15,000, less adjusted basis of $25,000). Thus, there would be a wash—$10,000 income reported from the collection of the accounts receivable followed by a $10,000 loss from the sale of his interest. However the character of the two amounts may not be the same and he may not recover the loss for many years after he reported the income.

b. **Alternatively, the partnership had made an election under Section 754.**

1. **What are the tax consequences to Ann and Carl?**

Ann: (The answer is the same as in a, above.) Upon the sale of her partnership interest, Ann has $10,000 of gain:

AR:	$15,000
AB:	5,000
Gain:	$10,000

Unrealized receivables: The accounts receivable are an unrealized receivable. (Section 751(c)) If the partnership had sold the accounts receivable for their fair market value, it would have gain recognized of $20,000:

AR:	$20,000
AB:	0
Gain:	$20,000

One-half, or $10,000, would have been allocated to Ann. To this extent Ann must recognize ordinary income. (Section 751(a); Treas. Reg. § 1.751-1(a)(2))

The amount that, when added to the amount of ordinary income of $10,000, results in the amount of gain Ann has on disposition of the partnership interest, $10,000, is zero.

Ordinary income:	$10,000
"X"	0
Gain on disposition:	$10,000

Accordingly, Ann must recognize $10,000 of ordinary income (and no capital gain). (Section 751(a); Treas. Reg. § 1.751-1(a)(2))

Carl: Because the partnership had made a Section 754 election, Carl receives his own inside basis in the partnership assets. First, determine the amount of adjustment to the inside basis. The amount of the adjustment is Carl's outside basis, $15,000, less his share of inside basis. (Treas. Reg. § 1.743-1(b))

outside basis
– share of inside basis
adjustment

To determine Carl's share of the partnership's inside basis of its assets, determine Carl's interest in the partnership's previously taxed capital (PTC) plus Carl's share of partnership liabilities. (Treas. Reg. § 1.743-1(d)(1))

Share of inside basis = Carl's PTC + share of partnership liabilities

Carl's interest in previously taxed capital is determined by considering a hypothetical disposition by the partnership of all its assets. (Treas. Reg. § 1.743-1(d)(1)) The assets are sold for cash equal to the asset's fair market value in a taxable transaction. The result would be:

Asset	Adj. Basis	FMV	Gain/Loss	Carl's share
Cash	$10,000	$10,000	0	0
Acct. Rec.	0	20,000	20,000	10,000

In a hypothetical liquidation, Carl would receive:

Share of cash:	$15,000
Share of tax loss:	+ 0
Share of tax gain:	– 10,000
Share of PTC:	$ 5,000

Because there are no partnership liabilities, his share of the inside basis would be $5,000:

Share of inside basis = Carl's PTC + share of partnership liabilities
= $5,000 + 0 = $5,000

His overall adjustment would be:

outside basis	$15,000
– share of inside basis	– 5,000
adjustment	10,000

Second, once the adjustment has been determined, that amount must be allocated among the partnership's assets. (Treas. Reg. § 1.743-1(e)) The accounts receivable are allocated to the ordinary asset group. (Treas. Reg. § 1.755-1(b)(2)(i)) There are no other assets.

The sale of the ordinary asset would result in a $10,000 gain allocable to Carl.

Asset	Adj. Basis	FMV	Gain/Loss	Carl's share
Acct. Rec.	$0	$20,000	$20,000	$10,000

Thus, an adjustment is made to Carl's inside basis in the items as follows:

Asset	Current Share of Basis	New Inside Adjustment	Basis
Cash	$5,000	0	$ 5,000
Acct. Rec.	0	10,000	10,000
Total:	$5,000	$10,000	$15,000*

* Note that this result makes sense. Carl paid $15,000 for the interest, and the total of his share of the inside basis is $15,000.

2. What are the tax consequences to Carl when the partnership collects the $20,000 of accounts receivable?

When the partnership collects the accounts receivable, the $20,000 is allocated equally to Carl and Bob, or $10,000 each. Bob must report the $10,000. Because Carl's basis in his share of the accounts receivable is $10,000 he reports nothing.

2.   Deb and Ellen are equal partners and had formed the partnership six years earlier. The partnership uses the cash method of accounting and all the asset were purchased by the partnership. At the end of the year, Deb sold her interest to Frank for $15,000. At the time of the sale, the balance sheet appeared as follows:

Asset	Adj. Basis	FMV	Partners	Adj. Basis	Cap. Acct.
Cash	$ 5,000	$ 5,000	Deb	$ 9,000	$15,000
Acct. Rec.	0	10,000	Ellen	9,000	15,000
Inventory	6,000	10,000		$18,000	$30,000
Land	7,000	5,000			
Total:	$18,000	$30,000			

a. The partnership has made no elections.

1. What are the tax consequences to Deb?

Upon the sale of her partnership interest, Deb has $6,000 of gain:

AR:	$15,000
AB:	9,000
Gain:	$ 6,000

Unrealized receivables: The accounts receivable are an unrealized receivable. (Section 751(c)) If the partnership had sold the accounts receivable for their fair market value, it would have gain recognized of $10,000:

AR:	$10,000
AB:	0
Gain:	$10,000

One-half, or $5,000, would have been allocated to Deb. To this extent Deb must recognize ordinary income. (Section 751(a); Treas. Reg. § 1.751-1(a)(2))

Inventory: The inventory and accounts receivable are inventory. (Section 751(d)) The accounts receivable have already been addressed. If the partnership had sold the inventory for its fair market value, it would have gain recognized of $4,000:

AR:	$10,000
AB:	6,000
Gain:	$ 4,000

One-half, or $2,000, would have been allocated to Deb. To this extent Deb must recognize ordinary income. (Treas. Reg. § 1.751-1(a)(2))

The total amount of ordinary income is:

Accounts receivable:	$5,000
Inventory:	2,000
Total ordinary income:	$7,000

The amount that, when added to the amount of ordinary income of $7,000, results in the amount of gain or loss the partner has on disposition of the partnership interest, $6,000, is a loss of $1,000.

Ordinary income:	$7,000
"X"	<1,000>
Gain on disposition:	$6,000

In sum, Deb must recognize (Section 751(a); Treas. Reg. § 1.751-1(a)(2)):

Ordinary income:	$7,000
Long term capital loss:	$1,000*

* Note that this makes sense. If the partnership disposed of the land, there would be a $2,000 loss ($5,000 amount realized, less $7,000 basis). Her share of the loss, $1,000, is represented in the sale of the interest.

2. What are the tax consequences to Frank?

Frank purchased the interest for $15,000. Thus, his outside basis in the partnership interest is $15,000. (Section 1012)

b. Alternatively, the partnership had made an election under Section 754.

1. What are the tax consequences to Deb?

(The answer is the same as in a, above.) Upon the sale of her partnership interest, Deb has $6,000 of gain:

AR:	$15,000
AB:	9,000
Gain:	$ 6,000

Unrealized receivables: The accounts receivable are an unrealized receivable. (Section 751(c)) If the partnership had sold the accounts receivable for their fair market value, it would have gain recognized of $10,000:

AR:	$10,000
AB:	0
Gain:	$10,000

One-half, or $5,000, would have been allocated to Deb. To this extent Deb must recognize ordinary income. (Section 751(a); Treas. Reg. § 1.751-1(a)(2))

Inventory: The inventory and accounts receivable are inventory. (Section 751(d)) The accounts receivable have already been addressed. If the partnership had sold the inventory for its fair market value, it would have gain recognized of $4,000:

AR:	$10,000
AB:	6,000
Gain:	$ 4,000

One-half, or $2,000, would have been allocated to Deb. To this extent Deb must recognize ordinary income. (Treas. Reg. § 1.751-1(a)(2))

The total amount of ordinary income is:

Accounts receivable:	$5,000
Inventory:	2,000
Total ordinary income:	$7,000

The amount that, when added to the amount of ordinary income of $7,000, results in the amount of gain or loss the partner has on disposition of the partnership interest, $6,000, is a loss of $1,000.

Ordinary income:	$7,000
"X"	<1,000>
Gain on disposition:	$6,000

In sum, Deb must recognize (Section 751(a); Treas. Reg. § 1.751-1(a)(2)):

Ordinary income:	$7,000
Long term capital loss:	$1,000*

* Note that this makes sense. If the partnership disposed of the land, there would be a $2,000 loss ($5,000 amount realized, less $7,000 basis). Her share of the loss, $1,000, is represented in the sale of the interest.

2. What are the tax consequences to Frank?

Because the partnership had made a Section 754 election, Frank receives his own inside basis in the partnership assets. First, determine the amount of adjustment to the inside basis. The amount of the adjustment is Frank's outside basis, $15,000, less his share of inside basis. (Treas. Reg. § 1.743-1(b))

$$
\begin{array}{l}
\text{outside basis} \\
\underline{-\ \text{share of inside basis}} \\
\text{adjustment}
\end{array}
$$

To determine Frank's share of the partnership's inside basis of its assets, determine Frank's interest in the partnership's previously taxed capital (PTC) plus Frank's share of partnership liabilities. (Treas. Reg. § 1.743-1(d)(1))

Share of inside basis = Frank's PTC + share of partnership liabilities

Frank's interest in previously taxed capital is determined by considering a hypothetical disposition by the partnership of all its assets. (Treas. Reg. § 1.743-1(d)(1)) The assets are sold for cash equal to the asset's fair market value in a taxable transaction. The result would be:

Asset	Adj. Basis	FMV	Gain/Loss	Frank's share
Cash	$5,000	$ 5,000	0	0
Acct. Rec.	0	10,000	10,000	5,000
Inventory	6,000	10,000	4,000	2,000
Land	7,000	5,000	<2,000>	<1,000>

In a hypothetical liquidation, Frank would receive:

Share of cash:	$15,000
Share of tax loss:	+ 1,000
Share of tax gain:	− 7,000 (= 5,000 + 2,000)
Share of PTC:	$ 9,000

Because there are no partnership liabilities, his share of the inside basis would be $9,000:

Share of inside basis = Frank's PTC + share of partnership liabilities
= $9,000 + 0 = $9,000

His overall adjustment would be:

outside basis	$15,000
− share of inside basis	− 9,000
adjustment	6,000

Second, once the adjustment has been determined, that amount must be allocated among the partnership's assets. (Treas. Reg. § 1.743-1(e)) The land is allocated to the capital and hotchpot (Section 1231) asset group and the accounts receivable and inventory are allocated to the ordinary asset group. (Treas. Reg. § 1.755-1(b)(2)(i))

The sale of the ordinary assets would result in a $14,000 gain, with $7,000 gain allocable to Frank.

Asset	Adj. Basis	FMV	Gain/Loss	Frank's share
Acct. Rec.	0	10,000	10,000	5,000
Inventory	6,000	10,000	4,000	2,000
Net change:				$7,000

Thus, a gain of $7,000 is allocated to the ordinary property.

The amount allocated to the capital and hotchpot (Section 1231) group is (Treas. Reg. § 1.755-1(b)(2)(i)):

Amount of total adjustment:	$6,000
Amount allocated to ordinary:	− 7,000
Allocation to capital/hotchpot:	<$1,000>

Next, for assets in the ordinary asset group, each asset is allocated an amount equal to the amount of income, gain, or loss that would be allocated to the partner from a hypothetical sale. (Treas. Reg. § 1.755-1(b)(3)(i)) Thus, $5,000 would be allocated to the accounts receivable and $2,000 allocated to the inventory.

For assets in the capital and hotchpot group, each item is allocated an amount equal to the amount of income, gain, or loss that would be allocated to the partner from the hypothetical sale of the item. (Treas. Reg. § 1.755-1(b)(3)(ii)) Thus, for the land, Frank would be allocated a loss of $1,000.

Adjustment would be made to Frank's inside basis in the items as follows:

Asset	Current share of basis	Adjustment	New inside basis
Cash	$2,500	0	$ 2,500
Acct. Rec.	0	5,000	5,000
Inventory	3,000	2,000	5,000
Land	3,500	<1,000>	2,500
Total:	$9,000	$6,000	$15,000*

* Note that this result makes sense. Frank paid $15,000 for the interest, and the total of his share of the inside basis is $15,000.

3. Greg and Hal are equal partners and had formed the partnership three years earlier. The partnership uses the cash method of accounting, all the assets were purchased by the partnership, and it holds the coins as collectibles. At the end of the year, Greg sold his interest to Ira for $20,000. At the time of the sale, the balance sheet appeared as follows:

Asset	Adj. Basis	FMV	Liabilities:		$ 2,000
Cash	$20,000	$20,000	Partners	Adj. Basis	Cap. Acct.
Acct. Rec.	0	14,000	Greg	$15,000	$20,000
Coins	2,000	4,000	Hal	15,000	20,000
Land	8,000	4,000		$30,000	$42,000
Total:	$30,000	$42,000			

a. The partnership has made no elections.

   1. What are the tax consequences to Greg?

Upon the sale of his partnership interest, Greg has $6,000 of gain:

AR:	$21,000	($20,000 cash + $1,000 of debt relief)
AB:	15,000	
Gain:	$ 6,000	

Unrealized receivables: The accounts receivable are an unrealized receivable. (Section 751(c)) If the partnership had sold the accounts receivable for their fair market value, it would have gain recognized of $14,000:

AR:	$14,000
AB:	0
Gain:	$14,000

One-half, or $7,000, would have been allocated to Greg. To this extent Greg must recognize ordinary income. (Section 751(a); Treas. Reg. § 1.751-1(a)(2))

Inventory: The accounts receivable are inventory. (Section 751(d)) The accounts receivable have already been addressed.

The total amount of ordinary income is $7,000.

The amount that, when added to the amount of ordinary income of $7,000, results in the amount of gain Greg has on disposition of the partnership interest, $6,000, is a loss of $1,000.

Ordinary income:	$7,000
"X"	<1,000>
Gain on disposition:	$6,000

If the partnership had sold the coins, a collectible, for their fair market value, it would have gain recognized of $2,000.

AR:	$4,000
AB:	2,000
Gain:	$2,000

One-half, or $1,000, would have been allocated to Greg. To this extent Greg has capital gain from collectibles. (Treas. Reg. §1.1(h)-1)

The amount that, when added to the amount of gain from collectibles, $1,000, results in the amount of capital gain Greg has on disposition of the partnership interest, $1,000 loss, is a capital loss of $2,000. Thus, Greg has $2,000 of adjusted net long-term capital loss.*

Lukewarm gain:	$1,000
"X"	<2,000>
Capital loss on disposition:	<$1,000>

In sum, from the sale of his partnership interest, Greg must report $7,000 of ordinary income, $1,000 capital gain from collectibles, and $2,000 of net long-term capital loss. (Section 751(a); Treas. Reg. §1.751-1(a)(2))

* Note that this makes sense. If the partnership disposed of the land, there would be a $4,000 loss (amount realized of $4,000, less basis of $8,000). His share of the loss, $2,000, is represented in the sale of the interest.

2. What are the tax consequences to Ira?

Ira purchased the interest for $21,000. Thus, his outside basis in the partnership interest is $21,000. (Section 1012)

b. Alternatively, the partnership had made an election under Section 754.

1. What are the tax consequences to Greg?

(The answer is the same as in a, above.) Upon the sale of his partnership interest, Greg has $6,000 of gain:

AR:	$21,000	($20,000 cash + $1,000 of debt relief)
AB:	15,000	
Gain:	$ 6,000	

Unrealized receivables: The accounts receivable are an unrealized receivable. (Section 751(c)) If the partnership had sold the accounts receivable for their fair market value, it would have gain recognized of $14,000:

AR:	$14,000
AB:	0
Gain:	$14,000

One-half, or $7,000, would have been allocated to Greg. To this extent Greg must recognize ordinary income. (Section 751(a); Treas. Reg. §1.751-1(a)(2))

Inventory: The accounts receivable are inventory. (Section 751(d)) The accounts receivable have already been addressed.

The total amount of ordinary income is $7,000.

The amount that, when added to the amount of ordinary income of $7,000, results in the amount of gain Greg has on disposition of the partnership interest, $6,000, is a loss of $1,000.

Ordinary income:	$7,000
"X"	<1,000>
Gain on disposition:	$6,000

If the partnership had sold the coins, a collectible, for their fair market value, it would have gain recognized of $2,000.

AR:	$4,000
AB:	2,000
Gain:	$2,000

One-half, or $1,000, would have been allocated to Greg. To this extent Greg has capital gain from collectibles. (Treas. Reg. § 1.1(h)-1)

The amount that, when added to the amount of gain from collectibles, $1,000, results in the amount of capital gain Greg has on disposition of the partnership interest, $1,000 loss, is a capital loss of $2,000. Thus, Greg has $2,000 of adjusted net long-term capital loss.*

Lukewarm gain:	$1,000
"X"	<2,000>
Capital loss on disposition:	<$1,000>

In sum, from the sale of his partnership interest, Greg must report $7,000 of ordinary income, $1,000 capital gain from collectibles, and $2,000 of net long-term capital loss. (Section 751(a); Treas. Reg. § 1.751-1(a)(2))

* Note that this makes sense. If the partnership disposed of the land, there would be a $4,000 loss (amount realized of $4,000, less basis of $8,000). His share of the loss, $2,000, is represented in the sale of the interest.

2. What are the tax consequences to Ira?

Because the partnership had made a Section 754 election, Ira receives his own inside basis in the partnership assets. First, determine the amount of adjustment to the inside basis. The amount of the adjustment is Ira's outside basis, $21,000, less his share of inside basis. (Treas. Reg. § 1.743-1(b))

outside basis
− share of inside basis
adjustment

To determine Ira's share of the partnership's inside basis of its assets, determine Ira's interest in the partnership's previously taxed capital (PTC) plus Ira's share of partnership liabilities. (Treas. Reg. § 1.743-1(d)(1))

Share of inside basis = Ira's PTC + share of partnership liabilities

Ira's interest in previously taxed capital is determined by considering a hypothetical disposition by the partnership of all its assets. (Treas. Reg. § 1.743-1(d)(1)) The assets are sold for cash equal to the asset's fair market value in a taxable transaction. The result would be:

Asset	Adj. Basis	FMV	Gain/Loss	Ira's share
Cash	$20,000	$20,000	$ 0	$ 0
Acct. Rec.	0	14,000	14,000	7,000
Coins	2,000	4,000	2,000	1,000
Land	8,000	4,000	<4,000>	<2,000>

In a hypothetical liquidation, Ira would receive:

Share of cash:	$20,000
Share of tax loss:	+ 2,000
Share of tax gain:	− 8,000 (= 7,000 + 1,000)
Share of PTC:	$14,000

His share of the inside basis would be $15,000:

Share of inside basis = Ira's PTC + share of partnership liabilities
= $14,000 + 1,000 = $15,000

His overall adjustment would be:

outside basis	$21,000
− share of inside basis	− 15,000
Adjustment	6,000

Second, once the adjustment has been determined, that amount must be allocated among the partnership's assets. The coins and land are allocated to the capital and hotchpot (Section 1231) asset group and the accounts receivable are allocated to the ordinary asset group. (Treas. Reg. § 1.755-1(b)(2)(i))

The sale of the ordinary assets would result in a $14,000 gain, with $7,000 allocable to Ira.

Asset	Adj. Basis	FMV	Gain/Loss	Ira's share
Acct. Rec.	0	14,000	14,000	7,000

Thus, a gain of $7,000 is allocated to the ordinary property.

The amount allocated to the capital and hotchpot (Section 1231) group is:

Amount of total adjustment:	$6,000
Amount allocated to ordinary:	− 7,000
Allocation to capital/hotchpot:	<$1,000>

Next, for assets in the ordinary asset group, each asset is allocated an amount equal to the amount of income, gain, or loss that would be allocated to the partner from a hypothetical sale. (Treas. Reg. § 1.755-1(b)(3)(i)) Thus, $7,000 would be allocated to the accounts receivable.

For assets in the capital and hotchpot group, each item is allocated an amount equal to the amount of income, gain, or loss that would be allocated to the partner from the hypothetical sale of the item. (Treas. Reg. § 1.755-1(b)(3)(ii)) Thus, for the coins and land, the allocation would be $1,000 to the coins and <$2,000> to the land, for a net allocation of <$1,000>.

Asset	Adj. Basis	FMV	Gain/Loss	Ira's share
Coins	2,000	4,000	2,000	1,000
Land	8,000	4,000	<4,000>	<2,000>
Net change:				<$1,000>

Adjustment would be made to Ira's inside basis in the items as follows:

Asset	Current share of basis	Adjustment	New inside basis
Cash	$10,000	0	$10,000
Acct. Rec.	0	7,000	7,000
Coins	1,000	1,000	2,000
Land	4,000	<2,000>	2,000
Total:	$15,000	$6,000	$21,000*

* Note that this result makes sense. Ira paid $21,000 for the interest, and the total of his share of the inside basis is $21,000.

4.   Jeb and Kent are equal partners and had formed the partnership three years earlier. The partnership uses the accrual method of accounting and all the assets were purchased by the partnership. At the end of the year, Jeb sold his interest to Len for $15,000. At the time of the sale, the balance sheet appeared as follows:

Asset	Adj. Basis	FMV	Partners	Adj. Basis	Cap. Acct.
Cash	$ 5,000	$ 5,000	Jeb	$16,000	$15,000
Acct. Rec.	10,000	10,000	Kent	16,000	15,000
Inventory	6,000	10,000		$32,000	$30,000
Stock	11,000	5,000			
Total:	$32,000	$30,000			

a. The partnership has made no elections.

   1. What are the tax consequences to Jeb?

Upon the sale of his partnership interest, Jeb has a loss of $1,000.

```
AR:    $15,000
AB:     16,000
Loss:  $ 1,000
```

Unrealized receivables: The accounts receivable are not an unrealized receivable under Section 751(c) because the income has already been included in income.

Inventory: The inventory and accounts receivable are inventory. (Section 751(d)) If the partnership had sold the accounts receivable for its fair market value, it would have no gain or loss.

```
AR:    $10,000
AB:     10,000
Gain:  $    0
```

If the partnership had sold the inventory for its fair market value, it would have gain recognized of $4,000:

```
AR:    $10,000
AB:      6,000
Gain:  $ 4,000
```

One-half, or $2,000, would have been allocated to Jeb. To this extent Jeb must recognize ordinary income. (Section 751(a); Treas. Reg. § 1.751-1(a)(2))

The total amount of ordinary income is $2,000.

The amount that, when added to the amount of ordinary income of $2,000, results in the amount of loss Jeb has on disposition of the partnership interest, $1,000, is a loss of $3,000.

Ordinary income:	$2,000
"X"	*<3,000>*
Loss on disposition:	<$1,000>

In sum, from the sale of his partnership interest, Jeb must report $2,000 of ordinary income and $3,000 of long-term capital loss.* (Section 751(a); Treas. Reg. § 1.751-1(a)(2))

* Note that this makes sense. If the partnership disposed of the stock, there would be a $6,000 loss (amount realized of $5,000, less adjusted basis of $11,000). His share of the loss, $3,000, is represented in the sale of the interest.

2. What are the tax consequences to Len?

Len purchased the interest for $15,000. Thus, his outside basis in the partnership interest is $15,000. (Section 1012)

b. Alternatively, the partnership had made an election under Section 754.

1. What are the tax consequences to Jeb?

(Same answer as in a, above.) Upon the sale of his partnership interest, Jeb has a loss of $1,000.

AR:	$15,000
AB:	16,000
Loss:	$ 1,000

Unrealized receivables: The accounts receivable are not an unrealized receivable under Section 751(c) because the income has already been included in income.

Inventory: The inventory and accounts receivable are inventory. (Section 751(d)) If the partnership had sold the accounts receivable for its fair market value, it would have no gain or loss.

AR:	$10,000
AB:	10,000
Gain:	$ 0

If the partnership had sold the inventory for its fair market value, it would have gain recognized of $4,000:

AR:	$10,000
AB:	6,000
Gain:	$ 4,000

One-half, or $2,000, would have been allocated to Jeb. To this extent Jeb must recognize ordinary income. (Section 751(a); Treas. Reg. § 1.751-1(a)(2))

The total amount of ordinary income is $2,000.

The amount that, when added to the amount of ordinary income of $2,000, results in the amount of loss Jeb has on disposition of the partnership interest, $1,000, is a loss of $3,000.

Ordinary income:	$2,000
"X"	<u><3,000></u>
Loss on disposition:	<$1,000>

In sum, from the sale of his partnership interest, Jeb must report $2,000 of ordinary income and $3,000 of long-term capital loss.* (Section 751(a); Treas. Reg. §1.751-1(a)(2))

* Note that this makes sense. If the partnership disposed of the stock, there would be a $6,000 loss (amount realized of $5,000, less adjusted basis of $11,000). His share of the loss, $3,000, is represented in the sale of the interest.

2. What are the tax consequences to Len?

Because the partnership had made a Section 754 election, Len receives his own inside basis in the partnership assets. First, determine the amount of adjustment to the inside basis. The amount of the adjustment is Len's outside basis, $15,000, less his share of inside basis. (Treas. Reg. §1.743-1(b))

$$\begin{array}{r} \text{outside basis} \\ \underline{-\text{ share of inside basis}} \\ \text{adjustment} \end{array}$$

To determine Len's share of the partnership's inside basis of its assets, determine Len's interest in the partnership's previously taxed capital (PTC) plus Len's share of partnership liabilities. (Treas. Reg. §1.743-1(d)(1))

Share of inside basis = Len's PTC + share of partnership liabilities

Len's interest in previously taxed capital is determined by considering a hypothetical disposition by the partnership of all its assets. (Treas. Reg. §1.743-1(d)(1)) The assets are sold for cash equal to the asset's fair market value in a taxable transaction. The result would be:

Asset	Adj. Basis	FMV	Gain/Loss	Len's share
Cash	$ 5,000	$ 5,000	$ 0	$ 0
Acct. Rec.	10,000	10,000	0	0
Inventory	6,000	10,000	4,000	2,000
Stock	11,000	5,000	<6,000>	<3,000>

In a hypothetical liquidation, Len would receive:

Share of cash:	$15,000
Share of tax loss:	+ 3,000
Share of tax gain:	<u>− 2,000</u>
Share of PTC:	$16,000

His share of the inside basis would be $16,000:

Share of inside basis = Len's PTC + share of partnership liabilities
= $16,000 + 0 = $16,000

His overall adjustment would be:

outside basis	$15,000
<u>− share of inside basis</u>	<u>− 16,000</u>
adjustment	<1,000>

Second, once the adjustment has been determined, that amount must be allocated among the partnership's assets. (Treas. Reg. § 1.743-1(e)) The stock is allocated to the capital and hotchpot (Section 1231) asset group and the accounts receivable and inventory are allocated to the ordinary asset group. (Treas. Reg. § 1.755-1(b)(2)(i))

The sale of the ordinary assets would result in a $4,000 gain, with $2,000 allocable to Len.

Asset	Adj. Basis	FMV	Gain/Loss	Len's share
Acct. Rec.	10,000	10,000	0	0
Inventory	6,000	10,000	4,000	2,000

Thus, a gain of $2,000 is allocated to the ordinary property.

The amount allocated to the capital and hotchpot (Section 1231) group is:

Amount of total adjustment:	<$1,000>
Amount allocated to ordinary:	− 2,000
Allocation to capital/hotchpot:	<$3,000>

Next, for assets in the ordinary asset group, each asset is allocated an amount equal to the amount of income, gain, or loss that would be allocated to the partner from a hypothetical sale. (Treas. Reg. § 1.755-1(b)(3)(i)) Thus, $2,000 would be allocated to the inventory.

For assets in the capital and hotchpot group, each item is allocated an amount equal to the amount of income, gain, or loss that would be allocated to the partner from the hypothetical sale of the item. (Treas. Reg. § 1.755-1(b)(3)(ii)) Thus, a $3,000 loss would be allocated to the stock.

Asset	Adj. Basis	FMV	Gain/Loss	Len's share
Stock	11,000	5,000	<6,000>	<3,000>

Adjustment would be made to Len's inside basis in the items as follows:

Asset	Current share of basis	Adjustment	New inside basis
Cash	$ 2,500	0	$ 2,500
Acct. Rec.	5,000	0	5,000
Inventory	3,000	2,000	5,000
Stock	5,500	<3,000>	2,500
Total:	$16,000	<$1,000>	$15,000*

* Note that this result makes sense. Len paid $15,000 for the interest, and the total of his share of the inside basis is $15,000.

5. Mike and Ned are equal partners and had formed the partnership three years earlier. The partnership uses the accrual method of accounting, all the assets were purchased by the partnership, and it holds collectibles. At the end of the year, Mike sold his interest to Opie for $20,000. At the time of the sale, the balance sheet appeared as follows:

Asset	Adj. Basis	FMV	Liabilities:		$10,000
Cash	$ 2,000	$ 2,000	Partners	Adj. Basis	Cap. Acct.
Acct. Rec.	14,000	14,000	Mike	$16,000	$20,000
Collectibles	7,000	20,000	Ned	16,000	20,000
Stock	9,000	14,000		$32,000	$50,000
Total:	$32,000	$50,000			

a. The partnership has made no elections.

1. What are the tax consequences to Mike?

Upon the sale of his partnership interest, Mike has a $9,000 gain.

AR:	$25,000	($20,000 cash + $5,000 debt relief)
AB:	16,000	
Gain:	$ 9,000	

Unrealized receivables: The accounts receivable are not an unrealized receivable under Section 751(c) because the income has already been included in income.

Inventory: The accounts receivable are inventory. (Section 751(d)) If the partnership had sold the accounts receivable for its fair market value, it would have no gain or loss.

AR:	$14,000
AB:	14,000
Gain:	$ 0

Mike is not required to recognize any ordinary income.

The amount that, when added to the amount of ordinary income of zero, results in the amount of gain or loss the partner has on disposition of the partnership interest, $9,000, is a gain of $9,000.

Ordinary income:	$ 0
"X"	9,000
Gain on disposition:	$9,000

If the partnership had sold the collectibles for its fair market value, it would have gain recognized of $13,000 (amount realized of $20,000, less $7,000 basis).

AR:	$20,000
AB:	7,000
Gain:	$13,000

One-half, or $6,500, would have been allocated to Mike. To this extent Mike has capital gain from collectibles. (Treas. Reg. § 1.1(h)-1)

The amount that, when added to the amount of gain from collectibles, $6,500, results in the amount of capital gain Mike has on disposition of the partnership interest, $9,000 gain, is a capital gain of $2,500. Thus, Mike has $2,500 of adjusted net long-term capital gain.

Lukewarm gain:	$6,500
"X"	2,500
Capital gain on disposition:	$9,000

In sum, from the sale of his partnership interest, Mike must report $6,500 of capital gain from collectibles, and $2,500 of net long-term capital gain.[*] (Section 751(a); Treas. Reg.§ 1.751-1(a)(2))

---

[*] Note that this makes sense. If the partnership disposed of the stock, there would be a $5,000 gain (amount realized of $14,000, less $9,000 adjusted basis). His share of the gain, $2,500, is represented in the sale of the interest.

2. What are the tax consequences to Opie?

Opie purchased the interest for $25,000. Thus, his outside basis in the partnership interest is $25,000. (Section 1012)

b. Alternatively, the partnership had made an election under Section 754.

1. What are the tax consequences to Mike?

(Same answer as in a, above.) Upon the sale of his partnership interest, Mike has a $9,000 gain.

AR:	$25,000 ($20,000 cash + $5,000 debt relief)
AB:	16,000
Gain:	$ 9,000

Unrealized receivables: The accounts receivable are not an unrealized receivable under Section 751(c) because the income has already been included in income.

Inventory: The accounts receivable are inventory. (Section 751(d)) If the partnership had sold the accounts receivable for its fair market value, it would have no gain or loss.

AR:	$14,000
AB:	14,000
Gain:	$ 0

Mike is not required to recognize any ordinary income.

The amount that, when added to the amount of ordinary income of zero, results in the amount of gain or loss the partner has on disposition of the partnership interest, $9,000, is a gain of $9,000.

Ordinary income:	$ 0
"X"	9,000
Gain on disposition:	$9,000

If the partnership had sold the collectibles for its fair market value, it would have gain recognized of $13,000 (amount realized of $20,000, less $7,000 basis).

AR:	$20,000
AB:	7,000
Gain:	$13,000

One-half, or $6,500, would have been allocated to Mike. To this extent Mike has capital gain from collectibles. (Treas. Reg. § 1.1(h)-1)

The amount that, when added to the amount of gain from collectibles, $6,500, results in the amount of capital gain Mike has on disposition of the partnership interest, $9,000 gain, is a capital gain of $2,500. Thus, Mike has $2,500 of adjusted net long-term capital gain.

Lukewarm gain:	$6,500
"X"	2,500
Capital gain on disposition:	$9,000

In sum, from the sale of his partnership interest, Mike must report $6,500 of capital gain from collectibles, and $2,500 of net long-term capital gain.* (Section 751(a); Treas. Reg.§ 1.751-1(a)(2))

* Note that this makes sense. If the partnership disposed of the stock, there would be a $5,000 gain (amount realized of $14,000, less $9,000 adjusted basis). His share of the gain, $2,500, is represented in the sale of the interest.

2. What are the tax consequences to Opie?

Because the partnership had made a Section 754 election, Opie receives his own inside basis in the partnership assets. First, determine the amount of adjustment to the inside basis. The amount of the adjustment is Opie's outside basis, $25,000, less his share of inside basis. Treas. Reg. § 1.743-1(b).

> outside basis
> − share of inside basis
> adjustment

To determine Opie's share of the partnership's inside basis of its assets, determine Opie's interest in the partnership's previously taxed capital (PTC) plus Opie's share of partnership liabilities. (Treas. Reg. § 1.743-1(d)(1))

> Share of inside basis = Opie's PTC + share of partnership liabilities

Opie's interest in previously taxed capital is determined by considering a hypothetical disposition by the partnership of all its assets. (Treas. Reg. § 1.743-1(d)(1)) The assets are sold for cash equal to the asset's fair market value in a taxable transaction. The result would be:

Asset	Adj. Basis	FMV	Gain/Loss	Opie's share
Cash	$ 2,000	$ 2,000	$ 0	$ 0
Acct. Rec.	14,000	14,000	0	0
Collectibles	7,000	20,000	13,000	6,500
Stock	9,000	14,000	5,000	2,500

In a hypothetical liquidation, Opie would receive:

> Share of cash: $20,000
> Share of tax loss: +   0
> Share of tax gain: − 9,000   (= 6,500 + 2,500)
> Share of PTC: $11,000

His share of the inside basis would be $16,000:

> Share of inside basis = Opie's PTC + share of partnership liabilities
> = $11,000 + 5,000 = $16,000

His overall adjustment would be:

> outside basis $25,000
> − share of inside basis   − 16,000
> Adjustment $ 9,000

Second, once the adjustment has been determined, that amount must be allocated among the partnership's assets. (Treas. Reg. § 1.743-1(e)) The collectibles and stock are allocated to the capital and hotchpot (Section 1231) asset group and the accounts receivable are allocated to the ordinary asset group. (Treas. Reg. § 1.755-1(b)(2)(i))

The sale of the ordinary assets would result not result in any gain.

Asset	Adj. Basis	FMV	Gain/Loss	Opie's share
Acct. Rec.	$14,000	14,000	0	0

The amount allocated to the capital and hotchpot (Section 1231) group is:

Amount of total adjustment:	$9,000
Amount allocated to ordinary:	– 0
Allocation to capital/hotchpot:	$9,000

For assets in the capital and hotchpot group, each item is allocated an amount equal to the amount of income, gain, or loss that would be allocated to the partner from the hypothetical sale of the item. (Treas. Reg. § 1.755-1(b)(3)(ii)) Thus, for the collectibles and stock, the allocation would be $6,500 to the collectibles and $2,500 to the stock, for a net allocation of $9,000.

Asset	Adj. Basis	FMV	Gain/Loss	Opie's share
Collectibles	$7,000	$20,000	$13,000	$6,500
Stock	9,000	14,000	5,000	2,500

Adjustment would be made to Opie's inside basis in the items as follows:

Asset	Current share of basis	Adjustment	New inside basis
Cash	$ 1,000	$ 0	$ 1,000 (no change)
Acct. Rec.	7,000	0	7,000
Collectibles	3,500	6,500	10,000
Stock	4,500	2,500	7,000
Total:	$16,000	$9,000	$25,000*

* Note that this result makes sense. Opie paid $25,000 for the interest, and the total of his share of the inside basis is $25,000.

Chapter VIII

Non-Liquidating Distributions from the Partnership to a Partner — General Rules

Just as Congress provided for the tax-free contribution of property to a partnership, it also provided, in most cases, for the tax-free withdrawal of property from a partnership.

A. Non-Liquidating Distribution of Cash

Impact on outside basis. A partner's withdrawal of cash from a partnership generally is not a taxable event to the partner or the partnership.[1] The partner's outside basis is reduced by the amount of cash distributed.[2] However, because the basis can never be negative, to the extent the cash distributed exceeds the partner's outside basis, the partner must recognize gain.[3] The gain is characterized as gain from the sale or exchange of a partner's partnership interest.

The rule applies to actual cash distributions and transactions that are treated as cash distributions. For example, a reduction in the partner's individual liabilities (*e.g.*, through assumption by the partnership) is treated as a cash distribution. Similarly, the forgiveness of a debt owed to the partnership is treated as a distribution of cash to the partner.[4]

Advance or draw. An advance or draw against a partner's distributive share of income is treated as a loan, and not a distribution of cash. On the last day of the partnership's taxable year, the advance or draw is treated as a cash distribution.[5]

---

1. Section 731(a).
2. Sections 705(a)(2); 733(1).
3. Section 731(a)(1).
4. Treas. Reg. § 1.731-1(c)(2).
5. Treas. Reg. § 1.731-1(a)(1)(ii).

Impact on capital account. When a partner withdraws cash from a partnership, he is reducing his economic investment in the partnership. Accordingly, his capital account is reduced by the amount of the distribution.

B. Non-Liquidating Distribution of Property

Impact on outside basis. The contribution of property to a partnership is not a taxable event. Similarly, a partner's withdrawal of property from a partnership generally is not a taxable event to the partner or the partnership.[6] Note, however, that a distribution of property to a partner may be taxable if:

- There is a disproportionate distribution of property;[7] or
- The distribution is part of a "mixing bowl" transaction.[8]

In general, the partner takes the property with the partnership's inside basis, a transferred basis. And, his outside basis is reduced by the basis of the property distributed.[9] Thus, just as the gain or loss inherent in property was preserved in the property upon contribution by a partner to the partnership, it also is preserved upon distribution of the property from the partnership to a partner.

To the extent the basis in the property distributed is larger than the partner's outside basis, the basis in the property is reduced to reflect the partner's outside basis before the asset is distributed.[10] Then, upon distribution of the asset, the partner will have a zero outside basis, and he takes the property with the reduced basis. For purposes of determining the length of time the partner has held the property, he can include (tack) the partnership's holding period onto his own holding period.[11]

If both cash and property are distributed, the consequences of the cash distribution are considered before the consequences of the property distribution.

Impact on capital account. The partner's capital account is reduced by the fair market value of the property. If the partner takes the property subject to a liability, his capital account is reduced by the net value of the property distributed. If the fair market value of the property is different than its book value, the book gain or loss must be reflected in the capital accounts prior to the distribution. Then, the distributee partner's capital account will be reduced based on the fair market value of the asset.[12] Alternatively, the partnership may elect to reflect its assets at fair market value and restate capital accounts to reflect current fair market values, then distribute the property.[13]

---

6. Section 731(a), (b).

7. See Section 751(b), discussed in Chapter IX.

8. Sections 704(c); 737, discussed in X.

9. Sections 731(a); 732(a)(1); 733(2). The partnership does not recognize any gain or loss on the distribution. Section 731(b); Treas. Reg. § 1.731-1(b).

10. Section 732.

11. Sections 735(b); 1223. For purposes of determining the length of time the partner has held inventory, the partner may not tack the partnership's holding period onto his own. Section 735(b).

12. Treas. Reg. § 1.704-1(b)(2)(iv)(e)(1).

13. Treas. Reg. § 1.704-1(b)(2)(iv)(f)(5)(ii).

1. Non-Liquidating Distribution of More Than One Property

The partnership may distribute several pieces of property to the partner. The partner takes each property with the partnership's inside basis. His outside basis is reduced by the bases of all the property distributed.

If the sum of the inside bases of all the property distributed is greater than the partner's outside basis, the basis of the property must be reduced so that the partner's outside basis is equal to the total of the bases in the assets distributed. The objective of the statute is to preserve the amount of ordinary income in any distributed unrealized receivables or inventory. Thus, the statutory scheme of reducing the basis in the distributed assets, to the extent possible, prevents a reduction in the basis of the unrealized receivables and inventory assets.

To reduce the basis of the assets distributed, first, identify all unrealized receivables and inventory items to be distributed to the partner. Allocate basis to those assets in an amount equal to the partnership's basis.[14] Unrealized receivables include, to the extent not previously included in income, any right to payment for services rendered. They also include the right to payment for goods delivered to the extent the proceeds would be treated as amounts received from the sale or exchange of property other than a capital asset. They also include any gain that would be characterized as ordinary income under the depreciation recapture provisions.[15] Inventory includes those assets held for sale to customers and any items held by the partnership that are not characterized as a capital or hotchpot (Section 1231) item.[16]

If the partner does not have sufficient basis to allocate to unrealized receivables and inventory, the partnership's basis in those assets must be reduced. If any of the properties have unrealized depreciation, reduce the basis by the amount of unrealized depreciation. If necessary, proportion the reduction based on the amount of depreciation in the assets.[17] If an additional reduction is needed, the bases of the assets are reduced in proportion to their respective (new) adjusted bases so as to equal the partner's outside basis.[18] The assets are distributed with the adjusted bases.

Second, if the partner has any remaining outside basis after making the allocation to unrealized receivables and inventory, the remaining portion is allocated to the other distributed property. First, allocate basis to those assets in an amount equal to the partnership's basis.[19]

If the partner does not have sufficient remaining basis to allocate to these other assets, the partnership's basis in these asset must be reduced. If any of the properties have unrealized depreciation, reduce the basis by the amount of unrealized depreciation. If necessary, proportion the reduction based on the amount of depreciation in the assets.[20] If an additional reduction is needed, the bases of the assets are reduced in proportion

---

14. Section 732(c)(1)(A)(i).
15. Section 751(c).
16. Section 751(d).
17. Section 732(c)(1)(A)(ii), (c)(3)(A).
18. Section 732(c)(1)(A)(ii), (c)(3)(B).
19. Section 732(c)(1)(B)(i).
20. Section 732(c)(1)(B)(ii), (c)(3)(A).

to their respective (new) adjusted bases so as to equal the partner's remaining outside basis.[21]

The partner takes each property with the partnership's inside basis, adjusted as provided above. His outside basis is reduced to zero.

2. Distributee Partner's Election

In certain circumstances, a different basis rule may apply. If the property is distributed:

- within two years from the time the partner acquired his interest by purchase, exchange, or inheritance;
- the partnership did not have a Section 754 election in effect at the time the partner acquired the interest; and
- the partner makes an election under Section 732(d),

then, the basis of the property will be determined as if the partnership had made the Section 754 election. The basis of the property is adjusted as provided for under Section 743(b). This basis is the basis used in determining the reduction in the partner's basis upon distribution of the property and the basis the partner takes in the property. The election only applies to the property distributed; it has no application with respect to property retained by the partnership.[22]

If the fair market value of the partnership property, excluding cash, at the time the partner acquired his interest is greater than 110 percent of the partnership's adjusted basis in the assets, the Internal Revenue Service may require the basis to be adjusted. The Service may require the adjustment even if the distribution is not made within two years of the time the partner acquired his interest.[23] Under the regulations, the adjustment will be required only in those situations when the absence of the election would cause a shift in basis from nondepreciable property to depreciable property.[24]

3. Distribution of Marketable Securities

Marketable securities include financial instruments (*e.g.*, stocks and bonds) and foreign currency that are actively traded. They include interests in a common trust fund, a mutual fund, and any financial instrument convertible into money or marketable securities.[25] Because the securities are easy to value and are liquid, when distributed from the partnership they are treated in the same manner as cash distributions. To the extent of the fair market value of the security on the date of distribution, the distribution is treated as a distribution of cash.[26] The basis in the hands of the partner is the basis

---

21. Section 732(c)()1)(B)(ii), (c)(3)(B).
22. Treas. Reg. § 1.732-1(d)(1)(vi).
23. Section 732(d).
24. Treas. Reg. § 1.732-1(d)(4)(ii).
25. Section 731(c)(2).
26. Section 731(c)(1). The amount of the distribution of marketable securities that is treated as a distribution of cash may be reduced in some circumstances. See Section 731(c)(3)(B).

as determined under the rules for distributions of property to a partner from the partnership.

If the fair market value of the security is greater than the partner's outside basis, the partner must recognize gain to the extent of the excess. When gain is recognized, the partner's basis in the security is its basis as determined under the above rules, increased by the amount of gain recognized.[27]

Exceptions. A distribution of marketable securities is not treated like a distribution of cash if:[28]

- The security was contributed to the partnership by the distributee partner; or
- The partnership is an investment partnership and the partner contributed only money and/or securities.

C. Ordering Rules

The order in which adjustments are made to a partner's outside basis can be important for several reasons, including determining if a loss must be deferred because of insufficient basis or gain must be reported because a cash distribution exceeds the partner's basis. Distributions to a partner are taken into consideration on the day the distribution is made. An advance or "draw" against a distributive share is treated as a distribution made on the last day of the partnership's taxable year. The order in which year-end allocations and distributions are taken into consideration is as follows:[29]

- First, on the last day of the partnership's taxable year, increase the partner's basis by the amount of the distributive share of partnership income.
- Second, decrease the outside basis for year-end distributions of cash, then of property.
- Third, decrease the basis by the amount of the distributive share of partnership losses.
- Fourth, if sufficient basis, decrease the basis by the amount of any losses carried forward.

D. Characterization of Subsequent Disposition of Property Distributed to a Partner

Congress was concerned about partners distributing property from the partnership to a partner and the partner selling it in an individual capacity to achieve a more favorable tax consequence (*i.e.*, converting ordinary income into long-term capital gain). Accordingly, the Code requires retaining the ordinary income treatment upon the distribution and sale of unrealized receivables, inventory, and recapture gain.

---

27. Section 731(c)(4).
28. Section 731(c)(3)(A).
29. Section 706(a).

Unrealized receivables. If the property distributed to the partner comes within the definition of an unrealized receivable, its character as ordinary continues in the hands of the partner, regardless of the use to which the partner may put the property or how long the partner holds the property before selling it.[30]

Inventory items. If the property distributed to the partner comes within the definition of inventory, for five years following distribution its character as ordinary continues in the hands of the partner, regardless of the use to which the partner may put the property. After five years, the character is determined in the hands of the partner.[31] If the property meets the definition of both an unrealized receivable and inventory, the character of the property in the hands of the partner is that of an unrealized receivable.

Recapture gain. If the property had any potential recapture income at the time of distribution, the recapture is preserved in the hands of the partner.[32]

E. Partnership Election

When a partnership distributes cash to a partner in excess of the partner's outside basis, the partner must recognize gain to the extent of the excess.[33] Because the partner recognizes gain, but no adjustments are made to the bases of the partnership property, the partnership's balance sheet may become distorted.

Similarly, when a partnership distributes property to a partner, the bases of the assets retained by the partnership are not affected.[34] This rule applies even in those situations where the partner was required to adjust the basis of the property being distributed (*i.e.*, the partner's outside basis was less than the basis of the asset being distributed).[35] Because the partner adjusted the basis in the distributed property, but no adjustments were made to any remaining partnership property, the partnership's balance sheet may become distorted.

> **Example:** Ann, Bob, and Carl are equal partners in a partnership. The partnership balance sheet appears as follows:

---

30. Section 735(a). If the partner disposes of the unrealized receivables in a transaction that qualifies for non-recognition, the characterization rule applies to the property received in the exchange in the same manner as it applied to the unrealized receivables. Section 735(c)(2).

31. Section 735(a). For purposes of determining the length of time the partner has held the inventory, the partner may not tack the partnership's holding period onto his own. Section 735(b). If the partner disposes of the inventory in a transaction that qualifies for non-recognition, the characterization rule applies to the property received in the exchange in the same manner as it applied to the inventory. Section 735(c)(2).

32. Sections 1245(b)(5); 1250(d)(5).

33. Section 731(a)(1).

34. Section 734(a).

35. Section 732(a)(2).

Asset	Basis	FMV	Partner	AB	Cap. Acct.
Cash	$6,000	$ 6,000	Ann	$3,000	$ 6,000
Land	3,000	12,000	Bob	3,000	6,000
	$9,000	$18,000	Carl	3,000	6,000
				$9,000	$18,000

The partnership distributes $6,000 of cash (equal to the amount of her capital account) to Ann in liquidation of her entire interest. Because Ann's outside basis is only $3,000, Ann must recognize $3,000 of gain (the excess of the cash distribution over Ann's outside basis). Note that the partnership assets reflect $9,000 of gain in the land, 1/3 of which, $3,000, would have been allocable to Ann if she had remained in the partnership and the asset were sold.

When a partnership distributes cash or property to a partner, the bases of the assets retained by the partnership are not affected. Thus, after the liquidation of Ann's interest, the partnership balance sheet would appear as follows:

Asset	Basis	FMV	Partner	AB	Cap. Acct.
Land	$3,000	$12,000	Bob	$3,000	$ 6,000
	$3,000	$12,000	Carl	3,000	6,000
				$6,000	$12,000

Even though the $3,000 gain in the land allocable to Ann was arguably reported by Ann, no adjustment has been made to the partnership's basis in the land. This distortion is reflected in the disparity between the inside basis of the partnership assets, $3,000, and the total of the partners' outside basis, $6,000.

If the partnership sells the land for $12,000, it will recognize gain of $9,000. One-half of the gain, $4,500, would be allocated to each of Bob and Carl and their outside basis would each be increased. They each would be recognizing $1,500 more gain than they would have if the property had been sold while Ann was still a partner in the partnership.

After the sale of the land, the partnership's balance sheet would appear as follows:

Asset	Basis	FMV	Partner	AB	Cap. Acct.
Cash	$12,000	$12,000	Bob	$ 7,500	$ 6,000
	$12,000	$12,000	Carl	7,500	6,000
				$15,000	$12,000

Again, there is a distortion, reflected in the disparity between the inside basis of the partnership's assets, $12,000, and the total of the partners' outside basis, $15,000. It also is reflected in the disparity between the partner's outside basis and capital accounts. If the partnership were to liquidate, the $12,000 of cash would be distributed equally between Bob and Carl, with each receiving $6,000. They would both recognize a loss of $1,500 (cash distribution of $6,000, less outside basis of $7,500), eventually recognizing a loss to offset the amount of gain that had previously been taxed to Ann, then again taxed to them upon the sale of the land.

Exception to the general rule. The partnership may make an election under Section 754 to adjust the inside basis of the partnership assets under Section 734(b). The adjustment corrects for an imbalance caused by a partner recognizing gain on the distribution of cash or adjusting the basis of distributed property.

When a partnership distributes cash to a partner in excess of the partner's outside basis, so that the partner must recognize gain in the amount of the excess, the amount of the Section 734(b) adjustment is the amount of gain recognized. The adjustment must be made to capital and hotchpot (Section 1231) assets.[36]

When a partner is required to adjust the basis of the property being distributed because the partner's outside basis is less than the basis of the asset being distributed, the amount of the adjustment is the amount of reduction in the property's basis. The upward adjustment is made to property of the same class of property that gave rise to the adjustment. Thus, the partnership property must be divided into two groups, one group containing capital and hotchpot (Section 1231) assets and the second group containing all remaining (ordinary) assets. Only the group with the same character of assets as that distributed by the partnership to the partner should be given a basis adjustment.[37]

Within the applicable group of assets, allocate the upward adjustment first to properties with unrealized appreciation in proportion to their appreciation (but only to the extent of the unrealized appreciation). Allocate any remaining adjustment in proportion to the fair market value of the property.[38]

If the partnership does not have assets of the character that must be adjusted, the adjustment is carried forward until the partnership acquires such property and an adjustment can be made.[39]

Depreciable assets. If the asset is depreciable and the basis has been increased because of the election, to the extent of the increase, the partnership is treated as having acquired a separate asset that was placed in service on the date of the distribution. That portion may be depreciated using an appropriate recovery method. The original portion of the basis continues to be depreciated using the traditional method used by the partnership.[40] If the asset is depreciable and the basis has been decreased, the decrease is taken into consideration over the property's remaining useful life.[41]

The allocation impacts the partnership and the partners going forward. It is not unique to the partner receiving the distribution. If the partnership makes an election under Section 754 to make a basis adjustment with respect to distributions of property by the partnership as provided in Section 734(b), the adjustment to the buyer-partner's basis in partnership assets as provided in Section 743(b) also applies.

Example: Ann, Bob, and Carl are equal partners in a partnership which has made an election under Section 754. The partnership balance sheet appears as follows:

Asset	Basis	FMV	Partner	AB	Cap. Acct.
Cash	$6,000	$ 6,000	Ann	$3,000	$ 6,000
Land	3,000	12,000	Bob	3,000	6,000
	$9,000	$18,000	Carl	3,000	6,000
				$9,000	$18,000

---

36. Treas. Reg. § 1.755-1(c)(1)(ii).
37. Treas. Reg. § 1.755-1(c)(1)(i).
38. Id.
39. Treas. Reg. § 1.755-1(c)(4).
40. Treas. Reg. § 1.734-1(e)(1).
41. Treas. Reg. § 1.734-1(e)(2).

The partnership distributes $6,000 of cash (equal to the amount of her capital account) to Ann in liquidation of her entire interest. Because Ann's outside basis is only $3,000, Ann must recognize $3,000 of gain (the excess of the cash distribution over Ann's outside basis).

Because the partnership has made a Section 754 election, it must adjust the inside basis of the partnership assets under Section 734(b). The amount of the adjustment is the amount of the excess (*i.e.*, the amount of gain recognized), or $3,000. The adjustment must be made to capital and hotchpot (Section 1231) assets. Because the land is a capital asset, the partnership increases its basis by $3,000. After the adjustment, the partnership balance sheet would be as follows:

Asset	Basis	FMV	Partner	AB	Cap. Acct.
Land	$6,000	$12,000	Bob	$3,000	$6,000
	$6,000	$12,000	Carl	3,000	6,000
				$6,000	$12,000

Summary

Distribution of Cash and/or Property from a Partnership: When cash and/or property is distributed to a partner:

Cash:

Step 1: Reduce the partner's basis by the amount of the cash distribution.

Step 2: If the amount of cash distribution exceeds the partner's basis, the partner must recognize gain to the extent of the excess, resulting in a zero basis.

Step 3: Reduce the partner's capital account by the amount of the cash distribution.

Property:

Step 4: Compare the inside basis of property to be distributed to the partner to the partner's outside basis.

Step 5: If the partner's outside basis is less than the property's inside basis, reduce the basis in the property to equal the partner's outside basis. Distribute the property.

Step 6: Reduce the partner's outside basis by the property's inside basis.

Step 7: If necessary, adjust the partners' capital accounts for any book gain or loss. Then, reduce the distributee partner's capital account by the fair market value of the property.

Partnership Election:

- The adjustment corrects for an imbalance caused by a partner recognizing gain on the distribution of cash or adjusting the basis of distributed property.
- When a partnership distributes cash to a partner in excess of the partner's outside basis, so that the partner must recognize gain in the amount of the excess, the amount of the Section 734(b) adjustment is the amount of gain recognized. The adjustment must be made to capital and hotchpot (Section 1231) assets.
- When a partner is required to adjust the basis of the property being distributed because the partner's outside basis is less than the basis of the asset being distributed, the amount of the adjustment is the amount of reduction in the property's basis. The upward adjustment is made to property of the same class of property that gave rise to the adjustment.

Questions

In the following questions, ignore any potential implications from the application of Section 751(b).

1.   Ann was a partner in the partnership. Her outside basis was $50,000 and her capital account balance was $70,000. What are the tax consequences to Ann when the partnership distributes $20,000 to her?

2.   Bob was a partner in the partnership. His outside basis was $5,000 and his capital account balance was $40,000. What are the tax consequences to Bob when the partnership distributes $15,000 to him?

3.   Carl was a partner in the partnership. His outside basis was $40,000 and his capital account balance was $50,000. What are the tax consequences to Carl when the partnership distributes stock to him? The stock has a basis of $10,000 and fair market value of $30,000.

4.   Deb was a partner in the partnership. Her outside basis was $10,000 and her capital account balance was $50,000. What are the tax consequences to Deb when the partnership distributes land to her? The land has a basis of $15,000 and fair market value of $30,000.

5.   Ellen was a partner in the partnership. Her outside basis was $50,000 and her capital account balance was $70,000. What are the tax consequences to Ellen when the partnership distributes $10,000 and stock to her? The stock has a basis of $20,000 and fair market value of $30,000.

6.   Frank was a partner in the partnership. His outside basis was $30,000 and his capital account balance was $70,000. What are the tax consequences to Frank when the partnership distributes $10,000 and land to him? The land has a basis of $30,000 and fair market value of $30,000.

7.   Greg was a partner in the partnership. His outside basis was $30,000 and his capital account balance was $80,000. What are the tax consequences to Greg when the partnership distributes Whiteacre and Blackacre to him? Whiteacre has a basis of $20,000 and fair market value of $30,000 and Blackacre has a basis of $30,000 and fair market value of $40,000.

8.   Hal was a partner in the partnership. His outside basis was $5,000 and his capital account balance was $60,000. What are the tax consequences to Hal when the partnership distributes accounts receivable and inventory to him? The accounts receivable have a zero basis and fair market value of $6,000 and the inventory has a basis of $3,000 and fair market value of $6,000.

9.   Ira was a partner in a partnership. The partnership distributed inventory to him. The inventory had a basis of $6,000 and fair market value of $10,000. Three years later, Ira sold the inventory for $15,000. What is the character of the gain?

10. Jeb was a partner in a partnership. The partnership distributed inventory to him. The inventory had a basis of $4,000 and fair market value of $10,000. Jeb held the inventory as investment property. Six years later, Jeb sold the inventory for $15,000. What is the character of the gain?

11. Kent was a partner in a partnership. The partnership distributed accounts receivable to him. The accounts receivable had a zero basis and fair market value of $10,000. Three years later, Kent sold the accounts receivable for $15,000. What is the character of the gain?

12. Len was a partner in a partnership. The partnership distributed accounts receivable to him. The accounts receivable had a zero basis and fair market value of $10,000. Six years later, Len sold the accounts receivable for $15,000. What is the character of the gain?

13. Mike, Ned, and Opie are equal partners in a general partnership. The partnership balance sheet was as follows:

Asset	Adj. Basis	FMV	Partner	AB	Cap. Acct.
Cash	$100,000	$100,000	Mike	$ 10,000	$100,000
Stock	70,000	160,000	Ned	60,000	100,000
Land	10,000	40,000	Opie	110,000	100,000
Total:	$180,000	$300,000		$180,000	$300,000

The partnership distributed $50,000 to Mike. After the distribution, Mike had a one-fifth interest worth $50,000.

(a) What are the consequences to Mike and the partnership if the partnership has not made a Section 754 election? Reconstruct the balance sheet after the distribution.

(b) What are the consequences to Mike and the partnership if the partnership has made a Section 754 election? Reconstruct the balance sheet after the distribution.

14. Paul, Quinn, and Roy are equal partners in a general partnership. The partnership balance sheet was as follows:

Asset	Adj. Basis	FMV	Partner	AB	Cap. Acct.
Cash	$140,000	$140,000	Paul	$ 20,000	$100,000
Inventory	9,000	10,000	Quinn	120,000	100,000
Stock	30,000	50,000	Roy	109,000	100,000
Land	70,000	100,000		$249,000	$300,000
Total:	$249,000	$300,000			

The partnership distributed the stock to Paul. After the distribution, Paul had a one-fifth interest worth $50,000.

(a) What are the consequences to Paul and the partnership if the partnership has not made a Section 754 election? Reconstruct the balance sheet after the distribution.

(b) What are the consequences to Paul and the partnership if the partnership has made a Section 754 election? Reconstruct the balance sheet after the distribution.

Solutions

1. **Ann was a partner in the partnership. Her outside basis was $50,000 and her capital account balance was $70,000. What are the tax consequences to Ann when the partnership distributes $20,000 to her?**

The distribution of cash to Ann is not a taxable event to her or the partnership. (Section 731(a)(1)) Her outside basis is reduced by the amount of cash distributed, or reduced from $50,000 to $30,000. (Section 733(1))

Basis:	$50,000
Distribution:	− 20,000
Basis:	$30,000

The distribution to Ann has reduced her economic investment in the partnership. Accordingly, her capital account is reduced by the amount of the distribution, or reduced from $70,000 to $50,000.

Cap. account:	$70,000
Distribution:	− 20,000
Cap. account:	$50,000

2. **Bob was a partner in the partnership. His outside basis was $5,000 and his capital account balance was $40,000. What are the tax consequences to Bob when the partnership distributes $15,000 to him?**

The distribution of cash to Bob, by itself, is not a taxable event to the partner or the partnership. (Section 731(a)(1)) His outside basis is reduced by the amount of cash distributed. However, because his basis can never be negative, to the extent the cash distributed exceeds his outside basis, Bob must recognize gain. (Section 731(a)(1)) The cash distribution exceeds his outside basis by $10,000. His basis in the partnership is reduced to zero (Section 733(1)) and the $10,000 gain is characterized as the gain from the sale or exchange of his partnership interest.

Basis:	$ 5,000	
Distribution:	− 15,000	
Basis:	$ 0	$10,000 gain

The distribution to Bob has reduced his economic investment in the partnership. Accordingly, his capital account is reduced by the amount of the distribution, or reduced from $40,000 to $25,000.

Cap. account:	$40,000
Distribution:	− 15,000
Cap. account:	$25,000

3. **Carl was a partner in the partnership. His outside basis was $40,000 and his capital account balance was $50,000. What are the tax consequences to Carl when the partnership distributes stock to him? The stock has a basis of $10,000 and fair market value of $30,000.**

The distribution of property to Carl from the partnership generally is not a taxable event. (Section 731(a)(1)) Carl takes the stock with the partnership's inside basis, or

$10,000. (Section 732(a)(1)) His outside basis is reduced by the basis of the property distributed, from $40,000 to $30,000. (Section 733(2))

Basis:	$40,000	
Distribution:	– 10,000	
Basis:	$30,000	His basis in the stock is $10,000.

The distribution to Carl has reduced his economic investment in the partnership. Accordingly, his capital account is reduced by the value of the property, or reduced from $50,000 to $20,000.

Cap. account:	$50,000
Distribution:	– 30,000
Cap. account:	$20,000

4.   Deb was a partner in the partnership. Her outside basis was $10,000 and her capital account balance was $50,000. What are the tax consequences to Deb when the partnership distributes land to her? The land has a basis of $15,000 and fair market value of $30,000.

The distribution of property to Deb from the partnership generally is not a taxable event. (Section 731(a)(1)) Deb takes the property with the partnership's inside basis. However, the partnership's basis in the land is larger than Deb's outside basis. Accordingly, the land's basis is reduced to reflect Deb's outside basis before the land is distributed, or to $10,000. (Section 732(a)(2)) Upon distribution of the land, Deb will have a zero outside basis. (Section 733(2))

Basis:	$10,000	
Distribution:	– 10,000	
Basis:	$ 0	Her basis in the land is $10,000.

The distribution to Deb has reduced her economic investment in the partnership. Accordingly, her capital account is reduced by the value of the property, or reduced from $50,000 to $20,000.

Cap. account:	$50,000
Distribution:	– 30,000
Cap. account:	$20,000

5.   Ellen was a partner in the partnership. Her outside basis was $50,000 and her capital account balance was $70,000. What are the tax consequences to Ellen when the partnership distributes $10,000 and stock to her? The stock has a basis of $20,000 and fair market value of $30,000.

If both cash and property are distributed, the consequences of the cash distribution are considered before the consequences of the property. The distribution of cash to Ellen is not a taxable event to her or the partnership. (Section 731(a)(1)) Her outside basis is reduced by the amount of cash distributed, or reduced from $50,000 to $40,000. (Section 733(1))

Basis:	$50,000
Cash distribution:	– 10,000
Basis:	$40,000

The distribution of property to Ellen from the partnership generally is not a taxable event. (Section 731(a)(1)) Ellen takes the stock with the partnership's inside basis, or

$20,000. (Section 732(a)(1)) Her outside basis is reduced by the basis of the property distributed, from $40,000 to $20,000. (Section 733(2))

Basis:	$40,000
Distribution:	− 20,000
Basis:	$20,000 Her basis in the stock is $20,000.

The distribution of cash and property to Ellen has reduced her economic investment in the partnership. Accordingly, her capital account is reduced by the cash and by the value of the property, or reduced from $70,000 to $30,000.

Cap. account:	$70,000
Cash distribution:	− 10,000
Distribution:	− 30,000
Cap. account:	$30,000

6. Frank was a partner in the partnership. His outside basis was $30,000 and his capital account balance was $70,000. What are the tax consequences to Frank when the partnership distributes $10,000 and land to him? The land has a basis of $30,000 and fair market value of $30,000.

If both cash and property are distributed, the consequences of the cash distributions are considered before the consequences of the property. The distribution of cash to Frank is not a taxable event to him or the partnership. (Section 731(a)(1)) His outside basis is reduced by the amount of cash distributed, or reduced from $30,000 to $20,000. (Section 733(1))

Basis:	$30,000
Cash distribuiton:	− 10,000
Basis:	$20,000

The distribution of property to Frank from the partnership generally is not a taxable event. (Section 731(a)(1)) Frank takes the property with the partnership's inside basis. However, the partnership's basis in the land is larger than Frank's outside basis. Accordingly, the land's basis is reduced to reflect Frank's outside basis before the land is distributed, or to $20,000. (Section 732(a)(2)) Upon distribution of the land, Frank will have a zero outside basis. (Section 733(1))

Basis:	$20,000
Distribution:	− 20,000
Basis:	$ 0 His basis in the land is $20,000.

The distribution of cash and property to Frank has reduced his economic investment in the partnership. Accordingly, his capital account is reduced by the cash and by the value of the property, or reduced from $70,000 to $30,000.

Cap. account:	$70,000
Cash distribution:	− 10,000
Distribution:	− 30,000
Cap. account:	$30,000

7. Greg was a partner in the partnership. His outside basis was $30,000 and his capital account balance was $80,000. What are the tax consequences to Greg when the partnership distributes Whiteacre and Blackacre to him? Whiteacre has a basis of

$20,000 and fair market value of $30,000 and Blackacre has a basis of $30,000 and fair market value of $40,000.

The distribution of property to Greg from the partnership generally is not a taxable event. (Section 731(a)(1)) Greg takes the property with the partnership's inside basis. However, the partnership's basis in Whiteacre and Blackacre is larger than Greg's outside basis. Accordingly, the lands' basis is reduced by a total of $20,000 to reflect Greg's outside basis before the land is distributed, or to $30,000. (Section 732(a)(2))

With respect to the distributed property, the amount by which the basis should be reduced is allocated first to assets with unrealized depreciation. (Section 732(c)(1)(A)) There is no unrealized depreciation. Thus, the decrease in basis is allocated in proportion to their respective adjusted basis. (Section 732(c)(1)(B), (c)(3)) The reduction is as follows:

Whiteacre: $20,000/$50,000 x $20,000 = $8,000
Blackacre: $30,000/$50,000 x $20,000 = $12,000

Whiteacre:	Blackacre:
$20,000	$30,000
− 8,000	− 12,000
12,000	18,000

Upon distribution of the property, Greg will have a zero outside basis. (Section 733(2))

Basis:	$30,000	
Whiteacre:	− 12,000	
Blackacre:	− 18,000	
Basis:	$ 0	His basis in Whiteacre is $12,000 and his basis in Blackacre is $18,000

The distribution of property reduced Greg's economic investment in the partnership. Accordingly, his capital account is reduced by the value of Whiteacre and Blackacre, or reduced from $50,000 to $20,000.

Cap. account:	$80,000
Whiteacre:	− 30,000
Blackacre:	− 40,000
Cap. account:	$10,000

8.   Hal was a partner in the partnership. His outside basis was $5,000 and his capital account balance was $60,000. What are the tax consequences to Hal when the partnership distributes accounts receivable and inventory to him? The accounts receivable have a zero basis and fair market value of $6,000 and the inventory has a basis of $3,000 and fair market value of $6,000.

The distribution of property to Hal from the partnership generally is not a taxable event. (Section 731(a)(1)) Hal takes the property with the partnership's inside basis, or a zero basis in the accounts receivable and $3,000 basis in the inventory. (Section 732(a)(1)) His outside basis is reduced by the basis of the property distributed, from $5,000 to $2,000. (Section 733(2))

Basis:	$5,000
Acct Rec.:	− 0
Inventory:	− 3,000
Basis:	$2,000

His basis in the accounts receivable is zero and his basis in the inventory is $3,000.

The distribution of property to Hal has reduced his economic investment in the partnership. Accordingly, his capital account is reduced by the value of the accounts receivable and inventory, or reduced from $60,000 to $48,000.

Cap. account:	$60,000
Acct. rec.:	− 6,000
Inventory:	− 6,000
Cap. account:	$48,000

9. Ira was a partner in a partnership. The partnership distributed inventory to him. The inventory had basis of $6,000 and fair market value of $10,000. Three years later, Ira sold the inventory for $15,000. What is the character of the gain?

The distribution of property to Ira is not a taxable event. (Section 731(a)(2)) Ira takes the property with the partnership's inside basis, or a $6,000 basis in the inventory. (Section 732(a)(1))

When he sells the inventory for $15,000, he will have $9,000 of gain.

AR:	$15,000
AB:	6,000
Gain:	$ 9,000

The inventory is inventory under Section 751(d). Thus, the character continues as ordinary in Ira's hands for five years. (Section 735(a)(2)) Ira has $9,000 of ordinary income.

10. Jeb was a partner in a partnership. The partnership distributed inventory to him. The inventory had a basis of $4,000 and fair market value of $10,000. Jeb held the inventory as investment property. Six years later, Jeb sold the inventory for $15,000. What is the character of the gain?

The distribution of property to Jeb is not a taxable event. (Section 731(a)(2)) Jeb takes the property with the partnership's inside basis, or a $4,000 basis in the inventory. (Section 732(a)(1))

When he sells the inventory for $15,000, he will have $11,000 of gain.

AR:	$15,000
AB:	4,000
Gain:	$11,000

The inventory is inventory under Section 751(d). Thus, the character continues as ordinary in Jeb's hands for five years. (Section 735(a)(2)) Because Jeb held the inventory more than five years after receiving it from the partnership, the character of the gain is determined in his hands.

11. Kent was a partner in a partnership. The partnership distributed accounts receivable to him. The accounts receivable had a zero basis and fair market value of $10,000.

Three years later, Kent sold the accounts receivable for $15,000. What is the character of the gain?

The distribution of property to Kent is not a taxable event. (Section 731(a)(2)) Kent takes the property with the partnership's inside basis, or a zero basis in the accounts receivable. (Section 732(a)(1))

When he sells the accounts receivable for $15,000, he will have $15,000 of gain.

AR:	$15,000
AB:	0
Gain:	$15,000

The accounts receivable are unrealized receivables under Section 751(c). Thus, the character continues as ordinary in Kent's hands. (Section 735(a)(1)) Kent has $15,000 of ordinary income.

12. Len was a partner in a partnership. The partnership distributed accounts receivable to him. The accounts receivable had a zero basis and fair market value of $10,000. Six years later, Len sold the accounts receivable for $15,000. What is the character of the gain?

The distribution of property to Len is not a taxable event. (Section 731(a)(2)) Len takes the property with the partnership's inside basis, or a zero basis in the accounts receivable. (Section 732(a)(1))

When he sells the accounts receivable for $15,000, he will have $15,000 of gain.

AR:	$15,000
AB:	0
Gain:	$15,000

The accounts receivable are unrealized receivables under Section 751(c). Thus, the character continues as ordinary in Len's hands, regardless of how long he holds them. (Section 735(a)(1)) Len has $15,000 of ordinary income.

13. Mike, Ned, and Opie are equal partners in a general partnership. The partnership balance sheet was as follows:

Asset	Adj. Basis	FMV	Partners	Adj. Basis	Cap. Acct.
Cash	$100,000	$100,000	Mike	$ 10,000	$100,000
Stock	70,000	160,000	Ned	60,000	100,000
Land	10,000	40,000	Opie	110,000	100,000
Total:	$180,000	$300,000		$180,000	$300,000

The partnership distributed $50,000 to Mike. After the distribution, Mike had a one-fifth interest worth $50,000.

   a. **What are the consequences to Mike and the partnership if the partnership has not made a Section 754 election? Reconstruct the balance sheet after the distribution.**

The distribution of cash to Mike, by itself, is not a taxable event to the partner or the partnership. (Section 731(a)(1)) His outside basis is reduced by the amount of cash distributed. However, because his basis can never be negative, to the extent the cash distributed exceeds his outside basis, Mike must recognize gain. (Section 731(a)(1)) The cash distribution exceeds his outside basis by $40,000. His basis in the partnership is reduced to zero (Section 733(1)) and the $40,000 gain is characterized as the gain from the sale or exchange of his partnership interest.

Basis:	$10,000
Distribution:	50,000
Basis:	$ 0 $40,000 gain

The distribution of cash reduced Mike's economic investment in the partnership. Accordingly, his capital account is reduced by the amount of the distribution, of from $100,000 to $50,000.

Cap. account:	$100,000
Cash distribution:	<50,000>
Cap. account:	$ 50,000

The balance sheet would appear as follows:

Asset	Adj. Basis	FMV	Partners	Adj. Basis	Cap. Acct.
Cash	$ 50,000	$ 50,000	Mike	$ 0	$ 50,000
Stock	70,000	160,000	Ned	60,000	100,000
Land	10,000	40,000	Opie	110,000	100,000
Total:	$130,000	$250,000		$170,000*	$250,000

* Note that there is a disparity between inside and outside basis and the amount of the disparity ($130,000 — $170,000) is the amount of gain Mike had to recognize, $40,000.

b. **What are the consequences to Mike and the partnership if the partnership has made a Section 754 election? Reconstruct the balance sheet after the distribution.**

The distribution of cash to Mike, by itself, is not a taxable event to the partner or the partnership. (Section 731(a)(1)) His outside basis is reduced by the amount of cash distributed. However, because his basis can never be negative, to the extent the cash distributed exceeds his outside basis, Mike must recognize gain. (Section 731(a)(1)) The cash distribution exceeds his outside basis by $40,000. His basis in the partnership is reduced to zero (Section 733(1)) and the $40,000 gain is characterized as the gain from the sale or exchange of his partnership interest.

Basis:	$10,000
Distribution:	– 50,000
Basis:	$ 0 $40,000 gain

The distribution of cash reduced Mike's economic investment in the partnership. Accordingly, his capital account is reduced by the amount of the distribution, of from $100,000 to $50,000.

Cap. account:	$100,000
Cash distribution:	<50,000>
Cap. account:	$ 50,000

The amount of the Section 734(b) adjustment is the amount of gain Mike had to recognize, or $40,000. (Section 734(b)(1)(A)) The upward adjustment is made to the same class of property that gave rise to the adjustment. (Treas. Reg. § 1.755-1(c)(1)(ii)) Thus, the partnership property should be divided into two groups, one group containing capital and hotchpot (Section 1231) assets and the second group containing all remaining (ordinary) assets. The stock and land are allocated to the capital and hotchpot group. There are no assets in the other group. Because cash was distributed, the adjustment must be made to capital and hotchpot (Section 1231) assets. (Treas. Reg. § 1.755-1(c)(1)(ii))

Within the group of capital and hotchpot assets, the upward adjustment is made first to properties with unrealized appreciation in proportion to their appreciation. (Treas. Reg. § 1.755-1(c)(2)(i))

Asset	Adj. Basis	FMV	Appreciation
Stock	$70,000	$160,000	$ 90,000
Land	10,000	40,000	30,000
Total:			$120,000

Stock: 90,000/120,000 x 40,000 = 30,000
Land: 30,000/120,000 x 40,000 = 10,000

The basis adjustment will be as follows:

Asset	Adj. Basis	Adjustment	New Basis
Stock	$70,000	$30,000	$100,000
Land	10,000	10,000	20,000
Total:			$120,000

After the adjustment, the partnership's balance sheet would appear as follows:

Asset	Adj. Basis	FMV	Partners	Adj. Basis	Cap. Acct.
Cash	$ 50,000	$ 50,000	Mike	$ 0	$ 50,000
Stock	100,000	160,000	Ned	60,000	100,000
Land	20,000	40,000	Opie	110,000	100,000
Total:	$170,000	$250,000		$170,000	$250,000

14. **Paul, Quinn, and Roy are equal partners in a general partnership. The partnership balance sheet was as follows:**

Asset	Adj. Basis	FMV	Partners	Adj. Basis	Cap. Acct.
Cash	$140,000	$140,000	Paul	$ 20,000	$100,000
Inventory	9,000	10,000	Quinn	120,000	100,000
Stock	30,000	50,000	Roy	109,000	100,000
Land	70,000	100,000		$249,000	$300,000
Total:	$249,000	$300,000			

The partnership distributed the stock to Paul. After the distribution, Paul had a one-fifth interest worth $50,000.

a. **What are the consequences to Paul and the partnership if the partnership has not made a Section 754 election? Reconstruct the balance sheet after the distribution.**

The distribution of property to Paul from the partnership generally is not a taxable event. (Section 731(a)(1)) Paul takes the property with the partnership's inside basis, or a basis of $30,000. (Section 732(a)(1)) However, the partnership's basis in the stock is larger than Paul's outside basis. Accordingly, the stock's basis is reduced to reflect Paul's outside basis before the stock is distributed, or to $20,000. (Section 732(a)(2)) Upon distribution of the stock, Paul will have a zero outside basis. (Section 733(1))

Basis:	$20,000
Stock:	– 20,000
Basis:	$ 0 His basis in the stock is $20,000.

The distribution of property to Paul has reduced his economic investment in the partnership. Accordingly, his capital account is reduced by the value of the stock, or reduced from $100,000 to $50,000.

Cap. account:	$100,000
Stock:	– 50,000
Cap. account:	$ 50,000

After the distribution, the partnership's balance sheet would appear as follows:

Asset	Adj. Basis	FMV	Partners	Adj. Basis	Cap. Acct.
Cash	$140,000	$140,000	Paul	$ 0	$ 50,000
Inventory	9,000	10,000	Quinn	120,000	100,000
Land	70,000	100,000	Roh	109,000	100,000
Total:	$219,000	$250,000		$229,000*	$250,000

* Note that there is a disparity between inside and outside basis and the amount of the disparity ($229,000–$219,000) is the amount of basis reduction in the stock prior to distribution, or $10,000.

b. **What are the consequences to Paul and the partnership if the partnership has made a Section 754 election? Reconstruct the balance sheet after the distribution.**

The distribution of property to Paul from the partnership generally is not a taxable event. (Section 731(a)(1)) Paul takes the property with the partnership's inside basis, or a basis of $30,000. (Section 732(a)(1)) However, the partnership's basis in the stock is larger than Paul's outside basis. Accordingly, the stock's basis is reduced to reflect Paul's outside basis before the stock is distributed, or to $20,000. (Section 732(a)(2)) Upon distribution of the stock, Paul will have a zero outside basis. (Section 733(1))

Basis:	$20,000
Stock:	– 20,000
Basis:	$ 0 His basis in the stock is $20,000.

The distribution of property to Paul has reduced his economic investment in the partnership. Accordingly, his capital account is reduced by the value of the stock, or reduced from $100,000 to $50,000.

Cap. account:	$100,000
Stock:	– 50,000
Cap. account:	$ 50,000

When a partner is required to adjust the basis of the property being distributed because the partner's outside basis is less than the basis of the asset being distributed, the amount of the adjustment under Section 734(b) is the amount of reduction in the property's basis, or under these facts $10,000. (Section 734(b)(1)(B)) The upward adjustment is made to the same class of property that gave rise to the adjustment. (Treas. Reg. § 1.755-1(c)(1)(i)) Thus, the partnership property should be divided into two groups, one group containing capital and hotchpot (Section 1231) assets and the second group containing all remaining (ordinary) assets. The land is allocated to the capital and hotchpot group. The inventory is allocated to the other group. Because stock was distributed, the adjustment must be made to capital and hotchpot (Section 1231) assets. (Treas. Reg. § 1.755-1(c)(1)(ii))

Within the group of capital and hotchpot assets, the upward adjustment is made first to properties with unrealized appreciation in proportion to their appreciation. (Treas. Reg. § 1.755-1(c)(2)(i)) Because there is only one asset in the capital and hotchpot group, the basis adjustment will be as follows:

Asset	Adj. Basis	Adjustment	New Basis
Land	$70,000	$10,000	$80,000

After the adjustment, the partnership's balance sheet would appear as follows:

Asset	Adj. Basis	FMV	Partners	Adj. Basis	Cap. Acct.
Cash	$140,000	$140,000	Paul	$ 0	$ 50,000
Inventory	9,000	10,000	Quinn	120,000	100,000
Land	80,000	100,000	Roy	109,000	100,000
Total:	$229,000	$250,000		$229,000	$250,000

Chapter IX

Disproportionate Distributions

While the general rule is that there are no tax consequences when property is distributed from a partnership to a partner, there are three exceptions to the rule. The first exception, disproportionate distributions, is discussed in this chapter. The second and third exceptions, distributions of property previously contributed by a partner and distributions to a partner who had previously contributed appreciated property, are discussed in next chapter.

A. Rationale

Each partner has an indirect ownership in the underlying partnership property. Each partner is also responsible for an allocable share of the underlying gain or loss in each partnership item. Determining how much of the partnership gain or loss a partner is responsible for is only part of the picture. The other part is the character of the gain or loss. In general, a partner will prefer long-term capital gain over ordinary gain and an ordinary loss over a capital loss, whether long term or short term. However, Congress does not permit the partners to effectively shift the character of the income, gain, or loss among the partners when making a distribution.

Example: Ann and Bob were equal partners in the partnership. The partnership owned the following assets, all of which were acquired by the partnership:

Asset	Adjusted Basis	Fair Market Value
Cash	$10,000	$10,000
Inventory	20,000	60,000
Land	10,000	50,000

The partnership purchased the land five years ago and holds it for investment purposes. If the partnership sold the inventory and the land, it would have $40,000 of ordinary income and $40,000 of long-term capital gain. The gain would be allocated as follows:

	Ann	Bob
Ordinary income:	$20,000	$20,000
Long-term capital gain:	20,000	20,000
Total gain:	$40,000	$40,000

In the alternative, if it distributed the inventory to Ann and the land to Bob and they both sold the property, they would each realize the following:

	Ann	Bob
Ordinary income:	$40,000	$ 0
Long-term capital gain:	0	40,000
Total gain:	$40,000	$40,000

While each partner still would be reporting a total of $40,000, Ann would have converted $20,000 of long-term capital gain into ordinary income, and Bob would have converted $20,000 of ordinary income into long-term capital gain.

The Code does not allow the partners to shift the character of the income, gain, or loss in this way.

If the partnership does make a distribution to a partner from just one category of property, the Code restructures the transaction and treats the partner as having received a proportionate amount from each category.

Example: If the partnership distributed the inventory to Ann, the distribution would be a disproportionate distribution. She is receiving too much of the ordinary income property and not enough of the capital asset property.

Under Section 751(b), the transaction is restructured and Ann is treated as if she had received one-half of the ordinary income property and one-half of the long-term capital gain property.

While the rationale behind the need for restructuring the transaction is not difficult to understand, the mechanics of the restructuring are a bit daunting.

B. Steps to Restructure the Transaction

First, divide the assets into two categories. The first category contains unrealized receivables and substantially appreciated inventory.

Unrealized receivables. Unrealized receivables include, to the extent not previously included in income, any right to payment for services rendered. They also include the right to payment for goods delivered to the extent the proceeds would be treated as amounts received from the sale or exchange of property other than a capital asset. They also include any gain that would be characterized as ordinary income under the depreciation recapture provisions.[1]

Substantially appreciated inventory. Inventory includes those assets held for sale to customers and any items held by the partnership that are not characterized as a capital

---

1. Section 751(c).

or hotchpot (Section 1231) item.[2] The inventory is substantially appreciated if the aggregate fair market value of the inventory exceeds 120 percent of the adjusted inside basis of the inventory.[3] If inventory was acquired for the principal purposes of causing the partnership's inventory to not be substantially appreciated, that inventory will be disregarded.[4]

If an item comes within the definition of both unrealized receivables and inventory items, it is considered in determining if the inventory is substantially appreciated. If the inventory is not substantially appreciated, and the asset meets the definition of unrealized receivables, it will continue to be considered an unrealized receivable.

Example: The partnership is an accrual basis taxpayer with a balance sheet as follows:

Asset	Adj. Basis	FMV	Partners	Adj. Basis	Cap. Acct.
Cash	$ 3,000	$ 3,000	Carl	$17,000	$20,000
Acct. Rec.	14,000	14,000	Deb	17,000	20,000
Lots for sale	10,000	20,000		$34,000	$40,000
Land	7,000	3,000			
Total:	$34,000	$40,000			

The accounts receivable do not come within the definition of unrealized receivables. The lots held for sale and the accounts receivable both come within the definition of inventory.

The aggregate fair market value of the inventory is $34,000. The aggregate adjusted basis is $24,000. The inventory is substantially appreciated because the aggregate fair market value, $34,000, exceeds 120 percent of the adjusted inside basis of the inventory, $28,800 (120% of $24,000).

The second category contains all remaining assets, generally cash and capital and hotchpot (Section 1231) assets.

Step One: Ellen, Frank, and Greg were equal partners in the partnership. The partnership's balance sheet appeared as follows:

Asset	Adj. Basis	FMV	Partner	AB	Cap. Acct.
Cash	$30,000	$30,000	Ellen	$18,000	$30,000
Inventory	18,000	30,000	Frank	18,000	30,000
Stock	6,000	30,000	Greg	18,000	30,000
Total:	$54,000	$90,000		$54,000	$90,000

The partnership distributes the inventory to Ellen in complete liquidation of her interest.

The inventory is substantially appreciated because the fair market value, $30,000, exceeds 120 percent of the adjusted inside basis of the inventory, or $21,600.

The assets are divided into two categories:

Unrealized receivables/inventory	Other
Inventory	Cash
	Stock

---

2. Section 751(d).
3. Section 751(b)(3)(A).
4. Section 751(b)(3)(B).

Second, determine the recipient partner's interest in each asset, based on his ownership interest in the partnership before the distribution.

Step Two: Ellen's interest in the partnership assets is as follows:		
Unrealized receivables/inventory	**Other**	
$10,000 Inventory	$10,000 Cash	
_____	$10,000 Stock	
Total: $10,000	$20,000	

Third, determine the recipient partner's interest in each asset after the distribution based on his ownership interest in the partnership. Include his interest in the distributed property.

Step Three: Ellen is no longer a partner in the partnership, so does not have an interest in its assets. But, the assets distributed to her are as follows:	
Unrealized receivables/inventory	**Other**
$30,000 Inventory	$ 0
Total: $30,000	$ 0

Fourth, comparing the partner's interests before and after the distribution, determine the category and amount of which she now owns too little and the category and amount of which she now owns too much.

Step Four: Ellen's interest in the partnership assets before distribution:	
Unrealized receivables/inventory	**Other**
$10,000	$20,000
Ellen's interest after distribution:	
Unrealized receivables/inventory	**Other**
$30,000	$ 0
Net: $20,000	<$20,000>
She received $20,000 more than her share of the inventory and received $20,000 too little of the other property.	

Fifth, take into consideration only the amount of the partnership assets the partner did not receive in a sufficient amount. Distribute those assets (in that amount) from the partnership to the partner. Use the same rules with respect to distributions of cash and property that generally apply to non-liquidating distributions. This step is sometimes referred to as a phantom distribution.

The partners may provide for a phantom distribution from any of the assets in the class; the distribution does not need to be a proportionate amount of each asset. If the partners do not have an agreement regarding the allocation, the regulations provide a default rule that the phantom distribution will be prorata.[5]

---

5. Treas. Reg. § 1.751-1(g).

Step Five: Ellen received $20,000 too little of the other property. Accordingly, the partnership distributes to her a prorata amount of each asset, or $10,000 of cash and $10,000 of stock.

Ellen's $18,000 basis is reduced first by the $10,000 cash distribution to $8,000. It is then reduced by the basis in the stock. The distribution to her is 10,000/30,000 of the value of the property. The correlative basis is $1/3 \times 6,000$, or $2,000. Thus, her basis is reduced from $8,000 to $6,000.

Ellen's capital account is reduced for the distributions, or from $30,000 to $10,000.

After the distribution of cash and stock, the balance sheet would appear as follows:

Asset	Adj. Basis	FMV	Partner	AB	Cap. Acct.
Cash	$20,000	$20,000	Ellen	$ 6,000	$10,000
Inventory	18,000	30,000	Frank	18,000	30,000
Stock	4,000	20,000	Greg	18,000	30,000
Total:	$42,000	$70,000		$42,000	$70,000

Sixth, the recipient partner sells the assets that were just distributed to him back to the partnership in exchange for a portion of the asset that was actually distributed to him. The general rules applicable to dispositions of property apply to the partner and the partnership. Thus, both parties recognize any gain or loss realized and take a cost basis in any asset purchased.

Step Six: Under the phantom distribution, the partnership distributed $10,000 of cash and stock with a basis of $2,000 and fair market value of $10,000 to Ellen.

Ellen sells these assets to the partnership in exchange for inventory. She sells the $10,000 of cash for $10,000 of inventory. She has no gain or loss on the disposition of the cash and her basis in the inventory is $10,000.

She sells the $10,000 of stock for $10,000 of inventory. She recognizes $8,000 of gain on the disposition ($10,000 amount realized, less $2,000 basis). Her basis in the inventory is $10,000, giving her a combined basis in the purchased inventory of $20,000.

The partnership has sold $20,000 of inventory. It recognizes $8,000 of gain (amount realized of $20,000, less $12,000 basis). The gain is allocated equally between Frank and Greg, increasing each of their bases by $4,000. The partnership has a cost basis in the stock of $10,000.

The balance sheet now appears as follows:

Asset	Adj. Basis	FMV	Partner	AB	Cap. Acct.
Cash	$30,000	$30,000	Ellen	$ 6,000	$10,000
Inventory	6,000	10,000	Frank	22,000	30,000
Stock	14,000	30,000	Greg	22,000	30,000
Total:	$50,000	$70,000		$50,000	$70,000

Seventh, considering the total amount distributed to the partner and the portion that was purchased by the partner in the previous step, determine the remaining amount that must be distributed to the partner. Use the same rules with respect to non-liquidating distributions of cash and property that generally apply to distributions.

Step Seven: As originally structured, the partnership distributed $30,000 of accounts receivable to Ellen. Through the phantom distribution and sale, Ellen purchased $20,000 of inventory from the partnership. Thus, she needs a distribution of $10,000 of inventory to end up with a total of $30,000 of inventory.

Ellen's basis of $6,000 is reduced by the basis in the inventory, or reduced to zero. Her capital account is reduced by $10,000 to zero. Her basis in the $30,000 of inventory is $26,000.

The balance sheet would appear as follows:

Asset	Adj. Basis	FMV	Partner	AB	Cap. Acct.
Cash	$30,000	$30,000	Frank	22,000	30,000
Stock	14,000	30,000	Greg	22,000	30,000
Total:	$44,000	$60,000		$44,000	$60,000

Summary

Objective: Preserve the character for everyone.

Steps:

Step 1: Divide the assets into two categories. The first category contains unrealized receivables and substantially appreciated inventory.

Step 2: Determine the recipient partner's interest in each asset, based on his ownership interest in the partnership before the distribution.

Step 3: Determine the recipient partner's interest in each asset after the distribution based on his ownership interest in the partnership. Include his interest in the distributed property.

Step 4: Comparing the partner's interests before and after the distribution, determine the category and amount of which he now owns too little and the category and amount of which he now owns too much.

- phantom distribution -

Step 5: *Take into consideration only the amount of the partnership assets the partner did not receive in a sufficient amount. Distribute those assets (in that amount) from the partnership to the partner.*

Step 6: *The recipient partner sells the assets that were just distributed to him back to the partnership in exchange for a portion of the asset that was actually distributed to him.*

———

Step 7: Considering the total amount distributed to the partner and the portion that was purchased by the partner in the previous step, determine the remaining amount that must be distributed to the partner and distribute that amount.

Problems

The balance sheet of the partnership was as follows:

Asset	Adj.	FMV	Partner	Adj. Basis	Cap. Acct.
Cash	$36,000	$ 36,000	Ann	$18,000	$ 36,000
Acct. Rec.	0	36,000	Bob	18,000	36,000
Stock	18,000	36,000	Carl	18,000	36,000
Total:	$54,000	$108,000		$54,000	$108,000

1.   What are the tax consequences if the partnership distributed $18,000 to Ann? After the distribution, she had a one-fifth interest in the partnership.

2.   Alternatively, what are the tax consequences if the partnership distributes one-half of the accounts receivable to Bob? After the distribution, he had a one-fifth interest in the partnership.

3.   Alternatively, what are the tax consequences if the partnership distributes one-half of the stock to Carl? After the distribution, he had a one-fifth interest in the partnership.

Solutions

The balance sheet of the partnership was as follows:

Asset	Adj.	FMV	Partner	Adj. Basis	Cap. Acct.
Cash	$36,000	$ 36,000	Ann	$18,000	$ 36,000
Acct. Rec.	0	36,000	Bob	18,000	36,000
Stock	18,000	36,000	Carl	18,000	36,000
Total:	$54,000	$108,000		$54,000	$108,000

1.   What are the tax consequences if the partnership distributed $18,000 to Ann? After the distribution, she had a one-fifth interest in the partnership.

First, divide the assets into two categories. The first category contains unrealized receivables and substantially appreciated inventory. The second category contains all remaining assets, generally cash and capital and hotchpot (Section 1231) assets.

Unrealized receivables/inventory	Other
Accounts receivable	Cash
	Stock

Second, Ann's interest in the partnership assets before the distribution was as follows:

Unrealized receivables/inventory	Other
$12,000 Accounts receivable	$12,000 Cash
_____	$12,000 Stock
Total: $12,000	$24,000

Third, Ann's interest in the partnership assets after the distribution and the distributed property is as follows:

Unrealized receivables/inventory	Other
As a one-fifth partner:	
$ 7,200 accounts receivable	$ 3,600 cash
	7,200 stock
Individually:	
$ 0	18,000 cash
Total: $7,200	$28,800

Fourth, determine the category and amount in which Ann now owns too little and the category and amount in which she now owns too much.
Ann's interest in the partnership assets before distribution:

Unrealized receivables/inventory	Other
Total: $12,000	$24,000

Ann's interest after distribution:

Unrealized receivables/inventory	Other
Total: $ 7,200	$28,800
Net: <$ 4,800>	$ 4,800

She received $4,800 too little of the inventory and $4,800 too much of the other property.

Fifth, since Ann did not get enough of the accounts receivable to the extent of $4,800, the partnership distributes $4,800 of accounts receivable to her. Because they have a zero basis, they do not reduce her basis. (Sections 732(a)(1); 733(2)) Her capital account is reduced by $4,800, from $36,000 to $31,200.

Basis	Cap. Account
$18,000	$36,000
− 0	− 4,800
$18,000	$31,200

Her basis in the accounts receivable is zero. (Section 732(a)(1))

After the distribution, the balance sheet would appear as follows:

Asset	Adj.	FMV	Partner	Adj. Basis	Cap. Acct.
Cash	$36,000	$ 36,000	Ann	$18,000	$ 31,200
Acct. Rec.	0	31,200*	Bob	18,000	36,000
Stock	18,000	36,000	Carl	18,000	36,000
Total:	$54,000	$103,200		$54,000	$103,200

* $36,000, less $4,800 distributed.

Sixth, Ann sells the accounts receivable to the partnership in exchange for cash (the asset she actually received). She recognizes $4,800 of gain on the disposition.

AR:	$4,800
AB:	$ 0
Gain:	$4,800

The partnership does not recognize any gain or loss on the disposition of the cash. It takes a cost basis of $4,800 in the accounts receivable. After the purchase of the accounts receivable, the balance sheet would appear as follows:

Asset	Adj.	FMV	Partner	Adj. Basis	Cap. Acct.
Cash	$31,200	$ 31,200*	Ann	$18,000	$ 31,200
Acct. Rec.	4,800	36,000**	Bob	18,000	36,000
Stock	18,000	36,000	Carl	18,000	36,000
Total:	$54,000	$103,200		$54,000	$103,200

* $36,000, less $4,800
** $31,200, plus $4,800

Seventh, distribute Ann's remaining portion of the asset that was distributed to her. The original distribution was $18,000 of cash. She received $4,800 upon the sale of the accounts receivable. The difference, $13,200, is now distributed to her. Her basis is reduced for the cash distribution, from $18,000 to $4,800. (Sections 731(a)(1); 733(1)) Her capital account is reduced by $13,200, or from $31,200 to $18,000.

Basis	Cap. Account
$18,000	$31,200
− 13,200	− 13,200
$ 4,800	$18,000

After the dust settles, Ann has $18,000 in cash and the partnership's balance sheet appears as follows:

Asset	Adj.	FMV	Partner	Adj. Basis	Cap. Acct.
Cash	$18,000	$18,000*	Ann	$ 4,800	$18,000
Acct. Rec.	4,800	36,000	Bob	18,000	36,000
Stock	18,000	36,000	Carl	18,000	36,000
Total:	$40,800	$90,000		$40,800	$90,000

* $31,200, less $13,200

2. **Alternatively, what are the tax consequences if the partnership distributes one-half of the accounts receivable to Bob? After the distribution, he had a one-fifth interest in the partnership.**

First, divide the assets into two categories. The first category contains unrealized receivables and substantially appreciated inventory. The second category contains all remaining assets, generally cash and capital and hotchpot (Section 1231) assets.

Unrealized receivables/inventory	Other
Accounts receivable	Cash
	Stock

Second, Bob's interest in the partnership assets before the distribution was as follows:

Unrealized receivables/inventory	Other
$12,000 Accounts receivable	$12,000 Cash
	$12,000 Stock
Total: $12,000	$24,000

Third, Bob's interest in the partnership assets after the distribution and the distributed property is as follows:

Unrealized receivables/inventory	Other
As a one-fifth partner:	
$ 3,600 accounts receivable	$ 7,200 cash
	7,200 stock
Individually:	
$18,000	—
Total: $21,600	$14,400

Fourth, determine the category and amount in which Bob now owns too little and the category and amount in which he now owns too much.

Bob's interest in the partnership assets before distribution:

	Unrealized receivables/inventory	Other
Total:	$12,000	$24,000

Bob's interest after distribution:

	Unrealized receivables/inventory	Other
Total:	$21,600	$14,400
Net:	$ 9,600	<$9,600>

He received $9,600 too little of the other assets and $9,600 too much of the accounts receivable.

Fifth, since Bob did not get enough of the other assets to the extent of $9,600, the partnership distributes $4,800 of cash and $4,800 of stock to him.

Cash: $36,000/72,000 \times \$9,600 = \$4,800$

Stock: $36,000/72,000 \times \$9,600 = \$4,800$

His basis is reduced by the amount of cash distributed (Sections 731(a)(1); 733(1)).

Basis:	$18,000
Cash:	− 4,800
Basis:	$13,200

The basis in the amount of stock distributed is:

$$\$4,800/\$36,000 \times 18,000 = \$2,400$$

His basis is reduced by the amount of basis in the property distributed (Sections 732(a)(1); 733(2)):

Basis:	$13,200
Stock:	2,400
Basis:	$10,800

His basis in the stock is $2,400. (Section 732(a)(1))

His capital account is reduced by the $4,800 cash and $4,800 stock distribution.

Cap Acct:	$36,000
Cash:	- 4,800
Stock:	- 4,800
Cap Acct:	$26,400

After the distribution, the balance sheet would appear as follows:

Asset	Adj.	FMV	Partner	Adj. Basis	Cap. Acct.
Cash	$31,200	$31,200*	Ann	$18,000	$36,000
Acct. Rec.	0	36,000	Bob	10,800	26,400
Stock	15,600**	31,200***	Carl	18,000	36,000
Total:	$46,800	$98,400		$46,800	$98,400

* $36,000, less $4,800

** $18,000, less $2,400

*** $36,000, less $4,800

Sixth, Bob sells the cash and stock to the partnership in exchange for $9,600 of accounts receivable (the asset he actually received). There is no gain on the disposition of the cash. He recognizes $2,400 of gain on the disposition of stock:

AR: $4,800
AB: _2,400_
Gain: $2,400

He takes a $9,600 cost basis in the accounts receivable. (Section 1012)

The partnership recognizes $9,600 gain on the sale of the accounts receivable.

AR: $9,600
AB: ___0___
Gain: $9,600

The gain is allocated equally between Ann and Carl. Each of their bases is increased by $4,800.

Basis: $18,000
Gain: _– 4,800_
Basis: $22,800

The partnership takes a cost basis of $4,800 in the purchased stock. (Section 1012)

After sale of the accounts receivable, the balance sheet would appear as follows:

Asset	Adj.	FMV	Partner	Adj. Basis	Cap. Acct.
Cash	$36,000	$36,000*	Ann	$22,800	$36,000
Acct. Rec.	0	26,400**	Bob	10,800	26,400
Stock	_20,400***_	_36,000****_	Carl	_22,800_	_36,000_
Total:	$56,400	$98,400		$56,400	$98,400

* $31,200, plus $4,800
** $36,000, less $9,600
*** $15,600, plus $4,800
**** $31,200, plus $4,800

Seventh, distribute Bob's remaining portion of the asset that was distributed to him. The original distribution was $18,000 of accounts receivable. He received $9,600 upon the sale of the cash and stock. The difference, $8,400, is now distributed to him. His basis is reduced for the accounts receivable. However, because the basis is zero, there is no adjustment to his basis. (Sections 732(a)(1); 733(2)) His capital account is reduced by $8,400, or from $26,400 to $18,000.

Cap. Acct: $26,400
Acct. rec.: _– 8,400_
Cap. Acct: $18,000

After the dust settles, Bob has $18,000 in accounts receivable with a basis of $9,600 and the partnership's balance sheet appears as follows:

Asset	Adj.	FMV	Partner	Adj. Basis	Cap. Acct.
Cash	$36,000	$36,000	Ann	$22,800	$36,000
Acct. Rec.	0	18,000*	Bob	10,800	18,000
Stock	_20,400_	_36,000_	Carl	_22,800_	_36,000_
Total:	$56,400	$90,000		$56,400	$90,000

* $26,400, less $8,400

3.   Alternatively, what are the tax consequences if the partnership distributes one-half of the stock to Carl? After the distribution, he had a one-fifth interest in the partnership.

First, divide the assets into two categories. The first category contains unrealized receivables and substantially appreciated inventory. The second category contains all remaining assets, generally cash and capital and hotchpot (Section 1231) assets.

Unrealized receivables/inventory	Other
Accounts receivable	Cash
	Stock

Second, Carl's interest in the partnership assets before the distribution was as follows:

Unrealized receivables/inventory	Other
$12,000 Accounts receivable	$12,000 Cash
_____	$12,000 Stock
Total: $12,000	$24,000

Third, Carl's interest in the partnership assets after the distribution and the distributed property is as follows:

Unrealized receivables/inventory	Other
As a one-fifth partner:	
$ 7,200 Accounts receivable	$ 3,600 stock
	7,200 cash
Individually:	
$ 0	18,000 stock
Total: $7,200	$28,800

Fourth, determine the category and amount in which Carl now owns too little and the category and amount in which he now owns too much.

Carl's interest in the partnership assets before distribution:

Unrealized receivables/inventory	Other
Total: $12,000	$24,000

Carl's interest after distribution:

Unrealized receivables/inventory	Other
Total: $7,200	$28,800
Net: <$4,800>	$ 4,800

He received $4,800 too little of the inventory and $4,800 too much of the other property.

Fifth, since Carl did not get enough of the accounts receivable to the extent of $4,800, the partnership distributes $4,800 of accounts receivable to him. Because they have a zero basis, they do not reduce his basis. (Sections 732(a)(1); 733(2)) His capital account is reduced by $4,800, from $36,000 to $31,200.

Basis	Cap. Account
$18,000	$36,000
– 0	– 4,800
$18,000	$31,200

His basis in the accounts receivable is zero. (Section 732(a)(1))

After the distribution, the balance sheet would appear as follows:

Asset	Adj.	FMV	Partner	Adj. Basis	Cap. Acct.
Cash	$36,000	$ 36,000	Ann	$18,000	$ 36,000
Acct. Rec.	0	31,200*	Bob	18,000	36,000
Stock	18,000	36,000	Carl	18,000	31,200
Total:	$54,000	$103,200		$54,000	$103,200

* $36,000, less $4,800

Sixth, Carl sells the accounts receivable to the partnership in exchange for stock (the asset he actually received). He recognizes $4,800 of gain on the disposition.

AR:	$4,800
AB:	0
Gain:	$4,800

He takes a cost basis in the stock, or $4,800. (Section 1012)

The partnership disposes of $4,800 of the stock. The basis in the stock sold is:

$4,800/$36,000 × 18,000 = $2,400.

AR:	$4,800
AB:	2,400
Gain:	$2,400

The gain is allocated equally between Ann and Bob, or $1,200 each. Their bases are increased by the amount of the gain.

Basis:	$18,000
Gain:	1,200
Basis:	$19,200

The partnership takes a cost basis of $4,800 in the accounts receivable, giving them a total basis of $4,800 (zero, plus $4,800). (Section 1012) After sale of the stock, the balance sheet would appear as follows:

Asset	Adj.	FMV	Partner	Adj. Basis	Cap. Acct.
Cash	$36,000	$ 36,000	Ann	$19,200	$ 36,000
Acct. Rec.	4,800	36,000*	Bob	19,200	36,000
Stock	15,600**	31,200***	Carl	18,000	31,200
Total:	$56,400	$103,200		$56,400	$103,200

* $31,200, plus $4,800
** $18,000, less $2,400
*** $36,000, less $4,800

Seventh, distribute Carl's remaining portion of the asset that was distributed to him. The original distribution was $18,000 of stock. He received $4,800 upon the sale of the accounts receivable. The difference, $13,200, is now distributed to him. The basis in the stock distributed is:

$13,200/31,200 \times 15,600 = \$6,600$

His basis is reduced for the stock distribution, from $18,000 to $4,800. (Sections 732(a)(1)); 733(2)) His capital account is reduced by $13,200, or from $31,200 to $18,000.

Basis	Cap. Account
$18,000	$31,200
− 6,600	− 13,200
$11,400	$18,000

His basis in the distributed stock is $6,600. (Section 732(a)(1))

After the dust settles, Carl has $18,000 of stock with a basis of $11,400 ($4,800 plus $6,600) and the partnership's balance sheet appears as follows:

Asset	Adj.	FMV	Partner	Adj. Basis	Cap. Acct.
Cash	$36,000	$36,000	Ann	$19,200	$36,000
Acct. Rec.	4,800	36,000	Bob	19,200	36,000
Stock	9,000*	18,000**	Carl	11,400	18,000
Total:	$49,800	$90,000		$49,800	$90,000

* $15,600, less $6,600
** $31,200, less $13,200

Chapter X

Mixing Bowl Transactions

While the general rule is that there are no tax consequences when property is distributed from a partnership to a partner, there are three exceptions to the rule. The first exception, disproportionate distributions, was discussed in the previous chapter. The second and third exceptions, distributions of property previously contributed by a partner and distributions to a partner who had previously contributed appreciated property, are discussed in this chapter.

A. Distribution of Previously Contributed Property

Under the second exception, there is a tax consequence when:[1]

- Property is distributed from a partnership to a partner;
- The property was previously contributed by a different partner to the partnership with a built-in gain or loss; and
- The property is distributed within seven years from the time of contribution.

Note that, in the absence of such a rule, a partner could escape the built-in gain or loss in contributed property by having the partnership distribute the property, rather than sell the property. In addition, because of the basis allocation rules of Section 732, the built-in gain or loss would be shifted to the recipient partner.

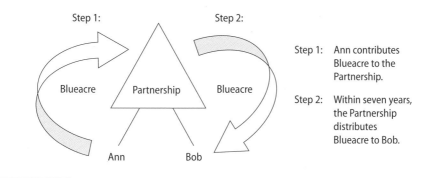

Step 1:   Ann contributes Blueacre to the Partnership.

Step 2:   Within seven years, the Partnership distributes Blueacre to Bob.

---

1. Section 704(c)(1)(B).

When property previously contributed by a partner with built-in gain or loss is subsequently distributed to another partner, several tax events occur. First, the contributing partner must recognize the built-in gain or loss on the property, determined as if the property had been sold for its fair market value as of the date of distribution. The character of the gain or loss is the same character that the partnership would have recognized upon sale of the property. The contributing partner's basis is adjusted by the amount of gain or loss.[2]

Next, the partnership's inside basis in the property is increased or decreased to reflect the gain or loss recognized by the contributing partner.[3] Then the property is distributed by the partnership to the partner.

The regulations contain an anti-abuse provision that allows the Internal Revenue Service to apply the rules in a manner that is consistent with the intent of the statute. The Service can restructure a transaction so that it is consistent with the applicable tax treatment.[4]

Exception to the general rule. The requirement that gain or loss be recognized does not apply in three situations. First, if the property is distributed to the same partner who originally contributed the property, no gain or loss is required to be recognized. Since the partner is receiving the property back, there is no opportunity for shifting of the built-in gain or loss. Accordingly, there is no need to recognize the built-in gain or loss upon distribution.[5]

Second, if:

- The partner who contributed the property also receives a distribution of property;
- The distributed property is like-kind; and
- The distribution occurs within 180 days of the distribution to the non-contributing partner or the due date of the contributing partner's tax return for the taxable year of the distribution,

then, the transaction is treated as a like-kind exchange. The contributing partner may reduce the amount of gain or loss that would be recognized upon the deemed sale of the contributed property by the amount of gain or loss in the like-kind property. In sum, to the extent the transaction would have qualified as a like-kind exchange if a third party had been used as an intermediary, the transaction should continue to qualify.[6]

Third, if the partner is a successor to the contributing partner and the property had been contributed with a built-in loss, the successor partner is not entitled to the built-in loss. Rather, the property is deemed to have been contributed to the partnership with a basis equal to its fair market value.[7]

---

2. Sections 704(c)(1)(B); 705(a)(1)(A), (a)(2)(A); Treas. Reg. §§ 1.704-4(a)(1)-(3), -4(b)(1), -4(e)(1).

3. Section 704(c)(1)(B)(iii); Treas. Reg. § 1.704-4(e)(2).

4. Treas. Reg. § 1.704-4(f).

5. Section 704(c)(1)(B). The same rule applies if the property is distributed to the contributing partner's successor-in-interest.

6. Treas. Reg. § 1.704-4(d)(3).

7. Section 704(c)(1)(C).

B. Distribution of Other Property to Partner Who Had Contributed Property — General Rule

Under the third exception, there is a tax consequence on the distribution of property to a partner when:[8]

- Property was previously contributed by the distributee partner to the partnership with a built-in gain; and
- Other property (not including money) is distributed by the partnership to the partner within seven years of the contribution; and
- The partnership retains the property contributed by the partner.

Note that, in the absence of such a rule, a partner could dispose of property with a built-in gain in exchange for other property but not recognize gain on the disposition.

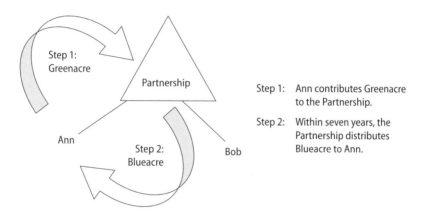

Step 1: Ann contributes Greenacre to the Partnership.

Step 2: Within seven years, the Partnership distributes Blueacre to Ann.

When a partner who previously contributed property with built-in gain to a partnership within seven years receives a distribution of other property, several tax events occur. The consequences of the distribution are considered after the consequences of any cash distributions.

First, the contributing partner must recognize gain in an amount that is the lesser of two amounts. The first amount is the fair market value of the distributed property, reduced by the partner's outside basis immediately before the distribution. The second amount is the amount of the net precontribution gain of the partner. Net precontribution gain is the net gain the distributee partner would have recognized under Section 704(c) if all the property contributed by that partner within seven years of the current distribution had been distributed to another partner at the time of the distribution to the contributing partner. The character of the gain is the same character that the partnership would have recognized upon sale of the contributed property.[9]

---

8. Section 737.
9. Section 737(a), (b).

Next, the partner's basis is increased by the amount of gain.[10]

Finally, the partnership's inside basis in the contributed property is increased to reflect the gain recognized by the partner.[11] The property is distributed by the partnership to the partner.

The regulations contain an anti-abuse provision that allows the Internal Revenue Service to apply the rules in a manner that is consistent with the intent of the statute. The Service can restructure a transaction so that it is consistent with the applicable tax treatment.[12]

Exception to the general rule. In general, if the property distributed was previously contributed by that partner, that property is not taken into consideration in determining the amount of gain the partner must recognize.[13]

Pre-emption by other provisions. If the disguised sales rules (of Section 707(a)(2)(B)) or the like-kind exchange treatment (of Section 704(c)(2)) also apply to the transaction, those Sections take precedence.[14] In addition, the provisions of Section 737 do not apply if Section 751(b), applicable to disproportionate distributions, applies.[15]

Distribution of marketable securities treated as distribution of cash. Marketable securities include financial instruments (*e.g.*, stock and bonds) and foreign currency that are actively traded. They include interests in a common trust fund, a mutual fund, and any financial instrument convertible into money or marketable securities.[16] Because the securities are easy to value and are liquid, to the extent of the fair market value of the security on the date of distribution, the distribution is treated as a distribution of cash.[17]

A distribution of marketable securities is not treated like a distribution of cash if:[18]

- The security was contributed to the partnership by the distributee partner; or
- The partnership is an investment partnership and the partner contributed only money and/or securities.

---

10. Section 737(c)(1).

11. Section 737(c)(2).

12. Treas. Reg. § 1.737-4.

13. Section 737(d)(1).

14. Treas. Reg. § 1.704-3(a)(5).

15. Section 737(d)(2).

16. Section 731(c)(2).

17. Section 731(c)(1). The amount of the distribution of marketable securities that is treated as a distribution of cash may be reduced in some circumstances. See Section 731(c)(3)(B).

18. Section 731(c)(3)(A).

Summary

Steps When Previously Contributed Property Is Distributed within Seven Years of Contribution:

Step 1: Determine the amount of built-in gain or loss that would have been generated if the property had been sold for its fair market value as of the date of distribution. Allocate that gain or loss to the contributing partner. Determine the character of the gain or loss as if the partnership had sold the property.

Step 2: Adjust the contributing partner's basis for the amount of gain or loss.

Step 3: Adjust the partnership's inside basis in the property by the amount of gain or loss recognized by the contributing partner.

Step 4: Distribute the property to the partner using the general rules applicable to distributions of property.

Steps When Previously Contributed Property Is Distributed within Seven Years of Contribution:

Step 1: First, reduce the fair market value of the distributed property (not including cash) by the partner's outside basis. The partner's basis is that basis immediately before the distribution, reduced, but not below zero, by any cash distributed.

Step 2: Second, compute the amount of the net precontribution gain of the partner. Net precontribution gain is the net gain the distributee partner would have recognized under Section 704(c) if all the property contributed by that partner within seven years of the current distribution had been distributed to another partner at the time of the distribution to the contributing partner.

Step 3: Determine which amount is the lesser amount, the amount determined under Step 1 or the amount determined under Step 2. The contributing partner must recognize gain equal to the lesser amount. The character of the gain is the same character that the partnership would have recognized upon sale of the contributed property.

Step 4: The partner's basis is increased by the amount of gain determined in Step 3.

Step 5: The partnership's inside basis in the contributed property is increased to reflect the gain recognized by the partner.

Step 6: Distribute the property to the partner using the general rules application to the distribution of property.

Problems

1.   Ann contributed land to the partnership. The land had a basis of $10,000 and fair market value of $25,000. Bob contributed $25,000. The partnership held the land for investment purposes.

Two years later, the partnership distributed the land to Bob. At the time of the distribution, the fair market value of the land was still $25,000. Ann's basis was $5,000 and Bob's basis was $50,000 and his capital account balance was $50,000. What are the tax consequences from the distribution?

2.   Carl contributed stock to the partnership. The stock had a basis of $10,000 and fair market value of $25,000. Deb contributed $25,000. The partnership used the traditional method for making Section 704(c) allocations.

Three years later the partnership distributed the stock to Deb. At the time of the distribution, its fair market value was $20,000, Carl's basis was $7,000 and Deb's basis was $30,000 and her capital account balance was $40,000. What are the tax consequences from the distribution?

3.   Ellen contributed stock to the partnership. The stock had a basis of $20,000 and fair market value of $25,000. Frank contributed $25,000. The partnership used the traditional method for making Section 704(c) allocations.

Three years later the partnership distributed the stock to Frank. At the time of the distribution, its fair market value was $15,000, Ellen's basis was $15,000 and Frank's basis was $30,000 and his capital account balance was $40,000. What are the tax consequences from the distribution?

4.   Greg contributed land to the partnership. The land had a basis of $30,000 and fair market value of $40,000. Hal contributed $40,000. The partnership held the land for investment purposes.

Four years later, the partnership distributed the land to Hal. At the time of the distribution, the fair market value of the land was $50,000. Greg's basis was $15,000 and Hal's basis was $50,000 and his capital account balance was $60,000. What are the tax consequences from the distribution?

5.   Ira contributed stock to the partnership. The stock had a basis of $10,000 and fair market value of $25,000. Jeb contributed $25,000.

Five years later, the partnership distributed the stock to Jeb. At the time of the distribution, the fair market value of the stock was still $25,000. Ira's basis was $5,000 and Jeb's basis was $10,000 and his capital account balance was $50,000. What are the tax consequences from the distribution?

6.   Kent contributed land to the partnership. The land had a basis of $10,000 and fair market value of $25,000. Len contributed $25,000. The partnership used the $25,000 to purchase stock. Two years later, when the stock was still worth $25,000, the partnership distributed it to Kent. At the time of the distribution Kent's basis was $5,000 and his capital account was $50,000. What are the tax consequences?

7.   Mike and Ned formed an equal partnership. Mike contributed land, which had a basis of $5,000 and fair market value of $30,000. Ned contributed $30,000. Three years later, the partnership used the $30,000 cash to purchase stock.

The following year, when the fair market value of the stock was still $30,000, the partnership distributed it to Mike. At the time of the distribution Mike's basis was $10,000 and his capital account was $50,000.

8.   Opie and Paul formed an equal partnership. Opie contributed stock which had a basis of $20,000 and fair market value of $30,000. Paul contributed $30,000. Three years later, the partnership used the $30,000 to purchase land.

The following year, when the fair market value of the land was still $30,000, the partnership distributed it to Opie. At the time of the distribution Opie's basis was $5,000 and his capital account was $50,000.

9.   Quinn and Roy formed an equal partnership. Quinn contributed land, which had a basis of $50,000 and fair market value of $20,000. Roy contributed $20,000. Three years later, the partnership used the $20,000 to purchase stock.

The following year, when the fair market value of the stock was still $20,000, the partnership distributed it to Quinn. At the time of the distribution Quinn's basis was $50,000 and his capital account was $60,000.

10. Sam and Tess formed an equal partnership. Sam contributed stock, which had a basis of $20,000 and fair market value of $30,000. Tess contributed land which had a basis of $10,000 and fair market value of $30,000.

Four years later, when the fair market value of the stock was still $30,000, the partnership distributed it to Tess. At the time of the distribution Tess's basis was $25,000 and her capital account was $50,000, and Sam's basis was $20,000.

11. Vince and Wes formed an equal partnership. Vince contributed land, which had a basis of $10,000 and fair market value of $40,000. Wes contributed stock which had a basis of $30,000 and fair market value of $40,000.

Four years later, when the fair market value of the land was still $40,000, the partnership distributed it to Wes. At the time of the distribution Wes's basis was $5,000 and his capital account was $50,000, and Vince's basis was $20,000.

Solutions

1.   Ann contributed land to the partnership. The land had a basis of $10,000 and fair market value of $25,000. Bob contributed $25,000. The partnership held the land for investment purposes.

Two years later, the partnership distributed the land to Bob. At the time of the distribution, the fair market value of the land was still $25,000. Ann's basis was $5,000 and Bob's basis was $50,000 and his capital account balance was $50,000. What are the tax consequences from the distribution?

Ann must recognize the built-in gain on the property, determined as if the property had been sold for its fair market value as of the date of distribution. (Section 704(c)(1)(B)(i)) If the property was sold at the date of distribution for its fair market value, the partnership would have recognized $15,000 of gain (fair market value of $25,000, less basis of $10,000). Because the partnership held the property for investment purposes, the gain is characterized as long-term capital gain. (Section 704(c)(1)(B)(ii)) Ann recognizes $15,000 of long term capital gain and her basis is increased by $15,000, from $5,000 to $20,000. (Section 704(c)(1)(B)(iii))

Ann:	Basis:
	$ 5,000
Gain:	15,000
Basis:	$20,000

The partnership's basis in the land is increased by $15,000, from $10,000 to $25,000. (Section 704(c)(1)(B)(iii))

Land:	$10,000
Gain:	15,000
Basis:	$25,000

Then the property is distributed by the partnership to Bob. Upon distribution of the property, his basis is reduced by $25,000, from $50,000 to $25,000. (Section 733(2)) His basis in the land is $25,000. (Section 732(a)(1)) His capital account is reduced by $25,000, from $50,000 to $25,000.

Bob:	Basis	Capital Account
	$50,000	$50,000
Distribution:	– 25,000	– 25,000
	$25,000	$25,000

2.   Carl contributed stock to the partnership. The stock had a basis of $10,000 and fair market value of $25,000. Deb contributed $25,000. The partnership used the traditional method for making Section 704(c) allocations.

Three years later the partnership distributed the stock to Deb. At the time of the distribution, its fair market value was $20,000, Carl's basis was $7,000 and Deb's basis was $30,000 and her capital account balance was $40,000. What are the tax consequences from the distribution?

Carl must recognize the built-in gain on the stock, determined as if the stock had been sold for its fair market value as of the date of distribution. (Section 704(c)(1)(B)(i)) If the stock was sold at the date of distribution for its fair market value, the partnership would have recognized $10,000 of gain (fair market value of $20,000, less basis of $10,000). All of this gain represents the built-in gain at the time Carl contributed the property to the partnership, as limited by the ceiling rule (and not corrected, as the partnership uses the traditional method). The gain is characterized as long-term capital gain. (Section 704(c)(1)(B)(ii)) Carl recognizes $10,000 of long term capital gain and his basis is increased by $10,000, from $7,000 to $17,000. (Section 704(c)(1)(B)(iii))

Carl:	Basis
	$ 7,000
Gain:	10,000
Basis:	$17,000

The partnership's basis in the stock is increased by $10,000, from $10,000 to $20,000. (Section 704(c)(1)(B)(iii))

Stock:	
	$10,000
Gain:	10,000
Basis:	$20,000

Then the stock is distributed by the partnership to Deb. Upon distribution of the stock, her basis is reduced by $20,000, from $30,000 to $10,000 (Section 733(2)), and her basis in the stock is $20,000 (Section 732(a)(1)). Her capital account is reduced $20,000, from $40,000 to $20,000.

Deb:	Basis	Capital Account
	$30,000	$40,000
Distribution:	– 20,000	– 20,000
	$10,000	$20,000

3.   **Ellen contributed stock to the partnership. The stock had a basis of $20,000 and fair market value of $25,000. Frank contributed $25,000. The partnership used the traditional method for making Section 704(c) allocations.**

Three years later the partnership distributed the stock to Frank. At the time of the distribution, its fair market value was $15,000, Ellen's basis was $15,000 and Frank's basis was $30,000 and his capital account balance was $40,000. What are the tax consequences from the distribution?

Ellen must recognize the built-in gain on the stock, determined as if the stock had been sold for its fair market value as of the date of distribution. (Section 704(c)(1)(B)(i)) If the stock was sold at the date of distribution for its fair market value, the partnership would have recognized a $5,000 loss (fair market value of $15,000, less basis of $20,000). There is no gain for Ellen to recognize.

The stock is distributed by the partnership to Frank. Upon distribution of the stock, his basis is reduced by $20,000, from $30,000 to $10,000. (Section 733(2)) His basis in the stock is $20,000. (Section 732(a)(1)) His capital account is reduced $15,000, from $40,000 to $25,000.

Frank:	Basis	Capital Account
	$30,000	$40,000
Distribution:	– 20,000	– 15,000
	$10,000	$25,000

4. Greg contributed land to the partnership. The land had a basis of $30,000 and fair market value of $40,000. Hal contributed $40,000. The partnership held the land for investment purposes.

Four years later, the partnership distributed the land to Hal. At the time of the distribution, the fair market value of the land was $50,000. Greg's basis was $15,000 and Hal's basis was $50,000 and his capital account balance was $60,000. What are the tax consequences from the distribution?

Greg must recognize the built-in gain on the property, determined as if the property had been sold for its fair market value as of the date of distribution. (Section 704(c)(1)(B)(i)) If the property was sold at the date of distribution for its fair market value, the partnership would have recognized $20,000 of gain (fair market value of $50,000, less basis of $30,000). However, only $10,000 of the gain represents built-in gain. Because the partnership held the property for investment purposes, the gain is characterized as long-term capital gain. (Section 704(c)(1)(B)(ii)) Greg recognizes $10,000 of long term capital gain and his basis is increased by $10,000, from $15,000 to $25,000. (Section 704(c)(1)(B)(iii))

Greg:		Basis
		$15,000
	Gain:	10,000
	Basis:	$25,000

The partnership's basis in the land is increased by $10,000, from $30,000 to $40,000. (Section 704(c)(1)(B)(iii))

Land:		$30,000
	Gain:	10,000
	Basis:	$40,000

Then the property is distributed by the partnership to Hal. Upon distribution of the property, his basis is reduced by $40,000, from $50,000 to $10,000. (Section 733(2)) His basis in the land is $40,000. (Section 732(a)(1)) His capital account is reduced by $50,000, from $60,000 to $10,000.

Hal:	Basis	Capital Account
	$50,000	$60,000
Distribution:	– 40,000	– 50,000
	$10,000	$10,000

5. Ira contributed stock to the partnership. The stock had a basis of $10,000 and fair market value of $25,000. Jeb contributed $25,000.

Five years later, the partnership distributed the stock to Jeb. At the time of the distribution, the fair market value of the stock was still $25,000. Ira's basis was $5,000 and Jeb's basis was $10,000 and his capital account balance was $50,000. What are the tax consequences from the distribution?

Ira must recognize the built-in gain on the stock, determined as if the stock had been sold for its fair market value as of the date of distribution. (Section 704(c)(1)(B)(i)) If the stock was sold at the date of distribution for its fair market value, the partnership would have recognized $15,000 of gain (fair market value of $25,000, less basis of $10,000). Ira recognizes $15,000 of gain and his basis is increased by $15,000, from

$5,000 to $20,000. (Section 704(c)(1)(B)(iii)) The gain is characterized as long-term capital gain. (Section 704(c)(1)(B)(ii))

Ira:	Basis
	$ 5,000
Gain:	15,000
Basis:	$20,000

The partnership's basis in the stock is increased by $15,000, from $10,000 to $25,000. (Section 704(c)(1)(B)(iii))

Stock:	$10,000
Gain:	15,000
Basis:	$25,000

Then the stock is distributed by the partnership to Jeb. Because the basis in the stock is greater than Jeb's basis, first the basis in the stock is reduced to $10,000. (Section 732(a)(2)) Then, the stock is distributed and his basis is reduced from $10,000 to zero. (Section 733(2)) His basis in the stock is $10,000. (Section 732(a)(2)) His capital account is reduced by $25,000, from $50,000 to $25,000.

Jeb:	Basis	Capital Account
	$10,000	$50,000
Distribution:	– 10,000	– 25,000
	$ 0	$25,000

6.   Kent contributed land to the partnership. The land had a basis of $10,000 and fair market value of $25,000. Len contributed $25,000. The partnership used the $25,000 to purchase stock. Two years later, when the stock was still worth $25,000, the partnership distributed it to Kent. At the time of the distribution Kent's basis was $5,000 and his capital account was $50,000. What are the tax consequences?

Kent had previously contributed property with built-in gain, then received a distribution of other property with seven years. Accordingly, he must recognize gain in an amount that is the lesser of two amounts. (Section 737(a)) The first amount is the fair market value of the distributed property, $25,000, reduced by his basis immediately before the distribution, $5,000, or $20,000. (Section 737(a)(1)) The second amount is the amount of the net precontribution gain. The amount of net precontribution gain in the land is $15,000 (fair market value of $25,000, less basis of $10,000). (Section 737(a)(2), (b)) The lesser of the two amounts is the second amount, $15,000.

Kent recognizes $15,000 of long term capital gain and his basis is increased by the amount of the gain. (Section 737(c)(1)) Accordingly, his basis is increased from by $15,000, from $5,000 to $20,000.

Kent:	Basis
	$ 5,000
Gain:	15,000
Basis:	$20,000

The partnership's basis in the land is increased to reflect the gain recognized by Kent, or increased by $15,000, from $10,000 to $25,000. (Section 737(c)(2))

Land:		$10,000
	Gain:	15,000
	Basis:	$25,000

Kent's basis and capital account are reduced to reflect the distribution of the stock. Because the basis in the stock is greater than Kent's basis, first the basis in the stock is reduced to $20,000. (Section 732(a)(2)) Then, the stock is distributed and his basis is reduced from $20,000 to zero. (Section 733(2)) His basis in the stock is $20,000. (Section 732(a)(2)) His capital account is reduced from by $25,000, from $50,000 to $25,000.

Kent:	Basis	Capital Account
	$20,000	$50,000
Distribution:	– 20,000	– 25,000
	$ 0	$25,000

7.   **Mike and Ned formed an equal partnership. Mike contributed land, which had a basis of $5,000 and fair market value of $30,000. Ned contributed $30,000. Three years later, the partnership used the $30,000 to purchase stock.**

The following year, when the fair market value of the stock was still $30,000, the partnership distributed it to Mike. At the time of the distribution Mike's basis was $10,000 and his capital account was $50,000.

Mike had previously contributed property with built-in gain, then received a distribution of other property within seven years. Accordingly, he must recognize gain in an amount that is the lesser of two amounts. (Section 737(a)) The first amount is the fair market value of the distributed property, $30,000, reduced by his basis immediately before the distribution, $10,000, or $20,000. (Section 737(a)(1)) The second amount is the amount of the net precontribution gain. The amount of net pre-contribution gain in the land is $25,000 (fair market value of $30,000, less basis of $5,000). (Section 737(a)(2), (b)) The lesser of the two amounts is the first amount, $20,000.

Mike recognizes $20,000 of long term capital gain and his basis is increased by the amount of the gain. (Section 737(c)(1)) Accordingly, his basis is increased by $20,000, from $10,000 to $30,000.

Mike:		Basis
		$10,000
	Gain:	20,000
	Basis:	$30,000

The partnership's basis in the land is increased to reflect the gain recognized by Mike, or increased from by $20,000, from $5,000 to $25,000. (Section 737(c)(2))

Land:		$ 5,000
	Gain:	20,000
	Basis:	$25,000

Mike's basis and capital account are decreased to reflect distribution of the stock. Upon distribution of the property, his basis is reduced by $30,000, from $30,000 to zero. (Section 733(2)) His basis in the stock is $30,000. (Section 732(a)(1)) His capital account is reduced by $30,000, from $50,000 to $20,000.

Mike:	Basis	Capital Account
	$30,000	$50,000
Distribution:	– 30,000	– 30,000
	$ 0	$20,000

8.   Opie and Paul formed an equal partnership. Opie contributed stock which had a basis of $20,000 and fair market value of $30,000. Paul contributed $30,000. Three years later, the partnership used the $30,000 to purchase land.

The following year, when the fair market value of the land was still $30,000, the partnership distributed it to Opie. At the time of the distribution Opie's basis was $5,000 and his capital account was $50,000.

Opie had previously contributed property with built-in gain, then received a distribution of other property within seven years. Accordingly, he must recognize gain in an amount that is the lesser of two amounts. (Section 737(a)) The first amount is the fair market value of the distributed property, $30,000, reduced by his basis immediately before the distribution, $5,000, or $25,000. (Section 737(a)(1)) The second amount is the amount of the net precontribution gain. The amount of net precontribution gain in the stock is $10,000 (fair market value of $30,000, less basis of $20,000). (Section 737(a)(2), (b)) The lesser of the two amounts is the second amount, $10,000.

Opie recognizes $10,000 of long term capital gain and his basis is increased by the amount of the gain. (Section 737(c)(1)) Accordingly, his basis is increased by $10,000, from $5,000 to $15,000.

Opie:	Basis
	$ 5,000
Gain:	10,000
Basis:	$15,000

The partnership's basis in the stock is increased to reflect the gain recognized by Opie, or increased from by $10,000, from $20,000 to $30,000. (Section 737(c)(2))

Stock:	$20,000
Gain:	10,000
Basis:	$30,000

Opie's basis and capital account are decreased to reflect distribution of the land. Because the basis in the land is greater than Opie's basis, first the basis in the land is reduced to $15,000. (Section 732(a)(2)) Then, the land is distributed and his basis is reduced from $15,000 to zero. (Section 733(2)) His basis in the land is $15,000. (Section 732(a)(2)) His capital account is reduced by $30,000, from $50,000 to $20,000.

Opie:	Basis	Capital Account
	$15,000	$50,000
Distribution:	– 15,000	– 30,000
	$ 0	$20,000

9.   Quinn and Roy formed an equal partnership. Quinn contributed land, which had a basis of $50,000 and fair market value of $20,000. Roy contributed $20,000. Three years later, the partnership used the $20,000 to purchase stock.

The following year, when the fair market value of the stock was still $20,000, the partnership distributed it to Quinn. At the time of the distribution Quinn's basis was $50,000 and his capital account was $60,000.

Because the land Quinn had previously contributed did not have a built-in gain, Section 737 does not apply. (Section 737(a)) Quinn's basis is reduced from $50,000 to $30,000 (Section 733(2)) and he takes a $20,000 basis in the stock (Section 732(a)(2)). His capital account is reduced by $20,000, from $60,000 to $40,000.

Quinn:	Basis	Capital Account
	$50,000	$60,000
Distribution:	− 20,000	− 20,000
	$30,000	$40,000

10. Sam and Tess formed an equal partnership. Sam contributed stock, which had a basis of $20,000 and fair market value of $30,000. Tess contributed land which had a basis of $10,000 and fair market value of $30,000.

Four years later, when the fair market value of the stock was still $30,000, the partnership distributed it to Tess. At the time of the distribution Tess's basis was $25,000 and her capital account was $50,000, and Sam's basis was $20,000.

Sam must recognize the built-in gain on the stock, determined as if the stock had been sold for its fair market value as of the date of distribution. (Section 704(c)(1)(B)(i)) If the stock was sold at the date of distribution for its fair market value, the partnership would have recognized $10,000 of gain (fair market value of $30,000, less basis of $20,000). Sam recognizes $10,000 of gain and his basis is increased by $10,000, from $20,000 to $30,000. (Section 704(c)(1)(B)(iii)) The gain is characterized as long-term capital gain. (Section 704(c)(1)(B)(ii))

Sam:	Basis
	$20,000
Gain:	10,000
Basis:	$30,000

The partnership's basis in the stock is increased by $10,000, from $20,000 to $30,000. (Section 704(c)(1)(B)(iii))

Stock:	$20,000
Gain:	10,000
Basis:	$30,000

Tess had previously contributed property with built-in gain, then received a distribution of other property within seven years. Accordingly, she must recognize gain in an amount that is the lesser of two amounts. (Section 737(a)) The first amount is the fair market value of the distributed property, $30,000, reduced by her basis immediately before the distribution, $25,000, or $5,000. (Section 737(a)(1)) The second amount is the amount of the net precontribution gain. The amount of net precontribution gain in the land is $20,000 (fair market value of $30,000, less basis of $10,000). (Section 737(a)(2), (b)) The lesser of the two amounts is the first amount, $5,000.

Tess recognizes $5,000 of long term capital gain and her basis is increased by the amount of the gain. (Section 737(c)(1)) Accordingly, her basis is increased by $5,000, from $25,000 to $30,000.

Tess:	Basis
	$25,000
Gain:	5,000
Basis:	$30,000

The partnership's basis in the land is increased to reflect the gain recognized by Tess, or increased from by $5,000, from $10,000 to $15,000. (Section 737(c)(2))

Land:	$10,000
Gain:	5,000
Basis:	$15,000

Tess's basis and capital account are decreased to reflect distribution of the stock. Upon distribution of the property, her basis is reduced by $30,000, from $30,000 to zero. (Section 733(2)) Her basis in the stock is $30,000. (Section 732(a)(1)) Her capital account is reduced by $30,000, from $50,000 to $20,000.

Tess:	Basis	Capital Account
	$30,000	$50,000
Distribution:	− 30,000	− 30,000
	$ 0	$20,000

11. **Vince and Wes formed an equal partnership. Vince contributed land, which had a basis of $10,000 and fair market value of $40,000. Wes contributed stock which had a basis of $30,000 and fair market value of $40,000.**

Four years later, when the fair market value of the land was still $40,000, the partnership distributed it to Wes. At the time of the distribution Wes's basis was $5,000 and his capital account was $50,000, and Vince's basis was $20,000.

Vince must recognize the built-in gain on the land, determined as if the land had been sold for its fair market value as of the date of distribution. (Section 704(c)(1)(B)(i)) If the land was sold at the date of distribution for its fair market value, the partnership would have recognized $30,000 of gain (fair market value of $40,000, less basis of $10,000). Vince recognizes $30,000 of gain and his basis is increased by $30,000, from $20,000 to $50,000. (Section 704(c)(1)(B)(iii)) The gain is characterized as long-term capital gain. (Section 704(c)(1)(B)(ii))

Vince:	Basis
	$20,000
Gain:	30,000
Basis:	$50,000

The partnership's basis in the land is increased by $30,000, from $10,000 to $40,000. (Section 704(c)(1)(B)(iii))

Land:	$10,000
Gain:	30,000
Basis:	$40,000

Wes had previously contributed property with built-in gain, then received a distribution of other property within seven years. Accordingly, he must recognize gain in an amount that is the lesser of two amounts. (Section 737(a)) The first amount is the fair market value of the distributed property, $40,000, reduced by his basis immediately before the distribution, $5,000, or $35,000. (Section 737(a)(1)) The second amount is the amount of the net precontribution gain. The amount of net precontribution gain in the stock is $10,000 (fair market value of $40,000, less basis of $30,000). (Section 737(a)(2), (b)) The lesser of the two amounts is the second amount, $10,000.

Wes recognizes $10,000 of long term capital gain and his basis is increased by the amount of the gain. (Section 737(c)(1)) Accordingly, his basis is increased by $10,000, from $5,000 to $15,000.

Wes:	**Basis**
	$ 5,000
Gain:	10,000
Basis:	$15,000

The partnership's basis in the stock is increased to reflect the gain recognized by Wes, or increased from by $10,000, from $30,000 to $40,000. (Section 737(c)(2))

Stock:	$30,000
Gain:	10,000
Basis:	$40,000

Wes's basis and capital account are decreased to reflect distribution of the land. Because the basis in the land is greater than Wes's basis, first the basis in the land is reduced to $15,000. (Section 732(a)(2)) Then, the land is distributed and his basis is reduced from $15,000 to zero. (Section 733(2)) His basis in the land is $15,000. (Section 732(a)(2)) His capital account is reduced by $40,000, from $50,000 to $10,000.

Wes:	**Basis**	**Capital Account**
	$15,000	$50,000
Distribution:	− 15,000	− 40,000
	$ 0	$10,000

Chapter XI

Liquidating Distributions

A partner can retire from the partnership either by liquidating his interest[1] or retiring by ceasing to be a partner under state law.[2] The tax consequences of the payments the partner receives from the partnership will depend on how they are characterized. All payments to a retiring partner, or a deceased partner's successor in interest, will fall into one of two categories, either a payment for the partner's interest in partnership property (Section 736(b)) or other payments (Section 736(a)).

A. Payments for Partner's Interest in Partnership Property (Section 736(b))

Payments covered. Subject to certain exclusions, Section 736(b) covers payments made to a partner for his interest in partnership property.

Tax Treatment. To the extent payments are made for a partner's interest in partnership property, the general rules for non-liquidating distributions (discussed in Chapter VIII) are applied.[3] For example:

- A partner does not recognize gain or loss when he receives a distribution of cash from a partnership,[4] except to the extent the cash distributed exceeds the partner's outside basis.[5] His outside basis is reduced by the amount of cash distributed.[6]
- A partner does not recognize gain or loss when he receives a distribution of property from a partnership. The partner's outside basis is reduced by the basis of the asset

---

1. Section 761(d); Treas. Reg. § 1.761-1(d). Liquidation is the termination of a partner's entire interest in a partnership by means of a distribution, or series of distributions, from the partnership to the partner. Section 761(d).
2. Treas. Reg. § 1.736-1(a)(1)(ii).
3. Section 736(b).
4. Section 731(a). The partnership does not recognize any gain or loss on the distribution. Section 731(b); Treas. Reg. § 1.731-1(b).
5. Section 731(a)(1).
6. Section 733(1).

distributed.[7] To the extent the basis in the property is larger than the partner's outside basis, the basis in the property is reduced to reflect the partner's outside basis, then the asset is distributed.[8] To the extent the basis in the property is less than the partner's outside basis, the basis in the property is increased, then the asset is distributed.[9]

- Ignoring unrealized receivables and unstated goodwill for purposes of defining unrealized receivables, if the distribution constitutes a disproportionate distribution under Section 751(b), the transaction will be restructured.
- If the partnership has made a Section 754 election, the basis in partnership assets will be adjusted as provided under Section 734(b).
- To the extent allowed, a retiring partner may tack the partnership's holding period in distributed assets.[10]
- If unrealized receivables or inventory are distributed, the character as ordinary is preserved (indefinitely for unrealized receivables and five years for inventory).[11]

Timing. Payments are taken into account in the year made by the partnership.[12] Under the rules related to non-liquidating distributions,[13] the partner's basis is reduced by each distribution.[14] The partner recognizes income only when a cash distribution exceeds his basis.[15] A partner who is receiving fixed payments may elect to effectively report a pro rata portion of the gain or loss each time he receives a payment.[16] If there is a loss and the property distributed consists only of cash, unrealized receivables, and inventory items, the partner will recognize the loss in the year the final payment has been made.[17]

Exceptions to the general rule. If the payment is:

- To a general partner;
- For his interest in partnership property;
- The partnership is a service partnership; and
- The payment is for — [18]
  - Unrealized receivables, or
  - Partnership goodwill when the partnership agreement does not expressly provide for such payment (sometimes called unstated goodwill);

then, the payment is not covered by Section 736(b).

A service partnership is one in which capital is not a material income producing factor. In turn, capital is not a material income producing factor if substantially all of

---

7. Sections 731(a); 733(2). The partnership does not recognize any gain or loss on the distribution. Section 731(b); Treas. Reg. § 1.731-1(b).
   8. Section 732(b), (c)(1)(A), (c)(3).
   9. Section 732(b), (c)(1)(B), (c)(2).
   10. Section 735(b).
   11. Section 735(a).
   12. Treas. Reg. § 1.736-1(a)(5).
   13. See Sections 731; 732.
   14. Sections 731; 732; 733.
   15. See Section 731(a)(1).
   16. Treas. Reg. § 1.736-1(b)(6).
   17. Treas. Reg. § 1.731-1(a)(2).
   18. Section 736(a), (b)(2), (b)(3).

the gross income of the business is from fees, commissions, or other compensation for personal services.[19] Accordingly, for this purpose, the extent to which the partnership owns capital is irrelevant. Rather, the source of the income is important.

> **Example:** Five doctors formed a partnership. The partnership acquired a large medical complex from which to run the partnership business. Even though the partnership has a large capital investment, its income is primarily from compensation for the services of its doctors. Accordingly, capital is not a material income producing factor.

For purposes of this provision, unrealized receivables do not include recapture gain.[20] Unrealized receivables include, to the extent not previously included in income, any right to payment for services rendered; they also include the right to payment for goods delivered to the extent the proceeds would be treated as amounts received from the sale or exchange of property other than a capital asset.[21]

The partners can provide for the payment of goodwill in the partnership agreement (stated goodwill). Or, they can include it in any modifications to the agreement, whether written or oral, made in a year prior to the date of filing the income tax return for the year of the liquidation.[22] To be respected, the payments must be reasonable.[23]

B. Other Payments (Section 736(a))

Payments covered. Two types of payments fall under Section 736(a). First, it includes those amounts excepted from coverage under Section 736(b). Thus, if the payment is:

- To a general partner;
- For his interest in partnership property;
- The partnership is a service partnership; and
- The payment is for—[24]
  - Unrealized receivables, or
  - Unstated goodwill,

then, the payment is covered by Section 736(a).

To the extent of the partner's share of the partnership's inside basis in unrealized receivables, the payment is treated as a distribution (*i.e.,* covered by Section 736(b)). The amount in excess of the partner's share of inside basis is covered by Section 736(a).[25]

Similarly, if the partnership agreement does not provide a payment for goodwill, to the extent of the partner's share of the partnership's inside basis in goodwill, the payment

---

19. Treas. Reg. § 1.704-1(e)(1)(iv).
20. Section 751(c).
21. Id.
22. Section 761(c); Treas. Reg. § 1.761-1(c).
23. Treas. Reg. §§ 1.736-1(b)(1), -1(b)(3).
24. Section 736(a), (b)(2), (b)(3).
25. Treas. Reg. § 1.736-1(b)(2).

is treated as a distribution (*i.e.*, covered by Section 736(b)). The amount in excess of the partner's share of inside basis is covered by Section 736(a).[26]

Second, a payment that is not for a partner's interest in the partnership's property (sometimes called a premium payment) is covered by Section 736(a).[27]

Tax Treatment. Payments that come within Section 736(a) are treated as either a distributive share of profits or a guaranteed payment.[28] If the amount of the payment depends on the income of the partnership, the payment is treated as a distributive share.[29] If the payment does not depend on the income of the partnership, it is treated as a guaranteed payment.[30] If the partnership uses its own assets to make the payment, it has disposed of property and must recognize any gain or loss realized.

Timing. A partner includes a distributive share in income for his taxable year within which the partnership's taxable year ends.[31] The partner includes a guaranteed payment in income in the year the partnership is entitled to claim a deduction.[32]

C. Allocation of Installment Payments

If the partner receives payments in installments, each installment must be allocated between the two possible types of payments (*i.e.*, between those covered by Section 736(a) and those covered by Section 736(b)). If the payments are of a fixed amount and paid over a fixed amount of time, the portion treated as a non-liquidating distribution (Section 736(b) payments) is the yearly installment payment, multiplied by the fixed payments related to payments for the partner's interest in the partnership property (Section 736(b) payments), divided by the total of all fixed payments. The remainder of each payment is for items that are treated as a distributive share of income or guaranteed payments under Section 736(a).[33]

If the payments are contingent (not of a fixed amount), the payment is allocated first to payments for items that come under Section 736(b) (payments for the partner's interest in the partnership assets). Any remaining amount is treated as payments for items that come under Section 736(a).[34]

Alternatively, the parties may agree as to the allocation of the payments. Under such an agreement, the amount allocated to items that come under Section 736(b) cannot exceed the partner's total value in partnership property at the time of retirement.[35]

---

26. Section 736(b)(2)(B), (b)(3); Treas. Reg. § 1.736-1(b)(3).
27. Treas. Reg. § 1.736-1(a)(3). It is irrelevant whether the partnership is a service partnership.
28. Treas. Reg. § 1.736-1(a)(3).
29. Section 736(a)(1), (a)(2); Treas. Reg. § 1.736-1(a)(3)(i).
30. Section 736(a)(1), (a)(2); Treas. Reg. § 1.736-1(a)(3)(ii).
31. Treas. Reg. §§ 1.736-1(a)(4); -1(a)(5).
32. Treas. Reg. §§ 1.736-1(a)(4); -1(a)(5).
33. Treas. Reg. § 1.736-1(b)(5)(i).
34. Treas. Reg. § 1.736-1(b)(5)(ii).
35. Treas. Reg. § 1.736-1(b)(5)(iii).

Summary

Section 736(a): Includes a payment to a general partner; for his interest in partnership property; where the partnership is a service partnership; and the payment is for unrealized receivables, unstated goodwill, or a premium.

With respect to unrealized receivables and unstated goodwill, it applies to just the amount in excess of the partner's share of inside basis.

The payments are treated as either a distributive share of profits or a guaranteed payment. If the amount of the payment depends on the income of the partnership, the payment is treated as a distributive share. If the payment does not depend on the income of the partnership, it is treated as a guaranteed payment.

Section 736(b): To the extent payments are made for a partner's interest in partnership property, the general rules for non-liquidating distributions apply.

Questions

1.   The partnership was a general partnership that leased commercial property. Carl retired from the partnership. At the time of his retirement, the partnership's balance sheet appeared as follows:

Asset	Adj.	FMV	Partner	Adj. Basis	Cap. Acct.
Cash	$100,000	$100,000	Ann	$ 25,000	$ 90,000
Stock	10,000	40,000	Bob	30,000	90,000
Whiteacre	10,000	60,000	Carl	80,000	90,000
Redacre	15,000	70,000		$135,000	$270,000
Total:	$135,000	$270,000			

The partnership paid Carl $90,000 in liquidation of his interest. No portion of the payment was for goodwill. What are the tax consequences to Carl?

2.   The partnership was a general partnership that provided consulting services. Ellen retired from the partnership. At the time of her retirement, the partnership's balance sheet appeared as follows:

Asset	Adj.	FMV	Partner	Adj. Basis	Cap. Acct.
Cash	$90,000	$ 90,000	Deb	$30,000	$ 50,000
Acct Rec	0	60,000	Ellen	30,000	50,000
Total:	$90,000	$150,000	Frank	30,000	50,000
				$90,000	$150,000

The partnership paid Ellen $50,000 in liquidation of her interest. No portion of the payment was for goodwill. What are the tax consequences to Ellen?

3.   The partnership was a general partnership that provided advertising services. Greg retired from the partnership. At the time of his retirement, the partnership's balance sheet appeared as follows:

Asset	Adj.	FMV	Partner	Adj. Basis	Cap. Acct.
Cash	$90,000	$ 90,000	Greg	$30,000	$ 50,000
Acct Rec	0	60,000	Hal	30,000	50,000
Total:	$90,000	$150,000	Ira	30,000	50,000
				$90,000	$150,000

The partnership paid Greg $60,000 in liquidation of his interest. Included in the payment was a $10,000 payment for goodwill, as provided in the partnership agreement. What are the tax consequences to Greg?

4.   The partnership was a general partnership that provided legal services. Jeb retired from the partnership. At the time of his retirement, the partnership's balance sheet appeared as follows:

Asset	Adj.	FMV	Partner	Adj. Basis	Cap. Acct.
Cash	$100,000	$100,000	Jeb	$ 45,000	$ 90,000
Stock	10,000	40,000	Kent	45,000	90,000
Whiteacre	10,000	60,000	Len	45,000	90,000
Redacre	15,000	70,000		$135,000	$270,000
Total:	$135,000	$270,000			

The partnership paid Jeb $100,000 in liquidation of his interest, with $10,000 representing a premium payment. What are the tax consequences to Jeb?

Solutions

1. The partnership was a general partnership that leased commercial property. Carl retired from the partnership. At the time of his retirement, the partnership's balance sheet appeared as follows:

Asset	Adj.	FMV	Partner	Adj. Basis	Cap. Acct.
Cash	$100,000	$100,000	Ann	$ 25,000	$ 90,000
Stock.	10,000	40,000	Bob	30,000	90,000
Whiteacre	10,000	60,000	Carl	80,000	90,000
Redacre	15,000	70,000		$135,000	$270,000
Total:	$135,000	$270,000			

The partnership paid Carl $90,000 in liquidation of his interest. No portion of the payment was for goodwill. What are the tax consequences to Carl?

While the payment to Carl is to a general partner for his interest in partnership property, the partnership is not a service partnership. Because the partnership is not a service partnership, the payments do not come within the exception of Section 736(a). The general rules for non-liquidating distributions apply (Section 736(b)) and Carl recognizes gain to the extent the cash distribution exceeds his basis. (Section 733(1))

Basis:	$80,000
Distribution:	– 90,000
Gain:	<$10,000>

Carl recognizes $10,000 of gain.

The liquidating distribution also reduces his economic investment in the partnership. His capital account is reduced by the amount of the distribution, or reduced from $90,000 to zero.

Cap account:	$90,000
Cash distribution:	<90,000>
Cap account:	$ 0

2. The partnership was a general partnership that provided consulting services. Ellen retired from the partnership. At the time of her retirement, the partnership's balance sheet appeared as follows:

Asset	Adj.	FMV	Partner	Adj. Basis	Cap. Acct.
Cash	$90,000	$ 90,000	Deb	$30,000	$ 50,000
Acct Rec	0	60,000	Ellen	30,000	50,000
Total:	$90,000	$150,000	Frank	30,000	50,000
				$90,000	$150,000

The partnership paid Ellen $50,000 in liquidation of her interest. No portion of the payment was for goodwill. What are the tax consequences to Ellen?

The payment of $30,000 for her share of the cash is covered by Section 736(b) and is treated in the same manner as a non-liquidating distribution. (Section 736(b)) Ellen recognizes gain to the extent the cash distribution exceeds her basis. (Section 733(1))

Basis:	$30,000
Distribution:	− 30,000
Gain:	$ 0

Ellen recognizes no gain.

Because Ellen is a general partner and the partnership is a service partnership, the accounts receivable are not treated as non-liquidating distributions (*i.e.*, they are treated as Section 736(a) payments). Because the remaining payment of $20,000 ($50,000, less $30,000) is made without regard to the partnership income it is treated as a guaranteed payment. Ellen includes the payments for the accounts receivable, $20,000, in her income in the year the partnership is entitled to a deduction. (Sections 736(a); 707(c))

The liquidating distribution also reduces her economic investment in the partnership. Her capital account is reduced by the amount of the distribution, or reduced from $50,000 to zero.

Cap account:	$50,000
Cash distribution:	<50,000>
Cap account:	$ 0

3. **The partnership was a general partnership that provided advertising services. Greg retired from the partnership. At the time of his retirement, the partnership's balance sheet appeared as follows:**

Asset	Adj.	FMV	Partner	Adj. Basis	Cap. Acct.
Cash	$90,000	$ 90,000	Greg	$30,000	$ 50,000
Acct Rec	0	60,000	Hal	30,000	50,000
Total:	$90,000	$150,000	Ira	30,000	50,000
				$90,000	$150,000

The partnership paid Greg $60,000 in liquidation of his interest. Included in the payment was a $10,000 payment for goodwill, as provided in the partnership agreement. What are the tax consequences to Greg?

Because the payment for goodwill was provided for in the partnership agreement, it is covered by Section 736(b). The payment of $40,000 for his share of the cash and the goodwill is covered by Section 736(b) and is treated in the same manner as a non-liquidating distribution. (Section 736(b)) Greg recognizes gain to the extent the cash distribution exceeds his basis. (Section 733(1))

Basis:	$30,000
Distribution:	40,000
Gain:	$10,000

Greg recognizes $10,000 of gain.

Because Greg is a general partner and the partnership is a service partnership, the accounts receivable are not treated as non-liquidating distributions (*i.e.*, they are treated as Section 736(a) payments). Because the remaining payment of $20,000 ($60,000, less $40,000) is made without regard to the partnership income it is treated as a guaranteed payment. Greg includes the payments for the accounts receivable, $20,000, in his income in the year the partnership is entitled to a deduction. (Sections 736(a); 707(c))

The liquidating distribution also reduces his economic investment in the partnership. His capital account is reduced by the amount of the distribution, or reduced from $50,000 to zero.

Cap account:	$50,000
Cash distribution:	<50,000>
Cap account:	$ 0 (plus he received a payment for goodwill)

4.   Partnership was a general partnership that provided legal services. Jeb retired from the partnership. At the time of his retirement, the partnership's balance sheet appeared as follows:

Asset	Adj.	FMV	Partner	Adj. Basis	Cap. Acct.
Cash	$100,000	$100,000	Jeb	$ 45,000	$ 90,000
Stock	10,000	40,000	Kent	45,000	90,000
Whiteacre	10,000	60,000	Len	45,000	90,000
Redacre	15,000	70,000		$135,000	$270,000
Total:	$135,000	$270,000			

The partnership paid Jeb $100,000 in liquidation of his interest, with $10,000 representing a premium payment. What are the tax consequences to Jeb?

The payment of $90,000 for his share of the Section 736(b) property is covered by Section 736(b) and is treated in the same manner as a non-liquidating distribution. (Section 736(b)) Jeb recognizes gain to the extent the cash distribution exceeds his basis. (Section 733(1))

Basis:	$90,000
Distribution:	45,000
	$ 0

Jeb recognizes $45,000 of gain.

Because Jeb is a general partner and the partnership is a service partnership, the premium payment is covered by Section 736(a). Because the payment is made without regard to the partnership income it is treated as a guaranteed payment. Jeb includes the $10,000 premium payment in his income in the year the partnership is entitled to a deduction. (Sections 736(a); 707(c))

The liquidating distribution also reduces his economic investment in the partnership. His capital account is reduced by the amount of the distribution, or reduced from $50,000 to zero.

Cap. Account:	$90,000
Cash distribution:	<90,000>
Cap. Account:	$ 0 (plus he received a premium payment)

Chapter XII

Transactions in Capacity Other Than as a Partner

A partner is not restricted to interacting with the partnership only as a partner. He may act in his capacity as an independent third party. In such cases, the tax consequences are consistent with a transaction between the partnership and a third party.

A. Compensation for Services, Rent, Interest

1. Services

Capacity as a partner. As a partner in a partnership, the partner may be expected to render services through the partnership. In exchange, the partner will receive a share of the partnership profits.[1] He will report any such profits as part of his allocable share of partnership items. His basis will be increased by the amount of gain or income allocated to him.

Not in capacity as a partner. If the partner is not acting in his capacity as a partner, he may render services as an independent contractor to the partnership.[2] In this case, the partner must recognize the payment he receives as compensation for services. He includes the amount in his gross income based on his individual accounting method.

The partnership may be able to claim an expense deduction if the payment qualifies as an ordinary and necessary expense under Section 162 or is deductible under some other provision.

Even though a partner generally is expected to contribute services to the partnership in his capacity as a partner (or be hired to provide services as an independent contractor), there is some support for the position that a partner may render services to the partnership

---

1. If the partner provides services in exchange for his partnership interest, he must report the value of the interest received as gross income. See discussion of receipt of a partnership interest in exchange for services in Chapter I.

2. Section 707(a)(1).

275

as an employee.[3] Any tax benefits that would be available to other employees would be available to the employee-partner.

Disguised services. Some payments, though in form structured as a distribution of partnership income, may be treated as compensation if they are in substance paid for services rendered by the partner not in his capacity as a partner. If:[4]

- A partner performs services for the partnership;
- There is a related direct or indirect allocation and distribution from the partnership; and
- When considered together, the transaction is properly characterized as a transaction between the partnership and a partner not acting in his capacity as a partner;

then the transaction will be treated as one between the partnership and a third party.

2. Rental of Property

Not in capacity as a partner. If the partner is not acting in his capacity as a partner and enters into an arrangement through which the partnership may use the partner's property, the transaction is treated as a rental or lease arrangement. The partner must recognize income upon receipt of the rental or lease payments. His includes the amounts in his gross income consistent with his individual accounting method.[5]

The partnership may be able to claim an expense deduction if it qualifies as an ordinary and necessary expense under Section 162 or is deductible under some other provision.

Similarly, if the partnership enters into an agreement allowing the partner to use partnership property, the transaction is treated as a rental or lease arrangement. The partnership must recognize the rental or lease payments as income, consistent with its accounting method.[6]

The partner may be able to claim an expense deduction if the payment qualifies as an ordinary and necessary expense under Section 162 or qualifies as a deduction under some other provision.[7]

3. Use of Money

Capacity as a partner. A partner may contribute money to a partnership. The contribution is reflected in his outside basis and in his capital account.

Not in capacity as a partner. The partner, not acting in his capacity as a partner, may loan the partnership money. The partner must include interest in his gross income and the partnership will be entitled to claim a deduction for the interest paid.

Similarly, the partnership may loan money to a partner not acting in his capacity as a partner. The partnership must include interest in its gross income and the partner will be entitled to claim a deduction for the interest paid.[8]

---

3. Armstrong v. Phinney, 394 F.2d 661 (5th Cir. 1968).
4. Section 707(a)(2)(A).
5. Section 707(a)(1).
6. Id.
7. Id.
8. Id.

4. Limitation

The deduction may be deferred in certain circumstances. For the deferral to be applicable, the following elements must be present as of the close of the payor-taxpayer's taxable year. First, the payor must be on the accrual basis of accounting, allowing the amount to be deducted, depreciated, or amortized regardless of whether it is paid.[9]

Second, the recipient must be on the cash basis of accounting or otherwise not be required to include the amount in gross income until it is paid.[10]

Third, the payor and recipient must have one of the following relationships:[11]

- A partnership and a partner;[12]
- The partnership and person if they are, directly or indirectly, partners in another partnership;[13] or
- If the transaction is related either to the operations of the partnership or to an interest in the partnership, any person related to one of the above partners.[14]

In determining who is a partner in a partnership, constructive ownership rules apply.[15]

If the three elements are present, the payor is not allowed to take a deduction until the amount is actually paid.[16] In essence, an accrual basis taxpayer is placed on the cash basis with respect to a related payee so that the inclusion in income and deduction occur in the same year. Note that the requirement that a deduction be deferred does not apply if the payment is a guaranteed payment.[17]

B. Transfer of property

1. Disposition of Property

Capacity as a partner. A partner may contribute property to a partnership. The contribution is reflected in both his outside basis and in his capital account.

Not in capacity as a partner. If a partner who is not acting in his capacity as a partner transfers property to a partnership, the transaction is treated as a sale. The partner must recognize gain or loss on disposition of the property. The partnership will take a cost basis in the property.

---

9. Section 267(a)(2)(B).

10. Section 267(a)(2)(A).

11. Section 267(a)(2)(B), (e).

12. Section 267(e)(1)(B)(i).

13. Section 267(e)(1)(C).

14. Section 267(e)(1)(D).

15. Section 267(e)(3). A partner is not considered as constructively owing a partnership interest owned by his partner. Section 267(e)(3)(A).

16. Section 267(a)(2), (e). The deferral provision is not applicable if the partnership owns low-income housing and pays qualifying expenses or interest to a qualified five-percent or less partner or any person related to a qualified five-percent or less partner. Section 267(e)(5).

17. Section 267(e)(4). See discussion of guaranteed payments in Chapter XIII.

Similarly, if the partnership transfers property to a partner not acting in his capacity as a partner, the transaction is treated as a sale. The partnership must recognize gain or loss on disposition of the property. The partner will take a cost basis in the property.[18]

Disguised sales. Some transactions, though in form structured as a distribution of partnership income, may be treated as a sale if the allocation is in substance a payment to purchase the partner's property. If:[19]

- A partner transfers property to a partnership;
- There is a related direct or indirect allocation and distribution from the partnership; and
- When considered together, the transaction is properly characterized as a transaction between the partnership and a partner not acting in his capacity as a partner;

then the transaction will be treated as one between the partnership and a third party.

Similarly, if the transaction is structured as a distribution of partnership property, it may be treated as a sale if the distribution is in substance a payment to purchase the partner's property. If:[20]

- A partner directly or indirectly transfers money or property to a partnership;
- There is a related direct or indirect transfer of money or other property by the partnership to the partner; and
- When considered together, the transaction is properly characterized as a sale of property;

then the transaction will be treated as a sale between the partners and the partnership or between partners acting not as partners.

If, within a two-year time frame, a partner transfers property to a partnership and the partnership transfers money or other consideration to the partner, the transfer is presumed to be a sale of the property by the partner to the partnership. The presumption can be rebutted, based on the facts and circumstances.[21] In contrast, if a partner transfers property to a partnership and the partnership transfers money or other consideration to the partner and the transfers occur more than two years apart, the transfer is presumed not to be a sale. The presumption can be rebutted, based on the facts and circumstances.[22]

2. Limitation

No deduction for a loss is allowed on sales between a partner and the partnership if the partner owns more than 50 percent of the capital interest or profits interest in the partnership.[23] In determining a partner's ownership in a partnership, constructive

---

18. Section 707(a)(2).
19. Section 707(a)(2)(A).
20. Section 707(a)(2)(B).
21. Treas. Reg § 1.707-3(c)(1). The order of the transactions is not relevant.
22. Treas. Reg § 1.707-3(d). The order of the transactions is not relevant.
23. Section 707(b)(1)(A); Treas. Reg § 1.707-1(b)(1)(i).

ownership rules apply.[24] The loss realized by a partner or the partnership must be otherwise allowable before the disallowance rule applicable to losses from the sale of property to a related party has any application.

Similarly, no deduction for a loss is allowed when a partnership sells property to another partnership where partners own more than 50 percent of the capital interest or profits interest in both partnerships.[25]

If a loss was disallowed because it was between a partner and a partnership or between two partnerships and there is a subsequent sale or exchange of the property, gain from disposition is recognized only to the extent it exceeds the loss that was disallowed.[26] The loss can be utilized to offset the gain only in situations where there is a gain on disposition of the property. Similarly, the loss can be utilized only to the extent of gain on disposition of the property. It cannot be used as a means of generating a loss. If gain from the sale of partnership property is not recognized because it was offset by a previously disallowed loss,[27] the basis of each partner's interest in the partnership is increased by the partner's share of the gain that is not recognized.[28]

3. Characterization Issues

If the sale occurs between certain related parties, the Code may dictate the character of the gain on disposition. If the sale occurs between:

- A partnership and a person owning, directly or indirectly, more than 50 percent of the capital interest or profits interest; or
- Two partnerships in which the same persons own, directly or indirectly, more than 50 percent of the capital interests or profits interests;

and, in the hands of the buyer, the asset would not be characterized as a capital asset; then the gain is characterized as ordinary. The rule applies regardless of whether it is a direct or indirect sale.[29]

C. Need for Making Determination

In some circumstances, the net tax results are the same, regardless of whether the partner is acting in his capacity as a partner or is acting as a third party. However, in some circumstances, determining the relationship of the partner to the partnership may be important.

First, if the partner can be classified as an employee, certain Code provisions may provide beneficial treatment. For example, in some circumstances, an employee may

---

24. Section 707(b)(3). A partner is not considered as constructively owing a partnership interest owned by his partner. Section 707(b)(3).

25. Section 707(b)(1)(B); Treas. Reg § 1.707-1(b)(1)(i).

26. Sections 707(b)(1); 267(d); Treas. Reg § 1.707-1(b)(1)(ii).

27. As provided for under Section 707(b)(1) and Section 267(d).

28. Rev. Rul. 96-10, 1996-1 C.B. 138.

29. Section 707(b)(2).

be able to exclude amounts that are paid for meals and lodging.[30] Or, an employee may be able to obtain employer-provided group life insurance and exclude the benefit from gross income.[31] Finally, other fringe benefits may be excludable from an employee's gross income.[32]

Second, if the payment is a distributive share, the character of the income will be determined at the partnership level.

Third, whether the partner is acting as a third party or in his capacity as a partner may impact the timing of including the income or claiming the deduction. If the amount is part of the partner's distributive share, it must be reported on the partner's individual return for the year during which the partnership year ends. If the partner is not acting in his capacity as a partner, the year he includes the amount in income or claims a deduction is determined by his accounting method. Similarly, the year the partnership includes the amount in income or claims a deduction is determined by the partnership's accounting method. However, the partnership's deduction may be limited by Section 267(a)(2) and (e).

Fourth, the classification of a payment may impact the overall tax consequences of the transaction to the partner and the partnership. For example, the partnership may attempt to obtain an advantage by disguising a payment that is in actuality to a partner acting in his capacity as a third party as an allocation of a partnership item.

Example: Ann, Bob, and Carl were equal partners in the partnership. During the year, Ann performed services for the partnership; the value of the services was $30,000. Because the services were paid in conjunction with the acquisition of a large triangular tract of land, the payment must be capitalized as part of the total cost and is not currently deductible. In addition, during the year, the partnership had $60,000 of gross income.

The transaction could be treated with Ann acting in her capacity as a third party. As an unrelated third party, Ann must include the $30,000 paid as compensation for services in her gross income. The partnership is not permitted to deduct any portion of the $30,000 it paid for Ann's services. Accordingly, it has $60,000 of net income that is allocated equally between the partners, or $20,000 each. The partners report the following amounts of income:

Ann:	$50,000	($30,000 plus $20,000)
Bob:	20,000	
Carl:	20,000	
Total:	$90,000	

Alternatively, the transaction could be treated with Ann acting in her capacity as a partner. The partners could agree to make a special allocation to Ann, allocating $30,000 to her, with the remainder divided equally between the partners. Thus, $30,000 would be allocated to Ann, and the remaining $30,000 would be allocated equally among the partners, or $10,000 each. The partners would report the following amounts of income:

---

30. See Section 119.
31. Section 79(a).
32. See, *i.e.*, Section 132.

Ann:	$40,000	($30,000 plus $10,000)
Bob:	10,000	
Carl:	10,000	
Total:	$60,000	

By treating Ann as acting in her capacity as a partner, the partners reduced the total amount of income reported by all the partners by $30,000. Or, seen from a different perspective, the form of the transaction allowed the partnership to effectively deduct the $30,000 paid to Ann. To the extent Ann is properly treated as not acting in her capacity as a partner, Section 707(a)(2)(A) prevents the partnership and partners from achieving this result.

D. Determining in Which Capacity a Partner Is Acting

In general. There is no bright line for determining whether a partner is acting in his capacity as a partner or acting as an independent third party. In general, a partner is not acting as a partner when the services are of a limited technical nature or in connection with a specific transaction;[33] a partner who performs services that are on-going and integral to the business of the partnership is acting in his capacity as a partner.[34] Ultimately, the determination must be made based on the substance of the transaction, and not its form.[35]

Legislative history. To assist in determining the character of a transaction, the legislative history of Section 707(a)(2)(A) sets forth factors to consider in determining if the payment is a disguised payment of compensation or disguised sale of property.

First: is there an appreciable risk that the payment will not be made or that it will not be made in full? In general, a partner assumes the risk that a partnership will not have profits. An independent third party does not assume any risk; he expects to be paid, regardless of the profitability of the partnership. The first factor is considered the most important factor.

Second: how long will the partner remain a partner in the partnership? This factor is only relevant if the partner could be described as transitory. Under such circumstances, the concern is that he may have joined the partnership for the sole purpose of structuring the transaction, in form, as an allocation to a partner when, in actuality, the payment is a fee or payment for property. However, if the partner continues in the partnership, the transaction could still be properly characterized as a transaction with an independent third party.

Third: how close in time is the allocation to the partner to the performance of services or use of property? The closer in time, the greater the indication the allocation is actually a disguised payment.

Fourth: based on all the facts and circumstances, does it appear that the partner joined the partnership solely to obtain favorable tax consequences for himself or the

---

33. Treas. Reg. § 1.707-1(a).

34. Pratt v. Commissioner, 64 T.C. 203 (1975), *aff'd in part, rev'd in part* 550 F.2d 1023 (5th Cir. 1977).

35. Treas. Reg. § 1.707-1(a).

partnership that could not have been obtained acting in his individual capacity? Any non-tax motives in becoming a partner are not taken into consideration.

Fifth: is the partner's interest in the partnership small in relation to the allocation? If the interest is small, it may be an indication that the payment is to the partner not in his capacity as a partner. However, if the partner's interest is substantial, it is not an indication the payment was part of his allocable share of partnership income.

The sixth factor is relevant only when dealing with the use of property (and not to the provision of services). Does the requirement that capital accounts be maintained as provided in the regulations make the income allocations[36] associated with the property unfeasible and, therefore, unlikely to be made?

---

36. For an allocation to have economic effect, the partners must agree to maintain the capital accounts in accordance with the regulations. See discussion of allocations in Chapter IV.

Summary

If the partner is acting in his capacity as a third party:

- The partner reports items as ordinary income (from compensation, rent, interest, etc.), including as required by the partner's method of accounting
- The partnership may claim an expense deduction or depreciation to the extent allowed by the Code, based on the partnership's accounting method. However, if:
  - The payor is required to make a payment to the payee;
  - The payor is on the accrual basis of accounting and the payment is otherwise deductible, depreciable, or amortizable;
  - The payee is on the cash basis of accounting or otherwise not required to include the amount in income until actually received;
  - No actual payment has been made; and
  - The payor and payee have a relationship defined in Section 267(e)(1);

then the payor is effectively placed on the cash basis of accounting and may claim a deduction only when the payment is actually made.

Presumption of sale: If, within a two-year time frame, a partner transfers property to a partnership and the partnership transfers money or other consideration to the partner, the transfer is presumed to be a sale of the property by the partner to the partnership. The presumption can be rebutted, based on the facts and circumstances.

Limitation on Loss: A loss realized on the sale of property may not be recognized if:

- There was a disposition of property;
- The taxpayer realized a loss;
- The loss would otherwise be allowed under the code; and
- The sale was between a more than 50-percent partner and a partnership or between two partnerships where the same parties own more than 50 percent of each partnership.

Characterization: If the sale occurs between:

- A partnership and a person owning, directly or indirectly, more than 50 percent of the capital interest or profits interest; or
- Two partnerships in which the same persons own, directly or indirectly, more than 50 percent of the capital interests or profits interests,

and, in the hands of the buyer, the asset would not be characterized as a capital asset, then the gain is characterized as ordinary.

Questions

1.   Ann, Bob, and Carl are equal partners in a general partnership. The partners and the partnership are accrual basis taxpayers. In the first year, Ann provided services to the partnership that were integral to the partnership's business in exchange for a special allocation of $10,000 of partnership income. The partners agree to allocate the remaining income equally. In the first year, the partnership has $70,000 of net ordinary income. What are the tax consequences to the partners?

2.   Deb, Ellen, and Frank are equal partners in a general partnership. The partners and the partnership are accrual basis taxpayers. In the second year, Deb provided accounting services to the partnership as an independent contractor in exchange for $20,000. Before considering the payment to Deb, the partnership had $80,000 of ordinary income. What are the tax consequences to the partners?

3.   Greg, Hal, and Ira are equal partners in a general partnership. The partners and the partnership are accrual basis taxpayers. In the third year, Greg provided services to the partnership that were integral to the partnership's business in exchange for a special allocation of $20,000 of partnership profits. The partners agree to allocate the remaining income equally. In the first year, the partnership has $120,000 of net ordinary income and $40,000 of long term capital gain. What are the tax consequences to the partners?

4.   Jeb, Kent, and Len are equal partners in a general partnership. The partners and the partnership are accrual basis taxpayers. In the fourth year, Jeb provided non-deductible legal services to the partnership as an independent contractor in exchange for $20,000. Before considering the payment to Jeb, the partnership had $90,000 of ordinary income and $30,000 of long term capital gain. What are the tax consequences to the partners?

5.   Mike, Ned, and Opie are equal partners in a general partnership. The partners are cash basis taxpayers and the partnership is an accrual basis taxpayer. In the third year, Mike leased land (in a non-partner capacity) to the partnership in exchange for a $20,000 payment. The partnership does not pay Mike at the end of the year. What are the tax consequences to Mike and the partnership?

6.   Paul owns 75 percent and Quinn owns 25 percent of a general partnership.

    a.   Paul sold stock to the partnership for $30,000. At the time of the sale, his basis in the stock was $50,000. What are the tax consequences to Paul?

    b.   Alternatively, Quinn sold stock to the partnership for $30,000. At the time of the sale, his basis in the stock was $50,000. What are the tax consequences to Quinn?

7.   Roy owns 60 percent of a general partnership. He sold land to the partnership for $100,000. He had previously purchased the land for $60,000 and held it as an investment. The partnership is in the business of subdividing property and offering lots for sale. What are the tax consequences to Roy?

Solutions

1. Ann, Bob, and Carl are equal partners in a general partnership. The partners and the partnership are accrual basis taxpayers. In the first year, Ann provided services to the partnership that were integral to the partnership's business in exchange for a special allocation of $10,000 of partnership income. The partners agree to allocate the remaining income equally. In the first year, the partnership has $70,000 of net ordinary income. What are the tax consequences to the partners?

Ann is acting in her capacity as a partner and enters into an arrangement through which the partnership agreed to make a special allocation to her. Thus, $10,000 of income is allocated to Ann.

Partnership income:	$70,000
Allocation to Ann:	– 10,000
Remaining income:	$60,000

The remaining $60,000 is allocated equally among the partners. Thus, Ann reports a distributive share of income of $30,000 and Bob and Carl each report $20,000 as their distributive share of partnership income. (Section 704(a))

Ann:	$30,000	($10,000 plus $20,000)
Bob:	20,000	
Carl:	20,000	
Total:	$70,000	

2. Deb, Ellen, and Frank are equal partners in a general partnership. The partners and the partnership are accrual basis taxpayers. In the second year, Deb provided accounting services to the partnership as an independent contractor in exchange for $20,000. Before considering the payment to Deb, the partnership had $80,000 of ordinary income. What are the tax consequences to the partners?

Deb is providing accounting services as an independent third party in exchange for a payment of $20,000. (Section 707(a)(1)) Thus, Deb must report $20,000 as compensation for services (Section 61(a)), and the partnership is entitled to claim a $20,000 expense deduction (Section 162(a)).

Partnership income:	$80,000
Section 162 deduction:	– 20,000
Net income:	$60,000

The net income is allocated equally between the partners, or $20,000 each. Deb reports a total of $40,000 ($20,000 in her non-partner capacity, and $20,000 as her distributive share) and Ellen and Frank each report $20,000 as their distributive share. (Section 704(a))

3. Greg, Hal, and Ira are equal partners in a general partnership. The partners and the partnership are accrual basis taxpayers. In the third year, Greg provided services to the partnership that were integral to the partnership's business in exchange for a special allocation of $20,000 of partnership profits. The partners agree to allocate the remaining income equally. In the first year, the partnership has $120,000 of net ordinary income and $40,000 of long term capital gain. What are the tax consequences to the partners?

Greg is acting in his capacity as a partner and enters into an arrangement through which the partnership agreed to make a special allocation to him. (Section 704(a)) The partnership has $160,000 of profits.

Ordinary income: $120,000/$160,000 × $20,000 = $15,000
Capital gain: $40,000/$160,000 × $20,000 = $5,000

Thus, the partnership allocates $15,000 of ordinary income and $5,000 of the long-term capital gain, totaling $20,000, to Greg for his services.

Partnership income:	$120,000
Allocation to Greg:	– 15,000
Remaining income:	$105,000

The remaining ordinary income, $105,000, is allocated equally among the partners, or $35,000 each.

Capital gain:	$40,000
Allocation to Greg:	– 5,000
Remaining income:	$35,000

The remaining long-term capital gain, $35,000, is allocated equally among the partners, or $11,667 each. (Section 704(a)) The partners report the following amounts.

Partner	Ordinary Income	LTCG
Greg	$ 50,000	$16,666
Hal	35,000	11,667
Ira	35,000	11,667
Total:	$120,000	$40,000

4.   Jeb, Kent, and Len are equal partners in a general partnership. The partners and the partnership are accrual basis taxpayers. In the fourth year, Jeb provided non-deductible legal services to the partnership as an independent contractor in exchange for $20,000. Before considering the payment to Jeb, the partnership had $90,000 of ordinary income and $30,000 of long term capital gain. What are the tax consequences to the partners?

Jeb is providing legal services as an independent third party in exchange for a payment of $20,000. (Section 707(a)(1)) Thus, Jeb must report $20,000 as compensation for services (Section 61(a)), and the partnership is not entitled to claim a $20,000 expense deduction.

The partnership income is allocated equally between the partners, or $30,000 each. Jeb reports a total of $50,000 ($20,000 in his non-partner capacity, and $30,000 as his distributive share) and Kent and Len each report $30,000 as their distributive share. (Section 704(a))

The capital gain is allocated equally between them, or $10,000 each. In sum, the partners report the following amounts.

Partner	Nonpartner Ordinary Income	Partner Ordinary Income	Partner LTCG
Jeb	$20,000	$30,000	$10,000
Kent	0	30,000	10,000
Len	0	30,000	10,000

5. Mike, Ned, and Opie are equal partners in a general partnership. The partners are cash basis taxpayers and the partnership is an accrual basis taxpayer. In the third year, Mike leased land (in a non-partner capacity) to the partnership in exchange for a $20,000 payment. The partnership does not pay Mike at the end of the year. What are the tax consequences to Mike and the partnership?

Mike is leasing the land as an independent third party in exchange for a payment of $20,000. (Section 707(a)(1)) Because Mike is a cash basis taxpayer and the partnership has not paid him, he does not have to include the $20,000 in his income.

Usually, the partnership would be entitled to deduct the lease payment. (Section 162(a)) The partnership's deduction may be deferred in certain circumstances. For the deferral to be applicable, first, the payor must be on the accrual basis of accounting, allowing the amount to be deducted, depreciated, or amortized regardless of whether it is paid. (Section 267(a)(2)(B)) The first element is met because the partnership is an accrual basis taxpayer.

Second, the recipient must be on the cash basis of accounting or otherwise not be required to include the amount in gross income until it is paid. (Section 267(a)(2)(A)) The second element is met because Mike is a cash basis taxpayer.

Third, the payor and recipient must have one of several identified relationships. (Section 267(a)(2)(B), (e)) One of the relationships is a partnership and a partner. (Section 267(e)(1)(B)(i)) Because Mike is a partner in the partnership, the third element is met.

Because the three elements are present, the partnership is not allowed to take a deduction until the amount is actually paid to Mike. (Section 267(a)(2), (e))

6. Paul owns 75 percent and Quinn owns 25 percent of a general partnership.

   a. Paul sold stock to the partnership for $30,000. At the time of the sale, his basis in the stock was $50,000. What are the tax consequences to Paul?

If a partner who is not acting in his capacity as a partner transfers property to a partnership, the transaction is treated as a sale. (Section 707(a)(1)) The partner must recognize gain or loss on disposition of the property. The partnership will take a cost basis in the property. (Section 1012) Paul would realize a $20,000 loss on the sale.

    AR: $30,000
    AB: 50,000
    Loss: <$20,000>

No deduction for a loss is allowed on sales between a partner and the partnership if the partner owns more than 50 percent of the capital interest or profits interest in the partnership. (Section 707(b)(1)(A); Treas. Reg. § 1.707-1(b)(1)(i)) Because Paul owns more 50 percent (he owns 75 percent), the limitation will apply to him and he is not allowed to recognize the loss.

   b. Alternatively, Quinn sold stock to the partnership for $30,000. At the time of the sale, his basis in the stock was $50,000. What are the tax consequences to Quinn?

If a partner who is not acting in his capacity as a partner transfers property to a partnership, the transaction is treated as a sale. (Section 707(a)(1)) The partner must recognize gain or loss on disposition of the property. The partnership will take a cost basis in the property. (Section 1012) Quinn would realize a $20,000 loss on the sale ($30,000 amount realized, less $50,000 basis).

AR: $30,000
AB: 50,000
Loss: <$20,000>

No deduction for a loss is allowed on sales between a partner and the partnership if the partner owns more than 50 percent of the capital interest or profits interest in the partnership. (Section 707(b)(1)(A); Treas. Reg. § 1.707-1(b)(1)(i)) Because Quinn owns less than 50 percent (he owns 25 percent), the limitation will not apply to him and he will be allowed to claim the loss if otherwise allowable.

7.   Roy owns 60 percent of a general partnership. He sold land to the partnership for $100,000. He had previously purchased the land for $60,000 and held it as an investment. The partnership is in the business of subdividing property and offering lots for sale. What are the tax consequences to Roy?

If a partner who is not acting in his capacity as a partner transfers property to a partnership, the transaction is treated as a sale. (Section 707(a)(1)) The partner must recognize gain or loss on disposition of the property. The partnership will take a cost basis in the property. (Section 1012) Roy would realize a $40,000 gain on the sale ($100,000 amount realized, less $60,000 basis).

AR: $100,000
AB: 60,000
Gain: $ 40,000

If the sale occurs between certain related parties, the Code may dictate the character of the gain on disposition. If the sale occurs between a partnership and a person owning, directly or indirectly, more than 50 percent of the capital interest or profits interest and, in the hands of the buyer (the partnership), the asset would not be characterized as a capital asset (as inventory, under these facts it would be ordinary), then the gain is characterized as ordinary. (Section 707(b)(2))

Because Roy owns more than 50 percent (he owns 60 percent), the re-characterization rule applies and the gain is characterized as ordinary.

Chapter XIII

Guaranteed Payments

A guaranteed payment is a fixed payment made by a partnership to a partner for services or use of capital that is not dependent on whether the partnership has income or profits. It is considered as having been made regardless of whether there is partnership income.[1]

The tax consequences to the partner and partnership reflect the hybrid nature of the payments.

Partner. If the parties agree to a guaranteed payment, the partner treats the payment as his distributive share of partnership profits. He must include the amount of the guaranteed payment in his gross income during the year that the partnership year ends in which the partnership deducted the amount or treated the amount as paid or accrued. Whether the partner has actually received the payment is irrelevant.[2]

The income is always characterized as ordinary income; its character does not depend on the character of income received or earned by the partnership for the year in which the payment is considered made.[3]

Partnership. If the partnership agrees to a guaranteed payment, it is allowed an expense deduction for the payment if otherwise allowed in the year deemed paid or accrued. If the payment is a capital expenditure, the partnership is allowed deprecation if the item is depreciable.[4]

---

1. Section 707(c).
2. Section 707(c); Treas. Reg. § 1.707-1(c).
3. Section 707(c); Treas. Reg. § 1.707-1(c).
4. Section 707(c); Treas. Reg. § 1.707-1(c). Because the payment must be included in the year the deduction is claimed, there is no need for deferral of the deduction under Section 267(a)(2).

Summary

Guaranteed payment: A fixed payment made by a partnership to a partner for services or use of capital that is not dependent on whether the partnership has income or profits.

Partner:
- Always characterized as ordinary income.
- Must be included in income in year deducted by the partnership, regardless of whether amount is actually paid.

Partnership: Permitted an expense or depreciation deduction to the extent allowed by the Code based on the partnership's accounting method.

Questions

1. Ann owned a 40 percent interest in a general partnership. The partnership agreed it would pay Ann $10,000 each year for consulting services regardless of whether the partnership had any income for the year.

   During the year, the partnership earned $110,000 and paid Ann $10,000. What are the tax consequences to Ann and the partnership?

2. Bob owned a limited partnership interest in a general partnership. The partnership agreed it would pay Bob a 10 percent return on the amount in his capital account. What are the tax consequences to Bob?

3. Carl owned a 40 percent interest in a partnership. The partnership agreed it would allocate to Carl 40 percent of income, but not less than $50,000. During the year, the partnership had $200,000 of income. What are the tax consequences to Carl?

4. Deb owned a 20 percent interest in a partnership. The partnership agreed it would allocate to Deb 20 percent of income, but not less than $50,000. During the year, the partnership had $100,000 of income. What are the consequences to Deb and the partnership?

Solutions

1.   Ann owned a 40 percent interest in a general partnership. The partnership agreed it would pay Ann $10,000 each year for consulting services regardless of whether the partnership had any income for the year.

During the year, the partnership earned $110,000 and paid Ann $10,000. What are the tax consequences to Ann and the partnership?

Because the payment is a fixed payment made by the partnership to Ann for her services and is not dependent on whether the partnership has income or profits, the payment is a guaranteed payment. She is required to include the payment in her gross income, regardless of whether it was paid. (Section 707(c); Treas. Reg. § 1.707-1(c)) The partnership may deduct the payment. (Section 162(a))

The net income, $100,000 ($110,000, less $10,000), is allocated among the partners based on their ownership interests, with $40,000 being allocated to Ann.

Ann must include $50,000 in her income, composed of the $10,000 guaranteed payment and $40,000 distributive share of income.

2.   Bob owned a limited partnership interest in a general partnership. The partnership agreed it would pay Bob a 10 percent return on the amount in his capital account. What are the tax consequences to Bob?

Because the payment is a fixed payment made by the partnership for the use of capital and is not dependent on whether the partnership has income or profits, the payment is a guaranteed payment. Bob must include the amount of the payment in his gross income, regardless of whether it was paid. The partnership may deduct the payment. (Section 707(c); Treas. Reg. § 1.707-1(c))

3.   Carl owned a 40 percent interest in a partnership. The partnership agreed it would allocate to Carl 40 percent of income, but not less than $50,000. During the year, the partnership had $200,000 of income. What are the tax consequences to Carl?

To the extent the amount is a fixed payment made by the partnership to Carl for his services and is not dependent on whether the partnership has income or profits, the payment is a guaranteed payment. (Section 707(c); Treas. Reg. § 1.707-1(c))

For services rendered in furtherance of the partnership business, Carl was entitled to receive 40 percent of partnership income, but not less than $50,000. During the year, the partnership had $200,000 of income. Carl's allocable share of the partnership's income was $80,000. (Section 704(a)) Because it is more than $50,000, no portion is a guaranteed payment.

4.   Deb owned a 20 percent interest in a partnership. The partnership agreed it would allocate to Deb 20 percent of income, but not less than $50,000. During the year, the partnership had $100,000 of income. What are the consequences to Deb and the partnership?

To the extent the amount is a fixed payment made by the partnership to Deb for her services and is not dependent on whether the partnership has income or profits, the payment is a guaranteed payment. She is required to include a guaranteed payment in her gross income, regardless of whether it was paid. (Section 707(c); Treas. Reg. § 1.707-1(c))

For services rendered in furtherance of the partnership business, Deb was entitled to receive 20 percent of partnership income, but not less than $50,000. During the year, the partnership had $100,000 of income. Deb's allocable share of the partnership's income is $20,000. (Section 704(a)) Thus, because her share of profits is less than $50,000 she is entitled to a guaranteed payment.

If the payment to Deb is deductible, the computation could be a bit difficult. But, you can solve for "X", where "X" is the amount of the guaranteed payment.

$$1/5 \ (\$100,000 - X) + X = \$50,000$$
$$\$20,000 - 1/5 \ X + X = \$50,000$$
$$4/5 \ X = \$30,000$$
$$X = \$37,500$$

Thus, if the partnership pays Deb a guaranteed payment of $37,500, it will have net income of

Income:	$100,000
Guaranteed payment:	< 37,500>
Net:	$62,500

The net income is allocated among the partners based on their ownership interests, with $12,500 allocated to Deb.

Net income:	$12,500	(62,500 x 1/5)
Guaranteed payment:	37,500	
Total:	$50,000	